Faith *and* Freedom

VINTAGE SPIRITUAL CLASSICS

General Editors
John F. Thornton
Susan B. Varenne

ALSO AVAILABLE

MARTIN LUTHER

Faith *and* Freedom

An Invitation to the Writings of Martin Luther

PREFACE BY

Richard Lischer

EDITED BY

John F. Thornton and *Susan B. Varenne*

VINTAGE SPIRITUAL CLASSICS

VINTAGE BOOKS
A DIVISION OF RANDOM HOUSE, INC.
NEW YORK

A VINTAGE SPIRITUAL CLASSICS ORIGINAL, APRIL 2002
FIRST EDITION

Editing and arrangement of the texts,
About the Vintage Spiritual Classics, Preface to the Vintage Spiritual
Classics Edition, Chronology of the Life of Martin Luther,
and Suggestions for Further Reading
Copyright © 2002 by Random House, Inc.

See page 375 for permissons acknowledgments

Library of Congress Cataloging-in-Publication Data is on file.

Vintage ISBN 0-375-71376-X

www.randomhouse.com
Book design by Fritz Metsch
Printed in the United States of America
10 9 8 7 6 5 4 3 2 1

ACKNOWLEDGMENTS

The editors wish to thank Dr. Richard Lischer of Duke Divinity School and Rev. Donald Baker of St. Gregory the Great Church in Manhattan for their generous help and valuable suggestions and advice in preparing the present volume.

Thanks are also due to the staff—and excellent resources—of the Burke Library of New York City's Union Theological Seminary.

CONTENTS

III. Sermons Through the Church Year

IV. Teachings

V. Letters, Table Talk

VI. PRAYERS, DEVOTIONS, AND HYMNS

ABOUT THE
VINTAGE SPIRITUAL CLASSICS

by John F. Thornton and Susan B. Varenne, General Editors

A turn or shift of sorts is becoming evident in the reflections of men and women today on their life experiences. Not quite as adamantly secular, and perhaps a little less insistent on material satisfactions, the reading public has recently developed a certain attraction to testimonies that human life is leavened by a Presence that blesses and sanctifies. Recovery, whether from addictions or personal traumas, illness, or even painful misalignments in human affairs, is evolving from the standard therapeutic goal of enhanced self-esteem. Many now seek a deeper healing that embraces the whole person, including the soul. Contemporary books provide accounts of the invisible assistance of angels. The laying on of hands in prayer has made an appearance at the hospital bedside. Guides for the spiritually perplexed have risen to the top of bestseller lists. The darkest shadows of skepticism and unbelief, which have eclipsed the presence of the Divine in our materialistic age, are beginning to lighten and part.

If the power and presence of God are real and effective, what do they mean for human experience? What does God offer to men and women, and what does He ask in return? How do we recognize Him? Know Him? Respond to Him? God has a reputation for being both benevolent and wrathful. Which will He be for me, and when? Can these aspects of the Divine somehow be reconciled? Where is God when I suffer? Can I lose Him? Is God truthful, and are His promises to be trusted?

Are we really as precious to God as we are to ourselves and to our loved ones? Do His providence and amazing grace guide our faltering steps toward Him, even in spite of ourselves? Will God abandon us if the sin is serious enough, or if we have episodes of resistance and forgetfulness? These are fundamental questions any person might address to God during a lifetime. They are pressing and difficult, often becoming wounds in the soul of the person who yearns for the power and courage of hope, especially in stressful times.

The Vintage Spiritual Classics present the testimony of writers across the centuries who have considered all these difficulties and who have pondered the mysterious ways, unfathomable mercies, and deep consolations afforded by God to those who call upon Him from out of the depths of their lives. These writers, then, are our companions, even our champions, in a common effort to discern the meaning of God in personal experience. For God is personal to us. To whom does He speak if not to us, provided we have the desire to hear Him deep within our hearts?

Each volume opens with a specially commissioned essay by a well-known contemporary writer that offers the reader an appreciation of its intrinsic value. A chronology of the general historical context of each author and his work is provided, as are suggestions for further reading.

We offer a final word about the act of reading these spiritual classics. From the very earliest accounts of monastic practice—dating back to the fourth century—it is evident that a form of reading called *lectio divina* (divine, or spiritual, reading) was essential to any deliberate spiritual life. This kind of reading is quite different from scanning a text for useful facts and bits of information, or advancing along an exciting plot line to a climax in the action. It is, rather, a meditative approach, by which the reader seeks to savor and taste the beauty and truth of every phrase and passage. This process of contemplative reading has the effect of enkindling in the reader compunction for past behavior that has been less than beautiful and true. At the same time, it increases the desire to seek a realm where all that is lovely and unspoiled may be found. There are four steps in *lectio divina:* first, to read; next, to meditate; then, to rest in the sense of God's nearness; and ultimately, to resolve to govern one's actions in the light of new understanding. This kind of reading is itself an act of prayer. And indeed, it is in prayer that God manifests His Presence to us.

by Richard Lischer

On April 16, 1521, the monk Martin Luther arrived at the city of Worms in triumphal procession. When he came to the outskirts of the city, he was escorted to its gate by one hundred mounted soldiers; two thousand townspeople came out to accompany him to his lodgings. Peasants and burghers alike hailed him as champion of the gospel and champion of the German people. To his astonishment, he had become a celebrity overnight.

Two days later, when challenged to recant his writings, he would refuse to do so on grounds familiar not only to scholars but in words memorized by every Lutheran schoolchild for the next four centuries: "My conscience is captive to the Word of God. Thus I cannot and will not recant, for going against my conscience is neither safe nor salutary. I can do no other, here I stand, God help me. Amen." His profession marked the beginning of an era in which the name *Luther* would symbolize faith, freedom, and the defiance of religious authority.

We live at the end of the epoch whose contours were shaped by the questions Luther asked and the answers he gave. Luther was indeed a world-historic figure who re-created the religion and language of the German people, but his dramatic moment before Holy Roman Emperor Charles V should not be allowed to obscure the less than dramatic circumstances in which he went about making his epoch. Luther spent the last thirty-five years of his life in Wittenberg, a walled town of 2,500 located on the Elbe River. His duties included lecturing in the theological faculty of the new university, theological writing and intrigue, voluminous correspondence, and an exhausting regimen of preaching. After he married, he lived with his wife and children in the former Augustinian cloister. There he also tended to his domestic responsibilities, which included playing the lute for his children and entertaining students and religious tourists who managed to find their way to his dinner table where, surrounded by eager listeners and note-takers, Dr. Luther was always "on."

Most of the works in this volume emerge from the pastoral ministry of the reformer. They witness to a gentler Luther than the master polemicist of *The Babylonian Captivity of the Church* or the hateful old man in *Of the Jews and Their Lies.* Luther's use of invective mirrors the traditions of public discourse in his day. It runs the gamut from playful to crude to tragic, but the bulk of his works consists of Bible commentary, catechetical treatises, sermons, and postils (sermonic treatments of scripture for the newly Evangelical clergy), whose tone is free of his harshest language.

It is customary among historians to debate whether Luther was the last medieval man or the first modern. In his anxiety over the devil, civil disorder, and the state of his own soul, mightn't he have been more comfortable living in the fourteenth rather than the six-teenth century? Or does the same spiritual *Angst,* with its rage against authority and preoccupation with freedom and personal faith, make him the godfather of us all? With Luther there are no easy answers. He is perhaps best understood as the bridge between two ways of relating to God, the medieval and the modern.

Luther entered the Augustinian monastery at Erfurt as St. Augustine had once come to Carthage, with a raging heart. As a monk he was soon confronted by his own demons in the form of *Anfechtungen,* spiritual terrors concerning his worthiness before God. Although he prayed unceasingly and pummeled his body, he couldn't shake them. Satan was sifting him like wheat in order to claim his soul and take it to hell. He pored over the Psalms and concluded, "A human heart is like a ship on a wild sea."

Only the pastoral care of his superior Johannes von Staupitz allowed him to survive his crisis. Staupitz recognized Luther's gifts and directed him to deepen his knowledge of scripture by obtaining a doctorate and teaching his fellow monks. Luther moved to Wittenberg in 1511 and gave his first lectures on the Psalms in 1513–15. In his lectures and sermons from this period he was still very much the scholastic theologian, employing the fourfold method of biblical interpretation—the literal, allegorical, moral, and eschatological—and structuring his argument along the lines of classical rhetoric.

Not long thereafter he began his practice of reading the Bible through twice a year. Driven by his *Anfechtungen,* he not only studied it but probed and tested it. He said one must read the scripture the way Moses struck the rock, by beating against it until it yields refreshing water. His scholastic training offered reasoned proofs, but he was looking for a promise that would release him from his terrible uncertainty.

Within two years, his lectures on the Psalms and Romans revealed a dramatic shift in his theology. For Luther *the* issue he repeatedly struck like a rock was Paul's treatment of the righteousness of God in the epistle to the Romans. This is the righteousness (or justice) by which God may condemn or acquit sinners. He began to perceive two sides of the holy God and two distinct expressions of God's righteousness. There is a righteousness that is so pure that it can delight only in itself and punish those who offend against it. This is the thunder of God's *No* spoken through the law. Such righteousness cannot be placated by good deeds or pious monastic practices. This was the justice—and the God—that had always terrified Luther. But there is another righteousness, also holy, pure, and good, but its perfection is such that it can't help but impart something of itself to others. Far from a threat, such goodness in God motivates His love for sinners.

The only way to approach such righteousness is to open one's heart to it in faith, to embrace it. Faith is not a proposition or a deed; it is the open hand that receives the promise. That's all. Between these two visions of divine goodness—one austere and walled like a castle, the other generous to the point of death— Luther's soul hung in the balance. As an old man he remembered his passage from one form of righteousness to the other:

> Though I lived as a monk without reproach, I felt
> that I was a sinner before God with an extremely
> disturbed conscience. I could not believe that He
> was placated by my satisfaction. I did not love,
> yes, I hated the righteous God who punishes sinners,
> and secretly, if not blasphemously, certainly murmuring

greatly, I was angry with God. . . . Thus I raged with a fierce
　　and troubled conscience. Nevertheless I beat importunately
upon Paul at that place, most ardently desiring to know
　　what St. Paul wanted.

At last, by the mercy of God, meditating day and
　　night, I gave heed to the context of the words, namely,
"In it the righteousness of God is revealed, as it is
　　written, 'He who through faith is righteous shall live.'"
There I began to understand that the righteousness of
　　God is that by which the righteous lives by a gift of
God, namely by faith. . . . Here I felt that I was
　　altogether born again and had entered paradise itself
through open gates.

It is clear from the record of his lectures and sermons that
Luther's discovery occurred over a period of years. Later in his life,
he telescoped his personal quest for the gospel into an epiphany of
undetermined length, his so-called tower experience. It is named
for the room in the Black Cloister in Wittenberg where he made
his exegetical breakthrough. That Luther *may* have been referring
to the toilet in the tower, the *cloaca,* only adds to the abject lowli-
ness out of which he made his discovery.

But after all, what could be more lowly and degrading than the
spectacle of a crucified messiah? As the gates of paradise opened for
Luther, all other avenues to religious knowledge and power closed,
save for one, the cross. If you wish to know *if* there is a God, you
may admire the wonders of nature; but if you want to know *who*
God is and what His disposition toward you, a sinner, is, you must
go to the cross, for only in the cross has God revealed the depth of
His gracious love *pro nobis,* for us. And only in the cross do we
understand the nature of our responsibilities toward one another.
All the methods of understanding God upon which Scholasticism
had relied—reason, Aristotle, tradition—closed before Luther.
All the paths to the Divine trod by later cultural forms of Protestantism—sentiment, nature, morality—sealed as well. God is out
there all right, but He might as well be in hiding or living on the
dark side of the moon, for all the good He does *pro nobis.*

If one wishes to understand the later Lutheran ethos of indifference to religion and its sometimes reckless abandonment to the gospel, one can only begin with Luther's theology of the cross. For, apart from the Crucified One, so *little* of God is available to Lutherans, and yet as Luther (and St. Paul) would insist, the cross is everything! It is the power and the wisdom of God [1 Cor. 1:24]. Luther would have enjoyed John Donne's punning advice, "Hang upon him who hangs upon the cross."

The dark sense of Lutheran irony, especially *vis-à-vis* the Protestant tendency to whisper, whimper, and otherwise emote God into life, owes its origins not to the frigid Scandinavian weather, as the humorist Garrison Keillor suggests, but to Luther's theology of the cross. Such a hard yet joyful narrowing of grace does not allow for grandiosity, self-importance, pulpit princes, religious entrepreneurs, entertainers, or Lutheran TV evangelists. Radio is permitted—but no video.

Luther's theological breakthrough did not free him from the mighty sense of conflict that characterized his earlier religious life. It only clarified its true terms. The monkish conflict with his own bodily desires settled into a lifelong battle with the devil. The struggle within his own soul he projected onto the wider screen of the Reformation, where it manifested itself as a battle to preserve the gospel. He begins an open letter to Pope Leo X with this remarkable phrase: "Living among the monsters of this age with whom I am now for the third year waging war . . ." In his person Luther effected a merger of private and public religion: his own quest for justification would be enacted in a Church yearning for freedom but ruled by external obligation.

One of the clearest indicators of Luther's premodern sensibility is his preoccupation with the devil. Satan is not a rhetorical device or symbol of evil but an ever-present reality with whom Luther suffers an almost cordial familiarity. Satan is "a mighty, malicious, and turbulent spirit," he warns his Wittenberg congregation. Once he appeared to him in the form of a pig, he confesses. Never debate him when you're alone. If you are having difficulty praying, it is usually the Adversary's fault. Sometimes it works to make fun of him. Satan hates to be mocked.

Between the absolute priority of God's grace and the vexing reality of the Prince of Darkness, Luther found no space for self-

induced spiritual development. In his debate with Erasmus, he
went so far as to describe the human being as a horse that is ridden
either by God or Satan. Erasmus was a precursor of Enlightenment religion, which ascribed a great deal of autonomy to the
human spirit. Nineteenth-century idealism and romanticism went
on to make freedom the essence of humanity. Luther experienced
his life in another way altogether, as a battlefield on which large,
transcendent armies were contending. By faith he knew that
Christ has conquered sin, death, and the devil, and to that extent
Luther considered himself little more than a spectator to the
events going on around and within him. This perhaps explains the
remarkable insouciance—some would say naiveté—with which
he dealt with political matters. "And then while I slept or drank
Wittenberg beer with my Philip and with Amsdorf, the Word so
greatly weakened the papacy, that never an emperor inflicted such
damage upon it. I did nothing, the Word did it all."

Paradoxically, the person who is little more than the battlefield
of Christ and Satan experiences life as an exhilarating burst of freedom. Nearly half a millennium later, Luther's namesake would cry
out, "Free at last, free at last! Thank God almighty, I'm free at
last!" As a still-segregated black man, Martin Luther King, Jr., was
not free but was announcing the imminent arrival of eschatological
freedom in America. Better than anyone at mid-twentieth century,
King would have understood the famous paradox with which
Luther opens his 1520 treatise, *The Freedom of a Christian:*

> A Christian is a perfectly free lord of all, subject to none.
>   A Christian is a perfectly dutiful servant of all, subject
> to all.

When one receives the grace of God in Jesus Christ, what sometimes passes for freedom is unmasked and its true character
revealed. The multiple bondages to pleasure, self-absorption, law,
and fear are destroyed, and something new takes their place. No
longer is the human being *incurvatus in se,* to use one of Luther's
more vivid metaphors—turned in upon himself. The openness
that is given with life in Christ does not entail absolute political or
psychological self-determination. Jesus does not make us the master of our fate or the captain of our souls. Rather, the new freedom

takes the shape of servanthood toward others. Yet because it is service to the beloved Christ, with whom the believer is organically joined, it is marked by joy and freedom. In Luther, the dialectic between freedom and servanthood never ceases.

Luther found it hard to flesh out the dialectic in public policy. Inevitably, it proved impossible to inject freedom and servanthood into European politics in such a way that would maintain the tension between freedom in Christ and obedience to civil authorities. His teaching on the *callings* of the Christian did much to encourage ordinary believers to exercise their faith through their secular occupations. It caused them to see their work as a vehicle of faith and praise. His teaching also recognized the prince, magistrates, and a stable government as a divinely sanctioned order within which the Christian may live a faithful witness. He once said in a sermon that only the Christian can appreciate the peace guaranteed by the state because only Christians truly understand the depth of Satan's potential for disordering the world. The civil state exists only because Christians continue to pray for it. But the Lutheran dialectic never solved the problem of how Christians may legitimately challenge or change their government. His characteristic defiance of religious authority did not have a political correlative, nor did he wish it. There is no Lutheran politics. The political ramifications of the freedom of the gospel were left for others to sort out.

Where Luther did maintain the paradox and brilliantly teach and practice it was among believers in the Church. Once grasped by his evangelical insight, Luther applied it to every corner of the Church's existence. He offered the Church the same radical pastoral care he himself had experienced, radical because it forsook palliative measures and recognized that all Christians live on the razor's edge of faith and despair, freedom and bondage. Even believers are threatened by the wiles of Satan, for the Christian is *simul iustus et peccator,* wholly saved and wholly sinful at the same time.

Here is a clue to the "modern" Luther, the one who refuses to reduce Christian existence to positive thinking or a series of easily digested spiritual laws. Many of his themes, such as anxiety, personal faith, and the revolt against authority, anticipate their secular development in modernity. Luther can and has been made out to be a neurotic, an existentialist, or a Marxist, respectively, but in these caricatures he only appears to be modern. Freud, Sartre, and

Marx will have to complete what he supposedly began. But in the matter of *simul iustus et peccator* Luther puts his finger on the human contradiction that haunts us all. We have seen the angel and the monster in the three-piece suit. He too saw the coexistence of evil and virtue in a blood-bought heart and could solve the mystery no better than we.

Luther's theology emerges from the believer's encounter with the crucified God. Unlike Calvin and later Reformed thinkers, his thought is not characterized by a highly rational structure or dogmatic symmetry, but it does have a single guiding principle. Emboldened by his key insight, Luther simply returns to every crevasse of human experience and every corner of Christian dogma and *rereads* them, as it were, in the light of his discovery of a gracious and not angry God.

To explain the doctrine of creation, for example, he does not begin with the sun and the moon and the stars. In the *Small Catechism,* when he explains the first article of the Apostles' Creed with the words, "I believe God has made *me* and all creatures," he is not using "me" as a rhetorical device to personalize an abstract doctrine. He is remembering the Tower in Wittenberg and confessing his own standing as a creature before God.

Luther would have agreed with William Faulkner's dictum, "The only thing worth writing about is the human heart in conflict with itself." Like Faulkner, he would never have limited himself to so small a canvas, but the gospel always begins by laying claim to the nearest available heart, in this case, that of the preacher. God speaks to *me.* The facts of the Bible record nothing but "dead history" until they are activated in the heart of the believer. The same "heart" is visible in many of his hymns, as in stanza four of "Dear Christians, Let Us Now Rejoice":

> Then God was sorry on His throne
>   To see such torment rend me;
> His tender mercy he thought on,
>   His good help He would send me.
> He turned to me His father-heart;
>   Ah! then was His no easy part,
> For of His best it cost Him.

If you don't believe in a gracious God, Luther often said, then you don't have one. That which you believe, you really have, he said, by which he meant to express the radical effectiveness of faith. The philosopher Ludwig Feuerbach (1804–72) seized upon the subjectivism of Luther to accuse Christianity of trading on projection and wish fulfillment. Those unattainable qualities we desire or value most we project onto a supernatural screen and call it God. God is nothing but humanity writ large. That argument has survived into the twenty-first century. The only way Luther knew to confound it was to beat upon the Word of God, whose authority he separated from the affections of the interpreter. In his sermons he repeatedly admonishes his hearers not to be guided by their feelings but by the promise found in the Word.

Luther did not believe that the interpretive community gives texts their meaning, but rather the text, because it cradles the objective promise of God, creates the community and bestows meaning on it. The same is true of the sacraments. Remember, he says, baptism does not work through water and anyone's personal faith but through water and the Word of God. Such comments do not sit well with current literary theory, which stresses the reader's formative role in creating the text of a novel or poem; nor are they compatible with popular spirituality, which makes the individual the final arbiter of divine truth. Feuerbach and Luther both understood the mechanism by which human beings imagine a god to suit their own fancy. What Feuerbach took as normative Christianity, however, Luther condemned as a deviation.

The heuristic of Luther's joyous discovery yielded a remarkable freedom in pastoral care. The whole point, he insisted, is to *use* the gospel in any circumstance for the comfort and renewal of human life. To know Christ is to know what He can do for you. In the light of the gospel the believer is free to embrace the whole marvel of nature and culture as the theater of God's grace. Art, architecture, and especially music can be vehicles by which the Spirit teaches and guides His people. Luther did not go in for glass-breaking in cathedrals and statue-wrecking. When such acts occurred in Wittenberg, he opposed them at great personal risk. He purified the Mass of its false doctrine but he did not discard it.

Thanks to Luther, his followers continue to worship according to the pattern of the ancient liturgy.

"Next after theology," he once said, "I give to music the highest place and the greatest honor." He saved his warmest accolades for the polyphonic chorale of the Netherlands, which was Catholic in origin. Luther himself gave to the Church many hymns and liturgical settings. His hymns, such as "From Heaven Above to Earth I Come" and "Dear Christians One and All, Rejoice," have enriched the Church worldwide. "A Mighty Fortress Is Our God" evokes the gray walls of a Saxon castle as a figure for God's steadfastness. His treatment of Psalm 130, "Out of the Depths," was sung at his funeral. Indeed, Luther's greatest interpreter is not a formal theologian but a church musician, Johann Sebastian Bach, whose transcendent genius took Luther's theology of the cross to its rational and affective limits.

Luther worked among ignorant people and backward priests who had no idea what to make of the Reformation sweeping their villages. In a torrent of treatises, letters, catechetical helps, sermons, and hymns, he never stopped telling them how to practice the gospel. Faith may be the open hand that receives the promise, but in his pastoral works it is also an "art" to be practiced by each believer. Luther fought for the Reformation village by village and heart by heart. To his barber, Master Peter, he patiently explains the ins and outs of prayer, not neglecting a realistic treatment of those moments when he himself is "cool and joyless" in prayer. His advice is characteristically practical and down to earth. He tells the barber to stay focused: keep your eye on the razor! And always speak the Amen firmly. He counsels parents to be lenient in corporal punishment. He muses over whether ministers of the gospel, too, may flee the plague. He addresses the problem of suffering from the Christian perspective ("it is better to have a cross than to be without one").

To be a pastor, Luther once said, requires a "motherly heart." His image of the pastor or preacher is the mother breast-feeding her young. He opens his own heart to women who have suffered miscarriage, reminding them that a prayer for a baby, even an unbaptized one, becomes "a great, unbearable cry in God's ears." Already before he married Katharina von Bora, Luther found himself defending women against the pagan habit of denigrating them for all but their biological contributions. Luther writes in *The Estate of Marriage,* "These are the words of blind heathen, who are ignorant of the fact that man and woman are God's creation. They blaspheme His work, as if man and woman just came into being spontaneously! I imagine that if women were to write books they would say exactly the same thing about men."

Even Luther's Bible translation served as an extension of his pastoral and educational ministry. He completed the New Testament in a miraculous twelve weeks while in hiding at the Wartburg. He was at great pains to produce a German Bible understandable to all. He used the court language of electoral Saxony as his standard, enriching it with other dialects with which he was familiar. In the process he created a single language of which all Germans would be proud. What he said of his translating applies to all his pastoral efforts: "Rather we must inquire about this of the mother in the home, the children on the street, the common man in the marketplace. We must be guided by their language, the way they speak, and do our translating accordingly." Perhaps that is why he was inclined to translate "Hail, Mary" with a salutation any German could warm to, *"Liebe Maria."*

It is in his preaching, however, that Luther explores the full range of his radical pastoral care. The sermon is his preferred vehicle because the Word of God was meant to be an oral event. Its capture by manuscript and the printed page constitutes a great loss, for the Church was never meant to be a *Federhaus,* a pen-house, but a *Mundhaus,* a mouth-house. Only the spoken word can do justice to the startling call of the gospel, which by its very utterance can create faith in the place of despair. "Word" and "promise" are not merely metaphors for something more basic in God, for God's salvation *is* "an acoustical affair."

Unlike his other pastoral duties, preaching for Luther bore its own special urgency. For the End was bearing down on Luther and his age. He believed the gospel was like a "passing shower which hurries on"; it can be taken away from us as it was from the Jews. Every sermon therefore embodies an act of hope in the preservation of the gospel until the End. Luther expressed little interest in the times and seasons of Christ's return. His question was not, Can Germany survive until the End? but the more theologically prescient, Can the Word of God survive in Germany?

In Wittenberg the reformers led three preaching services every Sunday and at least one on every day of the week. Luther preached constantly, several times per week, and sometimes every day. During Passiontide in 1529 he preached eighteen times in eleven days. He did not write his sermons in advance but ascended the pulpit with a *Konzept,* or organizing principle, and elaborated the substance of the lectionary text for each day. Since his method had no name, those who followed him dubbed it "the heroic method." Most of his 2,300 surviving sermons were recorded in shorthand by several stenographers, often with variations of wording and detail. He spoke at a moderate pace in a clear, sonorous voice. He claimed that he was afraid every time he mounted the pulpit stairs, so high a calling it is to proclaim God's Word, and he once reported a nightmare in which he had gotten up to preach but forgotten his *Konzept!* He is buried in the pavement beneath the canopied pulpit in the Castle Church.

Anyone who reads five-hundred-year-old sermons for their contemporary relevance must expect to be disappointed. But with Luther the reader is astonished by the clarity of the human voice and the discovery of luminous windows in his sermons whose beauty and insight open directly onto the modern consciousness.

Their power comes from Luther's intuitive apprehension of what is most human about the almighty God. In his arguments with Huldrych Zwingli over the Eucharist, Luther had argued the Catholic side, that the bread and wine do more than symbolize the body and blood of Christ. Thanks to the Incarnation, the finite really is capable of hosting the infinite. He brought his eucharistic arguments to fruition in the poetic power by which the biblical world became real in his sermons. In Mary and Joseph, the Canaanite woman, and the little boy with a few loaves and fishes—the infinite God appears in the vesture of ordinary people and events.

By reading Luther's sermons a social historian could map out sixteenth-century human nature in all its foolishness and tragedy. A theologian might read the same sermons as case studies in the doctrine of *simul iustus et peccator.* Luther's anthropology translates "the great dragon" in each of us into a host of three-dimensional clinical profiles of sin and redemption. The realism of his portraits demystifies and at the same time universalizes Christian dogma by giving it social size and psychological scope.

In his sermons they (we) are all there: the anxious mother who doesn't understand her precocious son—and then loses him on the way home from the Temple! A foreign woman who endures a racial insult in order to save her child; a prostitute who alone among her respectable critics understands the meaning of love; a rich burgher who disdains a beggar's cry but wishes to be known as a benefactor; a pious better-than-thou who sees the splinter in his neighbor's eye, but overlooks "planks large enough to build several hog troughs" in his own.

The peasants are there in full force, too. Like Augustine, Chrysostom, and countless other preachers, Luther frequently complained about the thickness and lethargy of his audience. "What? say these knaves, should I listen to the parson? Pass the beer, let us have a drink! O you shameful, miserable swine!" At a loftier theological level, they are "the poor" who suffer from a terrified conscience and religious confusion. He does not go to great lengths to sort out the emotional needs of his hearers to which the gospel provides the answer. Rather, he focuses on the experience of guilt before a holy God as the bond that unites all people. It is this transcendent need that transforms these "stupid folk" who "sit and stare at us like cows" into hearers of the Word.

What separates Luther's concrete analysis from sociology? One first notices the narrative cast of that analysis. He is viewing the misery of humankind as a part of a continuing saga of disobedience. The players change but the drama goes on. A more profound answer lies in the necessity of sin. Human evil is not to be analyzed or condemned before it is believed. Unlike the contemporary pulpit's reliance on the social sciences for its interpretation of the human being, Luther's assessment of people rested on a belief. Instead of proceeding from psychology toward faith, he moved from faith toward psychological realism.

Luther the preacher would not have approved of the Enlightenment's practice of disregarding the narrative while retaining the "points" or lessons to be derived from it. In fact, early in the Reformation he gave up the scholastic method of subdivisions and proofs, and in his best sermons he does not mechanically divide his exposition between doctrine and admonition. He simply tells the gospel with one voice, sometimes as if it were a message from another planet slicing through our sky, but most often as a "story about Christ, just as happens among men when one writes a book about a king or prince, telling what he did, said, and suffered in his day." Luther tells the story imaginatively, often by embellishing it with contemporary allusions, inventing additional dialogue, or performing a riff on the story like a jazz musician. By honoring the integrity of the story Luther allows the gospel to emerge from the narrative itself. The ultimate shape of the sermon follows the contour of human experience. The resolution is not so much pronounced as arrived at.

In his sermons it is difficult to find the seam dividing first-century Palestine and sixteenth-century Saxony—not because of clever applications of the past to the present, but because Luther still inhabited a tapestried world in which all the figures were woven together. The bane of "relevance" had not yet been imposed upon the sermon. It's not the preacher's job to make the Word of God interesting, only to speak it with one voice.

Nowhere is Luther's art more evident than in his treatment of the nativity. Of the peasant Mary about to give birth to her first-born, he says, "Nobody took to heart the heaviness of her body; and nobody cared that she was in strange surroundings and did not have any of the things which a woman in childbirth needs. Rather, she was there without anything ready, without light, without fire, in the middle of the night, alone in the darkness."

On the afternoon of Christmas day 1530 he told the same story in such a way that the reader is drawn into the event of Christ's birth as an awed observer. Luther pulls out all the stops, combining hyperbole, soliloquy, and apostrophe, all for the purpose of placing a solitary child in the spotlight on an otherwise darkened stage.

> And when the heavens and the stars and all creatures
> stare at me with horrible mien, I see nothing in heaven
> and earth but this child. . . . "Mary, you did not bear this child
> for yourself, but for me."

If a man could put out of his mind all that he is and
has except this child, and if for him everything—
money, goods, power, or honor—fades into darkness
and he despises everything on earth compared with
this child, so that heaven with its stars and earth
with all its power and all its treasures become as
nothing to him, that man would have the true gain
and fruit of this message of the angel.

The preacher's "I" is never far from this cosmic scene: "When I die I shall see nothing but darkness, and yet that light." Finally, after constructing a vast and brooding universe around this one point of light, he concludes, "And if this [account] is true—and it is the truth—then let everything else go." And from the shadows of a distant and more dangerous age, the reader is sorely tempted to *let everything else go* for the sake of this Christ.

Artistically, Luther laid open the Word as if it were the script of a village pageant and made his audience characters in its plot. Then, like pilgrims or amateur actors, his hearers advanced the story by performing it themselves and telling it to one another. This is the aesthetic of identification that underlay all Luther's pastoral care and preaching.

Theologically, he understood all too well the conflict churning at the heart of this story. Of that he was a carrier. Even the most gracious *Yes* of God is challenged by the fierce *No!* of this world and, more frightfully, by the continuing possibility of divine judgment. The sense of conflict gives even his pastoral treatises and sermons their eschatological tone—their *edge,* we might say. For their teller speaks the gospel with urgency and decisiveness and sometimes even anguish, knowing as he does that the story may be interrupted at any moment.

Early Life

1483 Born November 10 in Eisleben, east central Germany, second son of Hans and Margarethe. Martin is baptized the next day.

Charles VIII succeeds Louis XI to rule in France.

Richard of Gloucester murders his nephew Edward V and becomes king of England.

Raphael Sanzio, Italian painter, is born (d. 1520).

1484 The Luther family moves to nearby Mansfeld, where Hans becomes established in a mining firm and well able to support and educate his family, which eventually includes eight children. Martin attends the local school until he is fourteen.

Huldrych Zwingli, Swiss humanist and reformer, is born.

Sandro Botticelli, Italian painter (1445–1510), paints *Birth of Venus*.

1485 Henry Tudor, earl of Richmond, kills Richard III and succeeds him to the English throne as Henry VII.

Johannes Bugenhagen is born. He will be Luther's confidant and confessor at the University of Wittenberg, and the first Reformation priest to marry (1522). Pastor Bugenhagen will officiate at Martin and Katharina von Bora's wedding and will baptize their first child. He will be present at Luther's deathbed and preach the eulogy of his master.

1486 Johannes Eck is born. He will become the great Dominican theologian and opponent of Luther.

1488 Ulrich von Hutten, German humanist, is born. It is Hutten's edition of a treatise written sixty years earlier by Laurentius Valla that exposed the fifth-century Donation of Constantine as a forgery. This document had been effective in transferring the sovereignty over the Western world from Constantine to the pope. Luther will be galvanized by this revelation and conclude that the papacy is in the hands of the Antichrist.

1489 Thomas Cranmer, English reformer, is born (d. 1556). He is archbishop of Canterbury at the beginning of the English Reformation.

1490 Albert of Brandenburg, who will become a cardinal, is born. His administration as archbishop of Magdeburg and Mainz will be responsible for the sale of papal indulgences that precipitates Luther's protest in the form of the Ninety-five Theses.

1491 English king Henry VIII is born (d. 1547), as is Ignatius of Loyola (d. 1556), founder of the Jesuit order.

1492 Christopher Columbus (1451–1506), a Genoese supported by Isabella of Castile, sets sail west for India in the *Santa Maria*, landing instead in the Bahamas, October 12; in Cuba, October 18; and in Haiti, December 6. The *Santa Maria* goes down off Haiti, December 25.

The Inquisition drives the Jews from Spain. Granada is taken from the Muslims by Ferdinand of Aragon and Isabella of Castile, thus consolidating their monarchy.

Rodrigo Borgia (1431–1503), father of Cesare and Lucretia Borgia, becomes Pope Alexander VI following the death of Pope Innocent VIII.

Leonardo da Vinci (1452–1519) draws a flying machine.

1493 Columbus returns to Spain, then leaves on a second voyage (September 25, 1493–June 11, 1496) and lands in Puerto Rico, Dominica, and Jamaica.

Maximilian I becomes Holy Roman Emperor.

1494 Charles VIII of France invades Italy, sacks Rome, and forces the pope to take refuge in Castel Sant' Angelo, a Roman mausoleum built by Emperor Hadrian (d. 138).

1495 Charles VIII is crowned king of Naples, then returns to France. King Ferdinand II reconquers Naples and expels the French. A syphilis epidemic, introduced through French soldiers, spreads from Naples all over Europe.

The Jews are expelled from Portugal.

Hieronymus Bosch (1450–1516), of the Netherlands, paints *The Garden of Worldly Delights.*

Da Vinci paints *The Last Supper.*

John Taverner, English composer, is born (d. 1545).

Josquin des Prez (c. 1450–1521) is appointed organist and choirmaster at Cambrai cathedral.

1496 Ferdinand II of Naples dies and is succeeded by Frederick III.

1497 Martin is sent to Magdeburg to secondary school, where he becomes acquainted with the Brethren of the Common Life. They place great emphasis on devout reading of the scriptures and the inner life of the individual, with less regard for ritual and clerical hierarchy. Copies of the Bible are circulated and translation into the vernacular is promoted. The *Devotio moderna* of the Brethren reached its highest expression in the *Imitation of Christ* of Thomas à Kempis (1380–1471).

Philipp Melanchthon, German biblical humanist and reformer, is born (d. 1560). He is to become a close associate of Luther's. In 1530 he will compose the Lutheran formulation of faith known as the Augsburg Confession.

Girolamo Savonarola (1452–98), Dominican prior in Florence, attempts to depose Pope Alexander VI for corruption but instead is himself excommunicated.

John Cabot (c. 1450–c. 1499) and his son Sebastian voyage to the east coast of North America. He is an Italian under commission to Henry VII of England.

1498 Martin studies for three years at St. George Latin School in Eisenach with Trebonius, a well-known grammarian, who nurtures Martin's rhetorical skills.

Savonarola is burned at the stake in Florence as a result of his efforts to criticize and reform the papacy.

Charles VIII of France dies and is succeeded by Louis XII, duke of Orléans.

Vasco da Gama (c. 1460–1524) of Portugal discovers the sea route to India, putting Asia in direct communication with Europe by sea.

Albrecht Dürer (1471–1528), German Renaissance genius, completes *Self-Portrait, Apocalypse,* and *Knight, Death, and Devil.*

Michelangelo Buonarroti (1475–1564) sculpts the *Pieta* for St. Peter's in Rome.

1499 Amerigo Vespucci (1454–1512) sails from Spain to South America.

War between the Turks and Venice; Lepanto, on the Gulf of Corinth, surrenders to the sultan.

1500 Pope Alexander VI imposes a tithe for a crusade against the Turks.

Diet of Augsburg establishes the Council of Regency for administering the Holy Roman Empire and divides Germany into six regions.

1501 Desiderius Erasmus (1467–1536) of Rotterdam publishes the *Enchiridion,* a moral treatise intended to promote reform in the Church. A monk of the Augustinian Canons Regular, he turns against monastic life and criticizes its theological and sacramental structure. At first a supporter of Luther, later he and Luther become bitter enemies over differences on the relation between grace and freedom.

Michelangelo executes the sculpture *David*.

1502 Martin receives his bachelor's degree from Erfurt University.

Foundation of the University of Wittenberg by Frederick, elector of Saxony.

1503 Johannes von Staupitz (1468–1524) becomes vicar general of the Augustinian Hermits, an observant congregation. Staupitz, a scripture scholar, will become Martin's spiritual adviser and will appoint him his successor to the chair of scripture at the University of Wittenberg.

Venice signs a peace treaty with the Turks.

Pope Alexander VI dies and is succeeded by Pope Julius II, known for his military prowess.

Matthias Grünewald (1470–1528), a German painter and representative artist of the Reformation, paints *Crucifixion*. He is a good friend of Luther's.

Da Vinci paints the *Mona Lisa*.

Thomas Wyatt, English poet, is born (d. 1542).

1504 Lucas Cranach (1472–1553) paints *Rest on the Flight to Egypt*.

Dürer paints *Nativity*.

Raphael paints *Marriage of the Virgin*.

1505 On January 7 Martin receives his master's degree and on May 20 enters law school. On July 2 he is caught in a lightning storm at Stotternheim, near Erfurt. Terrified at the prospect of being struck, he vows to St. Anne that he will become a monk if she preserves him from peril. Apparently she did, and accordingly, on July 17 Martin enters the Augustinian monastery in Erfurt. Johannes von Staupitz is vicar general of the order. Frederick the Wise of Saxony is Martin's prince and protector. Martin's father, Hans, is greatly disappointed by his son's decision to forgo a career in law.

Pope Julius II calls Michelangelo to Rome.

Thomas Tallis, English composer, is born (d. 1585).

Luther's Life as a Monk

1506 Johann Tetzel (1465–1519), a Dominican monk, begins selling indulgences in Germany.

1507 Martin Luther is ordained a priest at the Cathedral Church of St. Mary in Erfurt on April 3. Overcome by the mystical implications of his duties as a priest, Martin falters at the altar in the midst of his first Mass, though he summons the strength to finish. His father's presence undoubtedly contributes to Martin's discomposure; he had suggested to Martin that his conversion experience could as likely have been prompted by the devil as by God.

Pope Julius II offers an indulgence for the rebuilding of St. Peter's in Rome.

1508 Luther is called to Wittenberg to teach.

Michelangelo begins to paint the ceiling of the Sistine Chapel in Rome.

Raphael enters the service of Julius II.

1509 Luther returns to Erfurt in October.

John Calvin is born (d. 1564). One of the major figures of the Reformation, his activity will be centered in Geneva. He is influenced by both Erasmus and Luther.

Henry VIII, Prince of Wales, succeeds his father as king of England and marries Catherine of Aragon.

1510 Luther is sent to Rome to represent his Augustinian order on the observant controversy. This dispute focused on strict withdrawal from the world as the ideal of monasticism, as opposed to conventualism, which was directed outward, toward preaching and ministering to the laity. There is no success in reuniting the two sides. Luther had expected to find Rome a holy place; instead he encounters rampant unbelief and immorality among all levels of clergy.

Titian Vecellio (c. 1488–1576), Italian, paints *The Gypsy Madonna*.

Louis Bourgeois, French musician, is born (d. after 1561).

1511 Luther is transferred from Erfurt to Wittenberg. For the next six years he will keep the rule of his order in the strictest manner, while lecturing on the Bible. These are called his "silent years."

The Holy League with Venice and Aragon is formed by Pope Julius II to drive the French out of Italy.

Albrecht Dürer paints *Adoration of the Trinity*.

1512 On October 19 Luther receives his doctorate in theology and assumes the chair of biblical theology at Wittenberg.

Threatened by the schismatic, antipapal council of Pisa, Pope Julius II convokes the Fifth Lateran Council, which will continue until 1517. It produces some little-heeded calls for reform and pronounces the dogma of the immortality of the soul.

Michelangelo finishes work on the Sistine Chapel.

1513 Luther begins lecturing in Latin on the book of Psalms. He sees Christ prefigured and speaking in the psalms, which manifest His righteousness.

Pope Julius II dies and is succeeded by Pope Leo X.

Vasco Núñez de Balboa (1475–1517) discovers the Pacific.

1514 Albert of Brandenburg is named archbishop of Mainz. To pay the papal fees entailed on the honor, he borrows 30,000 ducats from the banking house of Fugger in Augsburg. To finance the building of the Basilica of St. Peter in Rome, Pope Leo X issues a sale of indulgences. Albrecht agrees to allow the sale in Saxony and Brandenburg, and to split the profits fifty-fifty with the pope. Johann Tetzel, a German Dominican, preaches for the indulgence sale.

Thomas Wolsey (1471–1530), a butcher's son, is made archbishop of York.

Portuguese vessels sail as far as Chinese waters.

Correggio (Antonio Allegri, 1494–1534), Italian painter, discovers chiaroscuro, the interplay of light and dark in pictorial composition.

1515 Luther lectures on the epistle to the Romans. Verse 17 of chapter 1 is to become pivotal to his thought: "For in it [i.e., in the gospel] the righteousness of God is revealed through faith for

faith; as it is written, 'The one who is righteous will live by faith.'"
Luther emphasizes the word "live": for him, faith gives life. It is in
a small third-story office in one of the university towers that
Luther struggles with the concept of *iustitia* (righteousness, justice) and finally understands God's justice as God's divine mercy.
The transforming power of this insight will result in the designa-
tion of the moment as the "tower experience."

Louis XII of France dies and is succeeded by Francis I, who
conquers Milan.

Philip Neri (d. 1595) is born in Florence. He is destined to
become a leading figure of the Counter-Reformation.

Thomas Wolsey is appointed cardinal and lord chancellor of
England by Henry VIII. He personifies corruption in high church
office, seeking only secular advancement and power. He is dis-
graced in 1529 for his failure to help Henry secure a divorce.

1516 Luther begins his lectures on St. Paul's epistle to the Galatians, becoming ever more convinced in his view that all sin can be
reduced to unbelief. He also lectures on Hebrews and concludes
that fear of death is the result of disbelief in the Resurrection of
Christ. He believes that our fundamental attitude toward death is
a consequence of our confidence (or lack thereof) in the Resurrection.

Erasmus publishes his Greek New Testament, which will influence Luther's own German translation and other contemporary
vernacular editions.

Sir Thomas More (1478–1535) publishes *Utopia*. Friend of
Erasmus, eminent lawyer, devoted husband and father, and
ascetic, More will succeed Wolsey as lord chancellor of England
under Henry VIII.

Ferdinand II of Spain dies and is succeeded by King Charles I,
who later becomes Emperor Charles V.

Raphael paints the *Sistine Madonna*.

Titian paints *The Assumption*.

The Reformation Begins

1517 On October 31, Luther posts at the castle church of Wittenberg his Ninety-five Theses against the indulgence[1] that had been issued as a result of the arrangement between Pope Leo X, Archbishop Albert of Brandenburg, and the banking house of Fugger. Johann Tetzel actively promoted this sale. The posting of the theses marks the beginning of the Reformation in Germany. In just a few weeks, Luther becomes famous for his criticism of the papacy, as the Ninety-five Theses are translated from Latin into German and rushed into print to be sold far and wide. Luther's main point is to stress that the consequences of sin can be removed only by faith in the gospel. One must imitate Christ and repent continually of one's sins. No amount of money charitably donated can relieve one of this responsibility.

1518 Luther is summoned to the Diet of Augsburg by Cardinal Cajetan, papal legate to Germany, but refuses to recant his claims or his published works. A Dominican and court theologian of the Roman Curia, Sylvester Prierias, writes against Luther in his *Dialogue Concerning the Authority of the Pope*. Elector Frederick refuses to allow Luther to be either extradited or banished.

Luther's lifelong friend and fellow academician Philipp Melanchthon is appointed professor of Greek at the University of Wittenberg.

---

[1] An indulgence is a form of satisfaction for sin, provided the penitent is truly sorry and desires to make amends for the wrong committed. By means of an indulgence, the "temporal punishment" due to sin (punishment here on earth or in purgatory) is taken away. Moreover, by an act of intercessory prayer, an indulgence can be earned for a Christian who has died. Luther protested against the sale of indulgences because it led the faithful to believe that their donation of money guaranteed them a place in heaven and could free a soul from purgatory. Indulgence hawkers circulated far and wide, raising money that was sorely needed by the papacy. Luther was outraged by what he saw as a terrible abuse against true religion, motivated by greed.

1519 Luther is advised by the papal emissary sent to Wittenberg to write a letter of submission to the Holy See. When Luther then debates in Leipzig with Johannes Eck, he questions the infallibility of papal decisions as well as papal primacy by divine right. This is a decisive moment for Luther and for the Reformation. For Luther, Christ speaks not to an institution but to the individual heart.

Luther gives a second course of lectures on the psalms between June 27 and July 16, during which he comes to understand that God's righteousness is not His judgment against sinners but rather His gift of salvation.

On the death of Maximilian I, his grandson Charles I of Spain becomes Holy Roman Emperor Charles V.

Huldrych Zwingli begins the Swiss Reformation while preaching in Zurich.

Hernán Cortés (1485–1547) of Spain conquers and destroys the Aztec empire in Mexico (1519–21). The Portuguese Ferdinand Magellan (1480–1521) makes the first voyage around the world.

1520 Luther receives the papal bull *Exsurge Domine* (a binding letter with the papal seal, or *bulla*, attached), which threatens him with excommunication. Luther burns both the bull and a copy of canon law before the Elster Gate in Wittenberg. He writes three reform tracts: *To the Christian Nobility of the German Nation, The Babylonian Captivity of the Church,* and *The Freedom of a Christian.* Luther casts the pope as the Antichrist, the ruler of Babylon. He reduces the number of sacraments from seven to three, retaining baptism, the Eucharist, and penance. He redefines the Mass, rejecting the doctrine of transubstantiation (by which the Church taught that the bread and wine are changed in substance into the body and blood of Christ). He also rejects the notion of the Eucharist as a priestly sacrifice. He thus undercuts the dependence of the laity on the priesthood. Instead he proposes that the Mass is a promise of the remission of sins and that only faith in that promise makes the sacrament fruitful. He proclaims that the Christian, always justified and still sinning (*simul iustus et pecca-*

tor), is free from the domination of law because Christ dwells in the heart as the principle of salvation.

Luther's treatise *On Monastic Vows* rejects monasticism as a misguided attempt to please God and earn merit before Him with one's own works. Many monks and nuns, on reading it, feel justified to leave religious life. Luther remains a monk for five more years.

Johannes von Staupitz gives up his post as vicar general of the Augustinians. Deeply saddened by Luther's course of action, he joins the Benedictines, and will become an abbot in two years.

Pieter Brueghel the Elder, Dutch painter, is born (d. 1569).

Lucas Cranach paints a portrait of Luther (see cover).

1521 Luther is excommunicated on January 3 by Pope Leo X. In April Luther makes his stand at the Diet of Worms and refuses to recant. He is banned from the Holy Roman Empire but is hurried into protective custody at the Wartburg by his protector, Frederick the elector. There he begins his German translation of the Bible. He finishes the New Testament in eleven weeks (the Old Testament by 1534). Luther's translation of the Bible into High German marks one of the great milestones in the development of that language. Luther will be called the father of the German language.

Philipp Melanchthon writes *Loci communes,* the first systematic survey of Evangelical theology. The word "Evangelical" designates those who accept the doctrine of justification by faith and thus distinguish themselves from the Catholic Church. He apprises Luther of the Anabaptist currents, which are gathering strength. Luther is infuriated by their insistence on adult baptism and denial of infant baptism, since he holds that a child is not baptized because of its faith (it being too young for belief) but because of God's promise.

Pope Leo X confers the title "Defender of the Faith" on Henry VIII for his anti-Luther tract, *Assertio septem sacramentorum.* Luther responds with a furious tirade, *Against Henry, King of the English,* stung that Henry had labeled him a heretic without considering that there might be truth in his stand against the Roman church.

Ignatius of Loyola is wounded in battle defending Pamplona against the French. He undergoes conversion while convalescing. He then begins writing his *Spiritual Exercises,* in which he sets forth "Rules for Thinking with the Church."

The Expansion of Protestantism

1522 Luther returns to Wittenberg in March. His German New Testament is published in September.

The Wittenberg Augustinian cloister closes.

After the death of Leo X in December 1521, Adrian VI becomes pope. He favors reform.

1523 Luther resumes his lectures and writes *That Jesus Christ Was Born a Jew* and *Temporal Authority: To What Extent It Should Be Obeyed.* Luther's early tolerant attitude toward the Jews will develop into a fierce hostility when he comes to view them as obdurate foes of God who persist in rejecting the Father of Jesus Christ, who in Luther's eyes is their own God. He will consider them as public enemies of Christianity who deserve mercy only if they convert. Luther will strive to protect Christianity from what he perceives as their blasphemous denunciations of Christian beliefs.

On March 6 the enforcement of the Edict of Worms is postponed by the Edict of the Diet of Nuremberg. Adrian VI presents a program for renewal that includes an admission of papal guilt.

On July 1 the first Reformation martyrs are burned at the stake in Brussels: Augustinians Johann von Essen and Heinrich Voss.

Sir Thomas More is elected speaker of the House of Commons in England.

Adrian VI dies and is succeeded by Pope Clement VII.

1524 Luther abandons his religious habit on October 9.

Erasmus of Rotterdam writes against Luther in *Concerning Free Will.*

Johannes von Staupitz exchanges letters with Luther, rejecting with sad affection Luther's repudiation of monastic life. Staupitz dies without meeting Luther face-to-face again.

Zwingli abolishes the Catholic Mass in Zurich.

The Peasants' Revolt begins in southern Germany under the leadership of Thomas Münzer, Florian Geyer, and Michael Gaismair. This war is connected to the Reformation in that the gospel is invoked to justify the overthrow of existing authority. Luther takes the role of mediator between the peasants and the princes, but only at the outset.

1525 Luther marries Katharina von Bora (1499–1552), a former nun, on June 13. She is twenty-six, he is forty-one. Though the marriage was not a love match at the outset, Martin becomes devoted to this practical, energetic, and straightforward woman. They produce six children, of whom four will survive. Luther and Kate take great delight in their offspring. Hans will become a lawyer; Martin, a citizen of Wittenberg; and Paul, a doctor of medicine. Margaret will marry a Brandenburg nobleman. The Augustinian monastery of Wittenberg becomes their family dwelling. Luther's wedded state is a bold challenge to the ancient ideals of asceticism and virginity exalted by the church.

Luther writes tracts against religious enthusiasts, rebellious peasants, and, particularly, against Erasmus. *Concerning the Bondage of the Will* is Luther's treatise expounding his belief that by itself the human will is completely helpless—"captive, subject, and slave either of the will of God or the will of Satan." Against Luther's insistence on predestination, Erasmus had argued for man's free assent to God's saving grace. The break with Erasmus becomes bitter, total, and permanent.

English reformer William Tyndale's (1494–1536) translation of the New Testament is printed in Worms and Cologne (1525–1526). His translations of scripture will form the basis for the King James Version of the Bible (1611). An English Protestant, he shares many views with Luther, whom he met when he fled England under suspicion of heresy. Hunted down by order of Henry VIII, he will be executed as a heretic in Brussels.

The Peasants' Revolt is suppressed. Thomas Münzer is executed.

Death of Frederick the Wise, elector of Saxony. Elector John the Steadfast succeeds him. Both resist the interference of Catholic Rome in the temporal affairs of their government, understanding the state as God's legitimate authority in secular affairs. Luther's 1520 address *To the Christian Nobility of the German Nation,* an expression of his political views, was influenced by this conception. Both electors are sympathetic to Luther and guard his rights as a citizen against Rome's efforts to arrest him.

Charles V defeats France at Pavia and captures Francis I. Charles V becomes master of Italy.

Giovanni Pierluigi da Palestrina, Italian composer (d. 1594), is born. His polyphonic style, which he develops as a corrective for using profane melodies as settings for liturgical texts, is the model, along with Gregorian chant, for liturgical music.

1526 First Diet of Speyer postpones confronting the Reformation head-on and decrees instead that religious observance is to be determined on a territorial basis.

1527 Luther shows the first signs of serious heart disease. He is overcome by a violent depression, convinced that he has lost Christ and is being plunged into death and hell.

The first Protestant university is founded in Marburg, Germany.

The Lutheran reforms spread to Sweden.

Rome is sacked by a rogue imperial army of Emperor Charles V, and four thousand people are killed. Pope Clement VII is imprisoned in Castel Sant' Angelo.

Hans Holbein the Younger (1497–1543), court painter to Henry VIII, paints *Thomas More and His Family*.

1528 Henry VIII explains to the English public his motives for seeking a divorce from Catherine of Aragon.

The Reformation begins in Scotland, introduced by merchants who bring with them Lutheran teachings.

1529 Philip of Hesse arranges a meeting between Luther and Zwingli at Marburg in order to prompt them to achieve some measure of concord. Luther considers Zwingli's teaching on the Eucharist blasphemous because it rejects belief in the real presence of Christ in the elements of bread and wine. They fail to reach agreement on this point, and Luther refuses to shake hands with Zwingli at the end of the meeting.

Luther writes both his *Small Catechism* (in March) for the laity, and his *Large Catechism* (in May) for the clergy. Shocked by the ignorance of the fundamentals of Christian faith that he finds among both common people and clergy, Luther seeks to explain the teaching of the Church on the Ten Commandments, the Creed, and the Lord's Prayer.

Second Diet of Speyer opens with the Lutheran minority protesting against the decisions of the Catholic majority.

England joins Francis I and Charles V in the Treaty of Cambrai, which marks a peace agreement between France and Italy.

Turkish forces attack Austria and lay siege to Vienna.

Sir Thomas More becomes chancellor of England when Cardinal Wolsey falls from power. Wolsey dies before Henry VIII can have him tried for treason.

King Francis I founds the Collège de France.

1530 Luther remains at Coburg castle during the Diet of Augsburg (June 20–November 19). He sends off his tract *Exhortation to All Clergy Assembled at Augsburg*. The Augsburg Confession, prepared and read by Melanchthon, is signed by the Protestant princes. It is a definitive formulation of Lutheran doctrine. It is rejected by Emperor Charles V, his Catholic allies, and delegates from Rome. Western Christianity is henceforth divided.

Luther's father, Hans, dies. Luther retires with his psalter to grieve, and weeps until he is exhausted.

Charles V is crowned Holy Roman Emperor and king of Italy by Pope Clement VII.

1531 Luther's mother, Margarethe, dies.

Philip of Hesse forms the League of Schmalkalden, a powerful military alliance between the Protestant principalities.

Zwingli is killed in the battle of Kappel during the war in Switzerland between Protestant Zurich and the Catholic cantons.

Henry VIII takes upon himself the title of "Supreme Head of the Church in England."

Halley's comet arouses a wave of fear about the approaching end of the world.

1532 The Religious Peace of Nuremberg grants Protestants a free exercise of religion.

John Frederick I (1503–54), the Magnanimous, who is greatly influenced by Luther, becomes elector of Saxony.

Niccolò Machiavelli's (1469–1527) *The Prince* is published. It is a study of politics as divorced from ethics. It will be placed on the *Index of Forbidden Books* in 1559.

1533 Henry VIII marries Anne Boleyn, and a daughter, Elizabeth, is born. Anne is crowned queen, and Henry is excommunicated by the pope.

November 1, All Saints' Day, John Calvin (1509–64) hears Nicholas Cop, rector of the University of Paris, deliver a pro-Protestant address containing passages from Erasmus and Luther. Calvin determines to devote himself to the Protestant reform. He becomes its most formidable proponent after Luther himself.

1534 Luther completes his translation of the whole Bible into German.

Pope Clement VII dies and is succeeded by Pope Paul III, who considers calling a general council of the Church.

Anabaptists under John of Leiden form the kingdom of Zion at Münster.

Henry VIII, by his Act of Supremacy, dissolves English ties with the papacy.

The Jesuit order is founded by Ignatius of Loyola (1491–1556). In addition to poverty, chastity, and obedience to their order, Jesuits take a unique fourth vow, of direct obedience to the pope.

1535 Luther is made dean of the theological faculty at Wittenberg (until his death) and will lecture on the book of Genesis for the next ten years.

Negotiations take place with the papal nuncio to Germany, Pietro Paolo Vergerio, at Wittenberg castle about Protestant participation in the coming papal council.

Münster capitulates to the Hessian army at Zwickau, giving Catholics supremacy again. Anabaptist leader John of Leiden is tortured to death.

After efforts to avoid doing so, Thomas More finally refuses to take the oath of the king's supremacy. He is then tried for treason and beheaded on July 6.

Charles V conquers Tunis and frees twenty-thousand Christian slaves from their Ottoman captors.

Holbein, who earlier painted Thomas More, paints his portrait *King Henry VIII*.

1536 Luther is visited by south German Protestants, and the Wittenberg Concord is established. He produces the *Disputation Concerning Man* and the *Disputation Concerning Justification*.

Pope Paul III calls a council to be held in Mantua at Pentecost of 1537.

The Reformation is introduced into Denmark by King Christian III.

Catherine of Aragon dies. Queen Anne Boleyn is sent to the Tower of London and executed. Henry VIII marries Jane Seymour, his third wife. Over three hundred religious houses in England are dissolved by royal decree and taken over by the crown.

William Tyndale, English reformer, is burned as a heretic at Vilvoorde, in the Netherlands.

John Calvin writes the *Institutes of the Christian Religion,* the central work of Reformation theology.

Desiderius Erasmus, European humanist, dies.

Elector John Frederick of Saxony, Luther's patron and defender, decrees that Jews are to be expelled from his electorate. Jews, emboldened by predictions of the imminent coming of the Messiah, were speaking of the defeat of Christians and thus perceived as public enemies. Luther is approached by Josel von Rosheim to intercede for the Jews and convince the elector to change his mind. Luther refuses, insisting that the Jews were causing harm to the realm because of their blasphemous talk about Jesus of Nazareth.

1537 Luther experiences a serious attack of kidney stones during the *Bundestag* in Schmalkalden and comes close to death. He writes the Articles of Schmalkalden, a confession of faith and theology: "We hold that man is justified, without the works of law, through faith. . . . From this article no wavering is possible, even if heaven and earth pass away. . . . Upon this article rests all that we teach and live against the pope, devil, and world."

Disagreements with the duke of Mantua cause the Church council to be postponed.

Titian paints his portrait *King Francis I.*

1538 Calvin is forced by the war between Francis I and Emperor Charles V to detour on his way to Strasbourg and stop instead in Geneva. There he remains, with the result that Geneva becomes the center of Calvin's ministry and reform.

Holbein paints his portrait *Anne of Cleves.*

Charles Borromeo, future archbishop of Milan, is born (d. 1584). A model bishop, he will be prominent in the Counter-Reformation and a principal author of the Tridentine catechism.

1539 Luther writes *On the Councils and Churches.* He works on a further revision of his Bible translation.

A marriage agreement is signed at Hampton Court for Henry VIII to marry Anne of Cleves, his fourth wife.

Hernando de Soto explores Florida.

1540 Philip of Hesse commits bigamy, resulting in the loss of Protestantism's most powerful leader. This is a capital offense under imperial law, and Philip is forced to enter into a treaty with Charles V that undermines the Protestant League of Schmalkalden. As a result, Protestant ascendancy in Europe ceases.

Henry VIII marries Anne of Cleves, but the marriage is annulled almost immediately. He then marries Catherine Howard, his fifth wife.

The treaty between Venice and Turkey is signed at Constantinople.

The Society of Jesus is confirmed by Pope Paul III.

De Soto discovers the Mississippi River.

1541 Conferences in Worms and Regensburg produce agreements between Protestant and Roman theologians.

John Knox (1513–72) introduces the Calvinist reform into Scotland.

Henry VIII assumes the titles of king of Ireland and head of the Irish Church. Queen Catherine Howard is sent to the Tower of London, accused of immoral conduct.

Domenico Theotocopuli, El Greco, a Spanish-Greek painter, is born (d. 1614).

1542 War commences between the League of Schmalkalden, a Protestant alliance, and Duke Henry of Wolfenbüttel.

On September 20, Martin and Kate's daughter Magdalena dies at age thirteen of a viral infection. Kate is prostrate with grief, and Luther cannot endure the sound of the nails being driven into the coffin of his child.

Queen Catherine Howard is executed.

Pope Paul III convenes the Inquisition in Rome.

1543 Luther writes three anti-Jewish tracts, of which the most famous is *Of the Jews and Their Lies*. Luther's hope that the Jews will convert to Christianity and be saved is finally consumed by his increasing wrath over their refusal to accept Christ. In his rage, Luther wants Jews who refuse to convert to be expelled from Christian territories and their books and synagogues burned.

Henry VIII marries Catherine Parr, his sixth wife. She will survive him.

The *Index of Forbidden Books* is instituted and promulgated by Pope Paul III.

The first Protestants are burned at the stake by the Spanish branch of the Inquisition.

William Byrd, English composer, is born (d. 1623).

1544 Luther publishes a book of sermons called *The House Postils* and *Short Confession of the Holy Sacrament*.

Pope Paul III convokes the Council of Trent.

Torquato Tasso, Italian poet, is born (d. 1595). His greatest work is the romantic epic *Gerusalemme liberata,* which tells of the deliverance of the Holy City by the Crusaders from the Saracens in 1099.

1545 Luther writes the preface to the first volume of the complete Wittenberg edition of his Latin writings, *Against the Roman Papacy, an Institution of the Devil.*

The Council of Trent convenes. It will continue intermittently through 1564 to discuss the Reformation and the strategy for a Counter-Reformation.

Luther's Death and Beyond

1546 Luther preaches his last sermon in Eisleben on February 14. It is against the Jews. He dies on February 18, and his funeral is held at the castle church of Wittenberg on February 22. Philipp Melanchthon, his dearest and most faithful friend, preaches the funeral sermon.

Civil war begins in Germany between the Protestant League of Schmalkalden and Emperor Charles V.

Lucas Cranach the Younger (1515–86) paints his portrait *Martin Luther.*

1547 The Protestants are defeated at Mühlberg. Wittenberg capitulates. Elector John Frederick is forced to hand over his electoral dignity and lands to Duke Moritz. He is imprisoned for five years. So, too, is Philip of Hesse.

Henry VIII dies. He is succeeded by his and Jane Seymour's son, Edward VI.

Francis I of France dies and is succeeded by his son Henry II.

Miguel de Cervantes Saavedra, Spanish writer, is born (d. 1616). *Don Quixote* is his satirical masterpiece.

1555 The Peace of Augsburg declares the principle *Cuius regio eius religio* (each region would observe the religion of its ruler). The Lutheran states now enjoy equal rights with those of Roman Catholics.

1556 Thomas Cranmer is burned at the stake in England by order of Catholic Queen Mary I, daughter of Henry VIII and his first wife, Catherine of Aragon.

1558 After a brief reign and the end of her effort to extirpate Protestantism from the realm, Mary dies and is succeeded by her half sister, Elizabeth I (1533–1603).

1559 The coronation of Queen Elizabeth I.

King Henry II of France is killed in a tournament and he is succeeded by his son Francis II, whose wife, Mary Stuart, Queen of Scots, assumes the title of queen of England. Catholics regard her as having the legitimate right to the throne. After being deposed as queen in Scotland in 1567, she flees to England. Elizabeth imprisons Mary, and years later she is executed, on February 8, 1587.

1560 Philipp Melanchthon dies.

The beginnings of Puritanism stir in England when the first Calvinist refugees from Flanders arrive. They instigate a religious movement whose adherents seek to purge the Anglican Church of the remnants of its Catholic past.

King Francis II of France dies and is succeeded by Charles IX, with Catherine de Médicis, his mother, as regent.

The Church of Scotland is founded when John Knox and the Reformers expel the French, depose Mary of Guise, forbid the celebration of the Mass, abolish the jurisdiction of the pope, and approve the Scottish Confession.

1562 At the massacre of Vassy on March 1, twelve hundred French Huguenots are killed by forces of the Catholic duke of Guise. The first War of Religion begins. The massacre on St. Bartholomew's Day (August 24, 1572, in Paris) results in the murder of two thousand French Calvinists. There will be eight French civil wars involving the Catholics and the Huguenots. The religious freedom achieved by the Edict of Nantes in 1598 will be destroyed by Cardinal Richelieu in 1629 with the Peace of Alais. The civil and political rights of the Huguenots are revoked at this time, and many flee to seek sanctuary in other countries.

1563 The Council of Trent closes after setting the stage for the reform of Catholicism. The *Catechism of the Council of Trent* (1566) is very effective in disseminating Catholic doctrine as clarified by the council. However, the gulf between Catholics and Protestants is not bridged. This breach continues in Western Christendom to the present.

Faith *and* Freedom

Luther's Morning Prayer

My Heavenly Father, I thank You, through Jesus Christ, Your beloved Son, that You kept me safe from all evil and danger last night. Save me, I pray, today as well, from every evil and sin, so that all I do and the way that I live will please You. I put myself in Your care, body and soul and all that I have. Let Your holy Angels be with me, so that the evil enemy will not gain power over me. Amen.

I

"Here I Stand"

It has been well observed that revolutions are not freely created by one individual's will but rather involve setting loose larger forces that have accumulated and await their chance to pour forth. If ever there was a test of such a hypothesis, surely it was the day a Bible professor and monk, one Martin Luther, tacked his Ninety-five Theses on the door of the castle church of Wittenberg, an upstart university town in a backwater district of the Holy Roman Empire. Though, in fact, such an act, calling for yet another academic debate, was if anything routine, and though, in the end, no one ever came and the debate was never held, the effects of this one act by one man produced a sea change in Europe.

In the end what happened was not a revolution; it would properly be termed the Reformation. Although he challenged his colleagues and students in vain, within days, weeks, and months Luther's call had set loose an ever-widening debate. It would be difficult to conceive a better protagonist for it. One Franciscan prior, on receiving news of his friend Martin Luther's theses, told his monks, "He is here who will do the task."

These selections from the writings and sermons and letters and even the prayers and intimate conversations of Martin

Luther do not include this most famous and notorious document, the Ninety-five Theses. Their highly compressed and technical theological language do not serve well the needs of the reader we posit, who is in search of spiritual succor. Instead, to begin, we offer two other documents that dramatically and eloquently show the man and his core ideas. One was written three years after the theses and is the second part of The Freedom of a Christian, *a work, Luther was confident, that contained "the whole of Christian life in a brief form." In it he aimed to reconcile two paradoxical theses: "A Christian is a perfectly free lord of all, subject to none" and "A Christian is a perfectly dutiful servant of all, subject to all."*

The second reading is an excerpt from one of the most famous speeches ever made, Martin Luther's defense of his ideas before the assembled diet of the Holy Roman Empire at Worms. Interestingly, this occasion has come down to us as carefully recorded by officials of the Roman Catholic Church—who succeeded in having the diet ban Luther as an outlaw—as it was by his friends, who had come in his support. The resulting account shows us a man whose ringing affirmation of individual conscience over conformity to higher authority has stirred generations of thoughtful readers, as it did those then present.

The Freedom of a Christian

PART TWO

Many people have considered Christian faith an easy thing, and not a few have given it a place among the virtues. They do this because they have not experienced it and have never tasted the great strength there is in faith. It is impossible to write well about it or to understand what has been written about it unless one has at one time or another experienced the courage which faith gives a man when trials oppress him. But he who has had even a faint taste of it can never write, speak, meditate, or hear enough concerning it. It is a living "spring of water welling up to eternal life," as Christ calls it in John 4 [:14].

As for me, although I have no wealth of faith to boast of and know how scant my supply is, I nevertheless hope that I have attained to a little faith, even though I have been assailed by great and various temptations; and I hope that I can discuss it, if not more elegantly, certainly more to the point, than those literalists and subtle disputants have previously done, who have not even understood what they have written.

To make the way smoother for the unlearned—for only them do I serve—I shall set down the following two propositions concerning the freedom and the bondage of the spirit:

A Christian is a perfectly free lord of all, subject to none.

A Christian is a perfectly dutiful servant of all, subject to all.

These two theses seem to contradict each other. If, however, they should be found to fit together, they would serve our purpose beautifully. Both are Paul's own statements. He says in 1 Cor. 9, "For though I am free from all men, I have made myself a slave to all," and in Rom. 13 [:8], "Owe no one anything, except to love one another." Love by its very nature is ready to serve and be subject to him who is loved. So Christ, although He was Lord of all, was "born of woman, born under the law" [Gal. 4:4], and therefore was at the same time a free man and a servant, "in the form of God" and "of a servant" [Phil. 2:6–7].

Let us start, however, with something more remote from our subject, but more obvious. Man has a twofold nature, a spiritual and a bodily one. According to the spiritual nature, which men refer to as the soul, he is called a spiritual, inner, or new man. According to the bodily nature, which men refer to as flesh, he is called a carnal, outward, or old man, of whom the apostle writes in 2 Cor. 4 [:16], "Though our outer nature is wasting away, our inner nature is being renewed every day." Because of this diversity of nature, the scriptures assert contradictory things concerning the same man, since these two men in the same man contradict each other, "for the desires of the flesh are against the Spirit, and the desires of the Spirit are against the flesh," according to Gal. 5 [:17].

First, let us consider the inner man to see how a righteous, free, and pious Christian, that is, a spiritual, new, and inner man, becomes what he is. It is evident that no external thing has any influence in producing Christian righteousness or freedom, or in producing unrighteousness or servitude. A simple argument will furnish the proof of this statement. What can it profit the soul if the body is well, free, and active, and eats, drinks, and does as it pleases? For in these respects even the most godless slaves of vice may prosper. On the other hand, how will poor health or imprisonment or hunger or thirst or any other external misfortune harm the soul? Even the most godly men, and those who are free because of clear consciences, are afflicted with these things. None of these things touch either the freedom or the servitude of the soul.

It does not help the soul if the body is adorned with the sacred robes of priests or dwells in sacred places or is occupied with sacred duties or prays, fasts, abstains from certain kinds of food, or does any work that can be done by the body and in the body. The righteousness and the freedom of the soul require something far different, since the things which have been mentioned could be done by any wicked person. Such works produce nothing but hypocrites. On the other hand, it will not harm the soul if the body is clothed in secular dress, dwells in unconsecrated places, eats and drinks as others do, does not pray aloud, and neglects to do all the above-mentioned things which hypocrites can do.

Furthermore, to put aside all kinds of works, even contemplation, meditation, and all that the soul can do, does not help. One thing, and only one thing, is necessary for Christian life, righteousness, and freedom. That one thing is the most holy Word of God, the gospel of Christ, as Christ says in John 11 [:25], "I am the Resurrection and the life; he who believes in Me, though he die, yet shall he live"; and in John 8 [:36], "So if the Son makes you free, you will be free indeed"; and in Matt. 4 [:4], "Man shall not live by bread alone, but by every word that proceeds from the mouth of God." Let us then consider it certain and firmly established that the soul can do without anything except the Word of God and that where the Word of God is missing there is no help at all for the soul. If it has the Word of God it is rich and lacks nothing since it is the Word of life, truth, light, peace, righteousness, salvation, joy, liberty, wisdom, power, grace, glory, and of every incalculable blessing. This is why the prophet in the entire Psalm [119] and in many other places yearns and sighs for the Word of God and uses so many names to describe it.

On the other hand, there is no more terrible disaster with which the wrath of God can afflict men than a famine of the hearing of His Word, as He says in Amos [8:11]. Likewise there is no greater mercy than when He sends forth His Word, as we read in Psalm 107 [:20]: "He sent forth His Word, and healed them, and delivered them from destruction." Nor was Christ sent into the world for any other ministry except that of the Word. Moreover, the entire spiritual estate—all the apostles, bishops, and priests—has been called and instituted only for the ministry of the Word.

You may ask, "What then is the Word of God, and how shall it be used, since there are so many words of God?" I answer: the apostle explains this in Romans 1. The Word is the gospel of God concerning His Son, who was made flesh, suffered, rose from the dead, and was glorified through the Spirit who sanctifies. To preach Christ means to feed the soul, make it righteous, set it free, and save it, provided it believes the preaching. Faith alone is the saving and efficacious use of the Word of God, according to Rom. 10 [:9]: "If you confess with your lips that Jesus is Lord and believe in your heart that God raised Him from the dead, you will be saved." Furthermore, "Christ is the end of the law, that everyone who has faith may be justified" [Rom. 10:4]. Again, in Rom. 1 [:17], "He who through faith is righteous shall live." The Word of God cannot be received and cherished by any works whatever but only by faith. Therefore it is clear that as the soul needs only the Word of God for its life and righteousness, so it is justified by faith alone and not any works; for if it could be justified by anything else, it would not need the Word, and consequently it would not need faith.

This faith cannot exist in connection with works—that is to say, if you at the same time claim to be justified by works, whatever their character—for that would be the same as "limping with two different opinions" [1 Kings 18:21], as worshiping Baal and kissing one's own hand [Job 31:27–28], which, as Job says, is a very great iniquity. Therefore, the moment you begin to have faith you learn that all things in you are altogether blameworthy, sinful, and damnable, as the apostle says in Rom. 3 [:23], "Since all have sinned and fall short of the glory of God," and, "None is righteous, no, not one; . . . all have turned aside, together they have gone wrong" [Rom. 3:10–12]. When you have learned this you will know that you need Christ, who suffered and rose again for you so that, if you believe in Him, you may through this faith become a new man insofar as your sins are forgiven and you are justified by the merits of another, namely, of Christ alone.

Since, therefore, this faith can rule only in the inner man, as Rom. 10 [:10] says, "For man believes with his heart and so is justified," and since faith alone justifies, it is clear that the inner man cannot be justified, freed, or saved by any outer work or action at all, and that these works, whatever their character, have nothing to do with this inner man. On the other hand, only ungodliness and unbelief of heart, and no outer work, make him guilty and a damnable servant of sin. Wherefore it ought to be the first concern of every Christian to lay aside all confidence in works, and increasingly to strengthen faith alone, and through faith to grow in the knowledge, not of works, but of Christ Jesus, who suffered and rose for him, as Peter teaches in the last chapter of his first epistle [1 Pet. 5:10]. No other work makes a Christian. Thus when the Jews asked Christ, as related in John 6 [:28], what they must do "to be doing the work of God," He brushed aside the multitude of works which He saw they did in great profusion and suggested one work, saying, "This is the work of God, that you believe in Him whom He has sent" [John 6:29]; "for on Him has God the Father set His seal" [John 6:27].

Therefore true faith in Christ is a treasure beyond comparison, which brings with it complete salvation and saves man from every evil, as Christ says in the last chapter of Mark [16:16]: "He who believes and is baptized will be saved; but he who does not believe will be condemned." Isaiah contemplated this treasure and foretold it in chapter 10: "The Lord will make a small and consuming word upon the land, and it will overflow with righteousness" [cf. Isa. 10:22]. This is as though he said, "Faith, which is a small and perfect fulfillment of the law, will fill believers with so great a righteousness that they will need nothing more to become righteous." So Paul says, Rom. 10 [:10], "For man believes with his heart and so is justified."

Should you ask how it happens that faith alone justifies and offers us such a treasure of great benefits without works, in view of the fact that so many works, ceremonies, and laws are prescribed in the scriptures, I answer: First of all, remember what has been said, namely, that faith alone, without works, justifies, frees, and saves; we shall make this clearer later on. Here we must point out that the entire scripture of God is divided into two parts: commandments and promises. Although the commandments teach things that are good, the things taught are not done as soon as they are taught, for the commandments show us what we ought to do but do not give us the power to do it. They are intended to teach man to know himself, that through them he may recognize his inability to do good and may despair of his own ability. That is why they are called the Old Testament and constitute the Old Testament. For example, the commandment "You shall not covet" [Exod. 20:17], is a command which proves us all to be sinners, for no one can avoid coveting no matter how much he may struggle against it. Therefore, in order not to covet and to fulfill the commandment, a man is compelled to despair of himself, to seek the help which he does not find in himself elsewhere, and from someone else, as stated in Hosea [13:9]: "Destruction is your own, O Israel: your help is only in me." As we fare with respect to one commandment, so we fare with all, for it is equally impossible for us to keep any one of them.

Now when a man has learned through the commandments to recognize his helplessness and is distressed about how he might satisfy the law—since the law must be fulfilled so that not a jot or tittle shall be lost, otherwise man will be condemned without hope—then, being truly humbled and reduced to nothing in his own eyes, he finds in himself nothing whereby he may be justified and saved.

Here the second part of scripture comes to our aid, namely, the promises of God, which declare the glory of God, saying, "If you wish to fulfill the law and not covet, as the law demands, come, believe in Christ, in whom grace, righteousness, peace, liberty, and all things are promised you. If you believe, you shall have all things; if you do not believe, you shall lack all things." That which is impossible for you to accomplish by trying to fulfill all the works of the law—many and useless as they all are—you will accomplish quickly and easily through faith. God our Father has made all things depend on faith so that whoever has faith will have everything, and whoever does not have faith will have nothing. "For God has consigned all men to disobedience, that He may have mercy upon all," as it is stated in Rom. 11 [:32]. Thus the promises of God give what the commandments of God demand and fulfill what the law prescribes so that all things may be God's alone, both the commandments and the fulfilling of the commandments. He alone commands, He alone fulfills. Therefore the promises of God belong to the New Testament. Indeed, they *are* the New Testament.

Since these promises of God are holy, true, righteous, free, and peaceful words, full of goodness, the soul which clings to them with a firm faith will be so closely united with them and altogether absorbed by them that it not only will share in all their power but will be saturated and intoxicated by them. If a touch of Christ healed, how much more will this most tender spiritual touch, this absorbing of the Word, communicate to the soul all things that belong to the Word? This, then, is how through faith alone, without works, the soul is justified by the Word of God, sanctified, made true, peaceful, and free, filled with every blessing and truly made a child of God, as John [:12] says: "But to all who ... believed in His name, He gave power to become children of God."

From what has been said it is easy to see from what source faith derives such great power and why a good work or all good works together cannot equal it. No good work can rely upon the word of God or live in the soul, for faith alone and the Word of God rule in the soul. Just as the heated iron glows like fire because of the union of fire with it, so the Word imparts its qualities to the soul. It is clear, then, that a Christian has all that he needs in faith and needs no works to justify him; and if he has no need of works, he has no need of the law; and if he has no need of the law, surely he is free

from the law. It is true that "the law is not laid down for the just"
[1 Tim. 1:9]. This is that Christian liberty, our faith, which does
not induce us to live in idleness or wickedness but makes the law
and works unnecessary for any man's righteousness and salvation.

This is the first power of faith. Let us now examine also the second. It is a further function of faith that it honors Him whom it
trusts with the most reverent and highest regard, since it considers
Him truthful and trustworthy. There is no other honor equal to the
estimate of truthfulness and righteousness with which we honor
Him whom we trust. Could we ascribe to a man anything greater
than truthfulness and righteousness and perfect goodness? On the
other hand, there is no way in which we can show greater contempt for a man than to regard him as false and wicked and to be
suspicious of him, as we do when we do not trust him. So when the
soul firmly trusts God's promises, it regards Him as truthful and
righteous. Nothing more excellent than this can be ascribed to
God. The very highest worship of God is this: that we ascribe to
Him truthfulness, righteousness, and whatever else should be
ascribed to one who is trusted. When this is done, the soul consents
to His will. Then it hallows His name and allows itself to be treated
according to God's good pleasure, for clinging to God's promises,
it does not doubt that He who is true, just, and wise will do, dispose, and provide all things well.

Is not such a soul most obedient to God in all things by this
faith? What commandment is there that such obedience has not
completely fulfilled? What more complete fulfillment is there than
obedience in all things? This obedience, however, is not rendered
by works, but by faith alone. On the other hand, what greater
rebellion against God, what greater wickedness, what greater contempt of God is there than not believing His promise? For what is
this but to make God a liar or to doubt that He is truthful?—that
is, to ascribe truthfulness to oneself but lying and vanity to God?
Does not a man who does this deny God and set himself up as an
idol in his heart? Then of what good are works done in such
wickedness, even if they were the works of angels and apostles?
Therefore God has rightly included all things, not under anger or
lust but under unbelief, so that they who imagine that they are fulfilling the law by doing the works of chastity and mercy required
by the law (the civil and human virtues) might not be saved. They

are included under the sin of unbelief and must either seek mercy or be justly condemned.

When, however, God sees that we consider Him truthful and by the faith of our heart pay Him the great honor which is due Him, He does us that great honor of considering us truthful and righteous for the sake of our faith. Faith works truth and righteousness by giving God what belongs to Him. Therefore God in turn glorifies our righteousness. It is true and just that God is truthful and just, and to consider and confess Him to be so is the same as being truthful and just. Accordingly He says in 1 Sam. 2 [:30], "Those who honor Me I will honor, and those who despise Me shall be lightly esteemed." So Paul says in Rom. 4 [:3] that Abraham's faith "was reckoned to him as righteousness" because by it he gave glory most perfectly to God, and that for the same reason our faith shall be reckoned to us as righteousness if we believe.

The third incomparable benefit of faith is that it unites the soul with Christ as a bride is united with her bridegroom. By this mystery, as the apostle teaches, Christ and the soul become one flesh [Eph. 5:31–32]. And if they are one flesh and there is between them a true marriage—indeed the most perfect of all marriages, since human marriages are but poor examples of this one true marriage—it follows that everything they have they hold in common, the good as well as the evil. Accordingly the believing soul can boast of and glory in whatever Christ has as though it were its own, and whatever the soul has, Christ claims as His own. Let us compare these and we shall see inestimable benefits. Christ is full of grace, life, and salvation. The soul is full of sins, death, and damnation. Now let faith come between them and sins, death, and damnation will be Christ's, while grace, life, and salvation will be the soul's; for if Christ is a bridegroom, He must take upon Himself the things which are His bride's and bestow upon her the things that are His. If He gives her His body and very self, how shall He not give her all that is His? And if He takes the body of the bride, how shall He not take all that is hers?

Here we have a most pleasing vision not only of communion but of a blessed struggle and victory and salvation and redemption. Christ is God and man in one person. He has neither sinned nor died, and is not condemned, and He cannot sin, die, or be condemned; His righteousness, life, and salvation are unconquerable, eternal, omnipotent. By the wedding ring of faith He shares in the sins, death, and pains of hell which are His bride's. As a matter of fact, He makes them His own and acts as if they were His own and as if He Himself had sinned; He suffered, died, and descended into hell that He might overcome them all. Now since it was such a one who did all this, and death and hell could not swallow Him up, these were necessarily swallowed up by Him in a mighty duel; for His righteousness is greater than the sins of all men, His life stronger than death, His salvation more invincible than hell. Thus the believing soul by means of the pledge of its faith is free in Christ, its bridegroom, free from all sins, secure against death and hell, and is endowed with the eternal righteousness, life, and salvation of Christ, its bridegroom. So He takes to Himself a glorious bride, "without spot or wrinkle, cleansing her by the washing of water with the Word" [cf. Eph. 5:26–27] of life, that is, by faith in the Word of life, righteousness, and salvation. In this way He marries her in faith, steadfast love, and in mercies, righteousness, and justice, as Hos. 2 [:19–20] says.

Who then can fully appreciate what this royal marriage means? Who can understand the riches of the glory of this grace? Here this rich and divine bridegroom, Christ, marries this poor, wicked harlot, redeems her from all her evil, and adorns her with all His goodness. Her sins cannot now destroy her, since they are laid upon Christ and swallowed up by Him. And she has that righteousness in Christ, her husband, of which she may boast as of her own and which she can confidently display alongside her sins in the face of death and hell and say, "If I have sinned, yet my Christ, in whom I believe, has not sinned, and all His is mine and all mine is His," as the bride in the Song of Solomon [2:16] says, "My beloved is mine and I am his." This is what Paul means when he says in 1 Cor. 15 [:57], "Thanks be to God, who gives us the victory through our Lord Jesus Christ," that is, the victory over sin and death, as he also says there, "The sting of death is sin, and the power of sin is the law" [1 Cor. 15:56].

From this you once more see that much is ascribed to faith, namely, that it alone can fulfill the law and justify without works. You see that the First Commandment, which says, "You shall

worship one God," is fulfilled by faith alone. Though you were
nothing but good works from the soles of your feet to the crown of
your head, you would still not be righteous or worship God or fulfill the First Commandment, since God cannot be worshiped
unless you ascribe to Him the glory of truthfulness and all goodness which is due Him. This cannot be done by works but only by
the faith of the heart. Not by the doing of works but by believing
do we glorify God and acknowledge that He is truthful. Therefore faith alone is the righteousness of a Christian and the fulfilling of all the commandments, for he who fulfills the First
Commandment has no difficulty in fulfilling all the rest.

But works, being inanimate things, cannot glorify God,
although they can, if faith is present, be done to the glory of God.
Here, however, we are not inquiring what works and what kind
of works are done, but who it is that does them, who glorifies God
and brings forth the works. This is done by faith, which dwells in
the heart and is the source and substance of all our righteousness.
Therefore it is a blind and dangerous doctrine which teaches that
the commandments must be fulfilled by works. The commandments must be fulfilled before any works can be done, and the
works proceed from the fulfillment of the commandments [Rom.
13:10], as we shall hear.

That we may examine more profoundly that grace which our
inner man has in Christ, we must realize that in the Old Testament God consecrated to Himself all the firstborn males. The
birthright was highly prized, for it involved a twofold honor, that
of priesthood and that of kingship. The firstborn brother was
priest and lord over all the others and a type of Christ, the true and
only firstborn of God the Father and the Virgin Mary and true
king and priest, but not after the fashion of the flesh and the
world, for His kingdom is not of this world [John 18:36]. He
reigns in heavenly and spiritual things and consecrates them—
things such as righteousness, truth, wisdom, peace, and salvation.
This does not mean that all things on earth and in hell are not also
subject to Him—otherwise how could He protect and save us
from them?—but that His kingdom consists neither in them nor
of them. Nor does His priesthood consist in the outer splendor of
robes and postures like those of the human priesthood of Aaron
and our present-day Church; but it consists of spiritual things,

through which He by an invisible service intercedes for us in heaven before God, there offers Himself as a sacrifice, and does all things a priest should do, as Paul describes Him under the type of Melchizedek in the epistle to the Hebrews [Heb. 6–7]. Nor does He only pray and intercede for us, but He teaches us inwardly through the living instruction of His Spirit, thus performing the two real functions of a priest, of which the prayers and the preaching of human priests are visible types.

Now just as Christ by His birthright obtained these two prerogatives, so He imparts them to, and shares them with, everyone who believes in Him according to the law of the above-mentioned marriage, according to which the wife owns whatever belongs to the husband. Hence all of us who believe in Christ are priests and kings in Christ, as 1 Pet. 2 [:9] says: "You are a chosen race, God's own people, a royal priesthood, a priestly kingdom, that you may declare the wonderful deeds of Him who called you out of darkness into His marvelous light."

The nature of this priesthood and kingship is something like this: First, with respect to the kingship, every Christian is by faith so exalted above all things that, by virtue of a spiritual power, He is lord of all things without exception, so that nothing can do Him any harm. As a matter of fact, all things are made subject to Him and are compelled to serve Him in obtaining salvation. Accordingly Paul says in Rom. 8 [:28], "All things work together for good for the elect," and in 1 Cor. 3 [:21–23], "All things are yours, whether . . . life or death or the present or the future, all are yours; and you are Christ's." This is not to say that every Christian is placed over all things to have and control them by physical power—a madness with which some churchmen are afflicted—for such power belongs to kings, princes, and other men on earth. Our ordinary experience in life shows us that we are subjected to all, suffer many things, and even die. As a matter of fact, the more Christian a man is, the more evils, sufferings, and deaths he must endure, as we see in Christ the firstborn prince Himself, and in all His brethren, the saints. The power of which we speak is spiritual. It rules in the midst of enemies and is powerful in the midst of oppression. This means nothing else than that "power is made perfect in weakness" [2 Cor. 12:9] and that in all things I can find profit toward salvation [Rom. 8:28], so that the cross and death itself are compelled to serve me and to work together with me for my salvation. This is a splendid privilege and hard to attain, a truly omnipotent power, a spiritual dominion in which there is nothing so good and nothing so evil but that it shall work together for good to me, if only I believe. Yes, since faith alone suffices for salvation, I need nothing except faith exercising the power and dominion of its own liberty. Lo, this is the inestimable power and liberty of Christians.

Not only are we the freest of kings, we are also priests forever, which is far more excellent than being kings, for as priests we are worthy to appear before God to pray for others and to teach one another divine things. These are the functions of priests, and they cannot be granted to any unbeliever. Thus Christ has made it possible for us, provided we believe in Him, to be not only His brethren, coheirs, and fellow kings, but also His fellow priests. Therefore we may boldly come into the presence of God in the spirit of faith [Heb. 10:19, 22] and cry, "Abba, Father!" pray for one another, and do all things which we see done and foreshadowed in the outer and visible works of priests.

He, however, who does not believe is not served by anything. On the contrary, nothing works for his good, but he himself is a servant of all, and all things turn out badly for him because he wickedly uses them to his own advantage and not to the glory of God. So he is no priest but a wicked man whose prayer becomes sin and who never comes into the presence of God because God does not hear sinners [John 9:31]. Who then can comprehend the lofty dignity of the Christian? By virtue of his royal power he rules over all things, death, life, and sin, and through his priestly glory is omnipotent with God because he does the things which God asks and desires, as it is written, "He will fulfill the desire of those who fear Him; He also will hear their cry and save them" [cf. Phil. 4:13]. To this glory a man attains, certainly not by any works of his, but by faith alone.

From this anyone can clearly see how a Christian is free from all things and over all things so that he needs no works to make him righteous and save him, since faith alone abundantly confers all these things. Should he grow so foolish, however, as to presume to become righteous, free, saved, and a Christian by means of some good work, he would instantly lose faith and all its benefits, a foolishness aptly illustrated in the fable of the dog who runs along a stream with a piece of meat in his mouth and, deceived by the reflection of the meat in the water, opens his mouth to snap at it and so loses both the meat and the reflection.[2]

You will ask, "If all who are in the Church are priests, how do these whom we now call priests differ from laymen?" I answer: injustice is done those words "priest," "cleric," "spiritual," "ecclesiastic" when they are transferred from all Christians to those few who are now by a mischievous usage called ecclesiastics. Holy scripture makes no distinction between them, although it gives the name "ministers," "servants," "stewards" to those who are now proudly called popes, bishops, and lords and who should, according to the ministry of the Word, serve others and teach them the faith of Christ and the freedom of believers. Although we are all equally priests, we cannot all publicly minister and teach. We ought not do so even if we could. Paul writes accordingly in 1 Cor. 4 [1], "This is how one should regard us, as servants of Christ and stewards of the mysteries of God."

That stewardship, however, has now been developed into so great a display of power and so terrible a tyranny that no heathen empire or other earthly power can be compared with it, just as if laymen were not also Christians. Through this perversion the knowledge of Christian grace, faith, liberty, and of Christ Himself has altogether perished, and its place has been taken by an unbearable bondage of human works and laws until we have become, as the Lamentations of Jeremiah [1] say, servants of the vilest men on earth, who abuse our misfortune to serve only their base and shameless will.

To return to our purpose, I believe that it has now become clear that it is not enough, or in any sense Christian, to preach the works, life, and words of Christ as historical facts, as if the knowledge of these would suffice for the conduct of life; yet this is the fashion among those who must today be regarded as our best preachers. Far less is it sufficient or Christian to say nothing at all about Christ and to teach instead the laws of men and the decrees of the fathers. Now, there are not a few who preach Christ and

[2]Luther was fond of Aesop's Fables, of which this is one.

read about Him that they may move men's affections to sympathy with Christ, to anger against the Jews, and such childish and effeminate nonsense. Rather Christ ought to be preached to the end that faith in Him may be established, that He may not only be Christ but be Christ for you and me, and that what is said of Him and is denoted in His name may be effectual in us. Such faith is produced and preserved in us by preaching why Christ came, what He brought and bestowed, what benefit it is to us to accept Him. This is done when that Christian liberty which He bestows is rightly taught and we are told in what way we Christians are all kings and priests and therefore lords of all and may firmly believe that whatever we have done is pleasing and acceptable in the sight of God, as I have already said.

What man is there whose heart, upon hearing these things, will not rejoice to its depth, and when receiving such comfort will not grow tender so that he will love Christ as he never could by means of any laws or works? Who would have the power to harm or frighten such a heart? If the knowledge of sin or the fear of death should break in upon it, it is ready to hope in the Lord. It does not grow afraid when it hears tidings of evil. It is not disturbed when it sees its enemies. This is so because it believes that the righteousness of Christ is its own and that its sin is not its own, but Christ's, and that all sin is swallowed up by the righteousness of Christ. This, as has been said above,[3] is a necessary consequence on account of faith in Christ. So the heart learns to scoff at death and sin and to say with the apostle, "O death, where is thy victory? O death, where is thy sting? The sting of death is sin, and the power of sin is the law. But thanks be to God, who gives us the victory through our Lord Jesus Christ" [1 Cor. 15:55–57]. Death is swallowed up not only in the victory of Christ by also by our victory, because through faith His victory has become ours and in that faith we also are conquerors.

Let this suffice concerning the inner man, his liberty, and the source of his liberty, the righteousness of faith. He needs neither laws nor good works but, on the contrary, is injured by them if he believes that he is justified by them.

[3] Cf. page 11.

Luther at the Diet of Worms

APRIL 18, 1521
IN THE NAME OF JESUS

Most serene emperor, most illustrious princes, most clement lords, obedient to the time set for me yesterday evening, I appear before you, beseeching you, by the mercy of God, that your most serene majesty and your most illustrious lordships may deign to listen graciously to this my cause—which is, as I hope, a cause of justice and of truth. If through my inexperience I have either not given the proper titles to some, or have offended in some manner against court customs and etiquette, I beseech you to kindly pardon me, as a man accustomed not to courts but to the cells of monks. I can bear no other witness about myself but that I have taught and written up to this time with simplicity of heart, as I had in view only the glory of God and the sound instruction of Christ's faithful.

Most serene emperor, most illustrious princes, concerning those questions proposed to me yesterday on behalf of your serene majesty—whether I acknowledged as mine the books enumerated and published in my name and whether I wished to persevere in their defense or to retract them—I have given to the first question my full and complete answer, in which I still persist and shall persist forever. These books are mine and they have been published in my name by me, unless in the meantime, either through the craft or the mistaken wisdom of my emulators, something in them has been changed or wrongly cut out. For plainly I cannot acknowledge anything except what is mine alone and what has been written by me alone, to the exclusion of all interpretations of anyone at all.

In replying to the second question, I ask that your most serene majesty and your lordships may deign to note that my books are not all of the same kind.

For there are some in which I have discussed religious faith and morals simply and evangelically, so that even my enemies themselves are compelled to admit that these are useful, harmless, and clearly worthy to be read by Christians. Even the bull,[4] although harsh and cruel, admits that some of my books are inoffensive, and yet allows these also to be condemned with a judgment which is utterly monstrous. Thus, if I should begin to disavow them, I ask you, what would I be doing? Would not I, alone of all men, be condemning the very truth upon which friends and enemies equally agree, striving alone against the harmonious confession of all?

Another group of my books attacks the papacy and the affairs of the papists as those who both by their doctrines and by very wicked examples have laid waste the Christian world with evil that affects the spirit and the body. For no one can deny or conceal this fact, when the experience of all and the complaints of everyone witness that through the decrees of the pope and the doctrines of men the consciences of the faithful have been most miserably entangled, tortured, and torn to pieces. Also, property and possessions, especially in this illustrious nation of Germany, have been devoured by an unbelievable tyranny and are being devoured to this time without letup and by unworthy means. [Yet the papists] by their own decrees warn that the papal laws and doctrines which are contrary to the gospel or the opinions of the fathers are to be regarded as erroneous and reprehensible. If, therefore, I should have retracted these writings, I should have done nothing other than to have added strength to this [papal] tyranny and I should have opened not only windows but doors to such great godlessness. It would rage farther and more freely than ever it has dared up to this time. Yes, from the proof of such a revocation on my part, their wholly lawless and unrestrained kingdom of wickedness would become still more intolerable for the already wretched people; and their rule would be further strengthened and established, especially if it should be reported that this evil deed had been done by me by virtue of the authority of your most serene majesty and of the whole Roman Empire. Good God! What a cover for wickedness and tyranny I should have then become.

I have written a third sort of book, against some private and (as they say) distinguished individuals—those, namely, who strive to preserve the Roman tyranny and to destroy the godliness taught by me. Against these I confess I have been more violent than my

---

[4] Luther refers to the papal bull *Exsurge Domine,* issued in Rome on June 15, 1520.

religion or profession demands. But then, I do not set myself up as a saint; neither am I disputing about my life, but about the teaching of Christ. It is not proper for me to retract these works, because by this retraction it would again happen that tyranny and godlessness would, with my patronage, rule and rage among the people of God more violently than ever before.

However, because I am a man and not God, I am not able to shield my books with any other protection than that which my Lord Jesus Christ Himself offered for His teaching. When questioned before Annas about His teaching and struck by a servant, He said: "If I have spoken wrongly, bear witness to the wrong" [John 18:19–23]. If the Lord Himself, who knew that He could not err, did not refuse to hear testimony against His teaching, even from the lowliest servant, how much more ought I, who am the lowest scum and able to do nothing except err, desire and expect that somebody should want to offer testimony against my teaching! Therefore, I ask by the mercy of God, may your most serene majesty, most illustrious lordships, or anyone at all who is able, either high or low, bear witness, expose my errors, overthrowing them by the writings of the prophets and the evangelists. Once I have been taught, I shall be quite ready to renounce every error, and I shall be the first to cast my books into the fire.

From these remarks I think it is clear that I have sufficiently considered and weighed the hazards and dangers, as well as the excitement and dissensions aroused in the world as a result of my teachings, things about which I was gravely and forcefully warned yesterday. To see excitement and dissension arise because of the Word of God is to me clearly the most joyful aspect of all in these matters. For this is the way, the opportunity, and the result of the Word of God, just as He said, "I have not come to bring peace, but a sword. For I have come to set a man against his father . . ." [Matt. 10:34–35]. Therefore, we ought to think how marvelous and terrible is our God in His counsels, lest by chance what is attempted for settling strife grow rather into an intolerable deluge of evils, if we begin by condemning the Word of God. And concern must be shown lest the reign of this most noble youth, Prince Charles (in whom after God is our great hope), become unhappy and inauspicious. I could illustrate this with abundant examples from scripture—like Pharaoh, the king of Babylon, and the kings of Israel,

who, when they endeavored to pacify and strengthen their kingdoms by the wisest counsels, most surely destroyed themselves.
For it is He who takes the wise in their own craftiness [Job 5:13]
and overturns mountains before they know it [Job 9:5]. Therefore
we must fear God. I do not say these things because there is a need
of either my teachings or my warnings for such leaders as you, but
because I must not withhold the allegiance which I owe my Germany. With these words I commend myself to your most serene
majesty and to your lordships, humbly asking that I not be
allowed through the agitation of my enemies, without cause, to be
made hateful to you. I have finished.

*(When I had finished, the speaker for the emperor said, as if in
reproach, that I had not answered the question, that I ought not call
into question those things which had been condemned and defined in
councils; therefore what was sought from me was not a horned response
but a simple one, whether or not I wished to retract.*
Here I answered.)

Since, then, your serene majesty and your lordships seek a simple
answer, I will give it in this manner, neither horned nor toothed:
Unless I am convinced by the testimony of the scriptures or by
clear reason (for I do not trust either in the pope or in councils
alone, since it is well known that they have often erred and contra-
dicted themselves), I am bound by the scriptures I have quoted,
and my conscience is captive to the Word of God. I cannot and I
will not retract anything, since it is neither safe nor right to go
against conscience.
　I cannot do otherwise, here I stand, may God help me, Amen.[5]

---

[5]These words are given in German in the Latin text upon which this translation
is based. There is good evidence, however, that Luther actually said only: "May
God help me!"

II

Bible Prefaces and Exegeses

THE OLD TESTAMENT

Luther began his lifelong work of translating the Latin Vulgate Bible into German when he was in protective custody at the Wartburg, from May 1521 to March 1522, outlawed by the Edict of Worms. Summoned to the Diet of Worms in April 1521, Luther had refused to recant his repudiation of papal authority and insisted that the Christian be guided sola scriptura, *by scripture alone. He completed the New Testament in eleven weeks, and it appeared in print in September 1522. He immediately began work on the Old Testament. By 1524, Luther had finished translating the psalter and several earlier books. The complete Bible appeared in 1534.*

Moved as he was to great emotion by the power of scripture, it was Luther's aim to give his generation a vernacular version that would express the divine life he found there. He rejected literal translation and labored to find wording that would convey accurate and vivid meaning in German. Luther continued revising his work until the day of his death, using Erasmus's Greek text for the New Testament and consulting with his good friend Philipp Melanchthon and others whose expertise in Greek and Hebrew far exceeded his own. Together they studied commentaries by the Fathers of the Church, especially St. Augustine, and Jewish midrash. *Central to the entire Bible for Luther was Jesus Christ, crucified and resurrected, who offers redemption to every human being. It is the voice of Christ Himself Luther heard singing in the psalms.*

Preface to the Book of Job

1545 (1524)

The book of Job deals with the question whether misfortune comes from God even to the righteous. Job stands firm and contends that God torments even the righteous without cause other than that this be to God's praise, as Christ also testifies in John 9 of the man who was born blind.

Job's friends take the other side. They make a big and lengthy palaver trying to maintain God's justice, saying that He does not punish a righteous man, and if He does punish, then the man who is punished must have sinned. They have a worldly and human idea of God and His righteousness, as though He were just like men and His justice like the justice of the world.

To be sure, when Job is in danger of death, out of human weakness he talks too much against God, and in his suffering sins. Nevertheless Job insists that he has not deserved this suffering more than others have, which is, of course, true. Finally, however, God decides that Job, by speaking against God in his suffering, has spoken wrongly, but that in contending against his friends about his innocence before the suffering came, Job has spoken the truth. So the book carries this story ultimately to this conclusion: God alone is righteous, and yet one man is more righteous than another, even in the sight of God.

But this is written for our comfort, that God allows even His great saints to falter, especially in adversity. For before Job comes into fear of death, he praises God at the theft of his goods and the death of his children. But when death is in prospect and God withdraws Himself, Job's words show what kind of thoughts a man—however holy he may be—holds toward God: he thinks that God is not God, but only a judge and wrathful tyrant, who storms ahead and cares nothing about the goodness of a person's life. This is the finest part of this book. It is understood only by those who also experience and feel what it is to suffer the wrath and judgment of God, and to have His grace hidden.

The language of this book is more vigorous and splendid than that of any other book in all the scriptures. Yet if it were translated everywhere word for word—as the Jews and foolish translators would have it done—and not for the most part according to the sense, no one would understand it. So, for example, when he says something like this, "The thirsty will pant after his wealth" [Job 5:5], that means, "Robbers shall take it from him"; or when he says, "The children of pride have never trodden it" [Job 28:8], that means "the young lions that stalk proudly"; and many similar cases. Again, by "light" he means good fortune, by "darkness" misfortune [Job 18:8], and so forth.

Therefore I think that this third part will have to suffer and be accused by the know-it-alls of being an entirely different book from the Latin Bible. We just let them go. We have taken care to use language that is clear and that everybody can understand, without perverting the sense and meaning. We can allow anyone to do it better.[6]

Preface to the Psalter

1545 (1528)

Many of the holy fathers prized and praised the psalter above all the other books of the scripture. To be sure, the work itself gives praise enough to its author; nevertheless we must give evidence of our own praise and thanks.

Over the years a great many legends of the saints,[7] and passionals,[8] books of examples,[9] and histories, have been circulated; indeed, the world has been so filled with them that the psalter has been neglected. It has lain in such obscurity that not one psalm was rightly understood. Still, it gave off such a fine and precious fragrance that all pious hearts felt the devotion and power in the unknown words and for this reason loved the book.

I hold, however, that no finer book of examples or of the legends of the saints has ever come, or can come, to earth than the psalter. If one were to wish that from all the examples, legends, and histories, the best should be collected and brought together and put in the best form, the result would have to be the present psalter. For here we find not only what one or two saints have done, but what He has done who is the very head of all saints. We also find what all the saints still do, such as the attitude they take toward God, toward friends and enemies, and the way they conduct themselves amid all dangers and sufferings. Beyond that there are contained here all sorts of divine and wholesome teachings and commandments.

The psalter ought to be a precious and beloved book, if for no other reason than this: it promises Christ's death and Resurrection

---

[6]Readers are encouraged to look into the Vintage Spiritual Classics edition of *The Book of Job,* with a Preface by Cynthia Ozick (1998). [Eds.]

[7]The most famous collection of such legends was probably that of Jacobus de Voragine, compiled c. 1230–98.

[8]*Passionals* were picture books, with text, describing the life as well as the sufferings of Christ or the saints.

[9]*Exempel Bücher* were books in which the lives of the saints were set forth as examples for devout Christians to follow.

so clearly—and pictures His kingdom and the condition and
nature of all Christendom—that it might well be called a little
Bible. In it is comprehended most beautifully and briefly everything that is in the entire Bible. It is really a fine enchiridion, or
handbook. In fact, I have a notion that the Holy Spirit wanted to
take the trouble Himself to compile a short Bible and book of
examples of all Christendom or all saints, so that anyone who
could not read the whole Bible would here have anyway almost an
entire summary of it, comprised in one little book.

Beyond all that, the psalter has this noble virtue and quality.
Other books make much ado about the works of the saints, but say
very little about their words. The psalter is a gem in this respect. It
gives forth so sweet a fragrance when one reads it because it relates
not only the works of the saints, but also their words, how they
spoke with God and prayed, and still speak and pray. Compared
to the psalter, the other legends and examples present to us nothing but mere silent saints; the psalter, however, pictures for us real,
living, active saints.

Compared to a speaking man, a silent one is simply to be
regarded as a half-dead man; and there is no mightier or nobler
work of man than speech. For it is by speech, more than by his
shape or by any other work, that man is most distinguished from
other animals. By the carver's art even a block of wood can have
the shape of a man; and an animal can see, hear, smell, sing, walk,
stand, eat, drink, fast, thirst—and suffer from hunger, frost, and a
hard bed—as well as a man.

Moreover the psalter does more than this. It presents to us not
the simple, ordinary speech of the saints, but the best of their language, that which they used when they talked with God Himself in
great earnestness and on the most important matters. Thus the
psalter lays before us not only their words instead of their deeds,
but their very hearts and the inmost treasure of their souls, so we
can look down to the foundation and source of their words and
deeds. We can look into their hearts and see what kind of thoughts
they had, how their hearts were disposed, and how they acted in
all kinds of situations, in danger and in need. The legends and
examples, which speak only of the deeds and miracles of the saints,
do not and cannot do this, for I cannot know how a man's heart is,
even though I see or hear of many great deeds that he does. And

just as I would rather hear what a saint says than see the deeds he does, so I would far rather see his heart, and the treasure in his soul, than hear his words. And this the psalter gives us most abundantly concerning the saints, so that we can be certain of how their hearts were toward God and of the words they spoke to God and every man.

A human heart is like a ship on a wild sea, driven by the storm winds from the four corners of the world. Here it is stuck with fear and worry about impending disaster; there comes grief and sadness because of present evil. Here breathes a breeze of hope and of anticipated happiness; there blows security and joy in present blessings. These storm winds teach us to speak with earnestness, to open the heart and pour out what lies at the bottom of it. He who is stuck in fear and need speaks of misfortune quite differently than he who floats on joy; and he who floats on joy speaks and sings of joy quite differently than he who is stuck in fear. When a sad man laughs or a glad man weeps, they say, he does not do so from the heart; that is, the depths of the heart are not open, and what is in them does not come out.

What is the greatest thing in the psalter but this earnest speaking amid these storm winds of every kind? Where does one find finer words of joy than in the psalms of praise and thanksgiving? There you look into the hearts of all the saints, as into fair and pleasant gardens; yes, as into heaven itself. There you see what fine and pleasant flowers of the heart spring up from all sorts of fair and happy thoughts toward God, because of His blessings. On the other hand, where do you find deeper, more sorrowful, more pitiful words of sadness than in the psalms of lamentation? There again you look into the hearts of all the saints as into death; yes, as into hell itself. How gloomy and dark it is there, with all kinds of troubled forebodings about the wrath of God! So, too, when they speak of fear and hope, they use such words that no painter could so depict for you fear or hope, and no Cicero[10] or other orator so portray them.

And that they speak these words to God and with God, this, I repeat, is the best thing of all. This gives the words double earnest-

[10]Marcus Tullius Cicero (106–43 B.C.) was a Roman statesman distinguished as an orator and man of letters.

ness and life. For when men speak with men about these matters, what they say does not come so powerfully from the heart; it does not burn and live, is not so urgent. Hence it is that the psalter is the book of all saints; and everyone, in whatever situation he may be, finds in that situation psalms and words that fit his case, that suit him as if they were put there just for his sake, so that he could not put it better himself, or find or wish for anything better.

This also serves well another purpose. When these words please a man and fit his case, he becomes sure that he is in the communion of saints, and that it has gone with all the saints as it goes with him, since they all sing with him one little song. It is especially so if he can speak these words to God, as they have done; this can only be done in faith, for the words [of the saints] have no flavor to a godless man.

Finally there is in the psalter security and a well-tried guide, so that in it one can follow all the saints without peril. The other examples and legends of the silent saints present works that one is unable to imitate; they present even more works which it is dangerous to imitate, works which usually start sects and divisions, and lead and tear men away from the communion of saints. But the psalter holds you to the communion of saints and away from the sects. For it teaches you in joy, fear, hope, and sorrow to think and speak as all the saints have thought and spoken.

In a word, if you would see the holy Christian Church painted in living color and shape, comprehended in one little picture, then take up the psalter. There you have a fine, bright, pure mirror that will show you what Christendom is. Indeed you will find in it also yourself and the true *Gnothi seauton,*[11] as well as God Himself and all creatures.

So, then, let us see to it also that we thank God for all these unspeakable blessings. Let us receive them and use them diligently and carefully, exercising ourselves in them to the praise and honor of God, lest with our ingratitude we earn something worse. Heretofore, in the time of darkness, how one would have treasured a right understanding of a psalm, and a reading or hearing of it in intelligible German; but we did not have it. Now, however,

---

[11]"Know thyself," a well-known maxim from Greek philosophy, was the inscription on the temple of Apollo in ancient Delphi.

blessed are the eyes which see what we see, and the ears which hear what we hear.[12] And still I fear—no, sad to say, we see it!—that things are going with us as with the Jews in the wilderness, when they said of the bread from heaven, "We loathe this worthless food" [Num. 21:5]. We should remember, however, that at the same spot there stands also the story of how they were plagued and died [Num. 21:6], lest this same thing happen to us.

To this may God the Father of all grace and mercy help us, through Jesus Christ our Lord, to whom be praise and thanks, honor and glory, for this German psalter and for all His innumerable and unspeakable blessings to all eternity. Amen, amen.

Psalm 23

1. The Lord is my Shepherd, I shall not want.
2. He feeds me in a green pasture and leads me to the fresh water.
3. He restores my soul, He leads me in the right path for His name's sake.
4. Even though I walk through the valley of the shadow, I fear no evil; for Thou art with me; Thy rod and Thy staff, they comfort me.
5. Thou preparest a table before me against my enemies; Thou anointest my head with oil, Thou pourest my cup full.
6. Goodness and mercy shall follow me all the days of my life; and I shall dwell in the house of the Lord forever.

EXPOUNDED ONE EVENING AFTER GRACE AT THE DINNER
TABLE BY DR. MARTIN LUTHER

1536

In this psalm, David, together with every other Christian heart, praises and thanks God for His greatest blessing: namely, for the preaching of His dear Holy Word. Through it we are called,

---

[12]Cf. Matt. 13:16–17; Luke 10:23–24.

received, and numbered into the host which is God's communion, or church, where alone—and nowhere else—we can find and have pure doctrine, the true knowledge of God, and the right worship of God.

Blessed David, however, lauds and magnifies this noble treasure most beautifully in delightful figurative and picturesque language and also in metaphorical expressions taken from the Old Testament worship of God.

First he compares himself to a sheep. God Himself is carefully tending it as a faithful, diligent Shepherd. He is feeding it in a pleasant green pasture full of fine, heavy grass, where there is an abundance of freshwater and nothing at all is lacking. He is leading and guiding it with His rod on the right paths so that it may not stray. And He is protecting it with His Shepherd's staff so that the wolves may not rend it. Then he compares himself to a guest for whom God is preparing a table at which he finds strength and comfort, refreshment and joy in abundance.

The prophet accordingly applies many kinds of names to the Word of God. He calls it a fine, pleasant, green pasture; freshwater; the path of righteousness; a rod; a staff; a table; balm, or the oil of gladness [Ps. 45:7]; and a cup that is filled to overflowing. This he does quite appropriately, for the power of God is also of many kinds. Think of a sheep that is grazing in a fine, pleasant meadow, in green grass and near a cool body of water, that is, in the presence of its shepherd. He directs it with his rod or staff so that it may not go astray, and guards it with his staff that it may not suffer any harm but graze and rejoice in complete safety. Or think of a man who is sitting at a table at which there is an abundance of food and drink and all kinds of comfort and joy, and who is lacking nothing at all. And then think of those who are the sheep of this Shepherd about whom our psalm is singing, who abound much more in every good thing and are plentifully supplied not only in soul but also in body; as Christ says [Matt. 6:33], "Seek first the kingdom of God."

For whenever God's Word is preached properly and purely, it creates as many good things and results as the prophet here gives it names. To those that hear it diligently and seriously—and they are the only ones whom our Lord acknowledges as His sheep—it is pleasant green grass, a cool draft, by which the sheep of the Lord are satisfied and refreshed. It keeps them in the paths of righteousness and preserves them from suffering misfortune and harm. And it is to them an ever happy life, in which food and drink and all kinds of joy and pleasure abound. In other words, these sheep of the Lord are not only instructed and guided, refreshed, strengthened, and comforted by God's Word; but they are also continuously kept on the right path, protected in body and soul in all kinds of distress, and finally they conquer and overcome all tribulation and sorrow, of which they must endure only as much as verse 4 mentions. In short, they live in complete safety as men whom no sorrow can befall, because their Shepherd tends and protects them.

We should, then, learn from this psalm not to despise God's Word. We should hear and learn it, love and respect it, and join the little flock in which we find it, and on the other hand, flee and avoid those that revile and persecute it. Wherever this blessed light does not shine, there neither happiness nor salvation can be found, neither strength nor comfort of body or soul, but only dissension, fear, and terror, especially when sorrow, anxiety, and bitter death threaten. As the prophet says [Isa. 48:22], however, the wicked never have peace, regardless of whether they prosper or fail. For when they prosper, they grow presumptuous, haughty, and proud, and they forget our Lord God. Their only boast and trust is in their power, riches, wisdom, and holiness. These they are concerned to keep and increase while they persecute and suppress those that hinder them. But when their fortunes change, as eventually they surely must—for the tender Virgin Mary is a most truthful singer, and she has never missed even a single note in her song[13]—then they are the most miserable and sorrowful people, who speedily despair and lose heart. What ails them? They do not know where and how they may seek comfort. They do not have God's Word, which alone can properly teach patience and good cheer in affliction [Rom. 15:4].

This ought to warn and move us not to consider anything on this earth greater and more precious than the blessing of being able to have the dear, blessed Word and to be at a place where it may be preached and confessed freely and publicly. As often,

[13]Luther is referring to the Magnificat [Luke 1:46 ff.], in which [v. 51] the judgment of God is pronounced on the proud.

therefore, as the Christian who belongs to a church in which God's Word is taught enters this church, he should think of this psalm. With the prophet he should thank God with a happy heart for His ineffable grace in placing him, as His sheep, into a pleasant green meadow, where there is an abundance of precious grass and fresh-water—that is, for being enabled to be at a place where he can hear God's Word, learn it, and draw from it rich comfort for both body and soul.

Blessed David well knew how dear a treasure it is to have it thus. Therefore he could also glory and sing about it in so master-ful a fashion and exalt so great a blessing far above anything that is precious and splendid on earth, as can be seen from this psalm and others. We ought to learn this art from him and follow his exam-ple. Not only should we be thankful to God, our dear faithful Shepherd, and praise His inexpressible gift, which He has pre-sented to us purely out of kindness, as David does here in the first five verses; but we should also sincerely pray and ask Him, as he does in the last verse, that we may keep this possession and never fall away from His holy Christian Church.

Such a prayer, however, is extremely necessary, because we are very weak and have that treasure, as the apostle Paul says [2 Cor. 4:7], "in earthen vessels." And our adversary, the devil, is murder-ously hostile toward us because of this treasure. Therefore he does not rest, but goes about as a roaring lion and seeks how he may devour us [1 Pet. 5:8]. He also has another claim on us because of the old sack of our flesh, which we are still bearing on our necks and in which there are still many evil desires and sins. Moreover, the dear Christian Church is bespattered and befouled with so many horrible offenses that, because of them, many fall away from it. Therefore I say it is indeed necessary that we pray and preach the pure doctrine without ceasing, and thus protect ourselves against all offense, so that we may endure to the end and be saved [Matt. 10:22].

The mad, blind world knows nothing at all of this treasure and precious pearl. Like a sow or other irrational beast, it thinks only about filling its belly; or at best, it follows lies and hypocrisy and abandons truth and faith. Therefore it does not sing a psalm to God for His sacred Word. Rather, when He offers it the Word, it blasphemes and damns this Word as heresy. It persecutes and kills those who teach and confess it as corrupters and the worst scoundrels that the world bears. Therefore it will undoubtedly be up to the little flock to know this blessing and, together with the prophet, to sing to God a psalm or song of thanks for it.

But what do you say about those that cannot have the Word of God, for example, those that are dwelling here and there among tyrants and enemies of the Word? It is true: wherever God's Word is preached, there fruit will not be lacking, as Isaiah says in his fifty-fifth chapter [Isa. 55:11]; and pious Christians in such places have an advantage that they truly prize. For Christians consider it a great privilege to be at a place where God's Word is taught and confessed openly and publicly and the sacraments are administered according to Christ's command. But such Christians are not very plentiful, for there have always been many more false Christians than devout ones. The great throng cares nothing about God's Word, nor does it acknowledge it as a blessing that it can hear this Word without harm or danger. Indeed, it soon becomes sated and disgusted with it and considers it a burden to hear it and receive the sacraments. On the other hand, those who must submit to tyrants cry for it day and night with great longing. And if by chance they get even a small fragment of our bread, which Christ has richly distributed to us, they receive it with great joy and thanksgiving and make very good use of it. Our sows, however, who have this precious bread in abundance and many basketfuls of fragments [Matt. 14:20], are sated with it and do not even care to smell it. Indeed, they thrust it about with their snouts, root around in it, trample it with their feet, and run over it.

Thus the saying is true: when something is in common use, it is not appreciated but is despised, however precious it may really be. Unfortunately such a saying is proved especially true in the case of our dear Word. Where men have it, they do not want it. But where men do not have it, there they would be sincerely glad to have it. Where men have the Church, in which God's Word is taught, at their doorsteps, there they go strolling along the marketplace during the sermon and sauntering about the moat. Where they have to go ten, twenty, or more miles for it, there, as we read in Psalm 42:4, they would gladly go with the throng and lead them in procession to the house of God with glad shouts and songs of thanksgiving.

So this, in brief, is my answer to the question about those who live under tyrants. Blessed are they, be they scattered among the Turks or under the pope, who are robbed of the Word but would sincerely like to have it and meanwhile, until their lot improves, gratefully accept the fragments which come to them. If they are not far from places where God's Word is preached and the holy sacrament is administered according to Christ's command, they may, of course, travel to such places and make use of that treasure—as indeed many do and, on that account, are punished in body and possessions by their godless governments. If they live far away from such places, let them not stop sighing for the means of grace; and our Lord Jesus Christ will surely hear their sighing and in time restore their fortunes. But unhappy and more than unhappy are those that have this treasure at their doorsteps in abundance and still despise it. In the case of such, the Word of Christ will be fulfilled [Matt. 8:11]: "Many will come from east and west and sit at table with Abraham, Isaac, and Jacob in the kingdom of heaven"; in the case of others: "The sons of the kingdom will be thrown into the outer darkness." Let this be said by way of introduction. Now let us briefly consider the psalm.

1. The Lord is my Shepherd, I shall not want.

First of all the prophet, and every believing heart, calls God his Shepherd. Scripture gives God many friendly names, but especially dear and charming is the one that the prophet gives God here in calling Him a Shepherd and saying, "The Lord is my Shepherd." It is most comforting when scripture calls God our Refuge, our Strength, our Rock, our Fortress, Shield, Hope, our Comfort, Savior, King, etc. For by His actions and without ceasing He truly demonstrates in His people that He is exactly as scripture portrays Him. It is exceedingly comforting to know, however, that here and in other places in scripture He is frequently called a Shepherd. For in this single little word "shepherd" there are gathered together in one almost all the good and comforting things that we praise in God.

The prophet therefore uses these words with a happy, secure heart—a heart that is filled with faith and overflows with great joy and comfort. He does not say, "The Lord is my Strength, Fortress," etc., which would also be very comforting, but "my Shepherd"; as though he would say: "If the Lord is my Shepherd and I am His sheep, then I am very well supplied both in body and soul. He will feed me well, protect and preserve me from misfortune, care for me, help me out of all troubles, comfort me, and strengthen me. In short, He will do for me what a good shepherd can be expected to do." All of these blessings, and more, are comprehended in the single little word "shepherd"; and so he himself soon interprets it when he says, "I shall not want." Some of the other names which scripture gives God sound almost too splendid and majestic and at once arouse awe and fear when we hear them mentioned; for example, when scripture calls God our Lord, King, Creator. The little word "shepherd," however, is not of that kind but has a very friendly sound. When the devout read or hear it, it immediately grants them a confidence, a comfort, and a sense of security that the word "Father" and others grant when they are attributed to God.

Therefore this metaphor is one of the most beautiful and comforting and yet most common of all in scripture, when it compares His Divine Majesty to a pious, faithful, or as Christ says, "good shepherd" [John 10:14], and compares us poor, weak, miserable sinners to sheep. One can, however, understand this comforting and beautiful picture best when one goes to nature, from which the prophets have taken this picture and similar ones, and carefully learns from it the traits and characteristics of a natural sheep and the office, the work, and the care of a pious shepherd. Whoever does this carefully will not only readily understand this comparison and others in scripture concerning the shepherd and the sheep, but will also find the comparisons exceedingly sweet and comforting.

A sheep must live entirely by its shepherd's help, protection, and care. As soon as it loses him, it is surrounded by all kinds of dangers and must perish, for it is quite unable to help itself. The reason? It is a poor, weak, simple little beast that can neither feed nor rule itself, nor find the right way, nor protect itself against any kind of danger or misfortune. Moreover, it is by nature timid, shy, and likely to go astray. When it does go a bit astray and leaves its shepherd, it is unable to find its way back to him; indeed, it merely runs farther away from him. Though it may find other shepherds and sheep, that does not help it, for it does not know the voices of strange shepherds. Therefore it flees them and strays about until the wolf seizes it or it perishes some other way.

Still, however weak and small an animal a sheep may be, it nevertheless has this trait about it: it is very careful to stay near its shepherd, take comfort in his help and protection, and follow him however and wherever he may lead it. And if it can only so much as be near him, it worries about nothing, fears no one, and is secure and happy; for it lacks absolutely nothing. It also has this virtue—and this is to be marked well, because Christ praises it especially in His sheep [John 10:4]—that it very carefully and surely hears and knows its shepherd's voice, is guided by it, does not let itself be turned away from it, but follows it without swerving. On the other hand, it pays no attention at all to the voices of strange shepherds. Though they may tempt and lure it in the most friendly manner, it does not heed them, much less does it follow them.

It is the function of a faithful shepherd not only to supply his sheep with good pasture and other related things, but also to keep them from suffering harm. Moreover, he takes good care not to lose any of them. But if one of them should go astray, he goes after it, seeks it, and returns it [Luke 15:4]. He looks after the young, the weak, and the sick very carefully, waits on them, lifts them up and carries them in his arms [Isa. 40:11] until they are grown and are strong and well.

Just so it is in spiritual sheepherding, that is, in Christendom. As little as a natural sheep can feed, direct, guide itself, or guard and protect itself against danger and misfortune—for it is a weak and quite defenseless little animal—just so little can we poor, weak, miserable people feed and guide ourselves spiritually, walk and remain on the right path, or by our own power protect ourselves against all evil and gain help and comfort for ourselves in anxiety and distress.

How shall a man be able to govern himself in a God-pleasing manner when he knows nothing of God, is born and conceived in sin [Ps. 51:5], as we all are, and is by nature a child of wrath [Eph. 2:3] and an enemy of God? How shall we find the right path and stay on it when, as Isaiah says [Isa. 53:6], we cannot do otherwise than go astray? How is it possible for us to defend ourselves against the devil, who is a prince and ruler of this world and whose captives we all are, when with all our strength and power we cannot keep even a little leaf from hurting us or even command a weak fly? Why should we poor, miserable people desire to boast loudly of great comfort, help, and counsel against the judgments of God, the wrath of God, and eternal death, when every day and every hour we experience in ourselves and in others that even in trivial, bodily needs we can neither counsel and help ourselves nor seek comfort?

Let us therefore conclude freely: as little as a natural sheep can help itself in even the slightest degree but must simply depend on its shepherd for all benefits, just so little—and much less—can a man govern himself and find comfort, help, and counsel in himself in the things that pertain to his salvation. He must depend on God, his Shepherd, for all of that. And God is a thousand times more willing and ready to do everything that is to be done for His sheep than is any faithful human shepherd.

This Shepherd, however, of whom the prophet foretold so long before, is Christ, our dear Lord, who is a Shepherd much different from Moses. Moses is harsh and unfriendly toward his sheep. He drives them away into the desert, where they will find neither pasture nor water but only want [Exod. 3:1]. Christ, however, is the good, friendly Shepherd, who goes after a famished and lost sheep in the wilderness, seeks it there, and when He has found it, lays it on His shoulder rejoicing [Luke 15:4]. He even "gives His life for His sheep" [John 10:12]. He is a friendly Shepherd. Who would not be happy to be His sheep?

The voice of this Shepherd, however, with which He speaks to His sheep and calls them, is the holy gospel. It teaches us how we may win grace, forgiveness of sins, and eternal salvation: not by the law of Moses, which makes us even more shy, unstable, and discouraged, though even in times past we were excessively timid, shy, and frightened; but by Christ, who is "the Shepherd and Bishop of our souls" [1 Pet. 2:25]. For Christ has sought us miserable, lost sheep and has brought us back from the wilderness. That is, He has redeemed us from the law, sin, death, the power of the devil, and eternal damnation. By giving His life for us He has obtained for us grace, forgiveness of sin, comfort, help, strength, and eternal life against the devil and all misfortune. To the sheep of Christ this is a dear, sweet voice. They are sincerely glad to hear it, for they know it well and let themselves be guided by it. But a strange voice they neither know nor hear, because it sounds unfamiliar; they avoid it and flee from it [John 10:5].

The pasture with which Christ feeds His sheep is also the dear gospel, by which our souls are fed and strengthened, preserved from error, comforted in all temptations[14] and sorrows, protected against the devil's wile and power, and finally saved from all need. But His sheep are not all equally strong; in part they are still lost, scattered hither and yon, wounded, sick, young, and weak. He does not reject them for that reason but actually gives more attention to them and also cares for them more diligently than He does for the others who have no faults. As the prophet Ezekiel says in his thirty-fourth chapter [Ezek. 34:16], He seeks the lost, brings back the strayed, binds up the crippled, strengthens the sick. And the young lambs that have just been born, says Isaiah [40:11], He will gather in His arms and carry them so that they may not grow tired, and will gently lead those that are with young. All of this, Christ, our dear Shepherd, effects through the office of preaching and the holy sacraments, as is taught elsewhere frequently and with many words. It would take too long and require too many words to emphasize all these things adequately at this place. Besides, the prophet will indicate them later in the psalm.

From these words we can also see clearly how shamefully we have been led astray under the papacy. It did not depict Christ in so friendly a fashion as did the dear prophets, apostles, and Christ Himself, but portrayed Him so horribly that we were more afraid of Him than of Moses and thought that the teaching of Moses was much easier and more friendly than the teaching of Christ. Therefore we knew Christ only as an angry judge, whose anger we had to reconcile with our good works and holy life and whose grace we had to obtain through the merit and intercession of the dear saints. That is a shameful lie that not only deceives poor consciences miserably but also profanes God's grace to the extreme, denies Christ's death, Resurrection, ascension into heaven, etc., together with all His inexpressible blessings, blasphemes and damns His holy gos-

[14]Luther's word is *Anfechtung;* we have rendered it with "temptation" or "assault" or "affliction," but none of these does justice to its connotations in Luther.

pel, destroys faith, and sets up in its place nothing but horror, lies, and error.

If that is not darkness, then I do not know what darkness is. Up to now no one was able to notice it, but everyone considered it the pure truth. To the present day our papists wish to have it preserved as right and hence shed much innocent blood. Dear friend, if we can feed and rule ourselves, protect ourselves against error, gain grace and forgiveness of sins through our own merit, resist the devil and all misfortune, conquer sin and death—then all scripture must be a lie when it testifies of us that we are lost, scattered, wounded, weak, and defenseless sheep. Then we do not need a Christ either as a Shepherd who would seek, gather, and direct us, bind up our wounds, watch over us, and strengthen us against the devil. Then He has also given His life for us in vain. For as long as we can do and gain all these things through our own powers and piety, we do not need the help of Christ at all.

But here at once you hear the opposite, namely, that you lost sheep cannot find your way to the Shepherd yourself but can only roam around in the wilderness. If Christ, your Shepherd, did not seek you and bring you back, you would simply have to fall prey to the wolf. But now He comes, seeks, and finds you. He takes you into His flock, that is, into Christendom, through the Word and the sacrament. He gives His life for you, keeps you always on the right path, so that you may not fall into error. You hear nothing at all about your powers, good works, and merits—unless you would say that it is strength, good works, merit when you run around in the wilderness and are defenseless and lost. No, Christ alone is active here, merits things, and manifests His power. He seeks, carries, and directs you. He earns life for you through His death. He alone is strong and keeps you from perishing, from being snatched out of His hand [John 10:28]. And for all of this you can do nothing at all but only lend your ear, hear, and with thanksgiving receive the inexpressible treasure, and learn to know well the voice of your Shepherd, follow Him, and avoid the voice of the stranger.

If you wish, therefore, to be richly supplied in both body and soul, then above all give careful attention to the voice of this Shepherd, listen to His words, let Him feed, direct, lead, protect, and comfort you. That is: hold fast to His Word, hear and learn it gladly, for then you will be well supplied in both body and soul.

From what has been said until now one can, I hope, easily understand these words, "The Lord is my Shepherd," and indeed the whole psalm. The words "The Lord is my Shepherd" are brief but also very impressive and apt. The world glories and trusts in honor, power, riches, and the favor of men. Our psalm, however, glories in none of these, for they are all uncertain and perishable. It says briefly, "The Lord is my Shepherd." Thus speaks a sure, certain faith that turns its back on everything temporal and transitory, however noble and precious it may be, and turns its face and heart directly to the Lord, who alone is Lord and is and does everything. "He and none other, be he a king or an emperor, is my Shepherd," the psalmist says. Therefore he speaks out freely and with all boldness and says:

I shall not want.

Thus the prophet speaks, in a general way, of the various kinds of bodily and spiritual blessings that we receive through the office of preaching. It is as though he would say: "If the Lord is my Shepherd, then of course I shall not want. I shall have an abundance of meat, drink, clothing, food, protection, peace, and of all the necessities that pertain to the preservation of this life. For I have a rich Shepherd who will not let me suffer want." Chiefly, however, he speaks of the spiritual possessions and gifts that God's Word provides, and says: "Because the Lord has taken me into His flock and provides me with His pasture and care, that is, because He has richly given me His holy Word, He will not let me want anywhere. He will bless His Word so that it may be effective and bring forth fruit in me. He will also give me His Spirit, who will assist and comfort me in all temptations and distresses and will also make my heart safe and sure. My heart, therefore, will not doubt that I am my Lord's dear sheep and that He is my faithful Shepherd. He will treat me gently as His poor, weak sheep. He will strengthen my faith and provide me with other spiritual gifts; comfort me in all my troubles; hear me when I call upon Him; keep the wolf, that is, the devil, from being able to do me harm; and finally redeem me from all misfortune." This is what the psalmist has in mind when he says, "I shall not want."

"Yes," you may say, "but how shall I know that the Lord is my

Shepherd? I have not experienced that He is as friendly toward me as the psalm says; in fact, I have experienced the opposite. David was a holy prophet and a man dear and precious to God; so it was easy for him to speak of the matter and to believe what he spoke. But I cannot emulate him, for I am a poor sinner." Answer: I have shown above that in itself a sheep has chiefly this good attribute and fine virtue, that it knows the voice of its shepherd well and is guided more by its ears than its eyes. The same virtue Christ also praises in His sheep, when He says [John 10:4]: "My sheep know My voice." His voice, however, speaks thus [John 10:14, 15, 28]: "I am the Good Shepherd . . . and lay down My life for My sheep. . . . And I give them eternal life. And they shall never perish, and no man shall snatch them out of My hand." Give careful attention to this voice and be guided by it. If you do, then firmly believe that you are Christ's sheep and that He is your Shepherd, who knows you well and is able to call you by your name. But when you have Him as your Shepherd, you will surely not want. Yes, you already have what you shall have—eternal life. Nor will you ever perish. Nor shall any power be so great and mighty that it could snatch you out of His hand. Of that you can be sure. For this Shepherd's voice will surely not lead you astray. What more could you want?

But if you ignore this voice and are guided by what your eyes see and your old Adam feels, then you will lose the faith and the confidence that you ought, as a sheep, to have in Him as your Shepherd. Sometimes this thought, sometimes that one comes to you, so that you cannot be content but must argue with yourself and say: "If the Lord is my Shepherd, why does He impose this upon me, that the world torments and persecutes me so cruelly through no fault of mine? I am sitting in the midst of the wolves, I am not sure of my life for a moment; but I do not see any shepherd who would protect me." Again: "Why does He permit the devil to harm me so greatly with terror and doubts? Besides, I find myself quite unfit, weak, impatient, still laden with many sins. I feel no security but only doubt, no comfort but only fear and trembling because of God's wrath. When will He ever begin to manifest in me that He is my Shepherd?"

Such strange thoughts and many others will come to you if you fail to heed His voice and Word. But if you hold fast to them, you will be tempted neither by the devil's wile, the world's disfavor and raging, nor by your own weakness and unworthiness. You will go straight forward to speak freely: "Let the devil, the world, or my own conscience oppose me as violently as they may. I will not for that reason grieve myself to death. It must be so and it shall be so, that whoever is the Lord's sheep will surely be assailed by the wolves. Be it with me as it may, let them boil or roast me, it shall be my comfort that my Shepherd has given His life for me. Moreover, He has a sweet, kind voice, with which He comforts me and says that I shall never perish, neither shall any man snatch me out of His hand; I shall have eternal life [John 10:28]. And He will keep this promise, no matter what happens to me. If because of my weakness some sin or other fault by chance is still found in me, He will not reject me on that account. For He is a friendly Shepherd, who watches over the weak sheep, binds up their wounds, and heals them. And so that I may be all the more sure and not doubt, He has given me, as a token, His holy sacraments."

Just so it was with the prophet. He was not always happy, nor was he at all times able to sing, "The Lord is my Shepherd, I shall not want." At times he wanted much, almost too much. He would feel neither justice nor God's comfort and help, but only sin, God's wrath, terror, doubt, and the fear of hell, as he laments in many psalms. Nevertheless he abandons his feelings and holds God to His promise of a coming Messiah and thinks: "Be it with me as it may. This is still the comfort of my heart, that I have a gracious, merciful Lord, who is my Shepherd, whose Word and promise strengthen and comfort me. Therefore I shall not want." For this reason also he wrote this psalm and others, that we might be sure that in real temptation we can find counsel and comfort nowhere else, and that this alone is the golden art: to cling to God's Word and promise, to make judgments on the basis of this Word and not on the basis of the feelings of the heart. Then help and comfort will surely follow, and absolutely nothing will be wanting. The second verse follows.

2. *He feeds me in a green pasture and leads me to the freshwater.*

In the first verse the prophet briefly gathered together the meaning of the whole psalm, namely, that whoever has the Lord as a Shepherd will not want. He does not teach anything more in this psalm, but he does emphasize the thought further by means of fine figurative words and pictures and shows how it comes about that those who are the Lord's sheep want nothing, and says, "He feeds me," etc. Through almost the entire psalm, as he often does elsewhere, he uses words with a meaning different from their literal one. When he mentions the shepherd, the pasture, the green meadow, the freshwater, the rod, and the staff, therefore, we may well conclude that he wants something else to be understood by these words than we human beings are in the habit of saying with them. Such a way of speaking is very common in scripture, and therefore we should make every effort to get accustomed to it and learn to understand it.

But see how beautifully he can speak! "I am," he says, "the Lord's sheep; He feeds me in a green pasture." For a natural sheep nothing can be better than when its shepherd feeds it in pleasant green pastures and near freshwater. Where that happens to it, it feels that no one on earth is richer and more blessed than it is. For it finds there whatever it might desire: fine, lush, heavy grass, from which it will grow strong and fat; freshwater, with which it can refresh and restore itself whenever it likes; and it has its joy and pleasure there, too. At this point David would also say that God had shown him no greater grace and blessing on earth than this, that he was permitted to be at a place and among people where God's Word and dwelling place and the right worship were to be found. Where these treasures are found, there things prosper well, both in the spiritual and in the secular realm. It is as if he were saying: "All people and kingdoms on earth are nothing. They may be richer, more powerful, and more splendid than we Jews, and they may also boast mightily of what they have. Moreover, they may glory in their wisdom and holiness, for they, too, have gods whom they serve. But with all their glory and splendor they are a mere desert and wilderness. For they have neither shepherd nor pasture, and therefore the sheep must go astray, famish, and perish. But though we are surrounded by many deserts, we can sit and rest here, safe and happy in paradise and in a pleasant green pasture, where there is an abundance of grass and of freshwater and where we have our Shepherd near us, who feeds us, leads us to the watering place, and protects us. Therefore we cannot want."

That man had spiritual eyes and therefore saw plainly what is the best and noblest thing on earth. He does not glory in his royal splendor and power, for he knows well that such possessions are gifts of God. He does not run away from them either and let them lie idle, but uses them to the glory of God and thanks God for them. Above all he glories in this, that the Lord is his Shepherd and that he is in His pasture and in His care, that is, that he has God's Word. This blessing he can never forget, but speaks about it very beautifully and with great joy, and praises it far above all possessions on earth, as he also does in many other psalms. Thus he says [Ps. 119:72]: "The word of Thy mouth is dearer to me than thousands of gold and silver pieces"; and also [Ps. 19:11]: "It is more precious than gold, even much fine gold; sweeter also than honey and drippings of the honeycomb."

We, too, should learn this art, namely, to let the world glory forever in great riches, honor, and power. For these are indeed loose, uncertain, perishable wares that God lets men scramble for. It is a simple thing for Him to give to a scoundrel—who in turn blasphemes and slanders Him—a kingdom, a principality, or other honors and possessions on this earth. These are His chaff and His husks, with which He fills the bellies of His sows that He is about to slaughter [Luke 15:16]. To His children, however, as David says here, He gives the genuine treasure. Therefore, as the dear children and heirs of God, we ought to glory in neither our wisdom, nor strength, nor riches, but in this, that we have the "pearl of great value" [Matt. 13:46], the dear Word, through which we know God, our dear Father, and Jesus Christ, whom He has sent [John 17:3]. That is our treasure and heritage, and it is sure and eternal and better than all worldly possessions. Whoever has this treasure may let others gather money, live riotously, be proud and haughty. Let him not be troubled by such things, though he be despised and poor in the eyes of the world. But let him thank God for His inexpressible gift [2 Cor. 9:15] and pray that he may abide by it.

It does not matter how rich and glorious we are here on earth; if we keep this treasure, we are exceedingly rich and sufficiently honored. St. Paul was an unworthy, miserable man on earth, and the devil and the world assailed him most violently. To God he was a dear, worthy man. He was so poor, too, that he had to provide for himself with the work of his hands. And yet, despite such great poverty, he was richer than the emperor in Rome, though he had no other riches than the knowledge of Christ, in comparison with which, he says [Phil. 3:8]: "I count all things (nothing on earth is excluded) but loss and refuse."

May our dear God grant us grace that we, too, like David, Paul, and other saints, regard our treasure, which is the very same one they had, as something great and exalt it above all possessions on earth and thank God sincerely for having honored us with it above many other thousands. He might just as well have let us go astray as the Turks, Tartars, Jews, and other infidels, who know nothing of the treasure. He might have let us remain hardened like the papists, who blaspheme and damn our treasure. It is only because of His grace, however, that He has placed us into His green pastures and has provided us so richly with good food and freshwater. Therefore we should thank Him all the more.

The prophet, however, calls God's people and the Holy Christian Church a "green pasture," for it is God's pleasure ground, decorated and adorned with all kinds of spiritual gifts. The pasture, however, or the grass in it, is God's Word, with which our consciences are strengthened and restored. Into this green pasture our Lord God gathers His sheep, feeds them in it with precious grass, and restores them with freshwater. That is, He commits to the Holy Christian Church the office of a Shepherd, entrusts and gives to it the holy gospel and the sacraments, so that by means of these it may care for and watch over His sheep and so that these sheep may be richly provided with instruction, comfort, strength, and protection against all evil. But those who preach the law of Moses or the ordinances of men do not feed the sheep in a green pasture but in the desert, where they famish, and lead them to foul, smelly water, which will cause them to decay and die.

By means of the allegory of the green pasture, however, the prophet wants to indicate the great abundance and the riches of the holy gospel and of the knowledge of Christ among the believers. For just as the grass in a green pasture stands very thick and full and grows more and more, so it is with the believers: they not only have God's Word richly, but the more they use and apply it, the more it increases and grows among them. Therefore the psalmist expresses himself very plainly. He does not say, "He leads me once, or often, in a green pasture," but, "He leads me in them without ceasing, so that amid the grass and in the pasture I may lie, rest, and dwell securely and never suffer hunger or any other want." The word that he uses here means "lie" and "rest," as a four-footed animal lies and rests. In the same manner Solomon also speaks in the Seventy-second Psalm, where he prophesies that the kingdom of God and the gospel will prevail with might and go to all places, and says, "In the land, on the tops of the mountains, may the grain wave and blossom forth in the cities like the grass of the field" [Ps. 72:16]. David shows that he is speaking of the gospel also in this psalm when he says later, "He restores my soul," and, "Thy rod and Thy staff, they comfort me."

This, then, is the first fruit of the dear Word: that the Christians are instructed through it in such a way that they grow in faith and hope, learn to commit all their doings and ways unto God, and hope in Him for everything they need in soul and body.

He leads me to the freshwater.

This is the second fruit of the dear Word. It is not only the believers' pasture and grass with which they are satisfied and grow strong in the faith; to them it is also pleasantly cool freshwater, through which they gain refreshment and comfort. The psalmist therefore does not stop with saying, "He makes me lie down in green pastures," but also adds, "He leads me to the freshwater." It is as though he would say: "In great heat, when the sun smites hard [Ps. 121:6] and I can have no shade, He leads me to freshwater, gives me to drink, and refreshes me." That is, in all kinds of afflictions, anxieties, and distresses—spiritual and physical—when I cannot find help and comfort anywhere, I cling to the Word of grace. There alone, and nowhere else, do I find the right comfort and refreshment—and find it richly. What he says here in figurative language he expresses elsewhere in sober, clear words and says [Ps. 119:92]: "If Thy law had not been my delight, I should have perished in my affliction. I will never forget it, for with it Thou dost restore me."

But he still retains the metaphor of the shepherd and the sheep, which is a common thing among all the prophets. For the Jews had their best food from sheep and other animals and commonly

were shepherds, even as David himself and also the dear patriarchs were shepherds. Therefore this metaphor is often employed
in scripture. David, however, speaks of this matter in keeping
with the nature of the country; the Promised Land is a hot, dry,
sandy, stony land that has many deserts and little water. Therefore
the book of Genesis reports more than once how the shepherds of
the heathen quarreled with the shepherds of the patriarchs about
water.[15] They accordingly considered it a special treasure in that
land when they could have water for their cattle. In our countries
this is unknown, for there is enough water everywhere. David has
looked at his land and cites it as a special blessing that he is under
the protection of the Lord, who not only feeds him in a green pasture but during the heat also leads him to the freshwater.

In brief, he wishes to say this: as little as one can come to the
knowledge of God and the truth and to the right faith without the
Word of God, just so little can one find comfort and peace of conscience without it. The world has its comfort and joy, too, but
these last only a moment; when anxiety and distress and especially
the last hour comes, then it is as Solomon says [Prov. 14:13]: "After
laughter the heart is sad; and after joy comes grief." But those who
drink of this fresh and living water may indeed suffer affliction
and distress in the world, but they will never lack genuine comfort. Especially when the moment of crisis comes, the page turns
for them to the place where it says: "After brief weeping comes
eternal laughter; after a small sorrow comes glorious joy" [2 Cor.
4:17]. For they shall not weep and be sorrowful both here and
there, but it will be as Christ says [Luke 6:21]: "Blessed are you that
weep here, for you shall laugh."

*3. He restores my soul, He leads me in the right path for His name's
sake.*

Here the prophet himself explains what kind of pasture and
freshwater he has been discussing, namely, that kind by which the
soul is strengthened and restored. That, however, can be nothing
else than God's Word. But because our Lord God has a twofold

[15]Cf. Gen. 21:25; 26:19–22.

Word, the law and the gospel, the prophet makes it sufficiently clear that he is speaking here not of the law but of the gospel when he says, "He restores my soul." The law cannot restore the soul, for it is a Word that makes demands on us and commands us that we shall love God with all our hearts, etc., and our neighbors as ourselves [Matt. 22:37, 39]. It damns him that does otherwise and pronounces this sentence upon him [Gal. 3:10; Deut. 27:26]: "Cursed be everyone who does not do all the things written in the book of the law." Now, it is certain that nobody on earth does that; therefore the law comes in due time with its sentence and only grieves and frightens the souls. Where no help is provided, it presses them so that they must despair and be lost forever. St. Paul therefore says [Rom. 3:20]: "By the law comes only knowledge of sin," and [Rom. 4:15], "The law brings only wrath."

The gospel, however, is a blessed Word. It demands nothing of us but announces everything that is good, namely, that God has given us poor sinners His only Son and that He is to be our Shepherd; He will seek us famished and scattered sheep and give His life for us, to redeem us from sin, from eternal death, and from the power of the devil. That is the green grass and the freshwater with which the Lord restores our souls. Thus we are rid of our bad consciences and sad thoughts. More of that in the fourth verse.

He leads me in the right path.

"The Lord," he says, "does not stop with feeding me in a green pasture and leading me to the freshwater and thus restoring my soul. He also leads me in the right paths so that I may not go astray, get into the wilderness, and thus perish. That is, He keeps me in pure doctrine, that I may not be misled by false spirits or fall away from it because of temptation or offense; that I may know how I am to walk and live outwardly and not take offense at the holiness and the strict lives of hypocrites; and that I may also know what is the right doctrine, faith, and worship."

Another fine fruit and power of the dear Word is this: those who cling to it firmly not only receive from it strength and comfort for their souls but are also protected against false doctrine and false holiness. Many, it is true, receive this treasure but without being able to keep it. For when a man becomes smug and presumptuous and thinks he is safe, he will soon be lost; before he can look about, he has been led astray. The devil can also assume holiness and disguise himself, as St. Paul says [2 Cor. 11:14], as "an angel of light." His servants, then, pretend to be preachers of righteousness and enter the flock of Christ in sheep's clothing but inwardly are ravenous wolves [Matt. 7:15]. Therefore we should watch and pray, as the prophet does in the last verse, that our Shepherd will keep us true to the treasure He has given us. Those who fail in this surely lose the treasure, and as Christ says [Luke 11:26], their last state becomes worse than the first. For later they become the most venomous foes of Christianity and do much more harm with their false doctrine than the tyrants do with the sword. St. Paul indeed learned this from the false prophets who led his Corinthians and Galatians astray for a time and later carried off all of Asia [2 Tim. 1:15]. In our days we see this, too, in the Anabaptists and other schismatic spirits.

For His name's sake.

The name of God is the preaching of God, by which He is glorified and made known as the gracious, merciful, patient, truthful, and faithful one; although we are the children of wrath [Eph. 2:3] and are guilty of eternal death, He forgives us all our sins and receives us as His children and heirs. That is His name, and that name He causes to be proclaimed through the Word. He wants to be known, glorified, and honored by these means; and according to the First Commandment, He will also reveal Himself to us exactly as He has men preach of Him [Exod. 20:5, 6]. Thus, without ceasing, He strengthens and restores our souls spiritually and keeps us from falling into error, and also feeds us bodily and wards off all misfortune. But only those who cling to His Word, and who believe and confess boldly that all the gifts and possessions of body and soul that they own, they have received from God purely out of grace and kindness, that is, solely for His name's sake and not because of their own deeds and merits—only they give Him the honor of being exactly as we have just been told. They thank Him for His blessings and also proclaim these blessings to others. No haughty saints, such as heretics and schismatic spirits or enemies and blasphemers of the Word of God, can give Him this honor, for they glorify not His name but their own.

4. Even though I walk through the valley of the shadow, I fear no evil; for Thou art with me; Thy rod and Thy staff, they comfort me.

Until now the prophet has shown that those who have and love God's Word do not want, for the Lord is their Shepherd. This Shepherd not only feeds them in a green pasture and leads them to the freshwater so that they may become quite fat and strong and restored spiritually and physically; He also keeps them from becoming weary of the good pasture and the freshwater and from leaving the green pasture and straying from the right path, into the desert. That is the first part of this psalm. Now he goes on to teach that those who are this Lord's sheep are surrounded by much danger and misfortune. But the Lord, he says, not only protects them but also saves them from all temptations and distresses; for He is with them. He also shows beautifully in what way He is with them.

Here you can see that as soon as the Word is preached and as soon as there are people that accept and confess it, the devil quickly appears with all his angels and arouses the world with all its might against this Word, to stifle it and completely destroy those that have and confess it. Whatever our Lord God says or does must be swept clean and pass through the fire. It is very important for Christians to know this, else they may become perplexed and think: "How can this be harmonized? The prophet has said above, 'The Lord is my Shepherd, I shall not want,' and here he says the very opposite, that he must walk through the valley of the shadow, and in the following verse he admits that he has enemies. With these words he surely lets us know well enough that he does want—too much; yes, practically everything. For he who has enemies and wanders through the valley of the shadow can see no light, that is, he has neither comfort nor hope but is forsaken by everybody, and everything is black and dark before his eyes, even the beautiful, bright sun. How, then, can it be true that he does not want?"

Here you must not be guided by your eyes or follow your reason, as the world does. The world cannot see this rich, splendid comfort of the Christians, that they want nothing. Yes, the world considers it quite certain that the opposite is true, namely, that on earth there are no poorer, more miserable, and more unhappy people than these same Christians. And it helps very faithfully and boldly in having them most cruelly persecuted, exiled, reviled, and killed. And when the world does this, it thinks that thereby it has offered service to God [John 16:2]. Outwardly, then, it appears as if the Christians were the scattered sheep, forsaken by God and surrendered to the very jaws of the wolves, and that they wanted absolutely everything.

But those who serve the great god Mammon or Belly appear to the world to be the dear sheep which do not want and which, as the psalm says, God richly supports, comforts, and guards against all danger and misfortune. For they have what their hearts desire: honor, possessions, joy, pleasure, and everyone's favor. Nor do they have to fear that because of their faith they will be persecuted and killed. As long as they do not believe in Christ or confess Him, the only true Shepherd, they believe in the devil and his mother;[16] otherwise, too, they do as they will, for example, in covetousness. Not only do they prosper therein, but they also appear to be living saints, who are holding fast to the old faith and are not misled by any such heresy as this, that, as David teaches here, the Lord alone is a Shepherd. It is so horrible, great, and deadly a sin to believe in this Shepherd[17] and to confess Him that there has never been anything on earth like it. Even his Holiness the pope, who otherwise grants dispensation from all sins and even forgives them, is unable to grant forgiveness in the case of this sin only.

Therefore I say, do not follow the world in this matter, nor your reason, which, because it judges according to outward appearances, becomes a fool and considers the prophet a liar for saying, "I shall not want." You, however, cling to God's Word and promise, as was also said before. Listen to your Shepherd, however, and whatever He speaks to you. Judge according to His voice and not according to what your eyes see and your heart feels. Then you have gained the victory. That is how the prophet acts in his own

---

[16]This is perhaps a variation on Luther's more customary metaphor of the world as the devil's bride (cf. page 57).
[17]Either Luther is speaking ironically here or by the term "shepherd" he means the devil.

case. He confesses that he is walking through the valley of the shadow, that is, that he is surrounded by distresses, sadness, anxiety, and trouble, as can also be seen from his life's history and from other psalms. But his need of comfort is indicated sufficiently by the fact that he is grieved and has enemies. Nevertheless he says: "Though my temptations were even more numerous and great, and though my lot were even worse, and though I were already in the jaws of death, yet I will fear no evil. Not that I could assist myself through my own care, efforts, work, or help. Nor do I depend on my own wisdom, piety, royal power, or riches. Here all human help, counsel, comfort, and power are far too weak. This, however, avails for me, that the Lord is with me."

It is as if he would say: "As for me, I am indeed weak, sad, anxious, and surrounded by all kinds of danger and misfortune. Because of my sin, my heart and my conscience are not satisfied either. I experience such horrible terrors of death and hell that I almost despair. Yet though the whole world and also the gates of hell [Matt. 16:18] should oppose me, that will not dismay me. Yes, I will not be afraid of all the evil and sorrow that they may be able to lay on me; for the Lord is with me. The Lord is my counselor, comforter, protector, and helper—the Lord, I say, who has created heaven and earth and everything that is in it out of a more trifling thing than a speck of dust, that is, out of nothing. To Him all creation is subject: angels, devils, men, sin, death, etc.; in brief, He has everything in His power. And therefore I fear no evil."

Asaph also speaks thus in the Seventy-third Psalm. There he comforts the Christians because of the great offense that the wicked prosper so greatly on earth, while the dear saints of God are constantly tormented, and says [Ps. 73:23]: "If only I have Thee, Lord, I will ask nothing of heaven and earth. Even though my body and soul shall fail, Thou, O God, art the strength of my heart and my portion forever." But how the Lord is with him, he now goes on to show, and says:

Thy rod and Thy staff, they comfort me.

"The Lord," he says, "is with me, but not bodily so that I might see or hear Him. This presence of the Lord of which I am speaking is not to be grasped by the five senses. But faith sees it and believes

surely that the Lord is nearer to us than we are to ourselves."
How? Through His Word. He says therefore, "Thy rod and Thy
staff, they comfort me." It is as though he would say: "In all of my
anxieties and troubles I find nothing on earth that might help to
satisfy me. But then God's Word is my rod and my staff. To that
Word I will cling, and by it I raise myself up again. I will also learn
for sure that the Lord is with me and that He not only strengthens
and comforts me with this same Word in all distresses and temptations, but that He also redeems me from all my enemies contrary
to the will of the devil and the world."

With the words "Thy rod and Thy staff, they comfort me" he
returns to the metaphor of the shepherd and the sheep and would
speak thus: "Even as a bodily shepherd guides his sheep with his
rod or staff and leads them to freshwater, where they find food
and drink, and protects them with his staff against all danger; so
the Lord, the real Shepherd, leads and guides me also with His
staff, that is, with His Word, so that I may walk before Him with a
good faith and a happy conscience, remain in the right path, and
be able to protect myself against false doctrine and fictitious holiness. He also protects me against all danger and evil of spirit and
of body and saves me from all my enemies with His staff. That is,
with the same Word He strengthens and comforts me so richly
that no evil can be so great, be it of spirit or body, that I cannot
endure and overcome it."

You see, then, that the prophet is not speaking here of any
human help, protection, and comfort. He does not draw a sword.
Everything is done here in a hidden and mysterious manner
through the Word, so that no one becomes aware of any protection
and comfort but the believers alone. Here David lays down a common rule for all Christians, and it is to be well noted: that there is
no other way or counsel on earth to get rid of all kinds of temptation than this, that a man cast all his cares upon God, take Him at
His Word of grace, hold fast to it, and not let it be taken from him
in any way. Whoever does that can be satisfied, whether he pros-
pers or fails, whether he lives or dies. And in the end he can also
stand and must succeed against all devils, the world, and evil. That
is the way, I feel, to magnify the dear Word and to credit it with
much greater power than the power of all angels and men. And
that is the way in which also St. Paul magnifies it [Rom. 1:16]:

"The gospel," he says, "is a power of God that saves all who believe in it."

Here the prophet also touches upon the office of preaching. For through the oral preaching of the Word, which enters the ears and touches the heart by faith, and through the holy sacraments, our Lord God accomplishes all these things in His Christendom, namely, that men are brought to faith, are strengthened in faith, are kept in pure doctrine, and in the end are enabled to withstand all the assaults of the devil and the world. Without these means, Word and sacrament, we obtain none of these things. For since the beginning of the world God has dealt with all the saints through His Word and, in addition, has given them external signs of grace. This I say so that no one may venture to deal with God without these means or build for himself a special way to heaven, lest he fall and break his neck, as the pope has done to his followers and still does, and as today the Anabaptists and other schismatic spirits do.

But with the words "Thy rod and Thy staff, they comfort me" the prophet wishes to say something special. It is as though he would say: "Moses is also a shepherd and also has a rod and a staff. But he does nothing with them but drive and plague and burden his sheep with an unbearable burden [Acts 15:10; Isa. 9:3]. Therefore he is a terrible, horrible shepherd, whom the sheep only fear and from whom they flee. But Thou, O Lord, dost not drive and frighten Thy sheep with Thy rod and Thy staff, nor dost Thou burden them, but dost only comfort them."

Therefore he is speaking here about the office of preaching in the New Testament, which proclaims to the world that "Christ came into the world to save sinners" [1 Tim. 1:15] and that He has gained this salvation for sinners by giving His life for them. Whoever believes this should not perish but have eternal life [John 3:16]. That is the rod and the staff by which the souls obtain rest, comfort, and joy. In spiritual sheepherding, that is, in the kingdom of Christ, one should, therefore, preach to the sheep of Christ—the goats one must govern with Moses and the emperor's rod and staff—not the law of God, much less the ordinances of men, but the gospel, which the prophet with metaphorical words calls a rod of comfort and a staff of comfort. For through the gospel Christ's sheep obtain strength in their faith, rest in their hearts, and comfort in all kinds of anxieties and perils of death.

Those who preach this way conduct the office of a spiritual shepherd properly, feed the sheep of Christ in a green pasture, lead them to the freshwater, restore their souls, keep them from being led astray, and comfort them with Christ's rod and staff. Where men hear such preachers, they should believe for certain that they are hearing Christ Himself. They should also acknowledge such preachers as right shepherds, that is, as servants of Christ and stewards of God [1 Cor. 4:1], and pay no attention at all to the fact that the world proclaims and damns them as heretics and seducers. Those who preach something else than the gospel, who guide men to works, merit, and self-appointed holiness, may indeed praise themselves ten times over as the followers of the apostles, adorn themselves with the name and title of the Christian Church, and even raise the dead. Actually they are horrible wolves and murderers that do not spare the flock of Christ, but scatter, torture, and slaughter it not only spiritually but also bodily, as is now clearly and plainly to be seen.

Earlier the prophet called God's Word, or the gospel, grass, water, the right path, a rod, a staff. In the fifth verse he calls it a table that is prepared for us, an oil, and a cup that is filled to overflowing. He takes these metaphors of the table, oil, and cup from the Jews' Old Testament worship of God and says practically the same thing he had said before—namely, that those who have God's Word are richly supplied with all things of body and soul—except that here he indicates these blessings with other figures and allegories. First he presents the picture of the table on which the showbread had to be set at all times [Exod. 25:30; 40:23]. And he also shows what that means, and says:

5. *Thou preparest a table before me against my enemies; Thou anointest my head with oil, Thou pourest my cup full.*

Here the prophet confesses frankly that he has enemies. He says, however, that he defends himself against them and drives them back in this way, that the Lord has prepared a table before him against these same enemies of his. Is not that a wonderful protector? I should think He would prepare before him a mighty wall, a strong rampart, a deep moat, an armor, and other arms and weapons that have to do with battle, through which he might be safe from his enemies or put them to flight. But He prepares a table before him, at which he is to eat and to drink and in this way to defeat his enemies. I, too, would like to wage war if, without any danger, care, trouble, and work, one could conquer one's enemies by doing nothing more than sitting at a table and eating, drinking, and making merry.

By means of these words, "Thou preparest a table before me in the presence of my enemies," the prophet wishes to indicate the great, splendid, and wonderful power of the dear Word. It is as though he would say: "Thou, O Lord, dost offer me so many good things and feed me so splendidly and richly at the table that Thou hast prepared for me. That is, Thou dost overwhelm me so greatly with the boundless knowledge of Thy dear Word, that through this Word I not only have rich comfort inwardly, in my heart, despite my guilty conscience, despite sin, fear, the terror of death, and God's wrath and judgment; through it I also become outwardly so courageous and invincible a hero that all my enemies cannot prevail against me. The more raging and raving and insane they are toward me, the less I worry about them; yes, instead, I am secure, happy, and cheerful. And that is true only because I have Thy Word. It gives me such strength and comfort in the presence of all my enemies, so that even when they rage and rave most violently, I feel more at ease than when I am sitting at a table and have all that my heart desires: food, drink, joy, pleasures, music, and the like."

Here you shall hear how highly blessed David exalts and praises the dear Word, namely, by telling us that by means of it the believers gain the victory over the devil, the world, the flesh, sin, conscience, and death. When one has the Word and in faith clings to it firmly, these enemies, who otherwise are invincible, must all yield and let themselves be taken captive. It is, however, a wonderful victory and power, also a very proud and haughty boast on the part of the believers, that they may compel and conquer all of these horrible and, as it were, almighty enemies—not by raging, biting, resisting, striking back, avenging, seeking counsel and help here and there, but by eating, drinking, rejoicing, sitting, being happy, and resting. All of this, as we have said, is accomplished through the Word. For in scripture "eating and drinking" means believing and clinging firmly to the Word; and from this proceed peace, joy, comfort, strength, and the like.

Reason cannot accommodate itself to this wonderful victory of the believers. Here everything happens in a contradictory way. The world always persecutes and murders the Christians as the most harmful people on earth. When reason sees that, it must think that the Christians are succumbing and their enemies are supreme and victorious. Thus the Jews dealt with Christ, the apostles, and the believers, and executed them. When they had murdered or at least exiled them, they cried: "On to victory! Those who have done us harm no longer can confound us. Now we shall act according to our own pleasure." But when they felt most secure, our Lord sent the Romans against them, who treated them so horribly that it frightens one to hear it. Several hundred and more years later He also gave the Romans their reward, who had killed many thousands of martyrs throughout the Roman Empire. He had the city of Rome conquered by the Goths and Wends four times within a few years, and finally had it burned down and leveled, and let the empire perish. Who was victorious now? The Jews and the Romans, who had shed the blood of the dear saints like water? Or the poor Christians, who had been killed like sheep led to the slaughter, and had no other defense and weapons than the dear Word?

David is not speaking here only about his own person, but by means of these words he shows how the holy Christian Church fares. He gives it the proper coloration and paints a fine picture of it. Before God it is a pleasant green meadow, on which there is grass and water in abundance. That is, it is God's paradise and pleasure garden, adorned with all His gifts, and it has His inexpressible treasure: the holy sacraments, the dear Word, with which it instructs, governs, restores, and comforts His flock. To the world, however, it has a different appearance. It is a black, gloomy valley, where neither joy nor pleasure is to be seen, but only distress, anxiety, and trouble. The devil assails it with all his might because of its treasure. Inwardly he tortures it with his venomous, fiery arrows [Eph. 6:16]; outwardly he separates it with schisms and offenses [Rom. 16:17]. And he also incites his bride, the world,[18] against it, which imposes upon it all misery and heartache through persecution, slander, blasphemy, damnation,

---

[18]A favorite metaphor of Luther's for the world; cf. page 51.

and murder. It would not be surprising, therefore, if the dear Christian Church were completely destroyed in a moment's time through the great craft and might of both the devil and the world. For it cannot defend itself against its enemies: they are much too strong, crafty, and powerful for it. So it is, as the prophet depicts it here, an innocent, simple, defenseless lamb, which neither will nor can do anyone any harm, but at all times is ready not only to do good but to receive evil in return.

How, then, does it happen that Christendom, which is so weak, can withstand the craft and the tyranny of the devil and the world? The Lord is its Shepherd; therefore it does not want. He feeds and restores it spiritually and physically; He keeps it in the right path; He also gives it His rod and His staff as a sword. It does not, however, wield this sword with its hand but with its mouth. With it, it not only comforts the sad but also puts the devil and all his apostles to flight, no matter how craftily and shrewdly they may defend themselves. Moreover, the Lord has prepared a table, or paschal lamb, before it, in order to destroy its enemies completely when they rage greatly, gnash their teeth against it, become mad, insane, raging, and raving, and call to their aid all their craft, strength, and power. Thus the dear bride of Christ can sit down at the table of her Lord, eat of the paschal lamb, drink of the freshwater, be happy, and sing: "The Lord is my Shepherd, I shall not want." These are her weapons and guns, with which she has defeated and conquered all her foes until now. With these she will also retain the victory until judgment day. The more the devil and the world plague and torture her, the better she fares. For her betterment and growth come in persecution, suffering, and dying. Therefore one of the old fathers has said: "The blood of the martyrs is a seed."[19] Where one is executed, a hundred others rise again. Of this wonderful victory several Psalms sing; for example, the ninth, the tenth, and others.

In this way I also have been preserved by the grace of God the past eighteen years. I have let my enemies rage, threaten, slander, and damn me, take counsel against me without ceasing, invent many evil devices, and practice many a piece of knavery. I have let them worry anxiously how they might kill me and destroy my

---

[19]An allusion to Tertullian, *Apologeticus* 50, which had become proverbial.

teaching, or rather God's. Moreover, I have been happy and of good cheer—at one time better than at another—have not worried greatly about their raving and raging, but have clung to the staff of comfort and found my way to the Lord's table. That is, I have committed my cares to our Lord God, into which He had led me absolutely without my will or counsel; and meanwhile I spoke an Our Father or a psalm. That is all of the armor with which until now I have not only held off all my enemies, but by the grace of God have also accomplished so much that, when I look behind me and consider how matters stand in the papacy, I really must be surprised that things have gone so far. I should never have dared to imagine that even one-tenth of what is now evident would happen. He that has begun the good work will also bring it to completion [Phil. 1:6], even though nine more hells and worlds were gathered together in a heap. Therefore let every Christian thoroughly learn this art: to cling to this rod and this staff, and to find his way to this table when sorrow or other misfortune appears. Then he will surely gain strength and comfort for everything that worries him.

The second metaphor is that of the oil, which is often employed in holy writ. It was, however, a precious oil, such as a balsam or other sweet-smelling liquid. The priests and the kings were customarily anointed with it. Furthermore, when the Jews had their festivals and wished to be happy, they would anoint or sprinkle themselves with such precious oil, as Jesus also mentions [Matt. 6:17] when He says: "When you fast, anoint your head and wash your face." This custom, then, of using oil was common among these people when they wanted to be merry and happy [John 12:3]. Magdalene [Luke 7:38] also wished to make the Lord happy when she poured precious ointment of pure perfume on His head, for she saw that He was sad. The third metaphor is that of a cup, which they used in their worship when they brought drink offerings and rejoiced before the Lord.

With these words, "Thou anointest my head with oil, Thou pourest my cup full," the prophet, then, wishes to indicate the great, rich comfort that the believers have through the Word, that their consciences are sure, happy, and well satisfied amid all temptations and distresses, even death. It is as though he would say: "The Lord indeed makes an unusual warrior of me and arms me quite wonderfully against my enemies. I thought that He would have put armor on me, placed a helmet on my head, put a sword into my hand, and warned me to be cautious and give careful attention to the business at hand lest I be surprised by my enemies. But instead He places me at a table and prepares a splendid meal for me, anoints my head with precious balm or (after the fashion of our country) puts a wreath on my head as if, instead of going out to do battle, I were on my way to a party or a dance. And so that I may not want anything now, He fills my cup to overflowing so that at once I may drink, be happy and of good cheer, and get drunk. The prepared table, accordingly, is my armor, the precious balm my helmet, the overflowing cup my sword; and with these I shall conquer all my enemies." But is that not a wonderful armor and an even more wonderful victory?

David wishes to say this: "Lord, Thy guests, who are sitting at Thy table, the believers, not only become strong and bold giants in the presence of all their enemies, but they also become happy and drunk. That is due to the fact that Thou dost treat them well, as a rich man usually treats his guests. Thou dost feed them splendidly, make them happy and gay, and serve them so well with wine that they get drunk." All of that is done through the Word of grace. Through it the Lord, our Shepherd, feeds and strengthens the hearts of His believers, so that they defy all of their enemies and say with the prophet: "I am not afraid of the many hundreds of thousands of people who have set themselves against me round about" [Ps. 3:6]. And above, in the fourth verse, he said: "I fear no evil; for Thou, Lord, art with me." He accordingly gives them the Holy Spirit together with the Word; yes, through this same Word. The Holy Spirit makes them not only courageous and bold, but also so secure and happy that they get drunk with a great and boundless joy.

David is thus speaking here of spiritual power, joy, and intoxi-cation—the power of God [Rom. 1:16]; and a joy in the Holy Spirit, as St. Paul calls it [Rom. 14:17]; and a blessed intoxication, in which the people are filled not with wine, for that is debauch-ery, but with the Holy Spirit [Eph. 5:18]. And this is the armor and the weapons with which our Lord God equips His believers against the devil and the world; that is, He puts the Word into their mouths and puts courage, that is, the Holy Spirit, into their hearts. Unafraid and cheerful, they attack all their enemies with that equipment. They smite and conquer them despite all their power, wisdom, and holiness. Such warriors were the apostles on the day of Pentecost [Acts 2:1 ff.]. They stood up in Jerusalem against the command of the emperor and the high priest and acted as though they were veritable gods and all the others mere locusts, and they pressed forward with all strength and joy, as though they were intoxicated, as some actually mocked them and said they were filled with new wine. But St. Peter showed from the prophet Joel that they were not filled with wine but with the Holy Spirit. Afterward he flays about with his sword; that is, he opens his mouth and preaches, and with one stroke he rescues three thousand souls from the devil.

But such power, joy, and blissful intoxication are manifested in the believers not only when they prosper and have peace, but also when they suffer and die. When the council at Jerusalem, therefore, had the apostles flogged, they rejoiced that they had been counted worthy to suffer dishonor for the name of Christ [Acts 5:41]. And in Rom. 5:3 St. Paul says: "We also rejoice in our sufferings." Later on many martyrs, men and women, went to their deaths with happy hearts and laughing mouths as though they were going to a happy festival or dance. So we read of St. Agnes and St. Agatha,[20] who were virgins of thirteen or fourteen years, and of many others. They not only boldly and confidently conquered the devil and the world through their deaths, but were also cheerful with all their hearts, just as if they had been drunk with great joy. And it does vex the devil beyond measure when one can so confidently despise his great might and guile. In our times, too, many have died cheerfully because they have confessed Christ. Similarly we learn that many die in their beds with a fine understanding and faith and say with Simeon, "With peace and joy I now depart,"[21] so that it is a pleasure to behold, as I myself have often beheld it. And all this because, as the prophet says, they are anointed with the oil which the Forty-fifth Psalm [Ps. 45:7] calls

---

[20]Luther seems to be thinking primarily of St. Agnes here, combining with the details of her martyrdom the story of another virgin martyr, St. Agatha.
[21]Here Luther seems to be quoting his own versification of the *Nunc Dimittis* of 1524.

an oil of gladness and have drunk from the overflowing cup which the Lord has filled.

"Good!" you say, "but I do not yet find myself sufficiently well equipped to die cheerfully." That does not matter. As mentioned earlier, David did not always have the ability either; indeed, at times he complained that he had been cast away from the presence of God. Nor did other saints at all times have full confidence in God and an eternal pleasure and patience in their distresses and afflictions. St. Paul at times trusted so securely and surely in Christ that he would not have bothered even to stand up because of the law, sin, death, and the devil. "It is no longer I who live," he says [Gal. 2:20], "but Christ who lives in me." And [Phil. 1:23]: "My desire is to depart and to be with Christ." And [Rom. 8:32, 35]: "Who shall separate us from the love of God? He did not spare His own Son, but gave Him up for us all. Will He not also give us all things with Him? Shall tribulation, or distress, or persecution, or the sword separate us from Him?" When he speaks here of death, the devil, and all misfortune, he is as sure as though he were the strongest and greatest saint, for whom death would be pure joy. Elsewhere, then, he speaks as though he were the weakest and greatest sinner on earth: 1 Cor. 2:3, "I was with you in weakness and in much fear and trembling." Rom. 7:14, "I am carnal, sold under sin," which brings me into captivity. Rom. 7:24: "Wretched man that I am! Who will deliver me from the body of this death?" And in Gal. 5:17, he teaches that in the saints there is an eternal struggle of the flesh against the spirit. Therefore you ought not despair so soon, though you find yourself weak and fainthearted, but pray diligently that you might remain with the Word and grow in the faith and knowledge of Christ. This is what the prophet is doing here, teaching others to do by saying:

6. *Goodness and mercy shall follow me all the days of my life; and I shall dwell in the house of the Lord forever.*

Because the devil never stops tormenting the believers—inwardly with terror, outwardly with the wiles of false teachers and the power of the tyrants—the prophet here at the end earnestly asks that God, who has given him this treasure, would also keep him in it to the end. He says: "Oh, may the dear God grant His grace that goodness and mercy might follow me all the days of my life and that He might soon make manifest what He calls goodness and mercy," that is, that he might dwell in the house of the Lord forever. It is as though he would say: "Lord, Thou hast begun the matter. Thou hast given me Thy holy Word and received me among those who are Thy people, who know Thee, praise and magnify Thee. Continue to give Thy grace that I may remain with the Word and nevermore be separated from Thy holy Christendom." Thus he also prays in the Twenty-seventh Psalm [Ps. 27:4]: "One thing," he says, "I ask of the Lord, that will I seek after; that I may dwell in the house of the Lord all the days of my life, to behold the beautiful worship of the Lord, and to visit His temple."

Thus the prophet here teaches and admonishes all believers by his example not to become smug, proud, or presumptuous, but to fear and pray that they may not lose their treasure. Such an earnest admonition, however, should truly arouse us and awake us to pray diligently. Blessed David, a prophet enlightened with all kinds of divine wisdom and knowledge and endowed with so many kinds of great and splendid gifts of God, prayed often and very earnestly that he might remain in possession of the blessings of God. We, then, who surely must be considered as nothing at all in comparison with David and who, besides, live at the end of the world—and that, as Christ and the apostles tell us, is a horrible and dangerous time—ought much more to awake and to pray with all earnestness and diligence that we may remain in the house of the Lord all the days of our life, that is, that we may hear God's Word, through it receive the many kinds of blessings and fruit that were shown us above, and endure therein unto the end. May Christ, our only Shepherd and Savior, grant us this! Amen.

Comfort When Facing Grave Temptations

PSALM 142

First, such a person must by no means rely on himself, nor must he be guided by his own feelings. Rather, he must lay hold of the words offered to him in God's name, cling to them, place his trust in them, and direct all the thoughts and feelings of his heart to them.

Second, he must not imagine that he is the only one assailed about his salvation, but he must be aware (as St. Peter declares) that there are many more people in the world passing through the same trials [1 Pet. 5:9]. How often does David lament and cry out in the Psalms, "O God, I am driven far from Thy sight" [31:22], and, "I became like those who go into hell" [28:1]. These trials are not rare among the godly. They hurt, to be sure, but that is also in order, etc.

Third, he should by no means insist on deliverance from these trials without yielding to the divine will. He should address God cheerfully and firmly and say, "If I am to drink this cup, dear Father, may Your will, not mine, be done" [Luke 22:42].

Fourth, there is no stronger medicine for this than to begin with words such as David used when he said in Psalm 18 [:3], "I will call upon the Lord and praise Him, and so shall I be saved from all that assails me." For the evil spirit of gloom cannot be driven away by sadness and lamentation and anxiety, but by praising God, which makes the heart glad.

Fifth, he must thank God diligently for deeming him worthy of such a visitation, of which many thousands of people remain deprived.[22] It would be neither good nor useful for man to know what great blessings lie hidden under such trials. Some have wanted to fathom this and have thereby done themselves much harm. Therefore, we should willingly endure the hand of God in this and in all suffering. Do not be worried; indeed, such a trial is the very best sign of God's grace and love for man. At such a time it is well to pray, read, or sing Psalm 142, which is especially helpful at this point.

PSALM 142

I cry to the Lord with my voice,
　　with my voice I make supplication to the Lord.
I pour out my complaint before Him,
　　I lay my trouble before Him,
When my spirit is filled with fear,
　　Thou comest to my aid.

[22]Luther says elsewhere that the most dangerous trial is when there is none.

(That is, Thou hast concern about what happens to me and what should happen to me).

> In the path where I walk
> they have placed a snare for me.

(The devil does that by means of evil thoughts which fill man with uncertainty as to his fate and hinder him in his being and doing. However, we must commit this to God, who knows well what our course will be.)

> I look to the right and watch,
> there is no one who wants to know me.

(That is, the soul imagines that it does not belong in the company of the blessed. Here where the blessed are, no one knows the soul. Now it would flee in an attempt to rid itself of this grief, but, as seen in the following, this is impossible.)

> I cannot escape.

(That is, there can be neither escape nor flight, and I must remain here in my fear.)

> And no man is concerned about my soul.

(That is what the soul thinks, and that is also what it feels; but for all of that, the soul must not yield and give way to such thoughts and feelings.)

> I cry to Thee, dear Lord

(since nothing else wants to comfort or is able to help)

> and I say, "Thou art my refuge,
> my portion in the land of the living.

(That is, everything tells me that I must die and perish. But I fight against that and say, "No, I want to live, for this I look to Thee in faith.")

> Give heed to my lament,
>   for I am being greatly tormented.

> Save me from my persecutors,
>   for they are too powerful for me.
> Lead my soul out of prison

(That is, out of the distress and terror which hold me captive.)

> that I may give thanks to Thy name.
>   The righteous will gather around me

(to offer thanks with me and for me as a lost sheep [Luke 15:6])

> For Thou dealest bountifully with me.

(That is, rendereth me comfort in my need and help against evil.) Amen.

Sixth, it is necessary that one never doubt the promise of the truthful and faithful God. He promised to hear us; yes, He commanded us to pray, for the very reason that we might know and firmly believe that our petition will be heard. Thus Christ says in Matthew 21 [:22] and in Mark 11 [:24], "Therefore I tell you, whatever you ask in prayer, believe that you shall receive it, and you surely will." Also in Luke 11 [:9–13], "Ask, and it will be given you; seek, and you will find; knock, and it will be opened to you. What son is there among you who would ask his father for bread, and he would offer him a stone instead? etc. If you, then, who are evil, know how to give good gifts to your children, how much more will the heavenly Father give the Holy Spirit to those who ask Him?"

Such a person must also know Christ aright and know that by Him alone are all our sins paid and God's grace given to us, lest he presume to deal directly with God and without this mediator.

But if the inner assaults should become more severe after this medicine, he should do nothing else but abide by the above advice.

For this grave temptation is a good omen that this will soon end and that the devil is very nearly vanquished. He is merely making his strongest attempt now. Pharaoh, too, never persecuted the children of Israel as severely as he did toward the end.[24] One can also see this in a physical illness. Just before the medicine begins to help and heal the person, it makes him extremely sick. Therefore this person should be hopeful and of good cheer.

Preface to Solomon's Ecclesiastes
1524

This book is called in Hebrew *Qoheleth,* that is, "One who speaks publicly in a congregation." For *qahal* means a congregation assembled together, that which in Greek is called *ekklesia*. Now this book was certainly not written or set down by King Solomon with his own hand. Instead scholars put together what others had heard from Solomon's lips, as they themselves admit at the end of the book where they say, "These words of the wise are like goads and nails, fixed by the masters of the congregation and given by one shepherd" [Eccles. 12:11]. That is to say, certain persons selected by the kings and the people were at that time appointed to fix and arrange this and other books that were handed down by Solomon, the one shepherd. They did this so that not everyone would have to be making books as he pleased, as they also lament in that same place that "of the making of books there is no end" [Eccles. 12:12]; they forbid the acceptance of others.

These men here call themselves "masters of the congregation" [Eccles. 12:11], and books had to be accepted and approved at their hands and by their office. Of course, the Jewish people had an external government that was instituted by God, which is why such a thing as this could be done surely and properly. In like manner too, the book of the Proverbs of Solomon has been put together by others, with the teaching and sayings of some wise men added at the end. The Song of Solomon too has the appearance of a book compiled by others out of things received from the lips of Solomon. For this reason these books have no particular

[24]Cf. Exod. 1:8–14.

order either, but one thing is mixed with another. This must be the character of such books, since they did not hear it all from him at one time but at different times.

Now this book ought really to have a title [to indicate] that it was written against the free will.[25] For the entire book tends to show that the counsels, plans, and undertakings of men are all in vain and fruitless, and that they always have a different outcome from that which we will and purpose. Thus Solomon would teach us to wait in confident trust and to let God alone do everything, above and against and without our knowledge and counsel. Therefore you must not understand this book to be reviling God's creatures when it says, "All is vanity and a striving after wind." For God's creatures are all good, Gen. 1 [:31] and 2 Tim. 4 [1 Tim. 4:4]; and this book itself says that a man shall be happy with his wife and enjoy life, etc. [Eccles. 9:9]. It teaches, rather, that the plans and undertakings of men in their dealings with the creatures all go wrong and are in vain, if one is not satisfied with what is presently at hand but wants to be their master and ruler for the future. That's how it always goes—backward—so that a man has had nothing but wasted toil and anxiety; things turn out anyway as God wills and purposes, not as we will and purpose.

To put it briefly, Christ says in Matt. 6 [:34], "Do not be anxious about tomorrow, for tomorrow will have its own anxiety; it is enough that every day has its own evil." This saying is really the interpretation and content of this book. Anxiety about us is God's affair; our anxiety goes wrong anyhow, and produces nothing but wasted toil.

[25]At about the same time Luther was writing this preface, in the latter part of September 1524, Erasmus's famous treatise *De libero arbitrio* (*"Concerning Free Will"*), published at the beginning of the month in Basel, was making its appearance in Wittenberg.

THE NEW TESTAMENT

Luther was fierce in his desire to purge theology from what he saw as the corrupting influences of Aristotelian philosophy and Scholasticism. He believed that excessive reliance on human reason inclined people to self-sufficiency and thus obscured the mystery of faith. To live in faith is to live beyond what intellect and feeling can apprehend. Luther held that a Christian is justified only through trust in Christ, who alone can confer forgiveness. We cannot free ourselves from sin or from despair, nor can we trust our own conscience, because it is confused by sin. He observed that practices of the Church such as the issuance and sale of indulgences could lead the faithful astray because they inclined the sinner to forget to repent, and to rely instead on personal works to effect salvation. Over against the authority of the papal office and the teaching authority of the Church, the magisterium, Luther proposed the gospel alone as the source of divine truth. Scripture is the revelation of God in Jesus Christ, who clothes us with His righteousness when we come to have faith in Him and His infinite mercy. We are saved, Luther held, from sin and its effects sola fide (through faith alone), sola gratia (grace alone), and sola scriptura (scripture alone). Dogma, rites, and traditions are authentic only if they are in harmony with the biblical message. Luther's translation of the New Testament appeared in vivid, colloquial German in September 1522. It is commonly called the September Testament. Luther studied, preached, and lectured on scripture for thirty-four years, writing commentaries and revising his translation. He defined the central principle and reference point of his exegetical work as "that which proclaims Christ." This is the touchstone of Evangelical theology.

A Brief Instruction on What to Look for and Expect in the Gospels

It is a common practice to number the gospels and to name them by books and say that there are four gospels. From this practice stems the fact that no one knows what St. Paul and St. Peter are saying in their epistles, and their teaching is regarded as an addition to the teaching of the gospels, in a vein similar to that of

Jerome's introduction. There is, besides, the still worse practice of regarding the gospels and epistles as law books, in which is supposed to be taught what we are to do and in which the works of Christ are pictured to us as nothing but examples. Now where these two erroneous notions remain in the heart, there neither the gospels nor the epistles may be read in a profitable or Christian manner, and [people] remain as pagan as ever.

One should thus realize that there is only one gospel, but that it is described by many apostles. Every single epistle of Paul and of Peter, as well as the Acts of the Apostles, by Luke, is a gospel, even though they do not record all the works and words of Christ, but one is shorter and includes less than another. There is not one of the four major gospels anyway that includes all the words and works of Christ; nor is this necessary. Gospel is and should be nothing else than a discourse or story about Christ, just as happens among men when one writes a book about a king or a prince, telling what he did, said, and suffered in his day. Such a story can be told in various ways; one spins it out, and the other is brief. Thus the gospel is and should be nothing else than a chronicle, a story, a narrative about Christ, telling who He is, what He did, said, and suffered—a subject which one describes briefly, another more fully, one this way, another that way.

For at its briefest, the gospel is a discourse about Christ, that He is the Son of God and became man for us, that He died and was raised, that He has been established as a Lord over all things. This much St. Paul takes in hand and spins out in his epistles. He bypasses all the miracles and incidents [in Christ's ministry] which are set forth in the four gospels, yet he includes the whole gospel adequately and abundantly. This may be seen clearly and well in his greeting to the Romans [1:1–4], where he says what the gospel is, and declares, "Paul, a servant of Jesus Christ, called to be an apostle, set apart for the gospel of God, which He promised beforehand through His prophets in the holy scriptures, the gospel concerning His Son, who was descended from David according to the flesh and designated Son of God in power according to the Spirit of holiness by His Resurrection from the dead, Jesus Christ our Lord," etc.

There you have it. The gospel is a story about Christ, God's and David's Son, who died and was raised and is established as Lord.

This is the gospel in a nutshell. Just as there is no more than one Christ, so there is and may be no more than one gospel. . . .

Yes, even the teaching of the prophets, in those places where they speak of Christ, is nothing but the true, pure, and proper gospel—just as if Luke or Matthew had described it. For the prophets have proclaimed the gospel and spoken of Christ, as St. Paul here [Rom. 1:2] reports and as everyone indeed knows. Thus when Isaiah in chapter 53 says how Christ should die for us and bear our sins, he has written the pure gospel. And I assure you, if a person fails to grasp this understanding of the gospel, he will never be able to be illuminated in the scripture, nor will he receive the right foundation.

Be sure, moreover, that you do not make Christ into a Moses, as if Christ did nothing more than teach and provide examples as the other saints do, as if the gospel were simply a textbook of teachings or laws. Therefore you should grasp Christ, His words, works, and sufferings in a twofold manner. First as an example that is presented to you, which you should follow and imitate. As St. Peter says in 1 Pet. 4, "Christ suffered for us, thereby leaving us an example." Thus when you see how He prays, fasts, helps people, and shows them love, so also you should do, both for yourself and for your neighbor. However, this is the smallest part of the gospel, on the basis of which it cannot yet even be called gospel. For on this level Christ is of no more help to you than some other saint. His life remains His own and does not as yet contribute anything to you. In short, this mode [of understanding Christ as simply an example] does not make Christians, but only hypocrites. You must grasp Christ at a much higher level. Even though this higher level has for a long time been the very best, the preaching of it has been something rare. The chief article and foundation of the gospel is that before you take Christ as an example, you accept and recognize Him as a gift, as a present that God has given you and that is your own. This means that when you see or hear of Christ doing or suffering something, you do not doubt that Christ Himself, with His deeds and suffering, belongs to you. On this you may depend as surely as if you had done it yourself; indeed as if you were Christ Himself. See, this is what it means to have a proper grasp of the gospel, that is, of the overwhelming goodness of God, which neither prophet, nor apostle, nor angel was ever able fully to express, and which no heart could adequately fathom or marvel at. This is the great fire of the love of God for us, whereby the heart and conscience become happy, secure, and content. This is what preaching the Christian faith means. This is why such preaching is called "gospel," which in German means a joyful, good, and comforting "message," and this is why the apostles are called the "twelve messengers."

Now when you have Christ as the foundation and chief blessing of your salvation, then the other part follows: that you take Him as your example, giving yourself in service to your neighbor just as you see that Christ has given Himself for you. See, there faith and love move forward, God's commandment is fulfilled, and a person is happy and fearless to do and to suffer all things. Therefore make note of this, that Christ as a gift nourishes your faith and makes you a Christian. But Christ as an example exercises your works. These do not make you a Christian. Actually they come forth from you because you have already been made a Christian. As widely as a gift differs from an example, so widely does faith differ from works, for faith possesses nothing of its own, only the deeds and life of Christ. You have something of your own in them, yet they should not belong to you but to your neighbor.

So you see that the gospel is really not a book of laws and commandments which require deeds of us, but a book of divine promises in which God promises, offers, and gives us all His possessions and benefits in Christ. The fact that Christ and the apostles provide much good teaching and explain the law is to be counted a benefit just like any other good work of Christ. For to teach aright is not the least sort of benefit. We see too that unlike Moses in his book, and contrary to the nature of a commandment, Christ does not horribly force and drive us. Rather . . . He teaches so gently that He entices rather than commands. He begins by saying, "Blessed are the poor, blessed are the meek," and so on. And the apostles commonly use the expressions, "I admonish," "I request," "I beseech," and so on. But Moses says, "I command," "I forbid," threatening and frightening everyone with horrible punishments and penalties. With this sort of instruction you can now read and hear the gospels profitably.

When you open the book containing the gospels and read or hear how Christ comes here or there, or how someone is brought to Him, you should therein perceive the sermon or the gospel through which He is coming to you, or you are being brought to Him. For the preaching of the gospel is nothing else than Christ coming to us, or us being brought to Him.

Preface to the New Testament
1546 (1522)

It would be right and proper for this book to go forth without any prefaces or extraneous names attached and simply have its own say under its own name. However, many unfounded interpretations and prefaces have scattered the thought of Christians to a point where no one any longer knows what is gospel or law, New Testament or Old. Necessity demands, therefore, that there should be a notice or preface, by which the ordinary man can be rescued from his former delusions, set on the right track, and taught what he is to look for in this book, so that he may not seek laws and commandments when he ought to be seeking the gospel and promises of God.

Therefore it should be known, in the first place, that the notion must be given up that there are four gospels and only four evangelists.[26] The division of the New Testament books into legal, historical, prophetic, and wisdom books is also to be utterly rejected. Some make this division, thinking thereby (I know not how) to compare the New with the Old Testament. On the contrary it is to be held firmly that just as the Old Testament is a book in which are written God's laws and commandments, together with the history of those who kept and of those who did not keep them, so the New Testament is a book in which are written the gospel and the promises of God, together with the history of those who believe and of those who do not believe them.

For "gospel" (*euangelion*) is a Greek word and means in Greek a good message, good tidings, good news, a good report, which one sings and tells with gladness. For example, when David overcame

---

[26]Limiting the number of gospels to four was an ancient practice going back at least to Jerome, who based his position on the existence of but four living creatures in Ezek. 1 and Rev. 4—the man, lion, ox, and eagle.

the great Goliath, there came among the Jewish people the good report and encouraging news that their terrible enemy had been struck down and that they had been rescued and given joy and peace; and they sang and danced and were glad for it [1 Sam. 18:6].

Thus this gospel of God, or New Testament, is a good story and report, sounded forth into all the world by the apostles, telling of a true David who strove with sin, death, and the devil, and overcame them, and thereby rescued all those who were captive in sin, afflicted with death, and overpowered by the devil. Without any merit of their own He made them righteous, gave them life, and saved them, so that they were given peace and brought back to God. For this they sing, and thank and praise God, and are glad forever, if only they believe firmly and remain steadfast in faith.

This report and encouraging tidings, or Evangelical and divine news, is also called a New Testament. For it is a testament when a dying man bequeaths his property, after his death, to his legally defined heirs. And Christ, before His death, commanded and ordained that His gospel be preached after His death in all the world [Luke 24:44–47]. Thereby He gave to all who believe, as their possession, everything that He had. This included His life, in which He swallowed up death; His righteousness, by which He blotted out sin; and His salvation, with which He overcame everlasting damnation. A poor man, dead in sin and consigned to hell, can hear nothing more comforting than this precious and tender message about Christ; from the bottom of his heart he must laugh and be glad over it, if he believes it true.

Now, to strengthen this faith, God has promised this gospel and testament in many ways by the prophets in the Old Testament, as St. Paul says in Romans 1 [:1], "I am set apart to preach the gospel of God which He promised beforehand through His prophets in the holy scriptures, concerning His Son, who was descended from David," etc.

To mention some of these places: God gave the first promise when He said to the serpent, in Gen. 3 [:15], "I will put enmity between you and the woman, and between your seed and her seed; he shall bruise your head, and you shall bruise his heel." Christ is this woman's seed, who has bruised the devil's head, that is, sin, death, hell, and all his power. For without this seed, no man can escape sin, death, or hell.

Again, in Gen. 22 [:18], God promised Abraham, "Through your descendant shall all the nations of the earth be blessed." Christ is that descendant of Abraham, says St. Paul in Galatians 3 [:16]; He has blessed all the world through the gospel [Gal. 3:8]. For where Christ is not, there is still the curse that fell upon Adam and his children when he had sinned, so that they all are necessarily guilty and subject to sin, death, and hell. Over against this curse the gospel now blesses all the world by publicly announcing, "Whoever believes in this descendant of Abraham shall be blessed." That is, he shall be rid of sin, death, and hell, and shall remain righteous, alive, and saved forever, as Christ Himself says in John 11 [:26], "Whoever believes in Me shall never die."

Again God made this promise to David in 2 Sam. 7 [:12–14] when He said, "I will raise up your son after you, who shall build a house for My name, and I will establish the throne of His kingdom forever. I will be His father, and He shall be My son," etc. This is the kingdom of Christ, of which the gospel speaks: an everlasting kingdom, a kingdom of life, salvation, and righteousness, where all those who believe enter in from out of the prison of sin and death.

There are many more such promises of the gospel in the other prophets as well, for example Mic. 5 [:2], "But you, O Bethlehem Ephrathah, who are little to be among the clans of Judah, from you shall come forth for Me one who is to be ruler in Israel"; and again, Hos. 13 [:14], "I shall ransom them from the power of hell and redeem them from death. O death, I will be your plague; O hell, I will be your destruction."

The gospel, then, is nothing but the preaching about Christ, Son of God and of David, true God and man, who by His death and Resurrection has overcome for us the sin, death, and hell of all men who believe in Him. Thus the gospel can be either a brief or a lengthy message; one person can write of it briefly, another at length. He writes of it at length who writes about many words and works of Christ, as do the four evangelists. He writes of it briefly, however, who does not tell of Christ's works but indicates briefly how by His death and Resurrection He has overcome sin, death, and hell for those who believe in Him, as do St. Peter and St. Paul.

See to it, therefore, that you do not make a Moses out of Christ, or a book of laws and doctrines out of the gospel, as has been done heretofore and as certain prefaces put it, even those of St. Jerome.[27] For the gospel does not expressly demand works of our own by which we become righteous and are saved; indeed it condemns such works. Rather the gospel demands faith in Christ: that He has overcome for us sin, death, and hell, and thus gives us righteousness, life, and salvation not through our works, but through His own works, death, and suffering, in order that we may avail ourselves of His death and victory as though we had done it ourselves.

To be sure, Christ in the gospel, and St. Peter and St. Paul besides, do give many commandments and doctrines, and expound the law. But these are to be counted like all Christ's other works and good deeds. To know His works and the things that happened to Him is not yet to know the true gospel, for you do not yet thereby know that He has overcome sin, death, and the devil. So, too, it is not yet knowledge of the gospel when you know these doctrines and commandments, but only when the voice comes that says, "Christ is your own, with His life, teaching, works, death, Resurrection, and all that He is, has, does, and can do."

Thus we see also that He does not compel us but invites us kindly and says, "Blessed are the poor," etc. [Matt. 5:3]. And the apostles use the words "I exhort," "I entreat," "I beg," so that one sees on every hand that the gospel is not a book of law, but really a preaching of the benefits of Christ, shown to us and given to us for our own possession, if we believe. But Moses, in his books, drives, compels, threatens, strikes, and rebukes terribly, for he is a lawgiver and driver.

Hence it comes that to a believer no law is given by which he becomes righteous before God, as St. Paul says in 1 Timothy 1 [:9], because he is alive and righteous and saved by faith, and he needs nothing further except to prove his faith by works. Truly, if faith is there, he cannot hold back; he proves himself, breaks out into good works, confesses and teaches this gospel before the people, and stakes his life on it. Everything that he lives and does is

---

[27]Each of the four gospels had its own preface in Jerome's Vulgate. Luther's concern for the "one gospel" kept him from ever writing four such separate prefaces. Indeed at the beginning it seems likely that he envisioned but one preface for the entire New Testament.

directed to his neighbor's profit, in order to help him—not only to
the attainment of this grace, but also in body, property, and honor.
Seeing that Christ has done this for him, he thus follows Christ's
example.

That is what Christ meant when at the last He gave no other
commandment than love, by which men were to know who were
His disciples [John 13:34–35] and true believers. For where works
and love do not break forth, there faith is not right, the gospel does
not yet take hold, and Christ is not rightly known. See, then, that
you so approach the books of the New Testament as to learn to
read them in this way.

Which are the true and noblest books of the New Testament?

From all this you can now judge all the books and decide
among them which are the best. John's gospel and St. Paul's epistles, especially that to the Romans, and St. Peter's first epistle are
the true kernel and marrow of all the books. They ought properly
to be the foremost books, and it would be advisable for every
Christian to read them first and most, and by daily reading to
make them as much his own as his daily bread. For in them you do
not find many works and miracles of Christ described, but you do
find depicted in masterly fashion how faith in Christ overcomes
sin, death, and hell, and gives life, righteousness, and salvation.
This is the real nature of the gospel, as you have heard.

If I had to do without one or the other—either the works or the
preaching of Christ—I would rather do without the works than
without His preaching. For the works do not help me, but His
words give life, as He Himself says [John 6:63]. Now John writes
very little about the works of Christ, but very much about His
preaching, while the other evangelists write much about His
works and little about His preaching. Therefore John's gospel is
the one, fine, true, and chief gospel, and is far, far to be preferred
over the other three and placed high above them. So, too, the epistles of St. Paul and St. Peter far surpass the other three gospels,
Matthew, Mark, and Luke.

In a word, St. John's gospel and his first epistle, St. Paul's epistles, especially Romans, Galatians, and Ephesians, and St. Peter's
first epistle are the books that show you Christ and teach you all
that is necessary and salvatory for you to know, even if you were

never to see or hear any other book or doctrine. Therefore St. James's epistle is really an epistle of straw, compared to these others, for it has nothing of the nature of the gospel about it. But more of this in the other prefaces.

Exposition of Matthew 5:43–48

43. You have heard that it was said, "You shall love your neighbor and hate your enemy."

44. But I say to you, love your enemies and pray for those who persecute you,

45. so that you may be sons of your Father who is in heaven; for He makes His sun rise on the evil and on the good and sends rain on the just and on the unjust.

46. For if you love those who love you, what reward have you? Do not even the tax collectors do the same?

47. And if you salute only your brethren, what more are you doing than others? Do not even the gentiles do the same?

48. You, therefore, must be perfect, as your heavenly Father is perfect.

The statement that Christ quotes here does not appear in any single place in the Old Testament, but is scattered here and there throughout the book of Deuteronomy, where it talks about the enemies of Israel among the surrounding gentiles, like Moab, Ammon, and Amalek.[28] Although it does not expressly say that they should hate their enemies, still this follows from statements like the one in Deut. 23:6, that they should never do anything good for the Ammonites, the Moabites, and their other enemies, nor ever wish them good fortune or success. This was indeed a great concession and a generous grant to the Jews, and one which they used to good advantage. But here as elsewhere they misunderstood this, going to extremes and misusing it to gratify their own whims. Hence Christ has to reinterpret it and show them what the

[28]Cf., for example, Deut. 2:34, Deut. 3:2, and especially Deut. 7:1–5.

law really meant. They had neglected this and had laid emphasis only upon the statements that sounded as if they supported their position. Thus they provided backing for their own crookedness.

Here again you must note the distinction, and primarily the fact that He is speaking only about what Christians as Christians should do, and in particular what they should do on account of the gospel and their Christianity. My reply to someone else's hate or envy, slander or persecution should not be more hatred and persecution, slander and curses, but rather my love and help, my blessings and my prayers. For a Christian is the kind of man who knows no hatred or hostility against anyone at all, whose heart is neither angry nor vindictive, but only loving, mild, and helpful. That is how our Lord Christ is, and His heavenly Father Himself, to whom He points here as the pattern.

Now the question arises: what is to be said about the fact that the scriptures often talk about holy men cursing their enemies, even about Christ and His apostles doing so? Would you call that blessing their enemies? Or how can I love the pope when every day I rebuke and curse him—and with good reason, too? The answer, put as simply as possible, is this: I have often said that the office of preaching is not our office but God's. But whatever is God's, that we do not do ourselves; but He does it Himself, through the Word and the office, as His own gift and business. Now, it is written in John 16:8 that it is the office and work of the Holy Spirit to convince the world. But if He is to convince it, He cannot act the hypocrite or play the flattering gentleman and say what it would like to hear. He must rebuke it vigorously and attack it—the way Christ pronounces "Woe!" upon His Pharisees [Matt. 23]; the way Paul says to Elymas [Acts 13:10]: "You son of the devil . . . full of all villainy!"; the way Stephen reads a hard and sharp text to the high priests [Acts 7:51–53]; and especially the way St. Paul [Gal. 1:8] puts it all on one pile and calls everyone anathema, that is, excommunicated and cursed and sentenced to the abyss of hell, who does not preach the pure teaching about faith.

You see, that is how God's Word proceeds. It challenges the whole world. It reaches into the mouth of the lords and the princes and of everyone else, denouncing and cursing their whole way of life, something that is not proper for you or me to do as individual Christians except in our office and our teaching position. In

Ps. 2:10, 11 David dares to do this. He tells all the kings and lords to think, to humble themselves, to fall at the feet of the teaching about Christ, and to let themselves be rebuked and instructed. Otherwise they will be damned instantly and turned over to the devil. I would not dare to do that. But that is the way God's Word proceeds. It hammers the great and mighty mountains with its thunder and lightning and storms, so that they smoke. It shatters everything that is great and proud and disobedient, as Psalm 29 says. But on the other hand, it is also like a fruitful rain, sprinkling and moistening, planting and strengthening whatever is like the poor, parched plants that are weak and sickly.

Now, it is wrong for someone who is not a teacher and preacher, commissioned to administer the Word of God, to rush in, snapping and snarling and cursing. But whoever has been commissioned with this office must administer it. And it is wrong for him to neglect it or to be so scared that he refuses to open his mouth and to denounce what should be denounced, irrespective of personal considerations. For example, now we have to say to our bishops that they are tyrants and villains who flagrantly oppose both God and the law with their violent and capricious dealings. Now when I do this, I am not doing it on my own, but by virtue of my office. Otherwise, as far as my own person is concerned, I ought not to wish or say anything evil to any man on earth; rather I ought to wish everyone well and speak and act kindly toward him. It is not in this way that I am the enemy of the pope, the bishops, and all the enemies who persecute us and continually torment us. From my heart I am perfectly willing to let them have whatever temporal goods, power, and prestige God gives them; and I would do my best to help them keep it all. Indeed, I would be even happier if they were also as rich in spiritual goods as we are, and lacked nothing. And it would be our heart's delight if by surrendering our own body and life we could bring them to this, rescue them from their blindness, and save them from the power of the devil.

But they simply refuse to have this, and they cannot tolerate or accept any of the good things that we offer them. Therefore we must also let them go their own way, and say: "If we have to make a choice of which should perish, whether the Word of God and the kingdom of Christ or the pope with all his mob, then rather let him go to the abyss of hell, in the name of his god the devil, just so that the Word of God may abide!" If I must bless and praise one of them and curse and damn the other one, then I will bless the Word of God but curse them with everything they have. For I must place the Word of God above everything else. To keep it and to stay with Christ, who is my highest Treasure in heaven and on earth, I must be willing to risk my body and life, the popularity of the world, my goods, my reputation, and all my happiness. For one of these two things has to happen: either the Word of God will abide and conquer them or at least they will be unable to suppress it, even if they refuse to accept all its grace and goodness and salvation.

In this way a Christian can easily handle the situation and his relations toward both his enemies and his friends. So far as his neighbor's person is concerned, he will love and bless everyone. But on the other hand, so far as God and His Word are concerned, he will not put up with any transgression. He must give this precedence over everything else and subordinate everything else to it, irrespective of any person, be he friend or foe; for this cause belongs neither to us nor to our neighbor but to God, whom it is our duty to obey before anything else [Acts 5:29]. Consequently I say to my worst enemies: "Where it is only my own person that is involved, there I am very willing to help you and to do everything good for you, in spite of the fact that you are my enemy and that all you ever do for me is to harm me. But where it is the Word of God that is involved, there you must not expect any friendship or love that I may have for you to persuade me to do something against that, even if you were my nearest and dearest friend. But since you cannot endure the Word, I will speak this prayer and benediction over you: 'May God dash you to the ground!' I shall willingly serve you, but not in order to help you overthrow the Word of God. For this purpose you will never be able to persuade me even to give you a drink of water." In other words, our love and service belong to men. But they belong to God above all; if this is hindered or threatened, love and service are no longer in place. For the command is: "You shall love your enemy and do him good." But to God's enemies I must also be an enemy, lest I join forces with them against God.

Thus He has refuted this idea also against the delusion of the Jews, who gave a crooked twist to scripture by maintaining that they were permitted to hate their enemies. He has interpreted the law to mean that they were to have no enemy at all whom they should hate, in spite of the fact that Moses had told them not to establish or to maintain friendly relations with certain alien heathen, whom not they but God Himself had specifically designated as His enemies. But that they were to regard as their enemies anyone whom they chose, and that they were to curse, persecute, and torment such people—that was not what Moses meant to say. Solomon correctly understood and interpreted Moses, and he says [Prov. 25:21]: "If your enemy is hungry, give him bread to eat; and if he is thirsty, give him water to drink," a statement St. Paul also cites [Rom. 12:20]. Hating your enemy is proper to a public person and to an office that has been divinely established. But the commandment "You shall love your neighbor as yourself" [Lev. 19:18] applies to the common crowd and to each individual in particular.

Look at how high He puts the target. Not only does He denounce those who do harm to their enemies, but He also refuses to call those "pious" who neglect to do them good when they need it. He says first: "Love your enemies." But to love means to be good-hearted and to wish the best, to have a heart that is friendly, kind, and sweet toward everyone, not one that makes fun of misery or misfortune. He also wants us to express this by our words, as He says: "Bless those who curse you." Thus we should not speak a single harsh word against them, however terrible their abuse, slander, scolding, and curses may be, but only speak to them kindly and wish them well. This is the source of that beautiful Christian saying which some pious people use. When they hear that someone has done them wrong or has played some ugly trick upon them, they say: "May God forgive him!" They are concerned and sympathetic, and all they want is to keep this from bringing any harm to him in his relation to God. That is really a good tongue in response to the evil tongues of others, with both the mouth and the heart demonstrating nothing but love.

In the third place, He wants this kind of heart to become manifest in deeds as well, in all kinds of friendly and cordial works. He says: "Do good to those who hate you." This is really a very rare virtue. It is the kind of teaching that does not suit the world at all; nature finds it impossible to recompense all sorts of evil with nothing but good, not to be overcome by evil or by shameful ingratitude but to overcome evil with good, as St. Paul says [Rom. 12:21]. For this reason He had laid down the condition earlier [Matt. 5:20] that whoever wants to be a disciple of Christ and to enter the kingdom of heaven must have a righteousness that is different, one that is better than that of the Pharisees and the Jewish saints.

The fourth item, however, "Pray for those who spitefully abuse you and persecute you," applies more directly to our doctrine and faith than to our person and life. The fact that they persecute us is due to the Word of God: they claim that they are right and that we are wrong. Then it is our duty to pray and to commend our cause to God, for on earth there is no law or judge to vindicate us. Our persecutors are actually in competition not with us, but with God Himself; it is with His kingdom that they are interfering; they are doing the greatest injury not to us but to God Himself; and it is His wrath and condemnation that they have incurred. When we see all this, we should have pity on them and pray for them to be rescued from their blindness and their terrible doom. No one can do us any harm without doing it first to a far greater Lord, namely, to the High Majesty in heaven Himself.

Yet all this is valid only insofar as it goes on apart from one's official responsibility and does not interfere with it. As I have always said, it is necessary carefully to distinguish the teaching that pertains universally to each individual person from the teaching that pertains to persons in an office, whether it be spiritual or secular, whose task it is to punish and to resist evil. Therefore, even though personally they may be gentle, yet administering justice and meting out punishment is their official work, and it has to go on. It would be wrong if their pity moved them to neglect this, for that would be tantamount to helping, strengthening, and encouraging the evil. It is as if I were to say to our enemies, the pope, the bishops, the princes, and all the rest, who are persecuting the gospel and trampling its poor adherents underfoot: "Gentlemen, may the dear God reward you! You are pious people and holy fathers"; or as if I were to keep quiet, pay them homage, or kiss their feet. No, dear brother, this is what I ought to say: "I am a preacher. I have to have teeth in my mouth. I have to bite and salt and tell them the truth. And if they refuse to hear, then in the name of God I have to excommunicate them, lock them out of heaven, consign them to the fire of hell, and turn them over to the devil."

Now, whoever has this office of rebuking and denouncing, let him perform it. But apart from that office, let everyone stick to this teaching: You shall not denounce or curse anyone, but you shall wish him everything good and show this in your actions, even though he may act badly; thus you will disclaim all right to mete out punishment, and you will assign it to those whose office it is. Such a person will eventually find a Judge that will not spare him, even though you may not take vengeance or even seek it. God will not let any violence go unpunished, but He Himself will take vengeance on our enemies and will send home to them what they have deserved by the way they have treated us. As He Himself says [Deut. 32:35]: "Vengeance is Mine, I will repay." On the basis of this, St. Paul admonishes the Christians [Rom. 12:19]: "Never avenge yourselves, but leave it to the wrath of God." These words are not only instruction but also consolation, as if He were to say: "Do not take it upon yourselves to avenge yourselves on one another, or to speak curses and maledictions. The person that does you harm or injury is interfering with an office that is not his. He is presuming to inflict punishment or injury upon you without the command of God, indeed, contrary to it. Now, if you do the same, then you, too, are interfering with the office of God and sinning against God as gravely as this man has sinned against you. Therefore keep your fist to yourself. Leave it in the charge of His wrath and punishing, for He will not let it remain unavenged, and His punishment is more severe than you would like. This man has not assailed you but God Himself, and has already fallen into His wrath. He will not escape this. No one ever has. So why get angry with him when the anger of God, immensely greater and more severe than the anger and punishment of the whole world, has already come upon him and has already avenged itself more thoroughly than you ever could? Besides, he has not injured you one-tenth as much as he has injured God. When you see him lying under this severe condemnation, why so many curses and threats of vengeance? Rather you should take pity on his plight, and pray for him to be rescued from it and to reform."

As a confirmation and illustration of this teaching He cites two examples. He says in the first place: "So that you may be the sons of your Father who is in heaven; for He makes his sun rise on the evil and on the good and sends rain on the just and on the unjust." It is

as if He were to say: "If you want to be called true children of the
Father in heaven, then let His example move you to live and act
the way He does. But what does He do? He makes His sun rise
every day, and He sends rain on the pious and on the wicked
alike." Thus by mentioning these two things, the sun and the rain,
He has summarized in a few words all the earthly blessings that
God grants to the world. If it were not for these two things, or
even one of them, the whole world would long since have become
a wasteland, desolate and destroyed. If the sun did not rise every
day, there could be no daily work; the animals, along with the
trees, the plants, and the grass would all perish from the frost.
Therefore the sun alone is the source of the incalculable blessing
that fills the world and provides nourishment for all who seek it,
whether human or animal, as well as of the heat and warmth by
which everything stays alive, grows, and propagates itself, instead
of perishing. In other words, the benefits that God bestows
through the sun every hour and every moment are innumerable.
Yet where is there someone who acknowledges this or is thankful
for it?

Nevertheless, though God gives, produces, and preserves everything through the sun, still we must have rain as well. If the sun
kept on shining all the time, finally everything would dry up and
wither away on account of the heat, and no food or grain could
grow for man or beast. Therefore He has tempered it with the
rain, to revive it all and to preserve its moisture and strength.
Now, in these two there are included the four items that belong to
life, the items that the philosophers call the "primary qualities"—
cold and warm, dry and moist.[29] There must not be one member
of these pairs without the other. If there were nothing but cold, or
nothing but heat, there would be no life. Now, the sun brings two
of these items, the heat and the dryness; and the rain also brings
two, that it is, cold and moist. Thus to the whole world, to His enemies as well as His friends, God gives body and life and everything
it needs and uses, generously and freely every day. Indeed, He
rains most copiously on a desert, a wild forest, or an ocean, where

[29]From the basic discussion by Aristotle, *Categories,* chapter 8, the medieval
philosophers had developed the concept of "quality" in several directions, including the one Luther mentions here.

it is utterly useless, while He sends only scant showers where pious people live. And He gives the best kingdoms and countries and people and money and goods to the worst scoundrels, while to the pious He hardly gives enough bread to eat.

Everywhere throughout the wide world, God is displaying these examples to us, as if He wanted to admonish us by them and to say to us: "Don't you know what sort of man I am, and what sort of good I am doing for you? Ask the sun and the moon and the rain about it, ask everything that is cold or wet or warm or dry. Then you will see that I show innumerable benefits not only to My Christians but even more to the wicked people, who are not grateful to Me but repay Me with their intense persecution of My Son and of the pious Christians." Thus you must be ashamed of yourself when you look at the sun, which preaches this to you every day, ashamed even when you are in a field and you look at a little flower or at the leaf of a tree. For this is written all over the leaves and the grass. There is no bird so small, indeed, no fruit or berry or grain so tiny, that it does not show this to you and say: "For whom do I bear my beautiful fruits and berries? For the vilest rogues and rascals on earth." How you must reproach yourself, then, for your lack of love toward God, your failure to do any favors for your neighbor, and your refusal to show at least some regard for others, when He is continually doing you so much good by means of all the creatures.

There is not a single man on earth who has to put up with one percent of what He has to suffer every day from evil men. Not only are His possessions and all His creatures misused for sinful and shameful ends; but also the very men who have these possessions in the greatest abundance—kings, lords, and princes—hate Him and His Word as much as they do the devil himself. If they could, they would gladly exterminate it in one fell swoop. They incessantly fume against it with nothing but abuse, curses, and slander, and besides they batter it with their fists. So there is no one on earth that is the object of more hatred and envy, of more vicious tricks, than are His Christians. Now, this is what He has to put up with daily from the whole world. Still, He is so faithful that daily He sends the sunshine and His other superabundant blessings upon people who do not deserve even to have a blade of grass or a moment of sunshine, but to be showered with incessant hellfire

and to be pelted with thunderbolts and hailstones, spears and bul-
lets. He really ought to be called a faithful Father for letting such
desperate scoundrels have all those possessions, lands, servants,
and good weather, for letting them act like the lords of all and the
squires of His domain! Why, even the sun and the moon, together
with all the creatures, have to serve them, letting themselves be
misused in opposition to God by the whims and the wickedness of
such people. Now, if we want to be sons of the Father, we ought to
let this sublime example move us to live likewise.

The other example is that of the relation between the criminals
and murderers themselves. They, too, know the art of sticking
together and of backing one another up. They will even put their
bodies, their possessions, and their very lives at one another's dis-
posal; and yet their only aim is to do harm to other people, to rob
and murder, and this only for the sake of temporal and uncertain
possessions. "Therefore," He means to say, "you surely ought to be
ashamed of yourselves. You call yourselves Christians and sons of
God, and you want to get to heaven. You have such a good and
faithful Father, who promises and gives you everything good. And
yet you are no more devout than robbers and murderers; you are
just like all the criminals on earth." For there have never been
people so bad that they did not practice love and friendship
toward one another. Otherwise how could their business continue? Even the devils in hell cannot live in opposition to one
another, or their kingdom would soon be destroyed, as Christ
Himself says [Matt. 12:25, 26].

Do you see now how pious you are if you are friendly and kind
only to your friends? You are just about as pious as the thieves and
the scoundrels, as the whores and the criminals, or as the devil
himself. Yet in your smugness you go around supposing that you
are all right, you preen yourself and brag just as though you were
an angel. Thus our schismatic spirits now brag about the great
love they have in their midst, which makes it obvious that the
Holy Spirit is with them. But what is it that they do? They love
their own schismatic rabble; but meanwhile they hate us poison-
ously and murderously, though we have never done them any
harm. From this it is obvious what sort of spirit they really have!
Yet they have a right to brag that there is as much love among
them as among scoundrels, criminals, and murderers, or as much

as among the devils. On this basis, no man on earth would be called wicked. There is no one so desperately bad that he does not need to have someone for a friend. How, otherwise, could he live in human society if all he did were to snarl and snap at everyone? Now, if you want to draw the conclusion "He loves his friends, therefore he is pious and holy," you would finally have to make the devil and all his followers pious as well. Therefore the conclusion He intends to draw here, in opposition to the Pharisaic saints, is that everything they teach about love and the like is all wrong. He instructs them to turn the page and to look at the scriptures correctly if they want to be the people of God, to see correctly and to show love toward their enemies. In this way they could prove that their love was genuine and that they were God's children, as He shows His love to the ungrateful and to His enemies.

Moses himself had clearly said this, for example, in Exod. 23:4: "If you meet your enemy's ox or his ass going astray, you shall bring it back to him"; and again [Exod. 23:5]: "If you see it lying under its burden . . . you shall help it up." Here they should have discovered that they had an obligation to love their enemies, too, if they had really looked at the text instead of gliding over it, the way our blind theologians skim over the surface of the scriptures. For since the command here is to pick up and help an ass or an ox that belongs to an enemy, it means that they should do so all the more when danger threatens the enemy himself in his person or property, wife or children. In other words, this is what it says: "You shall not desire harm for your neighbor but prevent it, and if possible, help him and promote his advantage. In this way you can finally move him, and by your kindness you can overcome and soften him. Thus all he can do is to love you in return, because he sees and experiences nothing evil in your treatment of him, but only pure love and sheer goodness."

With this teaching and these examples Christ now concludes this chapter: "You, therefore, must be perfect, as your heavenly Father is perfect." Here our sophists have spun out many dreams about perfection and have applied them all to their orders and classes—as if only priests and monks were in a state of perfection, the one higher than the other, the bishops higher than all the others, and the pope the highest of all. By this means the word "perfection" becomes completely inapplicable to the ordinary Christian way of life, as if such people could not be called perfect or be perfect. But you hear Christ talking here not to bishops, monks, and nuns but in general, to all Christians who are His pupils, who want to be called the sons of God, and who do not want to be like the publicans and criminals as are the Pharisees and our clergy.

How does it come about that they are perfect? The answer—in brief, because elsewhere I have discussed it in more detail[30]—is this: we cannot be or become perfect in the sense that we do not have any sin, the way they dream about perfection. Here and everywhere in scripture, to be perfect means, in the first place, that doctrine be completely correct and perfect, and then, that life move and be regulated according to it. Here, for example, the doctrine is that we should love not only those who do us good, but our enemies, too. Now, whoever teaches this and lives according to this teaching teaches and lives perfectly.

But the teaching and the life of the Jews were both imperfect and wrong, because they taught that they should love only their friends, and they lived accordingly. Such a love is chopped up and divided, it is only half a love. What He wants is an entire, whole, and undivided love, where one loves and helps his enemy as well as his friend. So I am called a truly perfect man, one who has and holds the doctrine in its entirety. Now, if my life does not measure up to this in every detail—as indeed it cannot, since flesh and blood incessantly hold it back—that does not detract from the perfection. Only we must keep striving for it, and moving and progressing toward it every day. This happens when the spirit is master over the flesh, holding it in check, subduing and restraining it, in order not to give it room to act contrary to this teaching. It happens when I let love move along on the true middle course, treating everyone alike and excluding no one. Then I have true Christian perfection, which is not restricted to special offices or stations but is common to all Christians, and should be. It forms and fashions itself according to the example of the heavenly Father. He does not split or chop up His love and kindness, but by means of the sun and the rain He lets all men on earth enjoy them alike, none excluded, be he pious or wicked.

[30]One of Luther's more detailed discussions of perfection was in his treatise of 1521, *On Monastic Vows.*

Preface to the Epistle of St. Paul to the Romans[31]

1546 (1522)

This epistle is really the chief part of the New Testament, and is truly the purest gospel. It is worthy not only that every Christian should know it word for word, by heart, but also that he should occupy himself with it every day, as the daily bread of the soul. We can never read it or ponder over it too much; for the more we deal with it, the more precious it becomes and the better it tastes.

Therefore I too will do my best, so far as God has given me power, to open the way into it through this preface, so that it may be the better understood by everyone. Heretofore it has been badly obscured by glosses and all kinds of idle talk, though in itself it is a bright light, almost sufficient to illuminate the entire holy scriptures.

To begin with, we must have knowledge of its language and know what St. Paul means by the words "law," "sin," "grace," "faith," "righteousness," "flesh," "spirit," and the like. Otherwise no reading of the book has any value.

The little word "law" you must here not take in human fashion as a teaching about what works are to be done or not done. That is the way with human laws; a law is fulfilled by works, even though there is no heart in the doing of them. But God judges according to what is in the depths of the heart. For this reason, His law too makes its demands on the inmost heart; it cannot be satisfied with works, but rather punishes as hypocrisy and lies the works not done from the bottom of the heart. Hence all men are called liars in Psalm 116 [:11][32] because no one keeps or can keep God's law from the bottom of the heart. For everyone finds in himself displeasure in what is good and pleasure in what is bad. If, now, there is no willing pleasure in the good, then the inmost heart is not set on the law of God. Then, too, there is surely sin, and God's

---

[31]This was the preface which was being read in John Wesley's hearing when, by his own account, he felt his heart "strongly warmed" at the time of his conversion, May 24, 1738. This translation is based on the 1546 version appearing in the complete Bible of that year.

[32]Vulgate version, Ps. 115:11; cf. KJV.

wrath is deserved, even though outwardly there seem to be many good deeds and an honorable life.

Hence St. Paul concludes, in chapter 2 [:13], that the Jews are all sinners, saying that only the doers of the law are righteous before God. He means by this that no one, in terms of his works, is a doer of the law. Rather, he speaks to them thus, "You teach one must not commit adultery, but you yourself commit adultery" [2:22]; and again, "In passing judgment upon another you condemn yourself, because you, the judge, are doing the very same things" [2:1]. This is as if to say, "You live a fine outward life in the works of the law, and you pass judgment on those who do not so live. You know how to teach everyone; you see the speck that is in the eye of another, but do not notice the log that is in your own eye" [Matt. 7:3].

For even though you keep the law outwardly, with works, from fear of punishment or love of reward, nevertheless you do all this unwillingly, without pleasure in and love for the law, but with reluctance and under compulsion. For if the law were not there, you would prefer to act otherwise. The conclusion is that from the bottom of your heart you hate the law. What point is there, then, in your teaching others not to steal, if you yourself are a thief at heart, and would gladly be one outwardly if you dared? Though, to be sure, the outward work does not lag far behind among such hypocrites! So you teach others, but not yourself; nor do you yourself know what you are teaching—you have never yet understood the law correctly. Moreover the law increases sin, as St. Paul says in chapter 5 [:20], because the more the law demands of men what they cannot do, the more they hate the law.

For this reason he says, in chapter 7 [:14], "The law is spiritual." What does that mean? If the law were for the body, it could be satisfied with works; but since it is spiritual, no one can satisfy it—unless all that you do is done from the bottom of your heart. But such a heart is given only by God's Spirit, who fashions a man after the law, so that he acquires a desire for the law in his heart, doing nothing henceforth out of fear and compulsion but out of a willing heart. The law is thus spiritual in that it will be loved and fulfilled with such a spiritual heart, and requires such a spirit. Where that spirit is not in the heart, there sin remains; also displeasure with the law and hostility toward it, even though the law itself is good and just and holy.

Accustom yourself, then, to this language, that doing the works of the law and fulfilling the law are two very different things. The work of the law is everything that one does, or can do, toward keeping the law of his own free will or by his own powers. But since in the midst of all these works and along with them there remains in the heart a dislike of the law and compulsion with respect to it, these works are all wasted and have no value. That is what St. Paul means in chapter 3 [:20], when he says, "By works of the law will no man be justified in God's sight." Hence you see that the wranglers and sophists practice deception when they teach men to prepare themselves for grace by means of works.[33] How can a man prepare himself for good by means of works, if he does good works only with aversion and unwillingness in his heart? How shall a work please God if it proceeds from a reluctant and resisting heart?

[33]Two elements dominate the scholastic conception of grace: infusion and merit. By grace, Thomas (1225–74) meant not God's love, favor, or forgiveness but "a certain supernatural thing in man, coming into existence from God"—an infused condition, a supernatural ethical nature which makes man capable of good. Man's free will is thereby moved to prepare itself for, or dispose itself toward, further grace. Thomas always referred grace, and with it everything good in man, back to the agency of God as prime mover. Despite his emphasis on divine causality, however, his conception of grace as an infused substantial gift required—in order that the personal element not be lost entirely—that the personal agency of man and his free will be constantly brought to the fore. Thus Bonaventure taught that the purpose of God's infusing of grace is to make the sinner capable of merit; this merit can be attained, however, only through the free will.

The scholastics distinguished between two kinds of merit: the merit of worthiness (*meritum de condigno*—conduct insofar as it is purely a product of grace, and is deserving of eternal life) and the merit of fitness (*meritum de congruo*—conduct insofar as it results from the exercise of the free will, and merits from God a reward commensurate with its particular excellence). In the process of salvation God bestows initially a "grace gratuitously given." The resultant movements of the human will merit (congruously, by fitness), through cooperation, God's next gift of the "grace which makes acceptable." Again, the resultant movements of the human will merit (condignly, by worthiness), through cooperation, the gift of eternal life.

Without grace, of course, no merit is possible. To the attainment of justification, however, man can nevertheless dispose or prepare himself by fitness. Thus Gabriel Biel (c. 1425–92) says, "Good works morally performed without love merit by fitness . . . the grace of justification." So the idea of merit was made tolerable by the pious interpretation given to it in the appeal to prior grace; while into the conception of infused grace there was introduced through the scheme of merits that element which it otherwise lacked, namely, an element of personal relationship to God.

To fulfill the law, however, is to do its works with pleasure and love, to live a godly and good life of one's own accord, without the compulsion of the law. This pleasure and love for the law is put into the heart by the Holy Spirit, as St. Paul says in chapter 5 [:5]. But the Holy Spirit is not given except in, with, and by faith in Jesus Christ, as St. Paul says in the introduction. Faith, moreover, comes only through God's Word, or gospel, which preaches Christ, saying that He is God's Son and a man, and has died and risen again for our sakes, as He says in chapters 3 [:25], 4 [:25], and 10 [:9].

So it happens that faith alone makes a person righteous and fulfills the law. For out of the merit of Christ it brings forth the Spirit. And the Spirit makes the heart glad and free, as the law requires that it shall be. Thus good works emerge from faith itself. That is what St. Paul means in chapter 9 [:31]; after he has rejected the works of the law, it sounds as if he would overthrow the law by this faith. "No," he says, "we uphold the law by faith"; that is, we fulfill it by faith.

Sin, in the scripture, means not only the outward works of the body but also all the activities that move men to do these works, namely, the inmost heart, with all its powers. Thus the little word "do"[34] ought to mean that a man falls all the way and lives in sin. Even outward works of sin do not take place, unless a man plunges into it completely with body and soul. And the scriptures look especially into the heart and single out the root and source of all sin, which is unbelief in the inmost heart. As, therefore, faith alone makes a person righteous, and brings the Spirit and pleasure in good outward works, so unbelief alone commits sin, and brings forth the flesh and pleasure in bad outward works, as happened to Adam and Eve in paradise, Gen. 3.

Hence Christ calls unbelief the only sin, when He says in John 16 [:8–9], "The Spirit will convince the world of sin . . . because they do not believe in Me." For this reason too, before good or bad works take place, as the good or bad fruits, there must first be in the heart faith or unbelief. Unbelief is the root, the sap, and the chief power of all sin. For this reason, in the scriptures it is called the serpent's head and the head of the old dragon, which the seed

---

[34]*Thun,* i.e., "commit sin."

of the woman, Christ, must tread underfoot, as was promised to Adam, Gen. 3 [:15].

Between grace and gift there is this difference. Grace actually means God's favor, or the goodwill which in Himself He bears toward us, by which He is disposed to give us Christ and to pour into us the Holy Spirit with His gifts. This is clear from chapter 5 [:15], where St. Paul speaks of "the grace and gift in Christ," etc. The gifts and the Spirit increase in us every day, but they are not yet perfect since there remain in us the evil desires and sins that war against the Spirit, as He says in Rom. 7 [:5 ff.] and Gal. 5 [:17], and the conflict between the seed of the woman and the seed of the serpent, as foretold in Gen. 3 [:15]. Nevertheless grace does so much that we are accounted completely righteous before God. For His grace is not divided or parceled out, as are the gifts, but takes us completely into favor for the sake of Christ, our Intercessor and Mediator. And because of this, the gifts are begun in us.

In this sense, then, you can understand chapter 7. There St. Paul still calls himself a sinner; and yet he can say, in chapter 8 [:1], that there is no condemnation for those who are in Christ, simply because of the incompleteness of the gifts and of the Spirit. Because the flesh is not yet slain, we are still sinners. But because we believe in Christ and have a beginning of the Spirit, God is so favorable and gracious to us that He will not count the sin against us or judge us because of it. Rather He deals with us according to our faith in Christ, until sin is slain.

Faith is not the human notion and dream that some people call faith. When they see that no improvement of life and no good works follow—although they can hear and say much about faith—they fall into the error of saying, "Faith is not enough; one must do works in order to be righteous and be saved." This is due to the fact that when they hear the gospel, they get busy and by their own powers create an idea in their heart which says, "I believe"; they take this then to be a true faith. But it is a human figment and idea that never reaches the depths of the heart, nothing comes of it either, and no improvement follows.

Faith, however, is a divine work in us which changes us and makes us to be born anew of God, John 1 [:12–13]. It kills the old Adam and makes us altogether different men, in heart and spirit and mind and powers; and it brings with it the Holy Spirit. O it is a living, busy, active, mighty thing, this faith. It is impossible for it not to be doing good works incessantly. It does not ask whether good works are to be done, but before the question is asked, it has already done them, and is constantly doing them. Whoever does not do such works, however, is an unbeliever. He gropes and looks around for faith and good works, but knows neither what faith is nor what good works are. Yet he talks and talks, with many words, about faith and good works.

Faith is a living, daring confidence in God's grace, so sure and certain that the believer would stake his life on it a thousand times. This knowledge of and confidence in God's grace makes men glad and bold and happy in dealing with God and with all creatures. And this is the work which the Holy Spirit performs in faith. Because of it, without compulsion, a person is ready and glad to do good to everyone, to serve everyone, to suffer everything, out of love and praise to God, who has shown him this grace. Thus it is impossible to separate works from faith, quite as impossible as to separate heat and light from fire. Beware, therefore, of your own false notions and of the idle talkers who imagine themselves wise enough to make decisions about faith and good works, and yet are the greatest fools. Pray God that He may work faith in you. Otherwise you will surely remain forever without faith, regardless of what you may think or do.

Righteousness, then, is such a faith. It is called "the righteousness of God" because God gives it, and counts it as righteousness for the sake of Christ, our Mediator, and makes a man to fulfill his obligation to everybody. For through faith a man becomes free from sin and comes to take pleasure in God's commandments; thereby he gives God the honor due Him and pays Him what he owes Him. Likewise he serves his fellow men willingly, by whatever means he can, and thus pays his debt to everyone. Nature, free will, and our own powers cannot bring this righteousness into being. For as no one can give himself faith, neither can he take away his own unbelief. How, then, will he take away a single sin, even the very smallest? Therefore all that is done apart from faith, or in unbelief, is false; it is hypocrisy and sin, Rom. 14 [:23], no matter how good a showing it makes.

Flesh and spirit you must not understand as though flesh is only that which has to do with unchastity and spirit is only that which has to do with what is inwardly in the heart. Rather, like Christ in John 3 [:6], Paul calls everything "flesh" that is born of the flesh—the whole man, with body and soul, mind and senses—because everything about him longs for the flesh. Thus you should learn to call him "fleshly" too who thinks, teaches, and talks a great deal about lofty spiritual matters, yet does so without grace. From the "works of the flesh" in Gal. 5 [:19–21], you can learn that Paul calls heresy and hatred "works of the flesh." And in Rom. 8 [:3] he says that "the law is weakened by the flesh"; yet this is said not of unchastity, but of all sins, and above all of unbelief, which is the most spiritual of all vices.

On the contrary, you should call him "spiritual" who is occupied with the most external kind of works, as Christ was when He washed the disciples' feet [John 13:1–14], and Peter when he steered his boat and fished. Thus "the flesh" is a man who lives and works, inwardly and outwardly, in the service of the flesh's gain and of this temporal life. "The spirit" is the man who lives and works, inwardly and outwardly, in the service of the Spirit and of the future life.

Without such a grasp of these words, you will never understand this letter of St. Paul, nor any other book of holy scripture. Therefore beware of all teachers who use these words in a different sense, no matter who they are, even Origen, Ambrose, Augustine, Jerome, and others like them or even above them. And now we will take up the epistle.

It is right for a preacher of the gospel in the first place by revelation of the law and of sin to rebuke and to constitute as sin everything that is not the living fruit of the Spirit and of faith in Christ, in order that men should be led to know themselves and their own wretchedness, and to become humble and ask for help. This is therefore what St. Paul does. He begins in chapter 1 to rebuke the gross sins and unbelief that are plainly evident. These were, and still are, the sins of the heathen who live without God's grace. He says: Through the gospel there shall be revealed the wrath of God from heaven against all men because of their godless lives and their unrighteousness. For even though they know and daily recognize that there is a God, nevertheless nature itself, without grace, is so bad that it neither thanks nor honors God. Instead it blinds itself and goes steadily from bad to worse until, after idolatry, it blatantly commits the most shameful sins, along with all the vices, and also allows others to commit them unreprimanded.

In chapter 2 he extends his rebuke to include those who seem outwardly to be righteous and who commit their sins in secret. Such were the Jews and such are all the hypocrites who without desire or love for the law of God lead decent lives, but at heart hate God's law, and yet are quick to judge other people. This is the nature of all hypocrites, to think of themselves as pure and yet to be full of covetousness, hatred, pride, and all uncleanness, Matt. 23 [:25–28]. These are they who despise God's goodness, and in their hard-heartedness heap wrath upon themselves. Thus St. Paul, as a true interpreter of the law, leaves no one without sin, but proclaims the wrath of God upon all who would live well simply by nature or of their own volition. He makes them to be no better than the obvious sinners; indeed, he says they are stubborn and unrepentant.

In chapter 3 he throws them all together in a heap, and says that one is like the other: they are all sinners before God. Only, the Jews have had the word of God. Though not many have believed that word, this does not mean that the faith and truth of God are exhausted. He quotes incidentally a verse from Psalm 51 [:4], that God remains justified in His words. Afterward he comes back to this again and proves also by scripture that all men are sinners, and that by the works of the law nobody is justified, but that the law was given only that sin might be known.

Then he begins to teach the right way by which men must be justified and saved. He says: They are all sinners making no boast of God; but they must be justified without merit [of their own] through faith in Christ, who has merited this for us by His blood, and has become for us a mercy seat by God. God forgives all former sins to demonstrate that we are helped only by His righteousness, which He grants in faith, and which was revealed at that time through the gospel and was witnessed to beforehand by the law and the prophets. Thus the law is upheld by faith, though the works of the law are thereby put down, together with the boasting of them.

After the first three chapters, in which sin is revealed and faith's way to righteousness is taught, St. Paul begins in chapter 4 to meet certain remonstrances and objections. First he takes up the one that all men commonly make when they hear that faith justifies without works. They say, "Are we, then, to do no good works?" Therefore he himself takes up the case of Abraham, and asks, "What did Abraham accomplish, then, with his good works? Were they all in vain? Were his works of no use?" He concludes that Abraham was justified by faith alone, without any works, so much so that the scriptures in Gen. 15 [:6] declare that he was justified by faith alone even before the work of circumcision. But if the work of circumcision contributed nothing to his righteousness, though God had commanded it and it was a good work of obedience, then surely no other good work will contribute anything to righteousness. Rather, as Abraham's circumcision was an external sign by which he showed the righteousness that was already his in faith, so all good works are only external signs which follow out of faith; like good fruit, they demonstrate that a person is already inwardly righteous before God.

With this powerful illustration from the scriptures, St. Paul confirms the doctrine of faith he had set forth in chapter 3. He cites also another witness, David, who says in Psalm 32 [:1–2] that a man is justified without works—although he does not remain without works when he has been justified. Then he gives the illustration a broader application, setting it over against all other works of the law. He concludes that the Jews cannot be Abraham's heirs merely because of their blood, still less because of the works of the law; they must inherit Abraham's faith if they would be true heirs. For before the law—before the law of Moses and the law of circumcision—Abraham was justified by faith and called the father of all believers. Moreover the law brings about wrath rather than grace, because no one keeps the law out of love for it and pleasure in it. What comes by the works of the law is thus disfavor rather than grace. Therefore faith alone must obtain the grace promised to Abraham, for these examples too were written for our sakes [Rom. 15:4], that we too should believe.

In chapter 5 he comes to the fruits and works of faith, such as peace, joy, love to God and to every man, as well as confidence, assurance, boldness, courage, and hope amid tribulation and suffering. For all this follows, if faith be true, because of the superabundant goodness that God shows us in Christ, causing Christ to die for us before we could ask it of Him, indeed, while we were still enemies. Thus we have it that faith justifies without any works; and yet it does not follow that men are therefore to do no good works, but rather that the genuine works will not be lacking. Of these the work-righteous saints know nothing. They dream up works of their own in which there is no peace, joy, confidence, love, hope, boldness, or any of the qualities of true Christian work and faith.

After this he digresses and makes a pleasant excursion, telling whence come sin and righteousness, death and life, and comparing Adam and Christ. He means to say that Christ had to come as a second Adam bequeathing His righteousness to us through a new spiritual birth in faith, just as the first Adam bequeathed sin to us through the old fleshly birth. Thus he declares and proves that no one by his own works can raise himself out of sin into righteousness, any more than he can prevent the birth of his own body. This is proved also by the fact that the divine law—which ought to assist toward righteousness, if anything can—has not only not helped but has even increased sin. For the more the law forbids, the more our evil nature hates the law, and the more it wants to give reign to its own lust. Thus the law makes Christ all the more necessary, and more grace is needed to help our nature.

In chapter 6 he takes up the special work of faith, the conflict of the spirit with the flesh for the complete slaying of the sin and lust that remain after we are justified. He teaches us that we are not by faith so freed from sin that we can be idle, slack, and careless, as though there were no longer any sin in us. Sin is present; but it is no longer reckoned for our condemnation, because of the faith that is struggling against it. Therefore we have enough to do all our life long in taming the body, slaying its lusts, and compelling its members to obey the spirit and not the lusts. Thus we become like the death and Resurrection of Christ, and complete our baptism—which signifies the death of sin and the new life of grace—until we are entirely purified of sin, and even our bodies rise again with Christ and live forever.

All this we can do, he says, because we are under grace and not under law. He himself explains what this means. To be without the law is not the same thing as to have no laws and to be able to do what one pleases. Rather we are under the law when, without grace, we occupy ourselves with the works of the law. Then sin certainly rules [us] through the law, for no one loves the law by nature; and that is great sin. Grace, however, makes the law dear to us; then sin is no longer present, and the law is no longer against us but one with us.

This is the true freedom from sin and from the law. He writes about this down to the end of the chapter, saying that it is a freedom only to do good with pleasure and to live well without the compulsion of the law. Therefore this freedom is a spiritual freedom, which does not overthrow the law but presents what the law demands, namely, pleasure [in the law] and love [for it] whereby the law is quieted and no longer drives men or makes demands of them. It is just as if you owed a debt to your overlord and could not pay it. There are two ways in which you could rid yourself of the debt: either he would take nothing from you and would tear up the account, or some good man would pay it for you and give you the means to satisfy the account. It is in this latter way that Christ has made us free from the law. Our freedom is, therefore, no carefree fleshly freedom which is not obligated to do anything, but a freedom that does many works of all kinds, and is free of the demands and obligations of the law.

In chapter 7 he supports this with an analogy from married life. When a man dies, his wife is also alone, and thus the one is released entirely from the other. Not that the wife cannot or ought not take another husband, but rather that she is now for the first time really free to take another—something she could not do previously, before she was free from her husband. So our conscience is bound to the law, under the old man of sin; when he is slain by the Spirit, then the conscience is free, and the one is released from the other. Not that the conscience is to do nothing, but rather that it is now for the first time really free to hold fast to Christ, the second husband, and bring forth the fruit of life.

Then he depicts more fully the nature of sin and of the law, how by means of the law sin now stirs and becomes mighty. The old man comes to hate the law all the more because he cannot pay what the law demands. Sin is his nature and of himself he can do nothing but sin; therefore the law to him is death and torment.

Not that the law is bad, but the old man's evil nature cannot endure the good, and the law demands good of him; just as a sick man cannot stand it when he is required to run and jump and do the works of a well man.

Therefore St. Paul here concludes that the law, correctly understood and thoroughly grasped, does nothing more than to remind us of our sin, and to slay us by it, making us liable to eternal wrath. All this is fully learned and experienced by our conscience, when it is really struck by the law. Therefore a person must have something other than the law, something more than the law, to make him righteous and save him. But they who do not correctly understand the law are blind. They go ahead in their presumption, thinking to satisfy the law by means of their deeds, not knowing how much the law demands, namely, a willing and happy heart. Therefore they do not see Moses clearly; the veil is put between them and him, and covers him [Exod. 34:29–35; 2 Cor. 3:12–16].

Then he shows how spirit and flesh struggle with each other in a man. He uses himself as an example, in order that we may learn how properly to understand the work of slaying sin within us. He calls both the spirit and the flesh "laws"; for just as it is in the nature of the divine law to drive men and make demands of them, so the flesh drives men and makes demands. It rages against the spirit, and will have its own way. The spirit, in turn, drives men and makes demands contrary to the flesh, and will have its own way. This tension lasts in us as long as we live; though in one person it is greater, in another less, according as the spirit or the flesh is stronger. Nevertheless the whole man is himself both spirit and flesh, and he fights with himself until he becomes wholly spiritual.

In chapter 8 he comforts these fighters, telling them that this flesh does not condemn them. He shows further what the nature of flesh and spirit is, and how the Spirit comes from Christ. Christ has given us His Holy Spirit; He makes us spiritual and subdues the flesh, and assures us that we are still God's children, however hard sin may be raging within us, so long as we follow the spirit and resist sin to slay it. Since, however, nothing else is so good for the mortifying of the flesh as the cross and suffering, He comforts us in suffering with the support of the Spirit of love, and of the whole creation, namely, that the Spirit sighs within us and the creation longs with us that we may be rid of the flesh and of sin. So we see that these three chapters (6–8) drive home the one task of faith, which is to slay the old Adam and subdue the flesh.

In chapters 9, 10, and 11 he teaches of God's eternal predestination—out of which originally proceeds who shall believe or not, who can or cannot get rid of sin—in order that our salvation may be taken entirely out of our hands and put in the hand of God alone. And this too is utterly necessary. For we are so weak and uncertain that if it depended on us, not even a single person would be saved; the devil would surely overpower us all. But since God is dependable—His predestination cannot fail, and no one can withstand Him—we still have hope in the face of sin.

Here, now, for once we must put a stop to those wicked and high-flying spirits who first apply their own reason to this matter. They begin at the top to search the abyss of divine predestination, and worry in vain about whether they are predestinated. They are bound to plunge to their own destruction, either through despair or through throwing caution to the winds.

But you had better follow the order of this epistle. Worry first about Christ and the gospel, that you may recognize your sin and His grace. Then fight your sin, as the first eight chapters here have taught. Then, when you have reached the eighth chapter, and are under the cross and suffering, this will teach you correctly of predestination in chapters 9, 10, and 11, and how comforting it is. For in the absence of suffering and the cross and the perils of death, one cannot deal with predestination without harm and without secret anger against God. The old Adam must first die before he can tolerate this thing and drink the strong wine. Therefore beware that you do not drink wine while you are still a suckling. There is a limit, a time, and an age for every doctrine.

In chapter 12 he teaches what true worship is, and makes all Christians priests. They are to offer not money or cattle, as under the law, but their own bodies, with slaying of the lusts. Then he describes the outward conduct of Christians, under the spiritual government, telling how they are to teach, preach, rule, serve, give, suffer, love, live, and act toward friend, foe, and all men. These are the works that a Christian does; for, as has been said, faith takes no holidays.

In chapter 13 he teaches honor and obedience to worldly government. Although worldly government does not make people righteous before God, nevertheless it is instituted in order to accomplish at least this much, that the good may have outward peace and protection and the bad may not be free to do evil in peace and quietness and without fear. Therefore the good too are to honor it even though they themselves do not need it. Finally, he comprehends it all in love and sums it up in the example of Christ: as He has done for us, we are also to do, following in His footsteps.

In chapter 14 he teaches that consciences weak in faith are to be led gently, spared, so that we do not use our Christian freedom for doing harm but for the assistance of the weak. For where that is not done, the result is discord and contempt for the gospel; and the gospel is the all-important thing. Thus it is better to yield a little to the weak in faith, until they grow stronger, than to have the teaching of the gospel come to nothing. And this work is a peculiar work of love, for which there is great need even now, when with the eating of meat and other liberties, men are rudely and roughly—and needlessly—shaking weak consciences, before they know the truth.

In chapter 15 he sets up Christ as an example: we are to tolerate also those other weak ones who fail in other ways, in open sins or in unpleasing habits. We are not to cast them off, but to bear with them until they too grow better. For so Christ has done with us, and still does every day; He bears with our many faults and bad habits, and with all our imperfections, and helps us constantly.

Then, at the end, he prays for them, praises them, and commends them to God. He speaks of his own office and of his preaching, and asks them kindly for a contribution to the poor at Jerusalem. All that he speaks of or deals with is pure love.

The last chapter is a chapter of greetings. But he mingles with them a noble warning against the doctrines of men, which break in alongside the teaching of the gospel and cause offense. It is as if he had certainly foreseen that out of Rome and through the Romans would come the seductive and offensive canons and decretals and the whole squirming mass of human laws and commandments which have now drowned the whole world and wiped out this epistle and all the holy scriptures, along with the Spirit and faith itself; so that nothing remains anymore except the idol Belly, whose servants St. Paul here rebukes. God save us from them. Amen.

In this epistle we thus find most abundantly the things that a Christian ought to know, namely, what is law, gospel, sin, punishment, grace, faith, righteousness, Christ, God, good works, love, hope, and the cross; and also how we are to conduct ourselves toward everyone, be he righteous or sinner, strong or weak, friend or foe—and even toward our own selves. Moreover, this is all ably supported with scripture and proved by St. Paul's own example and that of the prophets, so that one could not wish for anything more. Therefore it appears that he wanted in this one epistle to sum up briefly the whole Christian and Evangelical doctrine, and to prepare an introduction to the entire Old Testament. For without doubt, whoever has this epistle well in his heart has with him the light and power of the Old Testament. Therefore let every Christian be familiar with it and exercise himself in it continually. To this end may God give His grace. Amen.

III

Sermons Through the Church Year

The last words delivered in public by Martin Luther were spoken from a pulpit. His belief in the sovereign power of God's Word properly preached to men never wavered. He once gave this impromptu advice on how to preach, in three brief steps: "First, you must learn to go up to the pulpit. Second, you must know that you should stay there for a time. Third, you must learn to get down again" (Table Talk, No. 5171b). Here are condensed all the needful elements: a constant aspiration to preach well, an understanding of what is right to say and how it must be said, and a belief that it is God's eloquent message, not prideful man's, that should be addressed to those present.

In Luther's day, as in the centuries before him, the pulpit was the indispensable means of communicating practically every sort of information, spiritual or not. Although printing, still in its infancy, had begun to amplify—at least to the educated elite, who could read—the sermons of preachers throughout Christendom, it was the living voice that commanded the interest and attention of all. The Reformation is simply inconceivable without the pulpit. Some three thousand of Luther's sermons survive, a fraction of the total delivered—sometimes at the rate of three or four a day—either in the form of outlines in his own hand or in versions transcribed by secretaries, colleagues, or admiring auditors. Since Luther's liturgical reforms nonetheless retained the traditional sequence of readings from the Bible long established by the Church for Sundays and holy days throughout the year, most of his sermons are based on these short readings, or pericopes, as they are technically known.

Like the biblical exegete and theologian he was, Luther, in the brief compass of the sermon form (he was by no means prolix in his delivery, a common failing of his day—and ours), managed always to give a clear and compelling interpretation of his text, to relate it to his own life and the lives of his congregation, and to make it absolutely clear that God's Word, not his, was what must dwell in our hearts. Many of the examples that follow are termed House Postils, or informal homilies, typically delivered in the former Augustinian monastery in Wittenberg, that became home to Luther's family, friends, and numerous visitors. Their conversational tone belies their strength and durability, which continue to reach and teach us across the centuries.

Christ fills me with more joy than any amount of suffering you [the devil] can impose on me. That kind of heart the angels wish for us sincerely with their song.

Concerning the message of the holy angels and their song.

1. Yesterday we heard the history and account of this festival, how the Son of God became a human being and was born into this world by the Virgin Mary. This scriptural account is proclaimed in sermons every year throughout Christendom, so that we might take it to heart and learn how to thank God with our whole hearts for this great and glorious blessing and grace which He has shown us through this birth of His Son.

2. Having again heard the gospel story, let us also listen to how the dear angels preach and sing about this birth. For as soon as Mary had given birth to her Son in the stall at Bethlehem, a heavenly sermon began to be proclaimed in the skies by the Lord's angel, who had appeared to the shepherds in the field, in a blinding light, proclaiming that Christ the Lord had been born in the city of David, and that He was wrapped in swaddling cloth and was lying in a manger. It is also an unheard of novelty, that our dear Lord God proclaims the birth of His Son to lowly shepherds. God leaves the mighty and influential "lords" sitting at Jerusalem and reveals the wonderful news from heaven to the "poor beggars," namely the shepherds in the field. The same angel bestows upon the shepherds the honor which their Lord Christ Himself has bestowed upon all human beings. Following the example of his Lord Christ, the angel humbles himself, and does not scorn proclaiming this news to the shepherds and the lowly beggars. Glorious though he is, the angel does not vaunt his glory; no, he humbles himself and delivers this marvelous message which shall continue to be proclaimed among Christians until the end of the world.

[35]Preached on St. Stephen's Day, December 26, at home, 1534.

3. What wonderful spirits those angels must be, angels in whom there isn't even a trace of pride! For just as the one angel humbles himself and preaches to the shepherds, so also the entire army of the heavenly hosts—as we shall briefly point out—unite in singing about the birth of Christ, allowing just the shepherds to listen to their song. But what is the Roman emperor, with all of his splendor, in comparison with just a single angel? That is why all the mighty lords, all the scholars, and all the saints do not by any stretch of the imagination even come close to being as great, or learned, or holy as the sweet angels are. No, all these human beings should observe diligently this example and learn from it not to overestimate their own knowledge, wisdom, saintliness, and other gifts; nor should they ever despise other people. For if these gifts had resulted in pride, then the blessed angels would have been justified in despising and looking down on the poor shepherds. But they do not do that. The shepherds may be ever so poor and wretched, yet the angels do not consider themselves so high and holy that they lose their joy and gladness while they proclaim this good news to the shepherds.

4. Here everything is done in harmony with the nature of Christ's kingdom, which is a totally different kingdom from the kingdom of this world. You see, in Christ's kingdom everyone is humble and busy in serving others, as Christ says in Matt. 20:25–28: "But Jesus called them unto Him, and said, 'Ye know that the princes of the gentiles exercise dominion over them, and they that are great exercise authority upon them. But it shall not be so among you: but whosoever will be great among you, let him be your minister; and whosoever will be chief among you, let him be your servant: even as the Son of Man came not to be ministered unto, but to minister, and to give His life a ransom for many.'"

5. That is what God also expects us to do. He wants us to use our own blessings in behalf of others, comforting them and meeting their needs, not despising anyone. The angels are a fine example for us, demonstrating that just as our Lord Jesus is a faithful Savior and serves all of us human beings, even so God's angels are faithful servants who gladly and willingly serve us. At the same time, the shepherds of that day must have been pious, God-fearing people who were looking forward to the coming of this Savior

with all their hearts. That is why they all came running, so that they could hear the proclamation of the Lord's angel. The people of our own day, especially the unruly mobs, deserve only to hear what the devil says. But the message which the angel proclaims to the shepherds is this: "Fear not: for, behold, I bring you good tidings of great joy, which shall be to all people. For unto you is born this day in the city of David a Savior, which is Christ the Lord. And this shall be a sign unto you; Ye shall find the babe wrapped in swaddling clothes, lying in a manger."

6. Anyone can understand this announcement if he just wants to do so, and then he could pass on this good news, repeating what the Lord's angel proclaimed, "Christ the Savior has been born in the city of David." He could retell the angel's message: On the night when Christ was born at Bethlehem, there was a blinding light; the Lord's angel proclaimed a marvelous message, followed by a lovely hymn of praise sung by the heavenly hosts. The message was "Fear not!" Anyone can understand that and remember it, provided only that he wants to glorify God in this way and assure himself of eternal blessedness.

7. In this proclamation, the angel summarizes the whole gospel, saying: This Savior, born in the stall, right next to the manger, will bring great joy to all people; He will free us from sin, death, and the devil, and is Christ the Lord Himself. All this took place in Bethlehem. These are not the words of men, nor can such a proclamation even be conceived by the mind of any human being; for not even the most learned people on earth know anything about this, for these are angelic words shouted down from heaven into this world; it is a message which praise be to God forever, has also been made known to us. It makes no difference whether you are reading or hearing this message today or whether you had heard the message directly from the angel himself. You see, not even the shepherds saw the angels (for they are invisible); they saw only the light and glory. But they did hear the words, and you are also hearing them today. For in these words which I read from the Bible in my sermon, you have a summary of the heavenly, angelic proclamation, provided only that we open our eyes and ears and are willing to hear and comprehend the message.

8. Now then, if you hope to be saved some other way, you ought seriously keep in mind this fact: here we have the first proclamation about the birth of Jesus Christ, shouted down from heaven, a proclamation that still holds true and will continue to be true until judgment day; this infant, born in Bethlehem by the Virgin, is the Savior, Christ the Lord, who will free us from sin and death and be our comfort to all eternity.

9. After the angel's proclamation, the whole army of the heavenly hosts sings a hymn of praise. A good message or sermon should be followed by a joyful hymn. That's why the dear angels rejoice over the birth of this Savior of all the world, and follow up the glorious proclamation with a joyful hymn in these words: "Glory to God in the highest, and on earth peace, goodwill toward men."

10. They divide their song into three assertions or points that form a triad, so that they cite three things: God, earth, mankind; and to each of these they attach an appropriate prayer request. To God be the glory; to the earth, peace; to all mankind, great joy. The word *Wohlgefallen* is bad German. The Greek text says *eudokia,* i.e., "joy and delight."

Their first assertion is: GLORY TO GOD IN THE HIGHEST.

11. What the blessed angels wish for God is glory, that is, they sing and wish that we people will recognize in this newly born infant the true God, and they thank God for the great, endless blessing that out of pure grace and mercy God has sent His Son, and permitted Him to become a true human being, in order that He might be able to redeem the entire human race. In effect they were saying: God has sent His Son, for which we should thank and praise Him to all eternity. For this grace and blessing we, the angels, want to praise and glorify God, and all peoples should follow our example by praising and glorifying Him.

The second assertion is: PEACE ON EARTH.

12. They also wish that there will be peace on earth, and that the kingdom of Christ, which is a kingdom of peace, will flourish on the earth. The kingdom of the world is characterized by stealing, robbery, murder, clubbing people to death, war, and bloodshed. In short, on the earth there is nothing but lack of peace, or turmoil. Each person harms the next person, no one practices

faithfulness toward his neighbor, each one beats the next person over the head. That is the essence of life on the earth! That is why the blessed angels wish for us Christians a peaceful life, so that we will be friendly toward one another, each one demonstrating to the other person love, faithfulness, and reciprocal service, bearing one another's burdens so that no one will be at odds with anyone else, and that everyone helps and shares good counsel to his neighbor. It is the wish and the prayer of the angels that God will provide these things on earth, so that our life on earth will be friendly and peaceful. That is the second assertion or petition of the angels.

And that is followed by their third request: GOODWILL TOWARD MEN.

13. In effect they are saying: It is our sincere desire that all men glorify God in the highest and that they live at peace with one another. Unfortunately it is impossible for these conditions to exist at all times because many people pay no attention whatsoever to the gospel. They refuse to accept this Son of God. Instead of that, they persecute both the gospel and the Son. May God, therefore, grant to the Christians a cheerful, joy-filled heart so that they will say: I have a Savior, who is Christ the Lord! If people mistreat me and persecute me because of this Savior, I'll rejoice over that too. I will maintain good cheer and joy in the midst of suffering. That is the kind of heart the blessed angels desire for us Christians, so that we may have joy in the face of hatred and go on singing when the devil goes on a rampage. The angels want us to be proud in Christ and in Him to defy all misfortune; and if the devil attacks us, that we mock and ridicule him by saying, Satan, you can only attack my body, my life, my property, and so on. You might as well give up on that, too, Satan, for you cannot harm me, since I have an eternal Savior, who will delight me with joy as a recompense for all my physical suffering here on earth.

14. That is the third assertion: that we will have a cheerful, joyful defiant state of mind in the face of whatever suffering we may experience, so that we can tell the devil, You do not have permission to make life so bitter for me that it would deprive me of the joy I find in this infant. That is the meaning of *eudokia:* a cheerful, unruffled, joyful, and courageous heart that pays little attention to misfortune and confidently tells the devil, Go ahead, be as mean

and poisonous as you wish; I will not let my joy be embittered or destroyed by your wrath. Christ fills me with more joy than any amount of suffering you can impose on me. That kind of heart the angels wish for us sincerely with their song.

15. Now if you reverse this angelic hymn, which is what unfortunately is often the case on earth, you then have the devil's hymn in which God is cursed and blasphemed in the highest, in which great havoc is wreaked, in which murder is practiced, in which government is carried out in such a way that no one can have a happy face, and cannot eat one morsel in peace and joy. That is what those abominable rabble-rousers practice. They are the devil's mouthpiece. The fanatics assist the devil in his crimes, blaspheming and disgracing God with their false doctrine.

16. Then they try to make sure that princes and lords fight against one another, that unfaithfulness and dissatisfaction are created, that "good things" must be said in the presence of witnesses, and that the worst possible crimes are proven against them. That's the way I like it, sings the devil. That is glory to the devil in hell: wars on earth, and to all mankind a heart that is filled with timidity and despair. As is often the case, God provides everyone with the basic necessities of life, but that doesn't satisfy them at all, at any time. Even though they have their cellars, rooms to spare, and though their tables are loaded with food, they still walk around with hanging heads, faces filled with grief; though they have everything, they find no pleasure in anything. That is the devil's song and wish. He doesn't want us to have any joy whatsoever in the gifts God has so graciously given to us. Now in sharp contrast to this, the blessed angels wish and request for us a courageous heart that is able to defy Satan and to boast of our Savior to Satan's face.

17. We had to say this about the hymn of the angels, so that you would learn and properly understand it. You won't find this written anywhere in any books; no, not so much as a single letter. For this hymn did not originate on earth but was brought down from heaven to the earth by the angels. May our dear Lord God help us with His Holy Spirit, so that we remember this hymn and live according to it, through Jesus Christ, His Son and our Lord. Amen.

THIRD SUNDAY AFTER EPIPHANY

1533

The Lord Christ singles out the centurion and lifts him higher than the whole people Israel . . . an example of holiness for all of the Jews. Let us hear today's gospel in praise of our dear Lord God.

Let us hear today's gospel in praise of our dear Lord God.

MATTHEW 8:1–13

When He was come down from the mountain, great multitudes followed Him. And, behold, there came a leper and worshiped Him, saying, Lord, if Thou wilt, Thou canst make me clean. And Jesus put forth His hand, and touched him, saying, I will; be thou clean. And immediately his leprosy was cleansed. And Jesus saith unto him, See thou tell no man; but go thy way, show thyself to the priest, and offer the gift that Moses commanded, for a testimony unto them. And when Jesus was entered into Capernaum, there came unto Him a centurion, beseeching Him, and saying, Lord, my servant lieth at home sick of the palsy, grievously tormented. And Jesus saith unto him, I will come and heal him. The centurion answered and said, Lord, I am not worthy that Thou shouldest come under my roof; but speak the word only, and my servant shall be healed. For I am a man under authority, having soldiers under me: and I say to this man, Go, and he goeth; and to another, Come, and he cometh; and to my servant, Do this, and he doeth it. When Jesus heard it, He marveled, and said to them that followed, Verily I say unto you, I have not found so great faith, no, not in Israel. And I say unto you, that many shall come from the east and west, and shall sit down with Abraham, and Isaac, and Jacob, in the kingdom of heaven. But the children of the kingdom shall be cast out into outer darkness: there shall be weeping and gnashing of teeth. And Jesus said unto the centurion, Go thy way; and as thou has believed, so be it done unto thee. And his servant was healed in the selfsame hour.

1. There are two marvelous works told in this gospel: first, the healing of the leper; second, the account of the centurion whose servant Christ restored to health.

2. However, the first and foremost thing in this story, which Jesus extols and commends so highly, is the faith of the centurion, a heathen, of whom Jesus says that He has not found such faith in Israel. It was indeed a wonder that a heathen, who did not have the promises as the Jews had, should nonetheless have had such great and excellent faith as to surpass all of Israel. The Lord welcomes such faith gladly and, as He longs to do, says to the centurion, "Go thy way, and as thou has believed, so be it done unto thee."

3. We see from this what is the best and most acceptable service before God, namely, nothing pleases our Lord God more than that we believe and trust in Him from the heart. The Lord our God does not ask for beautiful temples or splendid, shiny works, but rather for inner devotion of the heart, that is, for faith, as the prophet Jeremiah [5:3] asks, "O Lord, are not thine eyes upon the truth?" We should, therefore, know that when we serve God from the heart, with faith, we are then His servants, priests, children, and heirs, who will be with Him in heaven.

4. It is an especially beautiful sermon as the Lord Christ singles out the centurion and lifts him higher than the whole people Israel. He leaves out Annas, Caiaphas, and all the priests, the Pharisees and scribes, and makes out of the heathen centurion an example of holiness for all of the Jews. It is like having someone in our day say, I have found a Turk of such splendid faith that neither pope nor bishops, neither spiritual leaders nor secular, neither learned nor unlearned have a faith to compare, or as Christ says, I have not found a faith like it in Israel. The Jews were the native citizens, with the rights and status of children and heirs, under the covenant and the law, having the temple services and the promise; also, Christ originated from them according to the flesh [Rom. 9:5]. They heard Christ preaching daily and saw His miracles, yet did not believe in Him. The centurion, on the other hand, was a guest and stranger, outside of the citizenry of Israel, alien to the testaments concerning the promise [Eph. 2:12]. In short, he was a pagan, and this same heathen comes without circumcision and the law, and clings to the Lord Christ with such faith that he obtains more from Him than he could ever have wished or hoped for.

5. The evangelist informs us that the centurion's faith manifested two excellent features. First, with his faith there is great, deep humility, as he says, "Lord, I am not worthy that Thou shouldest come under My roof." This amounts to saying, O Lord, why would you even bother with me? I am wicked, you are holy; I am a sinner, you are righteous. Indeed, I have heard that you do great miracles in Israel, that you restore health to the sick, and I dearly wanted to have my sick servant helped; but I consider myself unworthy for you to come into my house.

6. Second, there is an effulgent magnificence to his faith in that he understands that Christ is true God, and attributes to Him such power and might that, even though absent, He could still heal his servant. He confesses not only his unworthiness that Christ should come into his house, but also that it would not actually require so much trouble, for Christ could effect that for which he petitioned merely by His word, even though not personally present. The centurion had heard that the Lord had previously raised the dead, and from the same report he had concluded within himself that it was not necessary for Christ personally to come to his servant. He need but speak the word and his servant would be well. So firmly does he believe this that he draws an example from his own life, "I am a man under authority, having soldiers under me; and I say to this man, Go, and he goeth; and to another, Come, and he cometh; and to my servant, Do this, and he doeth it." I am a man, he says, who is under authority. I am not a ruling magistrate with supreme power, but under authority. Yet I can with one word cause things to be done. If my word, then, is so powerful, your word is many more times so, because you are not mere man but the Lord God over all creatures, who demonstrates power and might everywhere by great signs and wondrous works.

7. That meant not only having faith, but also speaking and teaching about the nature and way of faith in the best, most vivid manner. For it is faith's rightful art to be moved to trust the word with the whole heart, as the one and only treasure and hope, never doubting the "Yea" and "Amen" to what the word promises. The centurion rested upon the word without wavering, fully confident of it. For that reason he said to Jesus, "Speak the word only, and my servant shall be healed." This was tantamount to his saying, If

I but have the word, I have everything, and nothing is lacking for my servant; he will be safe and sound.

8. This is such wonderful, excellent faith and such beautiful, deep humility on the centurion's part that Christ marvels over it, and bursts forth with joyful heart to say, "Verily I say unto you, I have not found so great faith, no, not in Israel. And I say unto you, that many shall come from the east and west . . ." The Jews, in other words, are unwilling to believe; the gentiles are beginning to come to faith. The tables are being turned. The Jews, the children of the kingdom who had the promises, will be cast away because of unbelief, while the heathen, who lack the promise, will be received into the kingdom because they believe.

9. The Lord is so pleased and so impressed with the centurion's humility and faith that He is ready straight on to do what the centurion desires. "Go thy way," he says, "and as thou hast believed, so be it done unto thee." The centurion has no need to petition further, nor explain anything more about his servant's illness. So deep is the Lord's love for him, that everything is "Yea" and "Amen" even before he petitions further. Even though the centurion was a heathen and unworthy, his fine faith pleases Jesus so very much, not because the centurion vaunts his unworthiness but because of his recognition of unworthiness, because he feels and confesses it. Such humility and faith prompts the Lord not only to heal the servant but also to praise and commend the centurion's faith.

10. That is one part of this lesson and it is recorded for our learning, to goad us, so that we may learn to believe, to regard ourselves as unworthy, and be led to say, Though I am not worthy of it, I accept it being unworthy; though I have not merited it—for I know nothing in myself by which I deserve it—yet will I take it as gift. That, indeed, is true faith and genuine humility, when a person fears because of his unworthiness and yet does not despair. As Ps. 147:11 states, "The Lord taketh pleasure in them that fear Him, in those that hope in His mercy." This is today's lesson, a glorious one, really too sublime for a house sermon; it really belongs in the Church's pulpit.

11. The leper is cleansed from his leprosy by the Lord and sent to the priests. Jesus does not deal with the centurion's servant in

this manner, nor with others whom He healed from their diseases, as He does here with the leper. He himself explains the reason why, when He says, "Go thy way, show thyself to the priest, and offer the gift that Moses commanded, for a testimony unto them." They have to give certification, and that I won't contest. Theirs is law and they have the authority to examine the lepers and to offer gifts for them; that prerogative I won't take from them. In the case of the centurion, however, He did not say, Go, let yourself be circumcised and become a Jew. Even less does He say now, Give up your vocation, run to the monastery and become a monk, or that the servant be given his freedom; rather He lets the centurion remain a centurion, the servant, a servant.

12. In this way Christ shows us that His kingdom does not overturn secular rule and the world's vocations. All stations in life, given and established by God, are good, and to become a Christian a person is not required to have a specified external station. A husband and wife need not part and run to the cloister in order to be Christians and serve God. They can bc Christians and serve God where they are, yes, be better Christians and serve God more than by leaving their vocations and running from each other. It is the pope who labeled all other vocations worldly, calling his alone spiritual, as also that of his monks and clerics. That is a perilous line for the world, and indeed false and fabricated. We see how the Lord lets the Jews retain their law and authority; and if they had received Him, He would have let the whole of Jerusalem, with Moses, the temple, the kingdom, and the priesthood stand and remain; even though they were wicked rascals, yet He would have let them abide.

13. That God later destroyed Jerusalem with the temple, its worship, and the kingdom came about because they refused to receive Him. This is His usual way: if they will not allow Him to abide, He will tear them to pieces. He was willing to let the Jews have their temple, if only the people would acknowledge Him and serve Him. But because they were unwilling, He let it all be smashed. It is similar to a great king and lord who storms a city, not intending to destroy, devastate, and demolish it totally, but wants it to give up, yield, pay tribute, and be subject to him instead of to his opponent and enemy. But if the city refuses to yield and

tries to destroy the king, he will demolish it. In like manner, Christ with His gospel does not wish to tear apart the government, family life, and external estates of the Jews, but simply said to them, Receive Me as your Lord, follow Me, and I will let you go on. But they did not want to receive Him as Lord nor follow Him. He warned them earnestly, admonished, entreated, and implored them, saying, I did not plan for you to oppose Me; I will be tolerant, but let Me continue to be your Lord. But they refused, saying, We don't want this one to rule over us. In fact, they did their utmost to destroy Him. But what happened? Indeed, they killed Him on the cross, but they could not be done with Him, and He destroyed them.

14. The same thing happened with the Roman Empire. Christ came to them, implored them to receive His gospel and follow Him in true fear, acknowledgment, and faith, willing to let them have their rule and government. He did not want to strip the Roman emperor of his authority, even teaching that people were to give the emperor his due [Matt. 22:21]. Indeed, as He stood before the governor of the land, Pilate, He deigned to give worldly rule its honor [John 18]. But the Roman emperor set himself and his empire against Christ, persecuted the gospel, crucified some Christians, killed others with the sword, and sought to destroy Christ and His followers. As a result, his government and empire fell, and Rome lay crumbled in the dust.

15. In short, we must receive Christ and His gospel ahead of everything else. When we do this, all else goes well; and even if for a time we lose sight of it, we shall not finally lose it. But if we do not accept Christ and His gospel, but persecute it, we will not hold anything else for long. If ever the dire necessity comes when I must choose either to deny Christ or leave behind my wife and children, the way out is clear. If I may continue to hold to Christ and retain my wife and child too, well and good, but if it's a choice between having wife, child, rule, power, and the like, and denying Christ, then I must forsake wife, child, rule, power, body, and life before I deny Christ.

16. Nowadays we are ready to grant the pope and his henchmen their power, glory, and honor, doing them no harm, if only

they will not lord it over the Church but will acknowledge Christ and allow Him alone to be Lord in the Church. And if they do not themselves want to receive Him, we would ask them only to allow us and others who want to trust in Him to do so, and not entice people to idolatry and blasphemy, nor kill people because of it. But the pope with his tonsured hordes are unwilling; they try to push Christ from His seat and set themselves in His place, throttling and killing those who want to belong to Christ. Bring on the fire, is their cry, burn the heretics, and their Christ be damned. For that reason Christ rebuffs them and says, Dear sirs, pope, bishops, lords, you intend Me evil, to push Me from My seat and set yourselves in my place; that will not happen. I will keep My throne, and all who want to unseat Me, pope, bishops, prelates, princes, lords, and all evil rascals, will lie in a heap anon.

17. To sum up, Christ wishes to let each man abide, but instead of serving Satan He wants him now to serve Him. Those who accede to His wish shall not only abide but will also be built up [Jer. 31:28]: "As I have watched over them, to pluck up, and to break down, and to throw down, and to destroy, and to afflict; so will I watch over them, to build, and to plant, saith the Lord." Whoever refuses will be destroyed. For God cannot and will not permit those to go unpunished who will not have Him to be Lord but serve Satan, as Moses testifies [Deut. 18:12:] "For all that do these things are an abomination unto the Lord: and because of these abominations the Lord thy God doth drive them out from before thee."

18. The world cannot and will not have Christ as Lord, nor serve Him. As a result land and people are destroyed and laid waste. If our town does not want to have Him who saved them as Lord, no injustice will be done to her when the same Lord and Savior destroys and lays her level with the ground, saying to her, Is this what you want? Will you not only forget all the benefits shown to you, but on top of it all drive Me out of the land and serve another master for having rescued you? Very well, let it be so, since you are so disloyal. No injustice is done those who cast Christ aside when they are punished and destroyed.

19. That is what Christ has in mind here, as He sends the leper to the priests. We are not to understand the Christian faith as the

fanatics do, who straightway overthrow constituted authority; nor as the papists, who define spiritual life in distinction from worldly life in terms of an outward discipline. On the contrary, we should know that a Christian and believer is one who has gotten another Lord. As far as his outward life goes, it remains as before, as St. Paul says [Gal. 3:28]: "There is neither Jew nor Greek, there is neither bond nor free, there is neither male nor female; for ye are all one in Christ Jesus." It does not follow that for the sake of Christian faith a person's external life itself is altered; rather it remains as before. Whatever you were when you were called to faith— husband, wife, servant, maid—continue so, as St. Paul teaches in 1 Cor. 7:20–24. We must rightly distinguish one's status as a Christian from the external existence, so that we properly spell out what it means to be a Christian, namely, to acknowledge Christ alone to be true Lord, who redeemed us and whose debtors we are.

20. This the pope and his minions have not understood, nor do they want to; but they mix and mingle together the outward way of life with the Christian station and make no distinction between the spiritual and worldly. The bishops and clerics have become worldly lords, ruling over land and people, and not least, have called their overlordship, properties, and possessions spiritual holdings, even though spiritual goods are those things which properly are not seen by the naked eye, nor taken in hand, like forgiveness of sins, righteousness which avails before God, life, and salvation. These are treasures which neither eye can see nor hand grasp, but faith only, which takes them in the Word.

21. It is gross blindness when a person is unable to distinguish Christian life from mere outward, worldly existence. As I have said, we need to learn this well, so that we can rightly define it verbally. A Christian life consists in this: that we receive the unseen Christ and believe that He is our only Lord and Savior, who rescued us from sin, death, devil, and hell. Then, once we have acknowledged Him as our Lord, we ought also serve Him with our whole life and pay tribute to Him, saying, Lord, previously I was under the devil's power and in His service, shamefully misusing Your gifts which also then I possessed, in part; but now I have learned and know for sure that You alone are my Lord and God. I believe in You, and therefore I also want to serve You in this faith,

trusting You from the heart, that You are my Lord and Savior, and want to be obedient to You in my station of life and do what pleases You. That means we must rightly distinguish Christian life from routine existence. Yet both are to be and remain subject under Christ, even though a Christian according to the body is subject to worldly rulers, for we would gladly yield body and life, goods and honor, in fact everything we have, rather than let go of Christ.

22. To this the Lord points as He says to the leper, "Go, show yourself to the priest." Along with evidencing His glory through miraculous healing, He does not want the impression in any way to be drawn, not even in slightest measure, that He taught and agitated insurrection against the Jewish rule and priesthood. It was as much as to say: The Jewish law and rule given to them by Moses would in no way displease Me, nor be a hindrance, if they would only receive Me as their Lord. To let themselves be circumcised, to deal with leprosy according to Moses' law, to bring sacrifices and to do other works of the law would be pleasing enough to Me, if only I might remain their Lord. But when they will not allow Me to be their Lord, then the friendship is at an end.

23. We see this everywhere in the gospels, how Christ did not assail the law of the Jews, had they only permitted Him to teach and do miracles, and received Him. But when they refused to accept Him, and on top of it reviled His teaching and His miracles, grounding their scolding and punishing of Him on their law, then He responded by smashing through their law as through a spiderweb, saying, "The Son of Man is Lord also over the sabbath." It is so yet today, as He says, Let everything be as it is, plain and honest, as long as the world receives Me as Lord. But if men will not receive Me, they shall be plucked up. For My Father will not tolerate My being despised and scorned. If men despise and reject Me, My Father will utterly destroy them, as Ps. 2:8–12 states, "Ask of Me, and I shall give Thee the heathen for Thine inheritance, and the uttermost parts of the earth for Thy possession. Thou shalt break them with a rod of iron; Thou shalt dash them in pieces like a potter's vessel. Be wise now therefore, O ye kings: be instructed, ye judges of the earth. Serve the Lord with fear, and rejoice with trembling. Kiss the Son, lest He be angry, and ye perish from the way, when His wrath is kindled but a little." It is as though God were saying, The world will

have good days, with body, life, and every good thing as largesse from God, if it will only acknowledge Him as Lord, receive Him, and serve Him. If it will not, its judgment is sealed.

24. We, who have learned this and been obedient, have pleased God and possess salvation. But the world has not responded in this way. Yes, the world says, If I were to receive Christ as Lord and serve Him, everything would be turned topsy-turvy and thrown into confusion. Indeed, God responds to the world: It will be as you say, total destruction, but not through fault of My word, but because of your stiff-neckedness for not receiving My word and acknowledging My Son as Lord. The Jews reasoned to themselves, If we let this man go, the Romans will come and take our land and people. Indeed, the Romans did come and, as the Jews themselves foresaw, left no stone upon another. And the Romans, too, later on said, Because these two beggars, Peter and Paul, have come, we've had nothing but trouble. And they were true prophets about their own necks! Our opponents today speak in the same way: Were we to accept the Lutheran gospel and believe on their Christ, everything—land and people—would be undone. They say this quite openly, knowing full well that it isn't true, for our gospel would allow them to be and remain, if only they are filled with fear. Put them and Christ together, however, and then see who is the stronger.

25. To the centurion Christ does not say that he should go to the priest, nor does He put him under the Jewish law, but allows him to remain a centurion under Roman imperial authority. The centurion's office was sanguinary business, and yet Jesus allowed him to keep the sword, lets him carry on in his bloody office, and does not forbid him from engaging in war and pursuing his bloody tasks. He, on the contrary, upholds the centurion in his post, and with His miraculous word heals his servant. Just as He did not take from the Jews their law and governance, so neither from the pagan Romans their offices and stations, not even from their military men. This is not to say that everything which their soldiers did pleased Him, but He permitted these stations and offices to remain. For one has to distinguish between the office and its abuse, as John the Baptist also taught when he said to the soldiers [Luke 3:14]: "Do violence to no man, neither accuse any falsely; and be content with your wages."

26. This is the nature of Christ's office and work, and for this reason He came, that the devil's kingdom might be taken off us, and that the people who formerly served the devil might now serve Him. So we teach too: whoever under the papacy served the devil with idolatrous practices, Masses, vows, and the like, should now take his stand against these and serve God, believing on Christ, that through Him alone, without worthiness of his own works, he is righteous before God and saved. If that remains sure and solid, then we rest at peace. If one tonsure is not enough, then let there be two; it makes no difference to God. But without and apart from Christ, to rely on caps and tonsures, God will not tolerate, but will smash it to smithereens. That's why Christ says, I will not take things from you; take nothing away from Me either; you remain you, and I will remain Myself. If then you die, you know where you will go. In short, Christ wants only to destroy the devil's kingdom, and beyond that He lets things be. God give us His grace to keep and hold on to this. For that we pray and beseech Him.

REMINISCERE SUNDAY — SECOND SUNDAY IN LENT

1534

She [the woman of Canaan] blinds her eyes and shuts her mind to the fact that she is a heathen, a gentile, and He a Jew. Her heart is so full of trust in Christ that she is convinced, He will not turn me away. By such faith she has wiped away the thought that she is a gentile and He a Jew.

MATTHEW 15:21–28

Then Jesus went thence, and departed into the coasts of Tyre and Sidon. And behold, a woman of Canaan came out of the same coasts, and cried unto Him, saying, Have mercy on me, O Lord,

Thou Son of David; my daughter is grievously vexed with a devil. But He answered her not a word. And His disciples came and besought Him, saying, Send her away; for she crieth after us. But He answered and said, I am not sent but unto the lost sheep of the house of Israel. Then came she and worshiped Him, saying, Lord, help me. But He answered and said, It is not meet to take the children's bread and to cast it to dogs. And she said, Truth, Lord: yet the dogs eat of the crumbs which fall from their masters' table. Then Jesus answered and said unto her, O woman, great is thy faith: be it unto thee even as thou wilt. And her daughter was made whole from that very hour.

1. This is a wonderful gospel lesson. Like others, it was chosen for this Sunday because it deals with driving out the devil, and by it they [our opponents] wanted to show that people were to strive to be pious, go to confession, and partake of the sacrament because the pope required these things. But this is a miserable, papistic piety, which lets a whole year go by until now, and then is satisfied—without scriptural warrant and without people's hearts being in it—by wretched fasting, involuntary confession, and compulsory attendance at the sacrament.

2. We must, therefore, first of all realize that this gospel is not treating of a trifling, insignificant matter, but of a very important and crucial teaching concerning faith's life-and-death struggle before God. From it we are to learn that nothing, not even the throes of death, must deter us from calling upon God in prayer— even though He has already said "No." The devil always needles us with thoughts of how God's face is turned away from us, that He wants nothing more to do with us. This is a terrible situation, and thick black clouds seem to cover and extinguish the lovely, bright sun—a wretchedness beyond telling.

3. That's the struggle pictured for us in the case of this woman. Not only her person but all other circumstances are so miserable that it's hard to imagine things being worse. First of all, she is a gentile, a difficult situation under the circumstances, for that means that she is not of Abraham's seed and, therefore, an outsider with no right to ask for help. The thought must have bounced around in

her mind, Why should I implore? It's of no use. I'm a stranger here, and in addition a gentile woman, and He is a Jew, sent to the Jews.

4. If such a staggering blow had hit our hearts, we probably would have succumbed and given up on prayer. For it is no joke when conscience tells us, You have no right to pray; you don't belong to Christ. Let St. Paul and St. Peter pray, but our Lord God won't listen to you; you have no faith, are probably not among the elect, and not worthy to be eligible for and deserving of stepping before God to ask for anything. With such thoughts and troubling doubts, the devil assaults and jabs at us.

5. But look at the woman now and learn from her how you ought to proceed under similar circumstances. She blinds her eyes and shuts her mind to the fact that she is a heathen, a gentile, and He a Jew. Her heart is so full of trust in Christ that she is convinced, He will not turn me away. By such faith she has wiped away the thought that she is a gentile and He a Jew. Another person, without faith, would not have withstood but would have thought, You are of the devil, and it's useless for you to petition; let His own people do the imploring, but it won't do you any good. Thus prayer would never have been uttered. But this woman lets nothing deter her, refuses to dispute within herself, You do not belong in the house; you are a locked-out gentile, not worthy that the earth carry you.

6. There is no more severe and malicious trial than when the devil shatters the heart, saying, Why do you keep on praying? You belong to me! Go to it, curse God, it doesn't matter, you won't be saved. Such devil-inspired thoughts can derail the unpracticed heart, so that it no longer prays and succumbs to doubts.

7. This incident, therefore, was recorded for our sakes, to keep us from stumbling when the evil foe confronts us with the charge "You are no Christian; your prayers won't accomplish a thing." No, not on your life, pay no attention, but say, I'm in charge here, there's no question about that; and even though I am a wicked sinner, I nonetheless know that my Lord Jesus is not a sinner and wicked, but forever righteous and gracious. Yes, the more sinful and wicked I perceive myself to be, the more passionately and

earnestly will I call upon Him and let nothing deter me. I haven't the time now to debate whether I am among the elect, but I do know that I need help and therefore I come humbly seeking for it.

8. Then you are following the woman's example to the letter, when with firm faith you counter the thoughts that would keep you from prayer and affirm: The Canaanite woman was a gentile and not among the chosen people, and yet she prayed and let nothing keep her from praying, nor will I, for I desperately require help from my various needs. Where else can I look for help, but with God in heaven, for the sake of His dear Son and my Redeemer, Christ Jesus? That's the kind of heroic, soldierlike faith the woman had, truly remarkable!

9. Now the text states how she cried, "Have mercy on me, O Lord, thou Son of David; my daughter is grievously vexed with a devil." In those words she explained her anguish, and Christ certainly heard her cry, but answered her not a word. Thus Christ added another blow on top of her dilemma. She is a gentile, an outsider, without any share in the inheritance of the chosen people. She runs after Christ and begs Him, but He remains impassively silent, as though He had nothing to do with her. Before a double onslaught like that, a tower, yes, a will made of iron would crumble. Through her mind the thought raced, Where is the man whom everyone was praising for His compassion, being quick to listen, eager to help? But all I see and meet with is that He hears only when He wants to and not when we need Him. But the poor woman does not let herself be scared off. But what else happens to her yet?

10. In the third place, the disciples become weary of her crying and are more compassionate, to their way of thinking, than Christ Himself. In fact they judge Him to be too hard and insensitive. So they get into the act and beseech Him in behalf of the woman, O Lord, give in and help her, otherwise she won't let up. Thus we have a priceless object lesson never to give up when we pray.

11. Tauler[36] offers an example of when it's time to stop; but it is wrong to suggest that in our preaching, for giving up praying is all

[36] A German mystic and eminent preacher of the Dominican order, in the fourteenth century, from Strasbourg. Wrote *The Book of Spiritual Poetry*.

too common among us already. So this is a wholesome example why we should on no account cease but continue to pray, and like this woman we ought to affirm: I will not now argue the question whether I am good or bad, worthy or unworthy. I have no time for that. There's something more important than that: my daughter is grievously vexed by the devil, and I need help and advice now. Her need was pressing her so heavily that she was ready for the hard cuffs and rebuffs she was encountering.

12. The third blow or shocking rebuff comes when Christ says, "I am not sent but to the lost sheep of Israel." And by so saying He also knocks the disciples on the head, disdaining to hear the woman or them as they plead for her.

13. They must have thought, This is a cruel man who won't even listen to other people who of their own accord, and unsolicited, plead in behalf of someone. And that is true. Christ is nowhere pictured as pitiless as in this gospel. Nonetheless she doesn't relent, but keeps right on, even though she's had to swallow three direct hits.

14. Since her cries and the entreaty of the disciples have not helped, she now follows along into the house (as Mark tells the story) like some ill-mannered woman, crying and running after Jesus. But even in the house He is not free of her, for she prostrates herself at His feet, begging Him. It's a lesson, indeed, recorded for our learning and comfort, teaching us that Christ is pleased at heart when we persist in prayer and do not give up.

15. Even then the Lord does not open Himself up to the woman's entreaty to help her, for listen to what He says: "It is not meet to take the children's bread and to cast it to dogs." If He had said such words to me, I would have charged out of there, convinced that it was useless and that my efforts were all in vain. It was surely the hardest blow of all that as she lies there at His feet He doesn't just let it rest with her being an impudent child and a gentile but also calls her a dog. This was worse, much worse than if He had said, You are a heathen and belong to the devil; now get to your feet and stop throwing yourself around; you have nothing to gain here. That certainly was a most traumatic trial. If He had spoken in this manner to me, I would have been scared off—words spoken

not just by St. Peter, St. Paul, or some other esteemed person, but
by Christ Himself! I would have been frightened to death.

16. What a superb and wonderful object lesson this is, therefore, to teach us what a mighty, powerful, all-availing thing faith
is. Faith takes Christ captive in His word, when He's angriest, and
makes out of His cruel words a comforting inversion, as we see
here. You say, the woman responds, that I am a dog. Let it be, I
will gladly be a dog; now give me the consideration that you give a
dog. Thus she catches Christ with His own words, and He is happy
to be caught. Very well, she says, if I am a dog, I ask no more than
a dog's rights. I am not a child nor am I of Abraham's seed, but you
are a rich Lord and set a lavish table. Give your children the bread
and a place at the table; I do not wish that. Let me, merely like a
dog, pick up the crumbs under the table, allowing me that which
the children don't need or even miss, the crumbs, and I will be
content therewith. So she catches Christ the Lord in His own
words and with that wins not only the right of a dog, but also that
of the children. Now then, where will He go, our dear Jesus? He
let Himself be made captive, and must comply. Be sure of this:
that's what He most deeply desires.

17. It is a true masterpiece, an especially vivid example that is
recorded for our sakes, in order that we might learn not to be
rebuffed by this man whom God permits to oppose us, as it were,
and to call us dogs and gentiles. As the woman said, also dogs must
have masters and crumbs, and also the gentiles must have a God.

18. By such tenacity and unflinching faith the Lord is taken
captive and pressed to answer, O woman, if you can tolerate and
survive such blows to your heart, so may it be granted to you, even
as you believe. Yours is not the typical pattern that I find. The Jews
are soon offended in Me and fall back at the slightest pretext, even
though I have shared with them a salutary teaching. You, however, cling firmly to the hope that I will help you and you don't let
go of Me.

19. We see here why the Lord presented Himself so unyielding
and refused to hear her, not because He wanted to present an
unfriendly image as not wanting to help her, but rather that her
faith might be so evident, that the Jews who were the children and

heirs of the kingdom might learn from the gentile, who was not among the children and had no inheritance, how they were to believe in Christ and place all confidence in Him. Her faith pleases Him so much that He can no longer hide His compassion and kindness, and He states, "O woman, great is thy faith: be it unto thee as thou wilt." Thus He gives her not merely a dog's rights, but is constrained to give her what she petitions for, healing her daughter, and places her among the descendants of Abraham. Her faith brings her to such a state of grace that she is no longer a dog or a gentile but is welcomed as a beloved daughter and a blessed woman.

20. This example serves us well in that, when our Lord God puts off answering, we do not let up but firmly trust that He will finally say "Yes," and even though He does not say it loudly and publicly, still says it privately in our hearts, until the time comes when we see and experience it in fact, provided that we don't meanwhile become lazy and lax in prayer and perseverance. We learn this from other examples as well. Joseph cried out in persevering prayer for more than twelve years before God willed to help him. In his case, the longer he waited, the worse the situation got; the more he prayed, the worse things became. Christ himself cried out urgently for help and deliverance at the time of His passion, but God held back, as we read in Ps. 22:2, "O my God, I cry in the daytime, but Thou hearest not; and in the night season, and am not silent." It is the same for Christians today. They very urgently and repeatedly call upon God and see no improvement, but like Joseph find that the longer and harder they have prayed, the worse things have become. If God had answered Joseph sooner and rescued him, then no doubt Jacob, his father, would have been happy but Joseph would have remained a sheepherder. But because God's answer was long delayed, he became ruler over all Egypt and the greatest among his brethren; and God through him accomplished much good both in the secular realm as well as in the Church.

21. This is also the manner of God's dealing with us. For a long time He denies our petition and the answer always is "No"; but if we hold fast to the "Yes," it will finally be "Yes," and no longer "No." For His Word does not lie [John 16:23]: "Whatsoever ye shall ask the Father in My name, He will give it you." Because the Word is true, His promise will not fail.

22. But our mind is greatly agitated by such delay and we would much rather that God would answer without delay. But we must not become aggravated. We must let our Lord God say "No," as He holds up our petition for a year, two years, three, or even longer, being on guard lest our hope and faith be wrenched from our hearts. We will in the end find that God will do far more for us than we asked for, just as in the case of this woman. Had she asked for even more, He would have granted it.

23. Our Lord God thus wishes to teach us that it is not always good to be heard immediately. In urgent need His answer is there, as for example, should we fall into the water, or be involved in warfare; the answer will not be long delayed. The same is true for great, difficult spiritual trials. But where the waiting and delay can be endured, we should learn that He usually holds back for our own good. It is as the prophet Habakkuk says [2:3]: "For the vision is yet for an appointed time, but at the end it shall speak, and not lie: though it tarry, wait for it; because it will surely come, it will not tarry."

24. That is also the situation now as He lets the pope and the Turk rage against us. We cry out woefully but He does not hear us, acts as though He doesn't know us, and lets us go on in our misery as though we had no God. But it won't go on like this forever; God will requite us. Let us, therefore, never doubt that we have a "Yes" in heaven, imbedded in the heart of our Lord Jesus Christ, and His Father's, and that in His time it will be revealed. Now He builds four or five iron walls in front of it, and the devil shoots off his futile "No" too. But we must learn to say, I will cling to the "Yes," that God will be merciful to His Church and rescue all who cry to Him for help. The "Yes" is deep in His heart, in keeping with Christ's promise [John 14:13]: "And whatsoever ye shall ask in My name, that will I do, that the Father may be glorified in the Son." Therefore I will not dispute whether I am among the elect, or a gentile and unworthy, but firmly persist that the "Yes" is there.

25. This episode, accordingly, is an especially beautiful example of true faith, that it needs to be practiced, that it will finally prevail and win out; also of how we, therefore, must not despise the Word, but cling firmly to its promise, never doubting that our prayer will be heard, even though for a time God delays. So, in the

case of this woman, she cries and implores, and will not let the "Yes" word be plucked from her heart—that Christ the Lord is friendly and will help.

26. May our dear Lord God help us to learn this lesson well, so that with our whole heart we firmly believe His Word and promises, and through Christ, with the Holy Spirit's help, are eternally saved. Amen.

ON BAPTISM

1528

Baptism is water comprehended and sanctified in God's commandment and Word, that is, a divine and holy water because of God's commandment.

You have heard the three parts, which we call the catechism [*Kinderlehre*], or common Christian teaching, set forth as simply and plainly as I can. On the two following days we shall deal with the two sacraments, which also belong here. For every Christian ought also to know these two sacraments.

Baptism is recorded in the last chapter of Mark: "Go into all the world and preach the gospel to the whole creation. He who believes and is baptized will be saved; but he who does not believe will be condemned" [Mark 16:15–16]. Even if a person is baptized but is without faith, he is lost. Be we shall at this time omit discussion of that which serves us in disputation and controversy with the adversaries. In connection with baptism the words themselves, which are recorded here, must be understood. These every person must know. In the first place, note the command of God, which is very stern when He says: "He who believes and is baptized will be saved; but he who does not believe will be condemned." This is a strict command; if a person wants to be saved, let him be baptized; otherwise he is in God's disfavor. Therefore, these words are in the first place a strict, earnest divine command. Hence you cannot hold the opinion that baptism is a human invention or any kind of command or thing, such as putting a wreath on one's head; it is God's command. Consequently, you must esteem baptism as something high, glorious, and excellent; for here there is a divine word and command, which institutes and confirms baptism. If in former times you considered it a splendid and precious thing when the establishment of an altar was confirmed by a letter of the pope, then esteem baptism a thousand times more, since it is instituted and ordained by God. If you look upon baptism as being only water, then you will consider it to be a paltry and ordinary thing.

Therefore, if you are asked what baptism is, you should not answer, as the fanatics do, that it is a handful of water, which is no good, that the Spirit, the Spirit must do it; the bathhouse servant, the minister, that is, effects nothing; therefore the Spirit should be present. But you should say: Baptism is water comprehended and sanctified in God's commandment and Word, that is, a divine and holy water because of God's commandment. The fanatics, the scoundrels rip off God's Word. If I skin a cow, it isn't worth much; but if I take the meat with the hide, it is worth four guldens. Therefore say that baptism is a living, saving water on account of the Word of God which is in it. The Word of God, however, is greater than heaven and earth, sun, moon, and all angels. Don't look at the water and see that it is wet, but rather that it has with it the Word of God. It is a holy, living, heavenly, blessed water because of the Word and command of God, which is holy. You cannot sufficiently extol it; who can ever sufficiently extol God's Word? And all this comes in baptism because God's Word is in baptism. This is the way I also speak of parents and neighbors. If I look at a father, seeing only that he has a nose, that he is flesh and blood, with bones, limbs, skin and hair, or likewise a mother, if I do not look upon her otherwise than that, I am not seeing her at all, but trampling her underfoot. But when the Fourth Commandment is added, then I see them adorned with a glorious crown and golden chain, which is the Word of God. And that shows you why you should honor this flesh and blood of your parents for the sake of God's Word. This the fanatics do not consider, nor can they do it, because they abominate the Word. The round halo which is painted around the heads of saints is around the heads of parents too. The golden halo, or diadem, came from the heathen. Later it became a garland, then flowers were added, and now it has become the bishop's miter. This Word of power is painted around the heads of parents as a diadem, just as if the majesty and the Word of God were painted about their heads.

So it is with baptism. Certainly when the devil sees baptism and hears the Word sounding, to him it is like a bright sun and he will not stay there, and when a person is baptized for the sake of the Word of God, which is in it, there is a veritable oven glow. Do you think it was a joke that the heavens were opened at Christ's baptism [Matt. 3:16]? Say, therefore, that baptism is water and God's Word comprehended in one. Take the Word away and it is the same water with which the maid waters the cow; but with the Word, it is a living, holy, divine water. He who considers the words: "will be saved" [Mark 16:16] will find it [salvation]; for with His words "will be saved," Christ puts salvation into baptism. Therefore it is impossible that this should be simple water when through it salvation, forgiveness of sins, and redemption from death and the devil is given.

But nobody believes what an excellent thing is in these words. The fanatics laugh at us and say: You neopapists teach the people to trust in water. But when I ask them: What do you say about these words, "He who believes and is baptized will be saved"? they flutter away. So you say to them: We do not teach that one should trust in water, but we do teach that the water, when it becomes one thing with God's Word, is baptism. The water does not do it because of itself, but rather because of the Word, which is connected with it. But if you take away the Word, then don't go telling us that baptism is useless water. Then it is a figment of the devil, who is seeking to sow bad seed among us. You hear your Savior say: If you believe and are baptized, then salvation follows, not because of the water, but because you believe the Word. It is not for nothing that I insist so emphatically that you say that baptism is natural, physical water connected with the Word of God. When these two come together, water and the Word of God, then it is a baptism.

But, you say, can water benefit me? No. What then? Baptism. But isn't it water? No; for it is water connected with the Word of God; therefore it must be something other than water. That's why we declare that the water amounts to nothing, but baptism does. Therefore baptism is water with the Word of God, and this is the essence and whole substance of baptism. When, therefore, water and God's Word are conjoined, it must necessarily be a holy and divine water, for as the Word is, so the water becomes also.

Furthermore, the benefit of baptism must also be learned. If baptism is water with the Word of God, what is its purpose, work, fruit, and benefit? It saves those who believe, as the words say. A child is baptized, not in order that it may become a prince; it is baptized in order that it may be saved, as the words say, that is, in order that it may be redeemed from sin, death, and the devil, that it may become a member of Christ, and that it may come into Christ's kingdom and Christ become its Lord. Accordingly, baptism is useful to the end that through it we may be saved. There you have the transcendent excellence of baptism. The first honor is that it is a divine water, and when you see a baptism remember that the heavens are opened. The fruit is that it saves, redeems you from sin, liberates you from the devil, and leads you to Christ. The fanatics insist that one must first become holy. But I am not contending with them now, but teaching the simple.

Thirdly, that we may know the person who should be baptized: who should receive baptism? The one who believes is the person to whom the blessed, divine water is to be imparted. If you believe that through this water you will be saved, it becomes a fact. The first point, therefore, is that baptism is water connected with God's Word. The second is the fruit, and the third is that the person who believes is the one who is worthy of baptism. Here some excellent things might be said; but you simple people, note these three points! The little word "believe" leaves no room for either works or monks' cowls. It does not say: He who obeys his parents, but: He who believes.

Here we meet the question whether children who are baptized believe. He who is simple, let him dismiss these questions and refer them to me or answer this way: I know that infant baptism pleases God; I know that I was baptized as a child; I know that I have the Holy Spirit, for this I have the interpretation of the scriptures themselves. If the baptism of children were nothing, then certainly there would not be a single person on earth who would truly speak a single word about Christ [i.e., a Christian]. But since Christ most certainly bestows the Holy Spirit [and thus confirms baptism], for Bernard, Bonaventure, Gerson, and John Hus had the Spirit, because this is God's work, believe therefore that infant baptism is true. How do you know this? I see the wonderful works of God, I see that He has sanctified many and given them the Holy Spirit. Therefore you tell [the adversaries] that children are truly baptized and say: I prove it by the works [of God]. It is known by its fruit; if there is fruit, there must be a tree. Furthermore, for me the Word of God weighs a thousand times more, etc. But this becomes a bit more learned[37] [than the thoughts of reason].

Note well, therefore, that baptism is water with the Word of God, not water and my faith. My faith does not make the baptism but rather receives the baptism, no matter whether the person being baptized believes or not; for baptism is not dependent upon my faith but upon God's Word. If today a Jew were to be baptized, who was seeking only the sponsor's christening gift, and we baptized him nevertheless, the baptism would be genuine, for it is God's Word with water. And even though the Jew did not believe, the baptism would nevertheless not be false. Likewise, if I administer the sacrament to someone who cherishes anger or the like, he nevertheless receives the true body [and the true blood of Christ]. Therefore it is false to say that infants do not believe and therefore should not be baptized. You have already heard that they do believe, because the fruits follow, namely, the gifts of the Holy Spirit. The sacrament [of the Lord's Supper] does not rest upon faith but upon the Word of God, who instituted it, and so it is with baptism also. Even if the children did not believe (which, however, is false), the baptism is not to be repeated. Therefore you should say: The baptism was genuine, but I, unfortunately, did not believe it.

These are crude spirits [the Anabaptists]. I am a learned man and a preacher and I go to the sacrament in the faith of others and in my own faith. Nevertheless, I don't stand on that, I stand on [His words]: "Take; this is My body" [Mark 14:22]. Upon these words I go, and I know that Christ invites me, for He said, "Come to Me, all who labor and are heavy-laden, and I will give you rest" [Matt. 11:28]; and this will not deceive me. Thus I certainly have the sacrament. Accordingly, I apply this to baptism and pray that faith may be given to it [the child]. But I do not baptize it upon its faith or someone else's faith, but upon God's Word and command. In my faith I may lie, but he who instituted baptism cannot lie. Therefore

[37]I.e, too advanced for a sermon addressed to children.

say: The children must necessarily be baptized, and their baptism is true, because God grants grace to children who are baptized immediately after their birth, namely, an excelling grace. Otherwise, if baptism were false, it would not manifest this [grace]. Secondly, even if the children did not believe, they must nevertheless not be rebaptized. You fanatics, you say that the earlier baptism was not genuine. This we by no means concede, for baptism is definitive, water with the Word. Therefore Augustine says, "The Word comes to the element, and it becomes a sacrament."

These two sacraments may be received also by an unbeliever. Thus the devil would secretly teach us to build upon our works, and in order to accomplish this more easily he makes a sham of faith and says: If you do not believe, then you are not baptized. But it simply does not follow that if I do not obey my parents, therefore I have no parents; if I do not obey the government, therefore the government is nothing. So it does not follow here: that person has not received baptism in faith, therefore the baptism is nothing or is not genuine. Indeed, the baptism was genuine precisely because you did not rightly receive it. The abuse confirms the baptism; it does not deny it. If all of you here were to be baptized today and there were hardly three among you who were holy, the baptism would still not be false, but rather the contrary; for our work and misuse neither make nor unmake God's work. A prince remains a prince, whether you are obedient or not. This the fanatics do not know, for they are blinded; that's why they look at the sacrament without the Word. There is rebellion concealed in this mind, because it always wants to separate God's Word from the person. It wants to tear down the Word; therefore it is a rebel, secretly.

THE LORD'S SUPPER

1528

The need [which drives us to the sacrament] is that sin, devil, and death are always present. The benefit is that we receive forgiveness of sins and the Holy Spirit.

In the first place, every one of you should know the words with which this sacrament was instituted—for one should not administer the sacrament to those who do not know these words and what they do and perform. Here we are not going to enter into controversy with the blasphemers of this sacrament. You must deal with this sacrament in the same way that you heard with regard to baptism, namely, that the chief point is God's Word and command, just as in the Lord's Prayer, the Creed, and the Ten Commandments. Even though you never believe or keep the Ten Commandments, the Ten Commandments nevertheless exist and remain, and so baptism and the sacrament of the altar also remain baptism and the sacrament of the altar. Even though you never obey your parents, they still remain your parents.

Therefore, the primary thing in the sacrament is the Word: "Jesus took bread, etc." [Matt. 26:26–28]. If you believe it, blessed are you; if not, Christ will still remain faithful. When we die and are snatched away, these errors will come. Nobody wants to look upon it as God's Word; if one does not have regard for it, then it is nothing. In the sacraments, the Ten Commandments, and the Creed, God's Word is the chief thing. Therefore, do not look only upon the water, the bread and wine, but rather connect with them the words "Take, eat," "Do this in remembrance of Me," and "Drink of it, all of you." Learn these words; in them the sacrament is summed up; if you have lost these words, you have lost the sacrament. The fanatics rip these words out, and the same goes for the pope, because he has concealed them. The Word of God is the chief thing in the sacrament. He who does not know them [the words of institution], let him not come to the sacrament.

Secondly: what is the sacrament of the altar? As baptism is water and God's Word conjoined, so it is here. Here the bread is not the kind of bread the baker bakes, nor is the wine the kind the vintner sells; for he does not give you God's Word with it. But the minister binds God's Word to the bread and the Word is bound to the bread and likewise to the wine, for it is said, "The Word comes to the element, and it becomes a sacrament." In all his lifetime Augustine never said anything better. It is not the word of our prince or the emperor, but of God. Therefore, when you hear this word "is,"[38]

---

[38] In the words of institution. I.e., how is it possible for the body to be under the bread?

then do not doubt. Thus the sacrament is bread and body, wine and blood, as the words say and to which they are connected. If, therefore, God speaks these words, then don't search any higher, but take off your hat; and if a hundred thousand devils, learned men, and spirits were to come and say, How can this be? you answer that one single word of God is worth more than all of these. A hundred thousand learned men are not as wise as one little hair of our God. In the first place, therefore, learn that the sacrament is not simply bread and wine, but the body and blood of Christ, as the words say. If you take away the words, you have only bread and wine. Hence the command of God is the greatest thing in the sacrament, as in the Lord's Prayer. Take hold only of the words; they tell you what the sacrament is. If a fornicator comes [to the table], he receives the true sacrament, because it does not lose power on account of his impiety and infidelity. Our unbelief does not alter God's Word. This I have often said. When a whore decks herself with gold, it is still gold. Misuse does not change God's Word. A robber abuses the light of day, the sun, and yet it remains the sun. Christ does not found His sacrament upon our use of it. What He says or ordains remains, no matter whether one uses it rightly or wrongly. The sacrament is body and blood, as the words say, whether it is received by one who is worthy or unworthy.

What is the use or fruit of the sacrament? Listen to this: "given for you"; "shed." I go to the sacrament in order to take and use Christ's body and blood, given and shed for me. When the minister intones, "This cup is the New Testament in My blood," to whom is it sung? Not to my dog,[39] but to those who are gathered to take the sacrament. These words must be apprehended by faith. Therefore I use the sacrament for the forgiveness of my sins; I say: I will go and take the body and the blood; it is a sure sign that it was instituted for me and against my death. "Which is given for you." There is the benefit.

Now follows: who are those who lay hold of this benefit? He who believes has baptism and he who does not believe does not have it. Likewise, he who believes that the body, which he receives, is given for him, has the fruit of this sacrament. Therefore, he who believes takes his rightful place at this sacrament. That's why I

---

[39]There is an untranslatable play on words here: *Cui canitur? Non cani meo.*

have said that these words are spoken, not to stones or a pillar, but to Christians. "For you." Who does "for you" mean? The door or the window, perhaps? No, those who today hear the words "for you." I am to believe it. If you believe, then you take the sacrament on the strength of these words "for you." Mark only those words! because the words "for you" make the devil more hostile to us. He says to us, My dear fellow, you must not believe this "for you." What is it to you? Drink at home and enjoy yourself! The sacrament doesn't concern you. It is this "you" that makes it our concern, just as in baptism: "He who believes and is baptized will be saved." So here it is: "for you." Therefore, note well and learn well these words! The benefit is: "given for you, shed for you." Why do you go to the sacrament? I go because it is a body and blood which is given and shed for me; that's why I go.

If the sacrament is rightly administered, one should preach, first, that the sacrament is the body and blood of the Lord under the bread and wine, as the words say. Secondly, the benefit: it effects the forgiveness of sins, as the words say, "which is shed for the remission of sins."

Beyond this I admonish you to prepare yourselves for it. Since it is the sacrament in which there is the forgiveness of sins, it is not to be despised. It is true that a large number of you come, and yet there are some among you who are so strong that they have not come once in five years. But you should go because you are the ones who need it most of all! And above all note these words, "for the remission of sins," as the pledge of the sacrament which assures us that we have the forgiveness of sins because it is proclaimed, not to a stone, but to you and to me. Otherwise the minister might as well keep silent. I remind you again of this small particle: "for you." Remember to include yourself in this "for you." Therefore let each one see to it that he comes to the sacrament himself and his family, if they want to be Christians. When you stay away so much, now that you have liberty to go to the sacrament, we see the attitude with which you came to it under the pope, when you came only by coercion. As only a few do good works, so only a few go to the sacrament. Formerly we were forced to go because we were driven. But now that nobody compels us we neglect it. I do not compel you to come to the preaching. But God ought to move you to come; for He requires it of you that you should hear and learn His Word. If you don't want to obey Him, [then don't]. So neither do I compel you to come to the sacrament. What does it matter to me and the chaplains if you don't want to listen and receive the sacrament? You have four doors here—go on out! But He who is above says: If you want to be a Christian, if you want to have forgiveness of sins and eternal life, then come here! There stands your God; He offers you His body and blood, broken and shed for you. If you want to despise God and neglect the forgiveness of sins, then stay away. So I do not compel you, but Christ pleads with you lovingly. If you despise this, then you see to it! We are saying what your God is offering to you. Accordingly, I beg you to hold to the sacrament, for your sakes, not ours. There are now few boys and girls and women who come. I know that you are not holier than Peter. It really grieves me that you are so cold in your attitude toward it. If you will not do it for God's sake and my sake, then do it for the sake of your own necessity, which is exceedingly great, namely, your sins and death. There is the temptation of adultery, of fornication, avarice, hatred, pride, envy, of unbelief and despair, and you do not consider how you are ever going to get out of them, and you grow altogether cold in that ungodliness. But listen to what Christ says here: "for you." He did not give it to you as a poison; He did not say: Take and eat, this shall be your poison, or that this food should harm us, but rather free us from sin, devil, and death. But that's the attitude we take, as if it were poison. Here you have medicine, not poison. When a person is sick he can soon find an apothecary, a doctor. But who seeks this physician, who has given His body? Do you still not see your sickness; don't you want forgiveness of sins? Why do you avoid it as if it were poison? It is true that it is poison to those who sin, as formerly the priests committed fornication. But in itself it is not a poison but an antidote, which means salvation, blessedness, life, forgiveness of sins. Certainly you will find that you are full of envy, inclined to all kinds of villainy, to greed and the like. You fear death, you sense your unbelief. This certainly is lack enough. Then say: the sacrament is not given to those who are sick as a poison but as a remedy. See to it, then, that you seek the sacrament for your betterment when you find yourself in an hour of peril of life, when the flesh drives you, the world entices you, and Satan assails you. And beyond this it is of even greater benefit, etc.

Therefore, do not be so cold toward it. We are not forcing you, but you ought to come of your own free will. It is my duty to instruct you as to the reason why you should come, namely, your need, not a command, for you feel the infirmity of your faith and your propensity to all evil. These perils should move you without any command whatsoever. It is not the pope, not the emperor, not the duke who compels me, but my own need compels me. Therefore, take a better attitude now toward the sacrament and also keep your children to it when they come to understanding. For this is how we know which are Christians and which are not. If you will not go, then let the young people come; for us so much depends upon them. If you do not do it, we shall take action against you. For even if you adults want to go to the devil, we shall nevertheless seek after your children.

The need [which drives us to the sacrament] is that sin, devil, and death are always present. The benefit is that we receive forgiveness of sins and the Holy Spirit. Here, not poison, but a remedy and salvation is given, insofar as you acknowledge that you need it. Don't say: I am not fit today, I will wait awhile. This is a trick of the devil. What will you do if you are not fit when death comes? Who will make you fit then? Say rather: Neither preacher, prince, pope, nor emperor compels me, but my great need and, beyond this, the benefit.

First, the sacrament is Christ's body and blood in bread and wine comprehended in the Word. Secondly, the benefit is forgiveness of sins. This includes the need and the benefit. Thirdly, those who believe should come.

ON CROSS AND SUFFERING

Preached on the Saturday before Easter,
Based on the Passion History

A HARMONY OF MATTHEW 27, LUKE 25, AND JOHN 19

1530*

So in our suffering we should so act that we give our greatest attention to the promise, in order that our cross and affliction may be turned to good, to something which we could never have asked or thought. And this is precisely the thing which makes a difference between the Christian's suffering and afflictions and those of all other men.

Dear friends, you know that it is customary in this season to preach on the passion, so I have no doubt that you have heard many times what kind of passion and suffering it was. You have also heard why it was that God the Father ordained it, namely, that through it He wanted to help, not the person for Christ, for Christ had no need at all for this suffering; but we and the whole human race needed this suffering. Thus it was a gift which was given and presented to us out of pure grace and mercy. But we shall not deal with these points now, for I have often spoken of them on other occasions.

But since there are many false fanatics abroad, who only distort the gospel and accuse us and say that we have nothing else to teach and preach except faith alone, that we leave out the doctrine of good works and the holy cross and suffering—and they also say that they have the true Spirit, who moves them to teach as they do—we shall at this time speak only of the example which this passion gives to us, what kind of cross we bear and suffer, and also how we should bear and suffer it.

Therefore we must note in the first place that Christ by His suf-

*This sermon was preached on the day after Luther's arrival at Feste Coburg, [April 16] where he stayed during the Diet of Augsburg, at which the Augsburg Confession was presented.

fering not only saved us from the devil, death, and sin, but also that His suffering is an example, which we are to follow in our suffering. Though our suffering and cross should never be so exalted that we think we can be saved by it or earn the least merit through it, nevertheless we should suffer after Christ, that we may be conformed to Him. For God has appointed that we should not only believe in the crucified Christ, but also be crucified with Him, as He clearly shows in many places in the gospels: "He who does not take His cross and follow Me," He says, "is not worthy of Me" [Matt. 10:38]. And again: "If they have called the master of the house Beelzebul, how much more will they malign those of his household" [Matt. 10:25].

Therefore each one must bear a part of the holy cross; nor can it be otherwise. St. Paul too says, "In my flesh I complete what is lacking in Christ's afflictions" [Col. 1:24]. It is as if he were saying: His whole Christendom is not fully completed; we too must follow after, in order that none of the suffering of Christ may be lacking or lost, but all brought together into one. Therefore every Christian must be aware that suffering will not fail to come.

It should be, however, and must be the kind of suffering that is worthy of the name and honestly grips and hurts, such as some great danger of property, honor, body, and life. Such suffering as we really feel, which weighs us down; otherwise, if it did not hurt us badly, it would not be suffering.

Beyond this, it should be the kind of suffering which we have not chosen ourselves, as the fanatics choose their own suffering. It should be the kind of suffering which, if it were possible, we would gladly be rid of, suffering visited upon us by the devil or the world. Then what is needed is to hold fast and submit oneself to it, as I have said, namely, that one know that we must suffer, in order that we may thus be conformed to Christ, and that it cannot be otherwise, that everyone must have his cross and suffering.

When one knows this it is the more easy and bearable, and one can comfort oneself by saying: Very well, if I want to be a Christian, I must also wear the colors of the court; the dear Christ issues no others in His court; suffering there must be.

This the fanatics, who select their own cross, cannot do; they resist it and fight against it. What a fine and admirable suffering that is! And yet they can reproach us, as if we did not teach aright concerning suffering and they alone can do it. But our teaching is this, that none should dictate or choose his own cross and suffering, but rather, when it comes, patiently bear and suffer it.

But they are wrong, not only with respect to their choosing their own cross, but also in that they flaunt their suffering and make a great merit of it and thus blaspheme God, because it is not a true suffering but a stinking, self-chosen suffering. But we say that we earn nothing by our suffering and therefore do not frame it in such beautiful monstrances as they do. It is enough that we know that it pleases God that we suffer in order that we may be conformed to Christ, as I have said.

So we see that the very ones who boast and teach so much about cross and suffering know the least either about the cross or of Christ, because they make their own suffering meritorious. Dear friends, it isn't that kind of thing at all; nor is anybody forced or compelled to it. If you don't want to do it for nothing and without any merit, then you can let it lie and so deny Christ. The way is at hand, but you must know that if you refuse to suffer you will also not become Christ's courtier. So you may do either one of these two, either suffer or deny Christ.

If you are willing to suffer, very well, then the treasure and consolation which is promised and given to you is so great that you ought to suffer willingly and joyfully because Christ and His suffering is being bestowed upon you and made your own. And if you can believe this, then in time of great fear and trouble you will be able to say: Even though I suffer long, very well then, what is that compared with that great treasure which my God has given to me, that I shall live eternally with Him?

Look what happens then: the suffering would be sweet and easy and no longer an eternal suffering, but only a modicum which lasts only a short time and soon passes away, as St. Paul [2 Cor. 4:17], and St. Peter [1 Pet. 1:6], and also Christ Himself says in the gospels [John 16:16–22]. For they look to that great, immeasurable gift, which is that Christ with His suffering and merit has become altogether ours. Thus the suffering of Christ has become so mighty and strong that it fills heaven and earth and breaks the power and might of the devil and hell, of death and sin. And then if you compare this treasure with your affliction and suffering, you will consider it but small loss to lose a little property, honor, health, wife, child, and even your own life. But if you refuse to regard this treasure and to suffer for it, so be it; go on and let it lie. He who does not believe will also receive none of these unspeakable goods and gifts.

Furthermore, every Christian should submit himself to this suffering that he is sure that it will work for his good and that Christ, for His Word's sake, will not only help us to bear this suffering but also turn and transform it to our advantage. And again what makes this cross more agreeable and bearable for us is the fact that our dear God is ready to pour so many refreshing aromatics and cordials into our hearts that we are able to bear all our afflictions and tribulations, just as St. Paul says in 1 Cor. 10 [:13], "God is faithful, and He will not let you be tempted beyond your strength, but with the temptation will also provide the way of escape, that you may be able to endure it." This is true. When the suffering and affliction is at its worst, it bears and presses down so grievously that one thinks he can endure no more and must surely perish. But then if you can think of Christ, the faithful God will come and will help you, as He has always helped His own from the beginning of the world; for He is the same God as He always has been.

Moreover, the cause of our suffering is the same as that for which all the saints have suffered from the beginning. Of course, the whole world must bear witness that we are not suffering because of public scandal or vice, such as adultery, fornication, murder, etc. Rather we suffer because we hold to the Word of God, preach it, hear it, learn it, and practice it. And since this is the cause of our suffering, so let it always be; we have the same promise and the same cause for suffering which all the saints have always had. So we too can comfort ourselves with the same promise and cling to it in our suffering and tribulation, as is highly necessary.

So in our suffering we should so act that we give our greatest attention to the promise, in order that our cross and affliction may be turned to good, to something which we could never have asked or thought. And this is precisely the thing which makes a difference between the Christian's suffering and afflictions and those of all other men. For other people also have their afflictions, cross, and misfortune, just as they also have their times when they can sit in the rose garden and employ their good fortune and their goods as they please. But when they run into affliction and suffering, they have nothing to comfort them, for they do not have the mighty promises and the confidence in God which Christians have. Therefore they cannot comfort themselves with the assurance that God will help them to bear the affliction; much less can they count on it that He will turn their affliction and suffering to good.

So it is, as we see, that they cannot endure even the small afflictions. But when the big, strong afflictions occur, they despair altogether, destroy themselves, or they want to jump out of their skin because the whole world has become too cramped for them. Likewise they cannot observe moderation either in fortune or misfortune. When things go well, they are the most wanton, defiant, and arrogant people you can find. When things go wrong, they are utterly shattered and despondent, more than any woman; as we see, those who are now pawing and bridling and bragging and boasting were so timid and nervous during the peasant uprising that they hardly knew where to go. So it must be when one does not have the promises and God's Word. But Christians have their consolation even in the worst of suffering and misfortune.

But in order that you may better understand this, I will give you a fine example in which the Christian's suffering is depicted. All of you are doubtless familiar with the way in which St. Christopher has at times been portrayed. But you should not think that there ever was a man who was called by that name or who actually did what is said about St. Christopher. Rather the person who devised this legend or fable was without a doubt a fine intelligent man who wanted to portray this picture for the simple people so that they would have an example and image of a Christian life and how it should be lived. And actually he did hit it off very well; for a Christian is like a great giant; he has great strong legs and arms, as Christopher is painted, for he bears a burden which the whole world, which no emperor, king, nor prince could carry. Therefore every Christian is a Christopher, that is, a Christ-bearer,[40] because he accepts the faith.

How goes it then with him? This way: when a man accepts the

---

[40] "Christopher" is derived from the Greek contraction of the name of Christ (*Christos*) and the verb *pherein* (to bear).

faith, he does not allow himself to think of it as something burdensome. He thinks of it as being like a little child, which is beautiful and well formed and easy to carry, as Christopher found. For at first the gospel looks like a fine, pleasant, and childlike teaching; as we saw at the beginning, when it started everybody got cracking and wanted to be an Evangelical. There was such a yearning and thirst for it that no oven is as hot as the people were then. But what happened? The same thing that happened with Christopher. He did not find out how heavy the child was until he got into the deep water.

So it was with the gospel; when it began to take hold, the waves rolled out and pope, bishops, princes, and the crazy rabble set themselves against it. Then we first began to feel how heavy the child is to carry. For it came so close to the good Christopher that he came very near to drowning. As you see, the same thing is happening now; on the other side, which is against the Word, there are so many tricks and stratagems, so much deceit and cunning, everything aimed at one purpose, to drown us in the water. There is such threatening and terror that we would be frightened to death if we did not have another consolation to oppose to it.

All right, then, anybody who has taken upon himself the burden of the Christ, the beloved child, must either carry Him all the way across the water or drown; there is no middle way. It's no good to drown; therefore we'll go through the water with the Christ, even though it looks again as though we would have to stay in it. After all, we have the promise that he who has Christ and relies and believes on Him can boldly say with David in Psalm 27, "Though a host encamp against me, my heart shall not fear; though war arise against me, yet will I be confident." Let them paw and stamp their feet, let them threaten and frighten as they please; were the water never so deep we shall nevertheless go through it with Christ.

So it is with all other things; when it gets going it becomes too heavy, whether it be sin, devil, hell, or even our own conscience. But how are we going to do it? Where shall we go and hide ourselves? For us it looks as if the whole thing would fall to the ground. But on the other side they are confident and proud; they think they already have won the day. I too see the good Christopher sinking; nevertheless he gets through, for he has a tree which he holds on to. This tree is the promise that Christ will do something remarkable with our suffering. "In the world," He says, "you shall have afflictions and tribulations, but in Me you shall have peace" [cf. John 16:33]. And St. Paul says, "We have a faithful God who helps us out of affliction, so that we can bear it" [cf. 1 Cor. 10:13]. These sayings are staves, yea, trees, which we can hold on to and let the waters roar and foam as they will.

So in Christopher we have an example and a picture that can strengthen us in our suffering and teach us that fear and trembling is not as great as the comfort and the promise, and that we should therefore know that in this life we shall have no rest if we are bearing Christ, but rather that in affliction we should turn our eyes away from the present suffering to the consolation and promise. Then we will learn that what Christ says is true: "In Me you shall have peace" [John 16:33].

For this is the Christian art, which we must all learn, the art of looking to the Word and looking away from all the trouble and suffering that lies upon us and weighs us down. But the flesh is utterly incapable of this art, it sees no farther than the present suffering. For this also is the way of the devil; he removes the Word far from one's eyes, so that one sees nothing but the present difficulty, just as he is doing with us now. What he wants is that we should deny and forget the Word altogether and gaze only at the danger which threatens us from the pope and the Turks. Then if he wins the play, he drowns us in the difficulty, so that we see nothing but its rush and roar. But this should not be. For this is what happens: when a person wants to be a Christian and acts according to his feelings, he soon loses Christ. Drive the suffering and cross from your heart and mind as quickly as you can; otherwise, if you think about it for long, the evil grows worse. If you have affliction and suffering, say: I have myself not chosen and prepared this cross; it is because of the Word of God that I am suffering and that I have and teach Christ. So let it be in God's name. I will let Him take care of it and fight it out who long ago foretold that I should have this suffering and promised me His divine and gracious help.

If you give yourself to scripture, you will feel comfort and all your concerns will be better, which otherwise you cannot control by any act or means of your own. After all, a merchant can bring himself, for the sake of gaining money and wealth, to leave house and home, wife and child, and risk his life for the sake of filthy lucre, and still have no sure promise or assurance that he will return home in health to wife and child; and yet he is foolhardy and rash enough to venture boldly into such danger without any promise whatsoever. Now, if a merchant can do that for money and riches, fie upon you, that we should not want to bear a little cross and still want to be Christians, even though, besides, we have in our hands the tree to which we cling against the waves, namely, the Word and the fine strong promises that we shall not be over- whelmed by the waves.

So the knight does too. He surrenders himself to battle, where innumerable spears, halberds, and firearms are directed against him. He too has no promise with which to console himself except his own mad spirit; and yet he goes on, even though his whole life is nothing but hard living and hard suffering.

And so it is with the papists too. They grudge no effort or labor to reestablish their abomination and idolatry. How often, just since the time when the gospel has been proclaimed anew, have they taken counsel together, even to this day, one deliberation after another, all of which have failed and fallen to ashes. And yet they want to imagine and are even sure they can sing this thing away and suppress the Word of God, so in sheer foolhardiness they go into it.

Now if merchants, knights, papists, and such riffraff can muster up such courage to take upon themselves and suffer such peril, effort, and labor, we should be simply ashamed that we rebel against suffering and the cross, even though we know, in the first place, that God has appointed that we should suffer and that it cannot be otherwise. In the second place, we also know our promise and assurance, that even though we are not such good Christians as we ought to be and are timid and weak both in life and faith, He will nevertheless defend His Word simply because it is His Word. Therefore we know that we can quite rightly bid defi- ance and say: Even though there were ten popes or Turkish emperors, I would like to see whether all of them together are a match for the Man who is called Christ. They may very well start a game which will grow too big for them to handle, but they will not demolish the Word. And this will happen even though we are weak in faith.

This then is the true art, that in suffering and cross we should look to the Word and the comforting assurance, and trust them, even as He said, "In Me you shall have peace, but in the world, tribulation" [cf. John 16:33]. It is as if He were saying: Danger and terror will surely hit you if you accept My Word; but let it come, this will happen to you because of Me. So be of good cheer; I will not forsake you, I will be with you and will help you. No matter how great the affliction may be, it will be small and light for you, if you are able to draw such thoughts from the Word of God.

Therefore in affliction every Christian should so arm himself that he may defend and guard himself with the fine, comfortable assurances which Christ, our dear Lord, has left us when we suffer for His Word's sake. But if we do not do this, if we let the comforting sayings go, then when the cross comes, the same thing that happened to Eve in paradise will happen to us. She had God's commandment and with it she should have beaten down the devil's suggestions and instigations. But what did she do? She let the Word go and kept thinking what a fine apple it was and that after all, such a little thing was of no great importance. So she went her way. And when one lets the Word go, there can be no other result. But when we stay with the Word and hold on to it, we shall certainly have the experience of conquering and coming out of it fine.

You see that we teach these two things when we preach on suffering and cross. And anybody who accuses us of teaching nothing about suffering is doing us an injustice. But this we do not do; we do not make our suffering meritorious before God. No, far from it. Christ alone did that and nobody else, and to Him alone belongs the glory.

In the third place we want also to consider why it is that our Lord God sends us such suffering. And the reason is that in this way He wants to make us conformed to the image of His dear Son, Christ, so that we may become like Him here in suffering, and there in that life to come in honor and glory [cf. Rom. 8:29; 8:17; 2 Tim. 2:11–12], as He says, "Was it not necessary that the Christ should suffer and enter into glory?" [cf. Luke 24:26]. But God cannot accomplish this in us except through suffering and affliction, which He sends to us through the devil or other wicked people.

The second reason is this, that even though God does not want to assault and torment us, the devil does, and he cannot abide the

Word. He is by nature so malicious and venomous that he cannot endure anything which is good. It irks him that an apple should be growing on a tree; it pains and vexes him that you have a sound finger, and if he were able he would tear everything apart and put it out of joint.

But there is nothing to which he is so hostile as the beloved Word. And the reason is that he can conceal himself beneath every created thing; only the Word exposes him so that he cannot hide himself, and shows everybody how black he is. Then he fights back and resists and draws together the princes and the bishops, thinking thus to conceal himself again. But it is of no avail; the Word nevertheless drags him out into the light. Therefore he too does not rest, and because the gospel cannot suffer him, so he cannot suffer the gospel, and that makes it equal. And if our dear God were not guarding us through His angels and we were able to see the devil's cunning, conspiring, and lying, we should die of the sight of it alone, so many are the cannon and guns he has ranged against us. But God prevents them from striking us.

So the two heroes meet, each doing as much as possible. The devil brews one calamity after another; for he is a mighty, malicious, and turbulent spirit. So it is time that our dear God be concerned about His honor; for the Word which we wield is a weak and miserable Word, and we who have and wield it are also weak and miserable men, bearing the treasure as Paul says [2 Cor. 4:7], in earthen vessels, which can easily be shattered and broken. Therefore the evil spirit spares no effort and confidently lashes out to see if he can smash the little vessel; for there it is under his nose and he cannot stand it. So the battle really begins in earnest, with water and fire to dampen and quench the little spark. Then our Lord God looks on for a while and puts us in a tight place, so that we may learn from our own experience that the small, weak, miserable Word is stronger than the devil and the gates of hell. They are to storm the castle, the devil and his cohorts. But let them storm; they will find something there that will make them sweat, and still they will not gain it; for it is a rock, as Christ calls it, which cannot be conquered. So let us suffer what comes upon us and thus we shall learn that God will stand by us to guard and shield us against this enemy and all his adherents.

Thirdly, it is also highly necessary that we suffer not only that

God may prove His honor, power, and strength against the devil, but also in order that when we are not in trouble and suffering this excellent treasure which we have may not merely make us sleepy and secure. We see so many people—unfortunately it is all too common—so misusing the gospel that it is a sin and a shame, as if now, of course, they have been so liberated by the gospel that there is no further need to do anything, give anything, or suffer anything.

This kind of wickedness our God cannot check except through suffering. Hence He must keep disciplining and driving us, that our faith may increase and grow stronger and thus bring the Savior more deeply into our hearts. For just as we cannot get along without eating and drinking, so we cannot get along without affliction and suffering. Therefore we must necessarily be afflicted of the devil by persecution or else by a secret thorn which thrusts into the heart, as also St. Paul laments [cf. 2 Cor. 12:7]. Therefore, since it is better to have a cross than to be without one, nobody should dread or be afraid of it. After all, you have a good strong promise with which to comfort yourself. Besides, the gospel cannot come to the fore except through and in suffering and cross.

Lastly, Christian suffering is nobler and precious above all other human suffering because, since Christ Himself suffered, He also hallowed the suffering of all His Christians. Are we not then poor, foolish people? We have run to Rome, Trier, and other places to visit the shrines; why do we not also cherish cross and suffering, which was much nearer to Christ and touched Him more closely than any garment did His body? This touched not only His body but His heart. Through the suffering of Christ, the suffering of all His saints has become utterly holy, for it has been touched with Christ's suffering. Therefore we should accept all suffering as a holy thing, for it is truly holiness.

Since we know then that it is God's good pleasure that we should suffer, and that God's glory is manifested in our suffering better than in any other way, and since we are the kind of people who cannot hold on to the Word and our faith without suffering, and moreover since we have the noble, previous promise that the cross which God sends to us is not a bad thing, but rather an utterly precious and noble holy thing, why should we not be bold to suffer? As for those who will not suffer, let them go and be cavaliers; we preach this only to the devout who want to be Christians, the others wouldn't carry it out anyhow. After all, we have so many assurances and promises that He will not allow us to stick in our suffering but will help us out of it, even though all men should doubt it. Therefore, even though it hurts, so be it, you have to go through some suffering anyhow; things cannot always go smoothly. It is just as well, nay, a thousand times better, to have suffered for the sake of Christ, who promised us comfort and help in suffering, than to suffer and despair and perish without comfort and help for the sake of the devil.

This, you see, is the way we teach concerning suffering, and you should also accustom yourself to distinguish carefully between the suffering of Christ and all other suffering and know that His is a heavenly suffering and ours is worldly, that His suffering accomplishes everything, while ours does nothing except that we become conformed to Christ, and that therefore the suffering of Christ is the suffering of a lord, whereas ours is the suffering of a servant. And those who teach otherwise know neither what Christ's suffering nor our suffering is. Why? Because reason cannot do otherwise; it likes to put on a display with its suffering, as with all other works, so that it may gain some merit. That's why we must learn to distinguish. We have said enough for this time concerning the example of the passion and our suffering. God grant that we may understand and learn it aright. Amen.

OF CHRIST'S RESURRECTION

For although we feel that sin is still in us, it is only permitted that our faith may be developed and strengthened, that in spite of all our feelings we accept the Word, and that we unite our hearts and consciences more and more to Christ. Thus faith leads us quietly, contrary to all feeling and comprehension of reason, through sin, through death, and through hell. Then we shall see salvation before our eyes, and then we shall know perfectly what we have believed, namely, that death and all sorrow have been conquered.

I. The Story of Christ's Resurrection

1. In the first place we shall briefly examine the text of this narrative, and afterward speak of the benefits of the Resurrection of Christ, and how we should build upon it. The text reads: "And when the sabbath was past." Here we must remember Mark writes of the sabbath according to the custom of the Hebrews, for according to the Jewish reckoning, the day began in the evening and lasted until the evening of the next day, as the first chapter of Genesis says: "And there was evening and there was morning, one day," "a second day," "a third day," and so forth. Thus the first and greatest sabbath began on the evening of the day when Christ was crucified, that is to say, at the time of sunset on the evening of Friday. Our reckoning conveys the wrong sense. Yesterday was the great sabbath, when Christ lay in the grave; in addition to this the Jews had seven full days which they celebrated, all of which they called sabbaths, counting them from the first holiday after the great sabbath and calling it *prima sabbatorum* (first of the sabbaths), and the third holiday *secunda sabbatorum* (second of the sabbaths), and so forth. On these days they ate only wafers and unleavened bread, for which reason they are also called by the evangelist the days of unleavened bread. From this we must conclude that Christ rose before sunrise and before the angel descended in the earthquake. Afterward the angel only came to open the empty grave, etc., as has been clearly described by the evangelists.

2. The question now arises: how can we say that He rose on the third day, since He lay in the grave only one day and two nights? According to the Jewish calculation it was only a day and a half; how shall we then persist in believing there were three days? To this we reply that He was in the state of death for at least a part of all three days. For He died at about two o'clock on Friday and consequently was dead for about two hours on the first day. After that night He lay in the grave all day, which is the true sabbath. On the third day, which we commemorate now, He rose from the dead and so remained in the state of death a part of this day, just as if we say that something occurred on Easter Day, although it happens in the evening, only a portion of the day. In this sense Paul and the evangelists say that He rose on the third day.

3. For this period and no longer Christ was to lie in the grave, so that we might suppose that His body remained naturally uncorrupted and that decomposition had not yet set in. He came forth from the grave so soon that we might presume that corruption had not yet taken place according to the course of nature; for a corpse can lie no longer than three days before it begins to decompose. Therefore Christ was to rise on the third day, before He saw corruption.

4. The great longing and love of the women for the Lord must also be particularly noted here, so that unadvised and alone they go early to the grave, not thinking of the great stone which was rolled before the tomb. They might have thought of this and taken a man with them. But they act like timid and sorrowing persons, and therefore they go on their way without even thinking of the most necessary things. They do not even think of the watchers who were clad in armor, nor of the wrath of Pilate and the Jews, but boldly they freely risk it and alone they venture on their way. What urged these good women to hazard life and body? It was nothing but the great love they bore to the Lord, which had sunk so deeply into their hearts that for His sake they would have risked a thousand lives. Such courage they had not of themselves, but here the power of the Resurrection of Christ was revealed, whose Spirit makes these women, who by nature are timid, so bold and courageous that they venture to do things which might have daunted a man.

5. These women also show us a beautiful example of a spiritual heart that undertakes an impossible task of which the whole world would despair. Yet a heart like this stands firm and accomplishes it, not thinking the task impossible. So much we say for the present on this narrative, and now let us see what are the fruits and benefits of the Resurrection of Christ.

II. The Fruits and Benefits of the Resurrection of Christ

6. St. Paul writes in Rom. 4:25 as follows: "Christ was delivered up for our trespasses, and was raised for our justification." Paul is indeed the man who extols Christ in a masterly manner, telling us exactly why and for what purpose He suffered and how we should

conform ourselves to His sufferings, namely, that He died for our sins. This is a correct interpretation of the sufferings of Christ, by which we may profit. And as it is not sufficient to know and believe that Christ has died, so it will not suffice to know and believe that He rose with a transfigured body and is now in a state of joy and blessedness, no longer subject to mortality, for all this would profit me nothing or very little. But when I come to understand the fact that all the works God does in Christ are done for me—nay, they are bestowed upon and given to me, the effect of His Resurrection being that I also will arise and live with Him—that will cause me to rejoice. This must be brought home to our hearts, and we must not merely hear it with the ears of our body or merely confess it with our mouth.

7.   You have heard in the story of the passion how Christ is portrayed as our exemplar and helper, and that He who follows Him and clings to Him receives the Spirit, who will enable him also to suffer. But the words of Paul are more Christian and should come closer home to our hearts and comfort us more, when he says: "Christ was raised for our justification." Here the Lamb is truly revealed, of whom John the Baptist testifies, when he says in John 1:29: "Behold the Lamb of God that taketh away the sin of the world." Here is fulfilled that which was spoken to the serpent: "I will put enmity between thee and the woman, and between thy seed and her seed: he shall bruise thy head," which means that for all those who believe in Him, hell, death, and the devil and sin have been destroyed. In the same manner the promise is fulfilled today which God gave to Abraham when He said in Gen. 22:18: "In Thy seed shall all the nations of the earth be blessed." Here Christ is meant, who takes away our curse and the power of sin, death, and the devil.

8.   All this is done, I say, by faith. For if you believe that by this seed the serpent has been slain, then it is slain for you; and if you believe that in this seed all nations are to be blessed, then you are also blessed. For each one individually should have crushed the serpent underfoot and redeemed himself from the curse, which would have been too difficult, nay impossible for us. But now it has been done easily, namely, by Christ, who has crushed the serpent once, who alone is given as a blessing and benediction, and

who has caused this gospel to be published throughout the world, so that he who believes, accepts it, and clings to it is also in possession of it, and is assured that it is as he believes. For in the heart of such a man the Word becomes so powerful that he will conquer death, the devil, sin, and all adversity, as Christ Himself did. So mighty is the Word that God Himself would sooner be vanquished than that His Word should be conquered.

9. This is the meaning of the words of St. Paul: "Christ was raised for our justification." Here Paul turns my eyes away from my sins and directs them to Christ, for if I look at my sins, they will destroy me. Therefore I must look unto Christ, who has taken my sins upon Himself, crushed the head of the serpent, and become the blessing. Now they no longer burden my conscience, but rest upon Christ, whom they desire to destroy. Let us see how they treat Him. They hurl Him to the ground and kill Him. O God; where is now my Christ and my Savior? But then God appears, delivers Christ, and makes Him alive; and not only does He make Him alive, but He translates Him into heaven and lets Him rule over all. What has now become of sin? There it lies under His feet. If I then cling to this, I have a cheerful conscience like Christ, because I am without sin. Now I can defy death, the devil, sin, and hell to do me any harm. As I am a child of Adam, they can indeed accomplish it that I must die. But since Christ has taken my sins upon Himself, has died for them, has suffered Himself to be slain on account of my sins, they can no longer harm me; for Christ is too strong for them, they cannot keep Him; He breaks forth and overpowers them, ascends into heaven, takes sin and sorrow captive, and rules there over all throughout eternity. Now I have a clear conscience, am joyful and happy and am no longer afraid of this tyrant, for Christ has taken my sins away from me and made them His own. But they cannot remain upon Him; what then becomes of them? They must disappear and be destroyed. This then is the effect of faith. He who believes that Christ has taken away our sin is without sin, like Christ Himself, and death, the devil, and hell are vanquished as far as he is concerned and they can no longer harm him.

10. Here we also refer to the passage in Hos. 13:14, which Paul quotes in reference to the victory that Christ has won by His Resur-

rection and by which He has conquered sin, death, hell, and all our enemies. Paul says that death is swallowed up in this victory, and he defies death with these words: "O death, where is thy victory? O death, where is thy sting?" just as if Paul would say: O death, where are thy teeth? Come, bite off one of my fingers. Thou formerly hadst a spear, what has become of it now? Christ has taken it from thee. Death, where is now thy spear, etc.? Sin, where is now the edge of thy sword and thy power? Paul says that the power of sin is the law. The more clearly we understand the law, the more sin oppresses and stings us. For this reason Paul says that Christ has completely destroyed and annihilated the spear and whetstone of death. Now, this gospel He has not taken with Him into heaven, but He caused it to be preached throughout the world, so that for him who believes in Christ, spear and whetstone, nay, sin and death, should be destroyed. This is the true gospel, which bestows life, strength, power, and marrow, and of which all the passages of scripture speak.

11. Therefore seek and learn to know Christ aright, for the whole scriptures confer upon us the righteousness of the true knowledge of Christ. But this must be brought about by the Holy Spirit. Let us therefore pray God that His gospel may prosper, that we all may truly learn to know Christ and thus rise with Him and be honored by God as He was honored.

12. The question now arises: if Christ has taken away death and our sins by His Resurrection and has justified us, why do we then still feel death and sin within us? For our sins torment us still, we are stung by our conscience, and this evil conscience creates the fear of hell.

13. To this I reply: I have often said before that feeling and faith are two different things. It is the nature of faith not to feel, to lay aside reason and close the eyes, to submit absolutely to the Word, and follow it in life and death. Feeling, however, does not extend beyond that which may be apprehended by reason and the senses, which may be heard, seen, felt, and known by the outward senses; for this cause feeling is opposed to faith and faith is opposed to feeling. Therefore the author of the epistle to the Hebrews writes

of faith: "Now faith is assurance of things hoped for, a conviction of things not seen." For if we would see Christ visibly in heaven, like the visible sun, we would not need to believe it. But since Christ died for our sins and was raised for our justification, we cannot see it or feel it, neither can we comprehend it with our reason. Therefore we must disregard our feeling and accept only the Word, write it into our heart, and cling to it, even though it seems as if my sins were not taken from me, and even though I still feel them within me. Our feelings must not be considered, but we must constantly insist that death, sin, and hell have been conquered, although I feel that I am still under the power of death, sin, and hell. For although we feel that sin is still in us, it is only permitted that our faith may be developed and strengthened, so that in spite of all our feelings we accept the Word and unite our hearts and consciences more and more to Christ. Thus faith leads us quietly, contrary to all feeling and comprehension of reason, through sin, through death, and through hell. Then we shall see salvation before our eyes, and then we shall know perfectly what we have believed, namely, that death and all sorrow have been conquered.

14. Take as an illustration the fish in the water. When they are caught in the net, you lead it quietly along, so that they imagine they are still in the water; but when you draw them to the shore, they are exposed and begin to struggle, and then they first feel they are caught. Thus it also happens with souls that are caught with the gospel, which Christ compares with a net, Matt. 13:47. When the heart has been conquered, the Word unites this poor heart to Christ and leads it gently and quietly from hell and from sin, although the soul still feels sin and imagines to be still under its power. Then a conflict begins, the feelings struggling against the Spirit and faith, and the Spirit and faith against our feelings; and the more faith increases, the more our feelings diminish, and vice versa. We have still sins within us, as for instance pride, avarice, anger, and so forth, but only in order to lead us to faith, so that faith may increase from day to day, and the man become finally a thorough Christian and keep the true sabbath, consecrating himself to Christ entirely. Then the conscience must become calm and satisfied and all the surging waves of sin subside. For as upon the

sea one billow follows and buffets the other, as though they would destroy the shore, yet they must disappear and destroy themselves, so also our sins strive against us and would fain bring us to despair, but finally they must desist, grow weary, and disappear.

15. In the second place, death is still at our elbow. It also is to exercise the faith of him who believes that death has been killed and all his power taken away. Now, reason feels that death is still at our elbow and is continually troubling us. He who follows his feelings will perish, but he who clings to the Word with his heart will be delivered. Now, if the heart clings to the Word, reason will also follow; but if reason follows, everything will follow, desire and love and all that is in man. Yea, we desire that all may come to the point when they may consider death to be dead and powerless. But this cannot come to pass until the old man, that is, the old Adam, be entirely destroyed, and meanwhile that process has been going on of which Christ speaks in Matt. 13:33, where He compares the kingdom of God to leaven, which a woman took and hid in three measures of meal. For even if the kneading has begun, the meal is not yet thoroughly leavened. So it is here. Although the heart clings to the belief that death and hell are destroyed, yet the leaven has not yet worked through it entirely. For it must penetrate and impregnate all the members of the body, until everything becomes leavened and pure and there remains nothing but a pure faith. This will not be brought about before the old man is entirely destroyed; then all that is in man is Christlike from center to circumference.

16. These two things, sin and death, therefore, remain with us to the end that we might cultivate and exercise our faith, in order that it may become more perfect in our heart from day to day and finally break forth, and all that we are, body and soul, become more Christlike. For when the heart clings to the Word, feelings and reasoning must fail. Then in the course of time the will also clings to the Word, and with the will everything else, our desire and love, till we surrender ourselves entirely to the gospel, are renewed, and leave the old sin behind. Then there comes a different light, different feelings, different seeing, different hearing, acting and speaking, and also a different outflow of good works. Now, our scholastics and papists have taught an external piety;

they would command the eyes not to see and the ears not to hear, and would put piety into our hearts from the outside. Ah, how far this is from the truth! But it comes in this way: when the heart and conscience cling to the Word in faith, they overflow in works, so that, when the heart is holy, all the members become holy, and good works follow naturally.

17. This is signified by the sabbath that was to be hallowed and on which the Lord lay quietly in the grave. It signifies that we should rest from all our works, should not stir, nay, should not allow any sin to stir within us, but we should firmly believe that death, hell, sin, and the devil are destroyed by the death of Christ, and we are righteous, pious, holy, and therefore contented, experiencing no longer any sin. Then all the members are calm and quiet, being convinced that sin and death are vanquished and prostrated. But this cannot be brought about, as I have said, until this impotent, wretched body and the old Adam are destroyed. Therefore it is indeed necessary that we are required to keep this sabbath. For as Christ lies in the grave on the sabbath, never feels or moves, so it must be with us, as we have heard: our feelings and actions must cease. And I say again that this cannot be accomplished before the old Adam is annihilated. Nevertheless we still experience sin and death within us, wrestle with them, and fight against them. You may tie a hog ever so well, but you cannot prevent it from grunting until it is strangled and killed. Thus it is with the sins in our flesh. As they are not yet entirely conquered and killed, they are still active, but when death comes, they must also die, and then we are perfect Christians and pure, but not before. This is the reason why we must die, namely, that we may be entirely freed from sin and death. These words on the fruits of the Resurrection of Christ may suffice for the present, and with them we will close. Let us pray God for grace that we may understand them and learn to know Christ aright.

SECOND SUNDAY AFTER EASTER —
MISERICORDIAS DOMINI

When I feel death approaching and know that I must die as do also those who do not believe in Christ, that makes no real difference. I still have the voice of my Shepherd, who has given me the most gracious promise, "Whoever keeps My word shall never see death." Also, "I lay down my life for the sheep." That is why I will never doubt that my faithful Shepherd knows me.

JOHN 10:11–16

I am the Good Shepherd: the Good Shepherd giveth His life for the sheep. But he that is an hireling, and not the Shepherd, whose own the sheep are not, seeth the wolf coming, and leaveth the sheep, and fleeth: and the wolf catcheth them, and scattereth the sheep. The hireling fleeth, because he is an hireling, and careth not for the sheep. I am the Good Shepherd, and know My sheep, and am known of Mine. As the Father knoweth Me, even so know I the Father: and I lay down My life for the sheep. And other sheep I have, which are not of this fold: them also I must bring, and they shall hear My voice; and there shall be one fold, and one Shepherd.

1. Our dear Lord Jesus Christ commenced the sermon on this gospel at the beginning of this chapter, basing it on the nature and characteristics of sheep. For the Lord God so created sheep that among all animals on earth there is none with better, sharper hearing than a sheep, as experience teaches. Suppose there are ten thousand men gathered together; a sheep will become skittish and run away except at the voice of its shepherd, which it recognizes and follows after, so certain, so acute is its awareness of the shepherd's voice. Similarly, there may be a thousand sheep in a flock, with all the ewes bleating, yet each lamb will recognize its mother's voice, and run after her until it finds her. Its hearing is extremely acute and perceptive, as I myself have often observed and wondered about.

2. Christ here takes note of this singular trait and states that He, too, has such lambs. For I am a Shepherd, He says, and My little sheep have this characteristic, to precisely recognize and know My voice. If My voice is not there, no one can lead them. With this He wants to teach us that if we wish to be Christ's sheep, we must have acute ears, ears that distinguish Christ's voice from all others, regardless how clear, beautiful, enticing, and friendly they may be.

3. From this, therefore, we ought to learn that we must not only diligently hear God's Word, but hear it in such a manner that we are immune to the input of the devil, who constantly seeks to plant all kinds of false teaching and mischief into our hearts. For a sheep not only has delicate and acute hearing, but also discriminating and sure, so that it distinguishes its shepherd's voice from all others and follows him. The sheep does not recognize a stranger's voice and so pays no attention to that voice. We are to be such little sheep and not only hear our Shepherd's voice, the voice of the Lord Jesus, but follow it faithfully and alone. Christ's voice says to us, You are a poor sinner, but I died for your sins; by clinging to Me you will be saved. We should listen to that and follow Him, always believing: That is my Shepherd's voice. If, however, we are overcome with fear and trepidation, so that our thoughts cause us to despair and forsake Christ and run away from Him, we must say to ourselves: That voice I will not hear; it is not my Shepherd, but the voice of a wolf.

4. Accordingly, with this parable of the shepherd and the sheep, our dear Lord Jesus Christ wants very much that we not only hear God's Word but also learn to hear it so exactly that we rightly distinguish it from every other word. It was tantamount to His saying, Those who hear and do God's Word know Me and are My lambs; these same little sheep are so dear to Me that I lay down My life for them and grant them eternal life; I take away their sin and death because they know Me, and I know and love them also.

5. Another reason this sermon is comforting and precious is that the Lord speaks of Himself as Shepherd over those who have and hear His Word, as His little sheep. It follows from this that we are not now, nor ever will be, forsaken, no matter how many temp-

tations and sorrows we have here on earth. One person lacks money and goods; another has poor health; a third, other problems. It seems we are surrounded by wolves and without a shepherd. It is just as Christ said to His disciples [Matt. 10:16]: "Behold I send you forth as sheep in the midst of wolves." And daily we see before our eyes that the Christian Church and Christian people are in the same predicament as the little sheep which the wolf has caught by the pelt, ready to devour it. It doesn't seem as though we have a shepherd who is concerned about us, but rather that the wolf has us in his jaws; nor do we seem at all to be so dear to Christ, but quite the opposite, the way things go in life and in death.

6. But maybe that's the way it has to be, namely, as if we actually are forsaken and without comfort, so that we may truly hear this Shepherd's piping and so learn truly to know Him. That happens when the voice says, "I know My own and My own know Me." Whoever is guided by this voice will not be dismayed when the devil makes him poor and sick, or when he is persecuted and plagued in the world; instead he hearkens to the voice of Christ, his Shepherd, calling out to him, I am your Shepherd, you are My dear little sheep, for which I have laid down My life. You hear My voice and so you recognize Me, and I know you. Such an understanding comes only from the Word and by faith, for as the Lord Himself said, "I know them, even as My Father knoweth, so even I know the Father."

7. When Christ, God's Son, walked on earth in person, it often seemed as if He were abandoned to all the devils and the most evil characters, who later also crucified Him, venting every conceivable act of malice upon Him. Surely it seemed as if God Himself had forgotten Him, that He was unaware of Him and did not know Him! Yes, it looked as if God His Father was not at home! And yet the Father did know Him, as He here says, "The Father knows Me and I know the Father." As if to say, Even when it appeared that the Father did not know Me, I nevertheless had shown that He did know Me, which in very truth He certainly did. Did He not fetch Me out of hell and rescue Me from death? So you should also act, My little sheep; don't let yourselves be led astray when it appears as if I knew you not. I do know you, My little sheep, and will not forsake you.

8. That's why Christians here on earth must, as it were, remain hidden under misfortune, heartache, sin, and all sorts of weaknesses and offenses—so much so that there may seem to be no difference between a Christian and an unbeliever. Outwardly considered, do not living and dying seem to be the same for both? Yes, sometimes it even seems that a Christian is worse off with our Lord God than a pagan! Doesn't he have more hard times, and also more offenses and temptations? But don't let that fool you; instead, keep remembering what your Shepherd says, "I know My sheep."

9. Granted, the devil and human reason interject: But how can He say that He truly knows you when things go so badly for you? Here you must reply: I am certain that He knows me, and even though I must suffer death and all kinds of misfortune, I will not let that thwart my faith; I know and hear and stay close to His voice! For even as a shepherd tenderly calls his little sheep, so Christ also encourages me: I am your Shepherd, I have laid down My life for you, I died for you! This is the Word I hear and believe. This is my one sure guarantee that He knows me and I know Him. If I should at times have different feelings than Christ here describes, that will not hurt me in the long run, for all such things are but an earthly trial. Contrariwise, here's what the Word teaches me about eternal life. When I feel death approaching and know that I must die as do also those who do not believe in Christ, that makes no real difference. I still have the voice of my Shepherd, who has given me the most gracious promise, "Whoever keeps My word shall never see death." Also, "I lay down My life for the sheep." That is why I will never doubt that my faithful Shepherd knows me.

10. Such knowing, however, is a hidden thing so that faith has space to function. Otherwise, as soon as we come from our baptism, clean and immortal, we would have no need either of the Word or faith. But because the Word is a living thing, it must be believed, even if not fully experienced, until that day when faith is no longer necessary, because then we will see and experience its reality. Never doubt, therefore, that when a man is baptized, he is as lovely and pure in God's sight as is the dear sun, no sin remaining, nothing but eternal righteousness. Christ Himself spoke that

way, "He who believes and is baptized will be saved." But this, of course, cannot be outwardly observed; regardless, however, it's true, provided we abide with the Word and the voice of the Shepherd. Everything depends, therefore, on our holding fast to the Word, remaining faithful until that blessed and eternal future when He will fully reveal what we now hear and believe from the Word. For just as our life now and hereafter in eternity involves two different ways of living, so it is impossible that in this life we can fully and entirely experience what we will feel and experience yonder.

11. Learning to know Christ is, therefore, truly a great art; there's always something new to learn. Just so, it's a great art truly to identify a Christian! Where is the man who can say that he's already experiencing eternal life? At the same time we must recognize the clear truth that a child, still laden with death, sin, and all kinds of miseries, with no visible marks of eternal life, nevertheless has begun eternal life on the day of his or her baptism. How can that be when the "old life" is still visible? Overarching that old and sinful life, God has prepared an eternal life, and it is already ours according to the Word and faith, even though we are not yet actually experiencing it. The world still sees us as sinners, even though we are righteous before God. Outwardly we are still foul, but in God's presence lovelier and brighter than the sun.

12. Recognizing a true Christian, therefore, involves far more than outward appearances; it's a matter of hearing the Word. That's exactly how it is with a little sheep; its very life depends upon hearing. If it doesn't hear the shepherd's voice, the wolves will soon be there. Without the shepherd's voice, all joy and assurance vanish and only fear and trembling remain. That's how it is also with a Christian: if he loses the Word, all comfort is gone; as long as he is faithful to the Word, he will behold Christ, his Shepherd, and therewith everything Christ has earned and promised him, namely, forgiveness of sins and eternal life. And that enables him to live out his life in full and certain hope; he eats, drinks, works, does what he is told to do, yes, will even gladly suffer whatever is laid upon him. He keeps his ears wide open for his Shepherd's voice and more and more trains himself not to judge according to what he sees and feels but solely according to the

sound of the Shepherd's voice, "I know My own and My own know Me, as the Father knows Me and I know the Father, and I lay down My life for the sheep."

13. This, then, we should learn, and we must discipline our-selves not to be offended when we see that Christians also must suffer and die like other people. Here is the true wisdom and the precious talent of Christians that they are able to say, On the sur-face, I see no difference between Christians and non-Christians; in fact, Christians are often worse off and must endure a hundred times more pain and evil than other people. On the basis of the Word, however, I see a great and outstanding difference, namely, that Christians and non-Christians differ not physically or as far as external goodness is concerned, but in this, that they have and hear the Shepherd's voice. This voice is not heard by the pagans, Turks, and Jews, or by hypocrites and false Christians who want to earn heaven by their good works; still less is His voice heard by tyrants or by that anti-Christian and luxury-loving crowd, the pope and his unspiritual followers. That voice is heard alone by the little sheep of Christ the Lord! Generally, then, judged by outward appearances and worldly standards, you will detect no difference between sheep and goats, between Christians and non-Christians.

14. The faithful and only Shepherd and Bishop of our souls, Jesus Christ, together with the Father and the Holy Spirit, grant us grace truly to recognize and follow His voice. Amen.

FIRST SUNDAY AFTER TRINITY[41]

Our old Adam remains an evil rascal. Once he knows that wealth in itself is not bad and poverty not good and that everything revolves around how a man handles them, he straightaway turns the distinction into a cover-up.

[41]Preached publicly at the parish church, 1535.

LUKE 16:19-31

There was a certain rich man, which was clothed in purple and fine linen, and fared sumptuously every day: and there was a certain beggar named Lazarus, which was laid at his gate, full of sores, and desiring to be fed with the crumbs which fell from the rich man's table: moreover the dogs came and licked his sores. And it came to pass that the beggar died, and was carried by the angels into Abraham's bosom: the rich man also died, and was buried; and in hell he lift up his eyes, being in torments, and seeth Abraham afar off, and Lazarus in his bosom. And he cried and said, Father Abraham, have mercy on me, and send Lazarus, that he may dip the tip of his finger in water and cool my tongue; for I am tormented in this flame. But Abraham said, Son, remember that thou in thy lifetime receivedst thy good things, and likewise Lazarus evil things: but now he is comforted, and thou art tormented. And beside all this, between us and you there is a great gulf fixed: so that they which would pass from hence to you cannot; neither can they pass to us, that would come from thence. Then he said, I pray thee therefore, Father, that thou wouldest send him to my father's house: For I have five brethren; that he may testify unto them, lest they also come into this place of torment. Abraham saith unto him, They have Moses and the prophets; let them hear them. And he said, Nay, Father Abraham: but if one went unto them from the dead, they will repent. And he said unto him, If they hear not Moses and the prophets, neither will they be persuaded, though one rose from the dead.

1. In this gospel lesson our Lord Jesus Christ sketches an easily understood example involving a rich man and a poor man. Everyone quickly grasps the meaning as God's judgment pertains to both of them; if only we would take it to heart and believe it.

2. Specifically and simultaneously, Christ directed this comparison against the Pharisees who were covetous. He wanted to castigate them for their greediness, not only by means of the parable and His earlier comments concerning the unjust steward, an account just previous to our text, but now by citing this example of divine judgment and punishment upon the rich man, in order to

alarm them, so that they might fear such judgment, repent, and amend their lives.

3. However, this warning spoken for the sake of the Pharisees on that occasion availed as little as do warnings addressed to rich and arrogant people of the world today. Unfortunately, as we know, such people most often think themselves pious and without greed. Vice has been turned into virtue. Greed nowadays has come to be viewed as talented, smart, careful stewardship. And as with greed, so sin in general is dressed up to look like virtue and not vice. Murder and harlotry, perhaps, are still considered sinful in some quarters, but other sins have in general come to be viewed more as virtues than vices. This is particularly the case with greed, now so dressed up and polished as no longer to be denominated as such. Neither prince nor peasant, nobleman nor average citizen is any longer considered greedy, but only upstanding, the common consensus being that the man who prudently provides for himself is a resourceful person who knows how to take care of himself.

4. The same holds true for other sins: pride is no longer pride, or sin, but honor. The proud man is no longer deemed arrogant but honorable, a commanding person, worthy of respect, a credit to his generation. Anger and envy are no longer that, or sin, but righteousness, zealousness, and virtue. The man who storms, or is envious, or who loses his cool is now considered industrious, with a passion for what is fair, and justly angry when high-handed injustice is done to him. Thus there are no more sinners in the world, but—God have mercy!—the world is full of holy people. In Seneca's words, when this happens, that vice is turned into virtue and honor, there no longer is hope or a way out; everything is lost.

5. The person who won't admit to being covetous is as unlikely to be struck by this parable as were the Pharisees. The proud man looks upon pride not as sin and arrogance, but as something deserving of honor and respect. He cannot be reprimanded for pride, because he considers himself holy and not a sinner deserving of punishment. Similarly, the person who believes that he has just cause for being envious, hateful, and vengeful will justify his anger and vengeance because of the injustice his neighbor has

done to him, which he cannot allow. Such a person cannot be helped. Who is going to correct and help those who have turned vice to virtue, sin to righteousness, shame and fault to something honorable? When greed is denominated productiveness; arrogance, honor; anger, zeal—then we have to leave it unrebuked, even as now.

6. That's the kind of person this rich man was. Even though infected with covetousness, he would have been unwilling to be known as greedy, or reprehensible for his greed, all the while allowing poor Lazarus to starve to death before his door. The Pharisees were the same sort, as St. Luke reports. Christ preached earnestly against Mammon and greed, but the Pharisees scoffed and refused to admit covetousness. They acted just like the noblemen of our day, who turn vice and shame into honor, fault into virtue, greed into industry, and so on. That is why Christ told them, You justify yourselves before men; but God knows your hearts. In other words, You Pharisees are pious; I cannot rebuke you, since you are no longer sinners, just plain and great saints. But you cannot deceive God. You are deceiving yourselves only. God will not judge you according to the measurements people have of you, for they do not know you. They esteem you as honorable men, not as covetous. God, however, knows your hearts, and it is according to your hearts that He judges.

7. So now the Pharisees and the rich man asked no questions about it, just as nowadays our noblemen, peasants, and townfolks also ask no questions about it, regardless what one preaches and says. It has now gotten to the point where gross vice, drinking, and carousing are no longer regarded a disgrace, but intemperance and drunkenness must now go by the name of gaiety. And just as all vices have become virtues, including greed, so nowadays no prince, duke, aristocrat, burgher, or peasant is known as greedy; and it's the going policy at the market, if they can get away with it, to charge four gulden for a bushel of corn. Everybody scratches, scrapes, manipulates, and juggles prices so that everyone, from the princely ranks down to the servant ranks, becomes a wheeler-dealer. In short, everything is leprous with greed, and yet no one wants to be thought of as greedy. And as it goes with greed, so it goes, as stated, also with other sins, such as anger, jealousy, hatred,

pride, and the like. What can we do about it? If we preach against it, people laugh and scoff; they do not want to acknowledge their sins or admit they have done wrong; worse, they want to travel the road to hell the way the rich man did here; and with the rich man they will indeed go to hell. For them, further appeal is useless. The fact is that when they are rebuked, they color and adorn their sins and vices with righteousness and virtue. How then can they be helped? Since that is the way they want it, there's no way out for them but the abyss of hell with the rich man. What can we do since they will not accept rebuke and do not want to repent or change for the better?

8. The gospels are at one when they speak about the fruits of faith and about the righteous works of a Christian, about what an upright man and righteous Christian should do. Yet, at the same time it is evident that the whole world is replete with greed and rushing toward hell, though no one wants to admit that he's greedy. We want to consider the words before us very closely and spell them out for you, so that if possible they might strike home and move someone's heart. Listen, says Christ, you greedy Pharisees, you who exonerate yourselves before men, I want to tell you a story:

There was a certain rich man, which was clothed in purple and fine linen, and fared sumptuously every day.

9. The Jews had a good pretense for dressing up their greed; for through Moses, God had promised that if they would be upright and keep His commandments, He would pour out blessing upon them in the field, in the kitchen, in the storehouses, and in the bedroom, so that every corner might overflow with rich abundance; at the end of the year they were to throw out the old so that they might store up the new. Such promise and teaching they could easily grasp, just as our people have now grasped the gospel since it is mellow. Then they went further and made this false inference from God's promise and faithful teaching: In His promise God says, whoever is upright shall have plenty; therefore, whoever has enough is upright; but whoever is in want or is poor is not upright. So, with them poverty had to be a punishment from God, like pestilence and other plagues. At the same time the false prophets, priests, and Levites furthered this with

their preaching, as Ps. 114:11–15 petitions against such false teachers, stating: "Rid me, and deliver me from the hand of strange children, whose mouth speaketh vanity, and their right hand is a right hand of falsehood: that our sons may be as plants grown up in their youth; that our daughters may be as cornerstones, polished after the similitude of a palace: that our garners may be full, affording all manner of store: that our sheep may bring forth thousands and ten thousands in our streets: that our oxen may be strong to labor; that there be no breaking in, nor going out; that there be no complaining in our streets. Happy is that people, that is in such case." That was the message of the false prophets among God's people, and they still had Moses on their side. For this reason, I say, the Jews had a good pretense with which to color their greed. If they were rich, they could adorn themselves with such teaching, as though they had kept God's commandment, and condemn the poor as though God had punished them for their sins and transgressions.

10. Against such false understanding Christ remonstrates here and says, You Pharisees exonerate yourselves as though you were godly; since you have plenty, you regard other people who suffer want as accursed; you dress up your greed and get your Mammon to be called God's blessing, meanwhile parading as though you have kept God's commandment. However, I wish to cite for you an example of a rich man and a poor man, one that presents an opposing view, one that speaks condemnation upon you rich people and, on the other hand, blessing upon the poor. Had you seen this rich man about whom I am speaking, you would have declared him blessed and said, To this man God gives blessings and everything in abundance, and allows him to live a good life, because it's evident that he has kept God's commandment. It's as Moses says, they who keep God's commandment should be filled with joy, should have peace, happiness, and everything in abundance; so it goes with this man, But I [Jesus] want to tell you what this means so that you discern and discard your false understanding. When God bestows riches and possessions, that is good and a blessing of God. But if one grubs and scratches for Mammon and through greed scrapes his possessions together, that is neither good nor a blessing of God.

11. That was the case with this rich man. He has many possessions; however, he is greedy and merciless. He does not keep a sin-

gle jot or tittle of God's law; and yet he has plenty of everything, a beautiful purple robe (for he thought of purple as we do of velvet), also the best and finest linen, thus decked out to the hilt. Besides, he has the best and choicest of things to eat and drink, pleasant and tranquil days, sleeps peacefully at night, rises in the morning whenever he wants to, is not plagued by misfortune as other people are, nor harassed in any way. In short, his life is filled to overflowing and happy. In your opinion he is thought to be a happy man; however, before God he is an ungodly man, who does not give a rap about God's commandment.

12. We ought to note this well so that we are on guard against the false understanding of the Pharisees and the false teachers. But now a greedy person is bound to object: Is it wrong, then, to be rich and have possessions? Didn't Abraham, David, and Job have possessions and yet were saved? Answer: Listen, you greedy belly; this rich man is not like Abraham, David, or Job; for whatever possessions he has he does not possess to the glory of God. Christ speaks here of those rich people who are greedy; He is portraying them in this example, and He paints them in their true color. Although this rich man is not stingy as regards his own body, nevertheless, he is greedy; he snatches up everything, gets hold of other people's possessions, then feasts and permits poor Lazarus to suffer want.

13. Thus it goes nowadays also. The whole world scratches and scrapes, and because of greed creates wanton privation; and yet for all that, our Lord God grants tolerable years. Now, then, I know for sure that you, skinflint, will take as little of your Mammon along with you into hell as did this rich man, if the meanwhile the devil does not run off with your wealth. In fact, you also will require luck if your children are to retain it after you are gone; for because of you the proverbs will remain true: *Male quaesit, male perdit,* that is, "Evil gotten, evil spent"; and *De male quaesitis non gaudet tertius heres,* or "The fortune ill-gotten rarely rejoices the third generation."

14. It was not a sin for this rich man to clothe himself, to eat and drink; for God created clothing, food, and drink, and says that it is blessing from Him. The one who receives it may use it in accord

with his needs. But to be greedy is wrong and a sin. Christ clearly says, "There was a rich man." Now the word "rich" is a very problematical word in many places of holy scripture. Abraham also is rich, but scripture does not for this reason call him a rich man; but "rich" in scripture means almost as much as an unscrupulous shyster or wicked man, as spoken of in Isa. 53:9: "He made his grave with the wicked, and with the rich in his death." There the prophet takes "rich" and "wicked" as one and the same thing. His point is, Christ died and was buried as an evildoer, rogue, and scoundrel, even though He had done wrong to no one. This is scripture's meaning for "rich." I would not dare to defame a rich man in this way. Now then! If someone is greedy and does not want to hear or accept it from us that he is greedy and wicked, he will still have to hear it just as this rich man had to hear it. The point here is whether we are going to deceive God in heaven, or ourselves.

15. This was the situation with the rich man, who considered himself pious, sitting contentedly in the midst of his riches before the world, adorning himself with the word spoken by God through Moses that whoever is pious God will bless; meanwhile allowing himself to think that he had no need to share with anyone, or allow anyone else to enjoy some of his wealth. His thinking was: If a man's poor, that's his curse; if rich, he's blessed; I am rich, and therefore, I am blessed and have kept God's commandment; Lazarus, on the other hand, is poor, and that's because he is a sinner and God has punished him.

And there was a certain beggar named Lazarus, which was laid at his gate full of sores, and desiring to be fed with the crumbs which fell from the rich man's table.

16. The Lord makes it very repulsive and puts a very heavy burden on the rich man. Poor Lazarus is covered with sores and lies at the gate of the rich man's house. For this reason the rich man cannot excuse himself or say, I did not know this; had I known there was such a poor man, I would have had him brought to me, given him food, had his sores treated, and provided for his

other needs, so that it would not have been necessary for him to lie in the street like a dog. Such excuse he couldn't plead. For poor Lazarus lies there at his doorstep, for the rich man to see every time he enters and leaves the house. Nevertheless, he lets Lazarus lie there and does nothing for him, but looks on him as doomed to misfortune, reasoning: This man has to be an ungodly, wicked person, because God has punished him and allowed him to lie there in his pus and sins. So poor Lazarus had to languish there in his stink before the eyes of the full-bellied rich man who fancies himself to be holy and yet is replete with all manner of sin, is without faith in God and love toward his neighbor, brimming over with greed, arrogance, and ruthlessness.

17. It is, of course, also dreadful that Lazarus himself comes and begs, not for bread, meat, or money, but only for what is thrown to the dogs. He desires only the scraps that are left over and fall from the table, whether they be bones or rinds, that someone might give them to him. It does not happen. It discomposes the rich man even more severely and contributes to his falling deeper into hell. Such an uncharitable and ruthless man is what greed and arrogance have made out of him; he is absolutely pitiless toward poor Lazarus, and there is not a spark of Christian love in his heart.

18. And what shall we say? Irrational animals and dogs come and take pity on the poor man. Had they had bread, they would have given it to him. They do what they are capable of doing; they use the best member they have, namely, their helpful tongues, and lick his sores and lap up the pus. How easily the rich man could have taken care of this; it would hardly have cost him a gulden and would hardly have put even a dent in his wealth. However, he despises and condemns the poor man burdened with sores as an accursed and condemned man.

19. Let this example be a warning to you, says Christ to the Pharisees. When you leave poor people lying hungry or thirsty, you think it's well and good. But turn over the page and look at the text aright. You think that only the rich belong in heaven because they alone are blessed of God. But listen, just the opposite is the

case! No rich man (as scripture denominates "rich") can enter heaven, but the poor will! For this reason, also, the gospel is preached not to the rich but to the poor. And that, too, is the plain truth. Were our Lord God to have received only the rich into heaven, then no one would be able to live peaceably with the rich. Yet beyond that, they are so contemptible with their little alms, with their wretched Mammon, that they regard other people as pure simpletons. What would have happened had God chosen rich people to be apostles? The rich would then have swaggered and said, Yes, take note, our Lord God did not want to choose any poor people to be evangelists, apostles, and the like, but selected only rich people for these purposes. But Christ turns it around and says, You rich people must become poor if the gospel is to be preached to you and you are to enter heaven. Although you are not poor when it comes to possessions, you are indeed poor in matters of the heart.

And it came to pass that the beggar died, and was carried by the angels into Abraham's bosom: the rich man also died, and was buried.

20. Poor Lazarus dies, with no one on earth to give him a decent burial; but the angels carry him into Abraham's bosom. The rich man dies, too, and is buried, undoubtedly in lordly manner, but in his case there are other kinds of angels waiting, to carry him to hell. Things are now reversed. Poor Lazarus, according to the Pharisees' judgment, was accursed and damned, while the same critics deemed the rich man blessed of God and a saved man. Yet our text states that Lazarus comes into Abraham's bosom; the rich man, however, enters into hell. We must, therefore, judge matters here rightly, not like the Pharisees, but as it is written.

21. We must make the proper distinction: the poor man doesn't come into heaven because he is poor, nor the rich man into hell because he is rich; rather it was a case that the poor man accommodated himself well to the fact that he was poor, while the rich man failed to handle his riches properly. A distinction easily made, but not easily kept! Our old Adam remains an evil rascal. Once he knows that wealth in itself is not bad and poverty not good and

that everything revolves around how a man handles them, he straightaway turns the distinction into a cover-up.

22. The distinction in itself is right and good: poverty is not by nature something good or wealth, evil. The person who handles his poverty properly and with patience, content that it is God's will, as St. Paul says [Phil. 4:11]: "I have learned, in whatsoever state I am, therewith to be content"—his poverty is a precious thing and a preparation for eternal life. By the same token, when a wealthy person perceives how God has blessed him with possessions and resolves that because God has bestowed riches upon him, he will rightly use his wealth and become neither proud nor greedy, he is ready to share his goods if and when a poor man comes to him for help in time of need. Such a rich man handles his riches well, like Abraham and David, who were wealthy, or Job, of whom it is said that he did not eat his morsel by himself alone [Job 31].

23. This distinction, I say, is a right one. But how many people, do you think, keep it? For the old Adam, as said, is a rogue who reasons this way: I know the distinction very well; poverty saves no one; riches condemn nobody; therefore, even though I'm rich, I'm not condemned by such wealth. He goes merrily on, becomes secure and proud, thinking that he can do with his wealth as he pleases. Our old nature is a rascal and is very adept at this. Accordingly, each person has to be on guard against the kind of self-deception that happened to this fat cat. God, the knower of hearts, will not be deceived; nothing is hidden from him.

24. Behold, what a rogue and scoundrel the rich man is; he has no consideration for this poor man but despises and regards him as accursed as he lies at his gate and begs merely for the rinds and crumbs; and before allowing him to have the rinds and crumbs that fall from his table, he lets the dogs devour them or lets them go to waste. This example is not cited here for no purpose, but so that the rich should be on guard lest because of their riches greed creep into them furtively.

25. The way things go today the whole world scrapes and scratches, and yet no one wants to be known as greedy, but everybody wants to be Evangelical and true Christians. And none

is affected by this parsimony quite as much as brother Studium (the zealous student) and the poor clergymen in the cities and villages. For there's nothing to be gotten from burghers and peasants, but only from poor people who have a houseful of children and can barely eke out a living by their hard work. Moreover, peasants, townsfolk, and nobles are able to increase their holdings of corn, barley, work, and business, double or triple their money, and thus all the more easily bear the greed and parsimony of others. But parish pastors and preachers, and those without a craft, who have to live on a pittance or, as the saying goes, on a shoestring, unable to augment or increase their money supply, are compelled to bear the brunt and allow themselves to be skinned and strangulated.

26. How many peasants, burghers, or nobles are there who give something to the poor Lazarus, who lies daily at their door? Yes, should they give to him? They rather skin him down to the bone, and what they extort they dissipate, squander, and show off with fancy food and clothing, guzzling drinks down their throats or hanging ornaments around the neck. For this reason I have often said, such conditions cannot continue much longer, but must come to an end. Either the Turk or Brother Vitus[42] will come and all of a sudden confiscate everything it took so long a time to extort, steal, rob, and amass, or judgment day will come rushing in and bring the game to a halt. For God is no longer able to tolerate the greed, wantonness, pride, sensuality, and stealing. He must step in and take control Himself since nothing else will stop it. People attribute all this to other things, rather than to the fact that they ought to aid poor Lazarus. Under the papacy people were charitable and gave willingly; however, now under the gospel no one gives anymore, but everyone simply extorts from the next person, and each wants to have it all to himself. And the longer one preaches the gospel, the deeper people are submerged in greed, arrogance, and sensuality, as if the poor beggar's pouch is to survive here forever. So completely has the devil taken hold of people.

27. There poor Lazarus now lies before the rich man's gate, and no one attends him. But the beloved holy angels are sitting by

---

[42]Reference to St. Vitus and the supposed cures from chorea, nerve disorder, through intercession.

and taking care of him because the rich man does not want to. Were I to change places, I would rather be poor Lazarus than the rich man, regardless of the fact that Lazarus lies before the gate of the rich man covered with sores, hungry, languishing, lonely, and without an attendant, while, on the other hand, the rich man has everything in abundance. For I would rather have an angel as guardian and keeper than a hundred Roman emperors with all their might. Now the text says that not one angel but many angels waited on Lazarus until his soul left him. O how badly the man was treated on earth, having had no one to take care of him! But now he has many angels who tend to him and carry his soul into Abraham's bosom. I would gladly let such nursemaids as Lazarus had also carry my soul. On the other hand, however, the rich man also has many servants waiting upon him. They stand around his bed in order to tend to him; behind him an entire dispensary is provided. Round about him, above him, under him, and on all sides are twenty or thirty devils, who are waiting for his soul to leave him and to carry it into hell. These are much different nurse-maids from those who wait upon the soul of poor Lazarus.

28. This is what the Lord is saying, and He means it in all seri-ousness, so that we might beware of greed and not become secure. We need such warning very much nowadays, in order that we do not make a virtue out of that shameful vice, accursed greed. Sad to say, it is now taking hold of so many. God knows our hearts, and judgment is imminent should we allow greed, the same greed which took hold of the rich man, to mislead us. If a person takes account of how much good he does in life, he will find that it is lit-tle enough. Why is it, then, that people scratch and scrape, and during the course of a year give very little, for God's sake, to church and school, the poor and needy? There is one coming who will reckon with us and say, You had poor Lazarus before your door and gave him nothing; you thought you were doing the right thing and doing well at that by not giving anyone a farthing; you allowed yourself to think that this was not greed, that God would not punish you; so now accept the reward which you have earned.

29. We preachers can no longer really prevent shameful greed. It lives and animates almost as if it were itself God and Lord in all lands, and to boot, adorns itself most beautifully. We sense it in the

marketplace and in the kitchen, for we hold on to neither penny nor farthing, while we don't so much as see the people who practice greed. We must therefore, let Him address it who says here that the devil led the rich man away. Accordingly, let everyone be forewarned and be vigilant. We are now witnessing a lot of greed among peasants, burghers, and nobility, displayed especially against poor clergymen. This cannot have a good ending. And this now is the picture being painted of the rich man and poor Lazarus, both in life and in death. But let us also now hear how things went for the rich man in hell.

And in hell he lift up his eyes, being in torments, and seeth Abraham afar off, and Lazarus in his bosom. And he cried out and said, Father Abraham, have mercy on me, and send Lazarus, that he may dip the tip of his finger in water, and cool my tongue; for I am tormented in this flame.

30. There lies the rich skinflint in hellish fire and torment; he looks up and sees a sight that is different from the one he saw before. For now he has revealed to him what he has done. The covering with which he had previously bedecked himself is gone. He can no longer say he had to dress so elegantly and live so lavishly and happily for the sake of his reputation. He sees poor Lazarus, whom he disdained before his gate, now lying in Abraham's bosom, just as a mother holds her child in her arms. This is an altogether different sight. Before he was not willing to accept such a sight; but now he sees that Lazarus is someone special in the eyes of God. Previous to this he saw nothing in the poor man but pus, sores, ridicule, and disdain; but now he sees him residing in pure glory and bliss.

31. He would so much like to be out of the torments of hell. "Father Abraham," he says, "have mercy on me, and send Lazarus, that he may dip the tip of his finger in water, and cool my tongue." This is portrayed as something especially horrible. Christ's words are very sharp and abrupt in this account or parable, for He is very much opposed to shameful, accursed greed. For that reason He represents the rich man to us as sitting in hell with a parched tongue and wanting desperately to have a drop of water to cool his

tongue; but that cannot be done, and he is given two different responses. First, Abraham rails at him and says:

Son, remember that thou in thy lifetime receivedst thy good things, and likewise Lazarus evil things: but now he is comforted, and thou art tormented.

32. In other words, You had your good things on earth; now suffer torment and agony for it. And you wanted it that way; therefore, you are not now suffering any injustice. You wanted to have your kingdom of heaven on earth; money and possessions were your salvation; beautiful clothes and a wonderful life were your paradise; let your money, your purple and beautiful clothes, your worldly desires, and joy save you now. Why should Lazarus, whom you abandoned and despised, help you when it went so badly for him? All this is the response of divine justice. He is comforted, and you are being tormented. To sum up: the rich belong in hell; but the poor, who conducted and resigned themselves rightly in their poverty, belong in heaven.

And beside all this, between us and you there is a great gulf fixed: so that they which would pass from hence to you cannot; neither can they pass to us, that would come from thence.

33. This is the second response. Even if we wanted to cross over to you and cool your tongue, it just cannot happen. On our own we cannot do it; for we are obligated to do God's will; we will do only what He wants. It is beyond our ability to do otherwise. Even though we wanted to help you, the chasm between us is so great that no one can pass from one side to the other. When you and Lazarus were together and were, so to speak, neighbors, he lay at your gate, where the one could have helped the other; there it was not necessary to step across a chasm; he was very close to you. You might at least have had him carried into your stable, if you had not wanted to give him a place in your home. But now he is too far away from you for you to be able to do him any good, and he in turn to help you. The gulf is too great; you cannot cross over to us, nor we to you. For this reason you cannot be helped. Such was the response given to the rich man.

34. The conclusion usually understood here is that the worst of the punishment for the rich and the damned will be that they will have to view the poor, whom they despised on earth, sitting in heaven. Accordingly, it pained the rich man in his heart to see Lazarus in Abraham's bosom. Hell's fire became twice as hot because he had to see the despised Lazarus enjoying such glory. And Abraham shows him nothing else but Lazarus. As the saying goes: Wherein one's sin consisted, with that will he be tormented [Wis. 11:17]. So also on judgment day! God will set the poor orphans and the rich, the covetous money grabbers, over against each other. While the usurer burns in hell, the poor man who was plagued and swindled by him will sit in Abraham's bosom. This is what the usurer will be compelled to see in his deep anguish.

35. That now is the judgment which the rich man in hell has to hear: We will not and cannot help you! He must despair of all help forever. I won't enter into a discussion concerning the nature of Abraham's bosom, nor is it necessary; people tend to pry and trouble themselves too much over unnecessary things and meanwhile allow primary things to slip by. We will understand very well the meaning of Abraham's bosom when we ourselves come there. Now we ought to content ourselves and learn from this example how Christ warns us against being greedy, rich people. If God blesses me with money and goods, I should be ready to benefit others therewith. If I refuse to do so, I see from the rich man's example what shall befall me.

36. Mammon is after all a damnable treasure which helps no one, yes, a burdensome weight that can only sink a person deeper in hell. However, if God blesses a person with possessions, wealth can be useful. But if not, if not rightfully utilized, it becomes sheer greediness and Mammon, belonging in hell. So let the question concerning Abraham's bosom rest, not disputing about it; let the scholastics argue about it if they must. The main point is that with reference to Abraham's bosom the rich man pleads:

I pray thee therefore, Father, that thou wouldest send him to my father's house: for I have five brethren; that he may testify unto them, lest they also come into this place of torment.

37. It amounts to his saying, If this is the way it must be—that I am lost and damned, while Lazarus is forever saved and comforted—then send Lazarus to my brothers; as yet there is no gulf fixed for them as there is for me in this place of torment. Let Lazarus go to my father's house and urgently tell my brothers how I am tormented here in the fires of hell, so that they might amend their lives and be saved. A pious, lost individual, indeed, who does not want the others to experience the torment and damnation in which he now is! However, this is not written in order for us to think that the damned are so minded, but that Christ might teach and warn people in a simple sort of way.

Abraham saith unto him, They have Moses and the prophets; let them hear them.

38. Every sabbath day, Jesus says, Moses and the prophets are read in their schools; let them pay attention to what they hear, as God commanded. Just as the Word of God is preached to us every Sunday, so the Jews were to listen to Moses and the prophets every sabbath. They should listen to them, Abraham says, and learn from them how to live and conduct themselves. So we should cling to the ministry of the Church and the external Word. God is not minded to begin something new and different for us.

And he said unto him, If they hear not Moses and the prophets, neither will they be persuaded, though one rose from the dead.

39. Even in his smallest request the condemned man cannot prevail. Now the rich man must endure the miserable fare and terrible thirst that Lazarus experienced while upon earth. Everything he pleads for and desires is denied. Christ says, If they refuse to listen to Moses and the prophets, that is, if they are going to deny the Word of God, even knowing that it is the Word of God, then they won't be swayed by someone rising from the dead either. This is the way it still is. Even today, were God to send an angel three or four times, people would take it in stride and think no more of it than they do of the preacher's sermons. It would make no difference even if one rose from the dead. If God's Word can-

not move a man, then nothing will avail, even though a dead man issued forth out of hell or an angel came from heaven.

40.   People engage in pretense and say, Sermons are old hat; but if someone rose from the dead, then people would believe. In the same vein, If the gospel were proclaimed by the high and mighty, like princes, kings, or rulers of the world, or by angels from heaven, then people would believe. How can we possibly believe if the people who do the preaching are nothing but lowly, despised fishermen? That's easily said, but basically it's of no count, for it is not the person of the preacher that makes the difference in bringing a man to faith, but the Word of God. To be sure, it is His Word that they are despising; and if they do that to the Word of God, what regard will they have for a word brought by an angel or by someone raised from the dead? Accordingly, Abraham says, "If they hear not Moses and the prophets, neither will they be persuaded, though one rose from the dead." For the word of Moses and the prophets is of greater weight and clout than a word from someone risen from the dead. The person who won't listen to Moses and the prophets will listen even less to someone raised from the dead. Maybe out of curiosity he might listen for a time, today, or tomorrow; but once tomorrow is past, that word will be despised also. Sirach states [51:33–34]: "Acquire wisdom for yourselves without money. Bring your necks under her yoke, and her burden let your soul bear," to which he sets himself as an example, "When I was yet young, before I wandered abroad, I desired her and sought her out without shame and made supplication in prayer."

41.   Devout believers, therefore, need to cling to the truth of God's Word as proclaimed in the church by faithful pastors. Were Paul, Peter, yes, Christ Himself to proclaim the Word, it would be to no avail if meanwhile we despised it. If we love and believe the Word, whether preached by Paul or Peter, Christ or John the Baptist, pastor or chaplain, it does not make any difference who the person is, for it is the Word that counts. If we base our baptism's worth on the fact that it was performed by the bishop of Mainz, by a cardinal, or the pope, then we are grounding it upon the person and not on baptism itself. It will not then endure. If we, however, esteem our baptism highly because it is God's sacrament, ordained

and commanded by Him, then we stand on sure and firm ground. The person of man does not make baptism better, whether done by the pope or some bishop, parish preacher or chaplain, than the baptism done by a midwife in time of emergency. Similarly, the Word preached by a parish preacher is not better than that of a chaplain. In short, it's a matter of the Word, not of the person.

42. Even if all the dead should rise and preach, that still would do no good; truly, one cannot rely at all on the preaching of the dead, for they could well be preaching lies. It is for this reason that God does not want the dead to preach; otherwise He would not have established the office of the ministry and ordained to such office apostles, bishops, pastors, and preachers. Through the office of the ministry He gives us His Word, which He has committed to men. He does not want to give us His Word through dead men, nor has He committed the preaching office to the dead. Thus is it written [Isa. 8:19–21]: "And when they shall say unto you, Seek unto them that have familiar spirits, and unto wizards that peep, and that mutter: should not a people seek unto their God? for the living to the dead? To the law and the testimony: if they speak not according to this word, it is because there is no light in them. And they shall pass through it, hardly bestead and hungry." This means that we should not seek guidance from, or listen to, the dead, but be guided by the law and the testimony, that is, by the Word. God has forbidden the dead to preach and commanded men, who have a calling, to preach His Word.

43. This is a strong testimony against the fantastic spirits. We see here that Lazarus was not to preach, but remain in Abraham's bosom; also the rich man was not to preach, but remain in hell. When these rambling spirits intrude into our houses, let us say, Devil, don't you know where you belong? Abraham holds Lazarus in his bosom, and the devil has the rich man in hell. If I want to hear preaching, I want to hear it there where God has ordained for it to be. Where? In the ministry of the Word, through the mouth of the parish preacher in the church, or of the fathers, mothers, masters, mistresses of the house. Whoever hears them, hears God. Whoever will not hear them, let him listen to the devil through the mouths of the dead and the fantastic spirits. Indeed, it is the devil when they claim to hear someone from the dead, for God has not

ordained that the dead should preach, but has directed us rather to the living, to whom he has commended His Word.

44. In this example of the rich man and poor Lazarus, we have a terrifying and earnest lesson against covetousness. It is a particularly shameful evil at work among greedy, loveless people, full of great injustice, thwarting all the fruits of the gospel. The Lord rebukes this evil, therefore, for good reason, especially, since it adorns itself as a virtue, refusing to be viewed as sin. If we find ourselves in it, may God help us, so that we come free of it. Amen.

THIRD SUNDAY AFTER TRINITY

1533

This gospel speaks of those sinners who draw close to Christ to hear Him, that is, that they may learn from His Word, confess their sins, begin to believe and to amend their lives. These sinners are the true sheep who cease from straying and are happy to be found by their Shepherd, Jesus Christ, because they want to hear God's Word and learn to amend their lives in harmony with it.

LUKE 15:1–10

Then drew near unto Him all the publicans and sinners for to hear Him. And the Pharisees and scribes murmured, saying, This man receiveth sinners, and eateth with them. And He spake this parable unto them, saying, What man of you, having an hundred sheep, if he lose one of them, doth not leave the ninety and nine in the wilderness, and go after that which is lost, until he find it? And when he hath found it, he layeth it on his shoulders, rejoicing. And when he cometh home, he calleth together his friends and neighbors, saying unto them, Rejoice with me; for I have found my sheep which was lost. I say unto you, that likewise joy shall be

*in heaven over one sinner that repenteth, more than over ninety
and nine just persons, which need no repentance. Either what
woman having ten pieces of silver, if she lose one piece, doth
not light a candle, and sweep the house, and seek diligently till
she find it? And when she hath found it, she calleth her friends
and her neighbors together, saying, Rejoice with me; for I have
found the piece which I had lost. Likewise, I say unto you, there
is joy in the presence of the angels of God over one sinner that
repenteth.*

1. This is one of the most comforting gospels of the entire year.
For it presents a beautiful picture of Christ, in which He compares
Himself with a shepherd who earnestly searches for poor sinners,
to bring them back, so that the wolf, the devil, doesn't get them
and they be eternally lost. Incredibly sweet are these words when
He says that the angels in heaven, those majestic creatures, rejoice
over one sinner who repents.

2. Herewith the Lord Christ pictures His office and kingdom,
that He is not a shepherd or king who has to do with the physical,
material sphere, or one who either turns the world upside down or
has nothing to do with it, but rather one who companies and mingles with poor sinners. His kingdom, therefore, is a spiritual kingdom, a kingdom of grace and mercy, a kingdom of forgiveness of
sins, and of eternal life.

3. The evangelist states that all kinds of people, tax collectors and
sinners, came to Jesus to hear Him. At the same time he explains
why so many tax collectors and sinners came, and why their coming
was so pleasing to the Lord Christ. Their coming was dear to Christ
because they were so eager to hear His Word and gospel. They
really, earnestly, wanted to hear His preaching. That's the way it was.

4. In contrast, the scribes and Pharisees taught and sacrificed in
the temple at Jerusalem, permitted themselves and their children to
be circumcised, carried out the precepts of the law, assiduously
attempted to live an irreproachable life of outward piety, and led an
outwardly honorable life in the people's eyes. They also reasoned
that the Messiah would be as holy as they and would associate with
holy people. His coming would be in line with outward holiness

and piety, and He would associate with holy people like the scribes and Pharisees. That would characterize Christ's reign and office. So, when they now saw the Lord Christ associating with tax collectors and sinners, receiving them with grace, interacting with them in a most friendly manner, they murmured against Him and said, "This one receives sinners and eats with them." Indeed the scribes and Pharisees were unable to judge differently, or come to any other conclusion, for they understood nothing of Christ's kingdom and office, that He had come to earth to redeem sinners, however great they were, however great or how many the sins were which they may have committed. The only requirement was that they hear His gospel, repent, and believe. Of this they understood nothing. They knew no more of God's Word than what Moses and the law taught.

5. The law always teaches—and reason concurs and can't do otherwise—that God is benevolent to those who are devout and obey His commandments, but that evildoers who do not keep his commandments are punished [Exod. 20:5–6]: "I the Lord thy God am a jealous God, visiting the iniquities of the fathers upon the children unto the third and fourth generation of them that hate Me; And shewing mercy unto thousands of them that love Me, and keep My commandments." Hence the conclusion that the Messiah was sent from God in order to deal with sinners as the law taught! Because the law states that God is angry with sinners and will not receive them, but rather punish them, it stands to reason that Christ would behave the same way, rejecting the tax collectors and sinners in unfriendly manner, and let them go their way.

6. The Lord Christ counters this thinking with two parables, the one about the shepherd and the lost sheep, the other about the woman and the lost coin. He could simply have answered by telling the gospel, that God is not at enmity with sinners, nor does He find satisfaction in their death and damnation, but rather sent His dear Son to redeem them. This is clearly articulated in Christ's remarks to Nicodemus, who was a Pharisee, in John 3:16–17: "For God so loved the world that He gave His only begotten Son, that whosoever believeth in Him should not perish, but have everlasting life. For God sent not His Son into the world to condemn the world; but that the world through Him might be saved." This is a teaching and preaching quite different from the law. He speaks not of God's

anger and displeasure with the sinner, but of grace and love. Therefore, Christ could have answered the Pharisees and scribes that one should not only know the law as the criterion of how to deal with sinners, but also the gospel, the preaching of grace, the teaching that we should receive sinners because God receives them. For Moses himself pointed to another prophet, another teaching and word given through him which was very much different from the law. At other places he refers to the special calling of this prophet. Thus in Matthew 9, when Christ was blamed and heckled by the Pharisees because He ate with publicans and sinners, He answered, "For I am not come to call the righteous, but sinners to repentance" [v. 13]. Here, too, He could have driven home the nature of His office by saying, I came to earth to save that which was lost. But He didn't wish only to answer the scribes and Pharisees, but to convince them by everyday examples drawn from human experience, so that He might muzzle their mouths, cause them to change their tune, and be won over.

7. With these parables He not only paints a sweet, comforting picture of His kingdom and ministry, but also shows therewith His deep concern for sinners, to seek them out and to do everything needful for their souls' salvation. A man, He says, with one hundred sheep, if he loses one, leaves the ninety-nine in the wilderness and goes to look for the lost one. He has neither peace nor rest until he finds the lost one. When he has found it, he places it upon his shoulder with joy and carries it home, calls his friends and neighbors and says, "Rejoice with me; for I have found my sheep which was lost." That's what a man would do for a dumb animal, a poor sheep. He is worried about the lost sheep, is much more concerned for the lost sheep than for all the others; he also rejoices more when he has found the lost sheep than over the ninety-nine which were not lost. Similarly, a woman who has ten coins and loses one, lights a lamp, sweeps the house, and looks with diligence until she finds it. When she has found it, she celebrates happily with her friends and neighbors. So it is in all circumstances: that which is lost causes much greater pain, sorrow, and concern. It is more loved, brings more joy, and is more of a solace than that which was never lost.

8. A mother who has many children loves them all and would not have any one of them suffer a mishap. But if one of them

becomes ill, the illness makes a difference between the other children and the sick child. The sickest now becomes the dearest. The mother's greatest care and concern are now for the sick child. Were we to judge the mother on the basis of her tender care, we would say that she loved only the sick child and not those who were well. It is the same for Him, our Lord Jesus says of Himself. Sinners are My purchases—valuable, earned property. I purchased them through My suffering and death at a price more costly and dear than a man a sheep, or a woman a coin, or even a mother her child. It cannot but distress Me and make Me deeply concerned if they should lose their way and slip through My hands. I cannot permit them to become the devil's property, because the price of their redemption is too high and has been too painful. For this reason, I cannot tolerate it if one of My sheep wanders off; and I respond as though the others didn't count, go after the lost, looking for it, lest it become prey to the wolves.

9. This certainly portrays the heart of our Lord Jesus in tenderest, most ardent terms. It would be impossible to paint in a more winsome and kindly manner the trouble, worry, toil, and concern that He has in setting right the wayward sinner. He strikes a responsive chord in our hearts when He reminds us of how we feel at the loss of something dear to us. Thus, His heart is greatly troubled and filled with compassion and concern, is His point here, when He sees the devil overcoming some poor sinner with sin and deception.

10. Moreover, just as He is tender minded toward the poor sinner, so also there is joy in heaven over one sinner who repents, more than over ninety-nine who require no repentance. He repeats those words once more, that the angels in heaven rejoice greatly over one sinner who repents. The dear angels and heavenly spirits celebrate with joy and sing a special *Te Deum Laudamus,* "We praise Thee, O God," when a poor sinner turns about and repents. If a man finds joy in finding a lost sheep, and a woman delights in finding a lost coin, and the angels in heaven rejoice over one sinner who repents, why do you scribes and Pharisees judge and rebuke Me, says Christ, when I receive publicans and sinners who come to Me to listen to My preaching with all diligence and heart's delight?

11. We should certainly be impressed by these beautiful comparisons and pictures, and such winsome and comforting words, so that from them we may learn to find comfort when a bad conscience and our sins accuse us. For we humans are all sinners and there isn't a one whom the devil hasn't frightened into the wilderness, nor anyone who after his baptism hasn't gone astray like a lost sheep and thus sinned against his God. Where there is sin, there the person is terrified before God. It is sin's nature to produce a frightened, discouraged spirit, troubled by disgrace and punishment. So, human reasoning, as well as the law's teaching, forces the conclusion that God is at enmity with sinners. A heart that knows itself to be guilty naturally feels fright, turns from grace, and anticipates punishment. But at this point is where power lies, that we, against our hearts and consciences, join with Christ to say, I am a poor sinner, that I will not deny; however, I will not for that reason despair, as though God did not want me, because my Lord Jesus Christ says that a poor sinner is just like a little sheep that has lost its shepherd and gone astray. Christ will not let such an erring sheep be lost, but will look for it and carry it back to the other sheep. That is attestation that because of sin He is not about to throw us out, but will rather, with all perseverance, endeavor to rescue us from sin and restore us again to grace. Moreover, He declares that He Himself, along with the angels in heaven, will rejoice when sinners come to repentance and are converted.

12. The parable of the sheep and the shepherd especially illustrates this. It is no small matter when a sheep in the pasture wanders away from the shepherd into the wilderness. It cannot think for itself; at any moment it is in danger from the wolf who slinks after it, to grab and devour it. In this predicament it has no recourse; it can neither protect itself nor get back. By nature no animal is more vulnerable and defenseless than a sheep. The same is true of a sinner whom the devil has turned from God and His Word and brought into sin. He is not safe even a moment, because our enemy, the devil, as Peter says, sneaks about like a roaring lion seeking whom he may devour.

13. In such jeopardy our only consolation is that we have a Shepherd, our dear Lord Jesus Christ, who accepts us and seeks us out, not to punish us for our sins and throw us into hell, but rather

finds us, places us on His shoulder, and rejoices to carry us home to safety from the wolf, where we have pasture and where every prospect pleases. You know how such search takes place, namely, that He permits His Word to ring out plainly, from which we learn how heinous and burdensome our sin is which would throw us into eternal damnation. But God, in His fatherly love, was compassionate toward us disobedient children and through His Son provided counsel and aid in our misery. It behooves us then to accept this gift with thanksgiving, believe in Christ, repent, and be converted to God.

14. This gospel not only comforts the poor sinner because Christ is such a caring Shepherd and King who searches out the straying sheep, picks them up, and carries them, but it also teaches us how we are to behave in relation to this Shepherd. It further teaches what we must do to be reinstated into Christ's kingdom and become beneficiaries of His grace and love, so that we who were once disoriented and lost might become loving and obedient sheep, now God's friends instead of His enemies. Like the publicans and sinners we should draw near to Christ, diligently and earnestly hear and learn His gospel, or as St. Paul states, The obedience of faith removes and annuls sin and all that is related to sin, namely, God's anger, eternal death, and damnation. It causes the sinner no longer to be a sinner, an enemy of God, but a justified friend of God and a joy to the angels in heaven.

15. In this way the gospel differentiates between sinners. It anticipates our squires, peasants, townspeople, nobility, princes, and all who praise themselves as being Evangelical but who misuse these beautiful, comforting comparisons and examples, asserting that Christ loves sinners and that the angels in heaven rejoice over one sinner who repents, and then they themselves forget about repentance. They continue in all types of sin, defiance, and wantonness before God and their fellowmen, without fear and timidity, shamefully secure. They sin freely against God's grace and mercy, and at the same time persecute and hate God's Word, as well as God's servants who preach His Word. They do not listen to the preaching sincerely, nor do they have heartfelt sorrow and repentance over their godless lives, their many sins and iniquity. They have learned nothing more from the gospel than to babble

that our Lord God will not cast a sinner away because Christ came
for the sake of the sinner, and so on.

16. This gospel lesson is not speaking of this sort of sinner, nor
ought they comfort themselves herewith, unless they want to
deceive themselves and play the hypocrite to their own harm and
destruction, going further astray, until the devil has them completely in a snare from which they cannot extricate themselves.
Rather, this gospel speaks of those sinners who draw close to
Christ to hear him, that is, that they may learn from His Word,
confess their sins, begin to believe and to amend their lives. These
sinners are the true sheep who cease from straying and are happy
to be found by their Shepherd, Jesus Christ, because they want to
hear God's Word and learn to amend their lives in harmony with
it. Christ makes the sign of the cross over such sinners and pronounces upon them a comforting, happy absolution: Your sins are
forgiven. You should know that God is merciful, nor should you
doubt, but rather firmly believe that it is so, even as I declare to
you. Because you hear My Word and believe in Me, I will take you
on My shoulders, carry you into the Church, yes, into the heavenly
kingdom. I will, yes, I have already provided for you, so that you
have a gracious God and Father in heaven.

17. This is what all poor sinners who love to hear God's Word
and acknowledge Christ as their Shepherd, Savior, and King
should remember, gleaning from it comfort and joy, and not
despairing because of their sin. For our dear Lord Jesus Christ
calls Himself a good, faithful Shepherd, which He truly is. For He
gave His life for such sinners, so that with all joy He might lead
and carry them into the heavenly kingdom and eternal life.

18. When God's Word is esteemed and praised as the only treasure, which can take away sin and all the misery resulting from
sin, like death, damnation, the devil, and hell, that is preaching in
a winsome and comforting way. Now we are no longer sinners
and enemies of God, but rather a joy to the dear angels in heaven
and all the saints on earth. For this reason we should hold God's
Word in highest honor and esteem, gladly hear it with open
hearts, and show respect and honor to those who preach the Word
to us. It will in turn bring us blessed fruit, freeing us from false

teaching and all danger from the troublesome devil, and save us eternally. May the faithful Shepherd and Bishop of our souls, the dear Lord Christ, impart this to us all through the Holy Spirit. Amen.

FOURTH SUNDAY AFTER TRINITY

I will not repay one evil with another evil. If someone else is a brier bush, capable of nothing but scratching, let him be a brier bush. I won't let that turn me into one; I'll remain a good, fruitful vine and produce good grapes. That is what my Father in heaven does too. He gives to the wicked scoundrels, as well as to those who are pious and just.

LUKE 6:36–42

Be ye therefore merciful, as your Father also is merciful. Judge not, and ye shall not be judged: condemn not, and ye shall not be condemned: forgive, and ye shall be forgiven: give, and it shall be given unto you; good measure, pressed down, and shaken together, and running over, shall men give into your bosom. For with the same measure that ye mete withal it shall be measured to you again. And He spake a parable unto them, Can the blind lead the blind? Shall they not both fall into the ditch? The disciple is not above his master: but everyone that is perfect shall be as his master. And why beholdest thou the mote that is in thy brother's eye, but perceivest not the beam that is in thine own eye? Either how canst thou say to thy brother, Brother, let me pull out the mote that is in thine eye, when thou thyself beholdest not the beam that is in thine own eye? Thou hypocrite, cast out first the beam out of thine own eye, and then shalt thou see clearly to pull out the mote that is in thy brother's eye.

1. In today's gospel lesson our dear Lord Christ teaches His disciples and all of us how we are to live as Christians in our relation-

ships with other people. For, if we have received faith and are considered to be Christians who have been saved from sin, death, and every kind of misfortune through our Lord Christ, then a new life must immediately follow, one in which we do what He desires. Our Lord summarizes this new life in the simple statement "Be ye therefore merciful, as your Father also is merciful."

2. Now everyone knows quite well that the term "merciful" describes a person who is ready to sympathize with his fellowman, a person who is kind and friendly toward this fellowman and is so genuinely concerned about his needs and misfortunes of soul and body, reputation and property, that he tries to think of ways in which he might be able to help his fellowman, and prove his concern by his deeds, doing them joyfully and gladly. That is what being "merciful" means. But He pointedly says, "as your Father also is merciful." With this assertion Jesus distinguishes between the mercy of a Christian and the mercy of non-Christians and wicked people who live in their midst. Sinners and tax collectors, who are mentioned shortly before this gospel, also practice mercy toward one another. They love one another, do friendly favors for one another, lend to one another; but they always do it with the expectation that this favor will be returned. That is a hoodlum's mercy, done with the hope of having that favor—or an even greater one—returned. Mercenary soldiers are murderers and insolent rascals, but they, too, practice mercy toward one another. The same is true of whores, rogues, and robbers. Even street gangs practice a certain kind of mercy, but their mercy extends only to their own group, and lasts only as long as their mutual criminal activities.

3. Christian mercy, however, is modeled after the mercy of our heavenly Father. A thief is not merciful to someone who is not a fellow thief, but only to his companions in theft. He might even not steal, if his buddies weren't helping and egging him on. That is a thieving, hypocrite's mercy. This also applies to our homes. If one of the family members is always making excuses for other family members, or if the members consistently cover up for a member who is not doing his share of work, that too is a hypocritical kind of mercy. As Christians, however, we are to be merciful in the same way our Father in heaven is merciful, not merely to those

who are our friends, nor merely to those who are fellow wrong-doers. That, too, is a hypocritical kind of mercy, yes, a devilish mercy. If we want to be Christians, we must be merciful in the same way our heavenly Father is merciful; not merely to our friends, nor only to those engaged in wrongdoing, but to everyone. That includes those whom we dislike, those who dislike and per-secute us, people of whom we think: They are not worth so much as a civil greeting. We know from experience how hard that is. Let's be honest; don't we say, Why should I be concerned about that rascal? He's done thus and so to me; so far as I'm concerned, he doesn't deserve to live; if it were up to me, I'd let the lice and worms destroy him. That is how our natural self always inclines us to a hypocritical mercy, which extends only to our compatriots in wrongdoing, but wants nothing to do with other people.

4. That is not what I mean, says Christ. What I mean is this: Even though your fellowman has wronged you, if you want to be a Christian, you must be merciful, in harmony with the example your heavenly Father has set. If you don't, you cannot be either the children or the brother of Him who with His blood has redeemed you from sin and death. The truth of the matter is that you have committed every kind of crime against your God and Father in heaven, and you've broken every one of His commandments, so that He would be fully justified in saying, Why should I sacrifice My Son for such hopeless rebels? I should let them go to the devil in the abyss of hell, for they don't fear, love, or trust in Me. What's more, they despise, blaspheme, and hate Me; they swear and curse by My name; they persecute and damn My Word; they disobey their parents and rulers; they are murderers, adulterers, and greedy thieves who charge exorbitant interest rates and commit perjury. In short, they commit every evil you can name. Therefore, let them go to hell, where they belong. Christ is saying that is what God could say to you, but He doesn't do that. Instead, despite your wickedness, He is good and gracious. He provides not only body and life, food and drink, wife and child, everything you need for this present life, but to top it all off, He gives you His Son and eternal life.

5. That is the kind of mercy we must learn to practice. For what is the mistreatment we have received from others in compar-ison with the gross offenses we have so often committed against

God? Now, if God has such great mercy that He gave His only begotten Son for His enemies, so that through Him they are freed from sin and death, and in addition to that, has also provided them with body and soul, property, and everything they need, when He could have justifiably punished them with hail, lightning, and hellfire in addition to every other kind of evil, we should certainly learn how to follow his example and say, Even though this fellow has mistreated me so badly that I have every right to chew him out, I won't do that. For that would be the reaction of a pagan rather than of a Christian. So, if he has mistreated me, just let it pass! But since he needs me and I'm in a position to help him, I will not pay him back in kind, because my Father in heaven has done the same for me.

6. On every hand we see the kind of wanton wickedness that the peasants are perpetrating. They, too, are merciful to one another, but their kind of mercy is far from being Christian. If they can sell their wares at the market for four times the going price—even when times are good—they'll do so. The same thing happens in the cities. Everyone is out to make money, regardless of what this does to other people. They gobble and guzzle, dance and prance, and live it up. They lie to and deceive one another whenever they can. That sort of conduct produces a bitterness of heart that says, I'll repay those rascals tit for tat, when they need my help. Those rascals should be driven out of the country and turned over to the devil for torture! A Christian, however, does not think such thoughts, but his reaction is rather, What ought I do? Although peasants who till the land are rude, that shall not move me to return their evil. No, I'll do what a good tree does: though this year's fruit is picked and enjoyed by good-for-nothing pickers, a year later it produces another crop of fruit, and doesn't get upset at all. I will react the same way, be a good tree and bear good fruit; I will not repay one evil with another evil. If someone else is a brier bush, capable of nothing but scratching, let him be a brier bush. I won't let that turn me into one; I'll remain a good, fruitful vine and produce good grapes. That is what my Father in heaven does too. He gives to the wicked scoundrels, as well as to those who are pious and just. He gives good things to everyone alike—cattle, oxen, calves, eggs, butter, cheese, house, home, wife, children,

money, property, body and soul, peace, good weather, and everything else we might need. He provides us with lovely sunshine,
even though we've deserved a rain of hellfire. But He does not do
that, not wanting to become a brier bush because of our ingratitude. Instead He says, Well, even if you insist on being wicked, I
shall continue to be beneficent, sending My sunshine and rain on
the good and the evil, on the righteous and the unrighteous alike.

7. That is the example our Lord Christ impresses on us, so that
we might continue in that kind of godliness, not letting the
wickedness of other people turn us into wicked people, the way
the worldly people do. They are quick to seek revenge and will
repay evil for evil. Christians should not live like that, however.
They should rather say, You are a brier bush; you've scratched me
up badly, but I refuse to become a brier bush because of your
actions. I shall, instead, do nothing but good for you when you are
in need. In addition to that, I shall ask God to forgive you and to
transform you from a brier bush into a beautiful, fruitful vine.
That is the meaning of "Be ye therefore merciful as your Father
also is merciful." He repays His greatest enemies and the most
wicked rogues with the highest possible good.

8. Now, we should not misunderstand this to mean that we
should never criticize or punish, for Christ is here speaking to His
disciples, who had no government or authority over them. Similarly, children in the home, peasants in the village, citizens in the
city, nobles on their estates, and princes in the empire have no
authority or power over one another in their respective groups. You
see, father and mother exercise authority in the home; in the village
it is the magistrate or judge who exercises authority; in the city it is
the burgomaster; on the estates it is the prince; in the empire it is the
emperor who wields authority. But children, peasants, burghers,
nobles, and princes are all equals in their respective groups.
Therefore, within their respective groups they should follow this
rule which the Lord here sets down: No one is to wrong his fellowman; but within their respective groups each one is to be merciful toward his equals. But when the persons are of different
ranks—for example, the emperor vis-à-vis the peasants—then we
must not use mercy in dealing with the wicked, but must punish
wrongdoing. Parents are not to practice mercy toward disobedient

children, but must discipline a misbehaving child immediately. Masters and mistresses are not to be merciful with their hired help, but must criticize whatever needs criticism, and they should not ignore any wrongdoing. God requires this of them, and if they fail to do it, God will call them to a severe accounting for such failure.

9. In other words, this command of Christ concerning mercy applies only to those who are equals. People who are of unequal status should be concerned only about their own particular responsibilities. The person to whom authority has been given must exercise that authority. But people who hold the same rank—burgher vis-à-vis burgher, and similarly, peasants, children, domestic servants over against others of their station—in such relationships a Christian must say, You have wronged me; may God forgive you! But it is not my responsibility to see to it that you are punished. That is what being merciful means.

10. So, whenever someone mistreats you, report it to your father, judge, magistrate, or prince, saying, Hank is doing so and so to me; Claus is doing so and so to me. You just see to it that you do not assume the role of judge or jury. In other words, no child, peasant, or burgher should beat up on another child, peasant, or burgher. No nobleman should go to war with another nobleman, as if he himself were God. He should, instead, report the matter to his prince, saying, This is what has happened to me; it is not my place to exact punishment, for I don't have that authority; so I'm reporting it to you, because you have been given the authority to adjudicate such matters. It is also being merciful when an aggrieved person prays to God in behalf of the offender, while simultaneously referring the matter to the proper authority for adjudication, so that the petulance of irresponsible people is held in check. Joseph, for example, did just that. He saw the many vices of his brothers, but he didn't try to discipline them himself, because that was not his duty. Instead, he reported it to his father: Father, Simeon is doing so and so; Levi is doing so and so. Won't you check on them and keep them from doing those things? That was a fitting and proper response and a good example of being merciful. Doing so, however, brought him nothing but disfavor, hatred, and envy, for his brothers couldn't believe that he really had their best interests at heart. It is truly being merciful when you report such

things to those who have been assigned the authority and responsibility of correcting them. That kind of reporting helps to save a
person's soul from the devil and his body from the hangman. In
contrast, if one person tries to destroy the next person by immediately taking him to task, you don't save either his soul or his body.

11. Children, hired help, and neighbors should conduct themselves in this way: they should not try to avenge themselves, but
should rather intercede with God in behalf of offenders, and then,
without any bitterness or rancor, inform superiors—parents, master, or mistress—about any injustice that has been committed.
That way we help one another with regard to the body, money, or
property and also with regard to the soul, so that we will improve
our lifestyle by no longer being so lazy, careless, indifferent,
impertinent, or unfaithful. The kind of mercy we need to practice
is the following: When your neighbor errs or does something
wrong, when you are treated unjustly, when you see something
illegal being done, do not personally jump in as judge and jury.
Instead of that, say, I'm concerned for you and sincerely wish you
had not done it; but it is not for me to judge, correct, or change
things; Christ doesn't want me to do that. Then you pray for that
person and you report the matter to a superior who has been
authorized to adjudicate the matter. For God has ordained more
than enough people for that purpose: princes, lords, magistrates,
father, mother, pastor, chaplain, and even an executioner. They
have the duty of punishing evildoers. Other people who have not
been appointed to such offices should leave the matter alone, exercise mercy, that is, give whatever counsel and help they can.

12. So let us carefully note that this command to practice mercy
is directed only to people of the same rank. In the case of people
who are of unequal rank—father, magistrate, ruler—they should
practice mercy toward their equals too, but not toward their infe-
riors who have acted unjustly. For they have been given the
responsibility of disciplining the misconduct of children, hired
help, and people of lower rank. But when the individuals are of
equal rank, they should treat one another in a way that is friendly,
kind, and sympathetic. They should help, admonish, and report to
the proper authority. That's what it means to live like a Christian.
And if people scold you for that—as children and hired help tend

to do—and if they call you a fink and informer, never mind. Their criticism is of no consequence. You just remember that you are a fig tree or a good vine and do not let yourself denigrate into a brier bush. That is what our lovely sun does too. It sees many a rascal who last night stole or committed adultery, but it goes right on being the lovely sun that it is, even if you don't deserve to ever see the sun again. You should think: Even if I can't help seeing your crimes, the time will come when I see you hanging on a gallows in full public view. Right now you are laughing at me because I can't avoid providing the light on your crimes. But what difference does that make? Unless you change your ways, the time is coming when I'll provide the light for your hanging!

13. Experience teaches us that God lets no crime go unpunished. Even though a person may run away from father and mother, he cannot run away from the executioner. You'll either have to repent and change your ways or await the inevitable punishment, for God lets nothing go unpunished unless there is a changing of ways. Many a person gets by for a time, is a fugitive from justice, and escapes punishment for a while. But if he doesn't change his ways, it will indeed be a miracle if he doesn't get what he has coming, if he doesn't receive his reward for his wrongdoing already here on earth. For the common proverb remains true: a person may escape from his parents, but he won't escape from God. God has arranged matters so that what a father cannot accomplish with the rod will be accomplished by the executioner's rope and sword. If you disregard the discipline of life, you'll have to suffer the discipline of death, which will be your just reward. That is what God has ordained and commanded. But we should not scold, bite, or vent our anger against one another. We should, instead, live a Christian life, so that we learn how to be merciful just as our Father in heaven is merciful.

14. Our Lord Christ explains this teaching in more detail with His parable of the splinter and the plank. This parable is directed primarily at those who try to excuse themselves by saying, This fellow did thus and so to me and I'm going to pay him back. He is a so-and-so! It is against such impatience and desire for vengeance that our Lord directs this parable, asking, What makes you so impatient and vengeful? Your neighbor must have riled you up

with something he said. But so what? That is a mere splinter. You, on the other hand, have a huge plank in your eye. Your neighbor has a tiny speck of dust in his eye, but your eye is filled by a huge plank. Your neighbor has wronged you by what he did, which is a sin, but you are guilty of a great and grievous sin against God, a sin you keep on committing every day.

15. So we should learn how to apply this parable when we see, hear, or suffer something unpleasant, so that we may be patient and say, What is that, compared to my great sin?! In the world you can expect a brother to strike, beat, stab, or murder someone because of the splinter, while he himself is responsible for a huge plank. The reason is that he has never kept God's commandment, despises God, curses by His holy name, refuses to obey God's Word, hates his neighbor, is a murderer at heart, lives a dissolute life, steals, robs, and perjures himself. In short, he does not keep the least of God's commandments even for a moment. But he ignores all this and proceeds to destroy someone who has made an ill-considered statement. Phooey on you, you plank toter! Is your vision so keen that you can spot a speck in your neighbor's eye but so stone blind that you cannot discern your own mountain of sin!

16. Therefore, when a Christian suffers injustice at the hands of his neighbor, he should say, I see a splinter in his eye, but if I look into the mirror, I see in my own eyes planks large enough to build several hog troughs. How important is this injustice my neighbor has done to me? He's done this at most once a month. And as old as I am, I have never kept a single one of God's commandments; I'm such a hopeless wretch that my sins are nothing but sow troughs. And I'm letting that tiny splinter in my neighbor's eye lead me astray? No, it cannot be true that the speck in my neighbor's eye is greater than all those planks in my eyes. I've committed a thousand more sins than he has. I should devote my thoughts to figuring out how to remove those planks from my eyes, and forget about the tiny speck of sawdust in my neighbor's eye. I've disobeyed God and my superiors and I keep right on sinning and—worthless sinner that I am!—I should get all worked up and turn a mean statement into a huge plank?

17. We must take to heart this friendly lesson and lovely parable which our dear Lord Christ here uses to teach us. You see,

what happens is this: our Lord God graciously forgives our many sins and is resolved to forget our big beam, but we do the exact opposite. Isn't that a totally inappropriate way to act? If we really think this through, we won't be so hasty in judging our neighbor, but will say to him, Dear brother, may God, who has overlooked my many planks, and has not only forgiven all my sins but daily showers His grace on me by letting His sun shine, also forgive your splinter of sin. That is what it means to live like a Christian. And if you are intent on seeing your neighbor punished, then report the matter to father, mother, judge, magistrate, and so on. Let them adjudicate the matter, so that judgment is carried out by those who have been commanded to exercise judgment. Meanwhile, let your thought be: It's merely a splinter, for which I forgive him; and for the sake of Him who has forgiven me far greater beams I will help him in any way I can.

Judge not, and ye shall not be judged: condemn not, and ye shall not be condemned: forgive, and you will be forgiven: give, and it will be given unto you; good measure, pressed down, and shaken together, and running over, shall men give into your bosom. For with the same measure that ye mete withal it shall be measured to you again.

18. There you have it! If you can stop judging others, God will stop judging you. If you can excuse and forgive your neighbor, God will forgive and excuse you. Not only that, but if you'll stop your temporal judgment, God will stop His eternal judgment. If you're willing to give a mite, God will give to you by the shovelful. If you forgive one sin, God has already forgiven all of your sins and is willing to forgive countless more sins. On the other hand, if you judge, condemn, refuse to forgive and help, the result will be that, because you refuse to leave the least offense unavenged, God will haul out the planks. In other words, if you point out a splinter of sin in your neighbor's life, God will point out a hundred huge beams of sin in your life.

19. Therefore, we must carefully note that in this text God is telling us, "Be merciful, as your Father also is merciful." God the Father is merciful, and He has been indescribably generous to me,

but with the expectation that I, too, should be generous. Yet, even if I forgive and give only a little, God will, in return, forgive and give without measure. If anyone is unmoved by such kindness, then nothing will move him! On the other hand, if someone is not terrified by the prospect that if we become brier bushes and nit-pickers, finding fault with our fellowman, then God will trot out a thousand beams of our sins. Anyone not moved by that prospect will not be terrified by anything. What fools we are, if we cannot overlook a neighbor's verbal insult, when God has almost drowned us with forgiveness and every other kind of gift! But on the other hand, He tells us that if we judge and condemn our fellowman, refusing to forgive or help him, then God will also throw the book at us, not overlooking one single sin. What a horrible judgment that would be!

20.   This is a comforting message for Christians. Non-Christians and pagans will ignore this message. Because of one verbal insult they will batter a person's head, and won't even hesitate to murder him. But if we really want to be Christians, we should be kind and merciful, gladly forgiving and helping our fellowman where possible. For our heavenly Father doesn't want to send anyone to hell. He wants to give generously, bless, and forgive people's sins, provided only that we in turn treat our fellowman in the same way, being merciful toward those who have wronged us. And such mercy must not be a hypocritical mercy, such as whores, hoodlums, and murderers practice toward their equals but don't hesitate to harm others in any way possible. No, our mercy is to be patterned after our Father in heaven. We should be kind to those who mistreat us in word or deed. That's how Christians should live. Turks and others do not have this teaching, but God has revealed it to us. We should thank Him for giving us such a pure and certain doctrine. That is a short explanation of this gospel lesson in terms that a child can understand.

ELEVENTH SUNDAY AFTER TRINITY

Just as God wants no one to flaunt his piety or talents, He likewise wants no one to despair when he realizes what a miserable sinner he is. Rather, one should trust in God's mercy, that even though he does not have as much as another, nevertheless he has the same merciful God. For this reason I will be content.

LUKE 18:9–14

He also told this parable to some who trusted in themselves that they were righteous and despised others: "Two men went up into the temple to pray, one a Pharisee and the other a tax collector. The Pharisee stood and prayed thus with himself, 'God, I thank thee that I am not like other men, extortioners, unjust, adulterers, or even like this tax collector. I fast twice a week, I give tithes of all that I get.' But the tax collector, standing far off, would not even lift up his eyes to heaven, but beat his breast, saying, 'God, be merciful to me, a sinner!' I tell you, this man went down to his house justified rather than the other; for everyone who exalts himself will be humbled, but he who humbles himself will be exalted."

1. In this gospel our dear Lord Jesus Christ presents us with a lesson based on two individuals, a Pharisee and a tax collector.

2. The Pharisees of the Jews had their counterpart in the monks of the papacy. They wore special clothing, observed special days for fasting and prayer, and pursued piety with such fervor as to make other people appear as nothing but woeful sinners in comparison. That's why they had the name Pharisee, because Pharisee means a singular person, one who wants to separate himself from the common herd as something special.

3. In stark contrast, the tax collectors were like extortioners and political hacks of our time. The Jewish tax collectors negotiated contracts with the Romans, for a designated sum of money, to collect water and land taxes. Then, in turn, they squeezed and

skinned the people for a percentage beyond that. That is why they were considered curmudgeons and flagrant sinners, for accepting a position whereby they greedily burdened and plagued the people. It was, therefore, thought to be inconceivable that a tax collector could be a pious individual, just as it was inconceivable that a Pharisee could be a scoundrel.

4. But our Lord Jesus Christ makes a different assessment here, stating that the tax collector is devout and righteous, while the Pharisee is a sinner, in fact a very great and despicable sinner. St. Luke makes the point unmistakably clear, much to people's wonderment in view of Christ's comparison, "And He spake this parable unto certain which trusted in themselves that they were righteous, and despised others."

5. His is an angry analysis of the Pharisees' two ugly vices, namely, they proudly considered themselves better than others, which in itself is a grievous sin (it is of the devil to consider oneself holy and righteous); and second, they despised others. Pray tell, how would it help such a proud wretch and hypocrite, even if he starved and prayed himself to death? The devil has occupied his heart and caused him arrogantly to boast, If I did not make myself holy, I'd have to wait a very long time for the Lord Jesus. But I fast a great deal; I say a lot of prayers; I do this and I do that, things other Jews do not do; I give my tithe while others would give the priests straw and stubble if they could get away with it. But I am not like that; I am much more pious, and so on.

6. Two shocking evils come home to roost in this so-called holy man. The first is an obnoxious arrogance that esteems itself so highly. Then, as though this sin weren't bad enough, there is his scurrilous disdain for other people. We see how the pesky devil gets the Pharisee to puff himself up; but then, not satisfied with that, he straightway judges and condemns others as nothing more than robbers, wrongdoers, and adulterers. That's his verdict upon the tax collector: Everybody sees that he cheats and robs the people, taking as much as he can. Such a scoundrel I am not; in contrast to him, I am a living saint. People generally find such pride and arrogance to be ill-tempered and slanderous. A common proverb states that if you are something, so be it, but let others

be something, too. But how can God tolerate such vicious evil? It must be thousands of times more reprehensible to God when an individual is arrogant toward Him.

7. In this gospel our Lord Jesus Christ pictures true righteousness for us and how it is to be distinguished from hypocrisy. It's as though He were saying, Consider the man who conducts himself like a living saint—he fasts, gives alms, does not commit adultery, does no one wrong, gladly attends divine service—can there be any other conclusion than that he is a pious man? But I tell you that if you truly wish to know an individual, then you must not look at outward pious show, which any scoundrel may simulate, but you must rather assess what is righteous before God. As far as his outward life, the Pharisee is pious; in fact, one would wish the whole world were like him. But such outward piety even a scoundrel can duplicate. Therefore, don't judge by outward appearances. You will find that hidden under such an apparent holy life is a devil's haughtiness. Because of such arrogance the devil could not abide in heaven; nor could Adam and Eve remain in paradise; how could this one remain in the Church?

8. To fast is commendable, to pray is commendable, not to commit adultery is commendable, not to rob, to do no one an injustice is all good and commendable in itself, but the Pharisee so overlaid his good deeds with arrogance that the result was nothing more than devil's filth. That's the way the world operates too. If someone does a person a kindness in order to ensnare him and to put him into his debt, he does the individual more harm than good. There is a proverb that says, Nothing costs more than what is given free. How can God take pleasure in such piety, which only aims to mock and flaunt Him? Such piety is double-dipped roguishness.

9. That's the story with the hypocrite here. God, he says, don't You see what a pious man You have in me? What is the rest of the world in comparison with me? These individuals are nothing but robbers, extortioners, and adulterers; but I am pious, and so on. With such arrogance, no matter what he does, yes, even if he were to sweat blood or permit himself to be burned, before God it is nothing more than an abomination and a great sin. That is why

Christ says that if you wish to be pious, fine, but guard against becoming an arrogant saint; for even if at times you stumble and fall into the mire, it is not as distressing to Me as when you presume to possess saintliness, when in fact it is self-righteousness.

10. Christ concludes this gospel with the statement "For everyone that exalteth himself shall be abased; and he that humbleth himself shall be exalted." With these words He teaches us to be humble and despise no one. Humility does not vaunt itself over others, but esteems them more highly. Whoever puffs himself up as more learned, attractive, rich, and pious than others is arrogant, just like the Pharisee, who because of his fasting, tithe giving, and other good works gloried in self-esteem. That the Lord forbids. In contrast, we note no self-righteousness on the part of the tax collector, but rather a genuine humility; he does not boast, but pleads that God would be merciful to him. Our Lord wants us also to learn that we have nothing whereof to boast—whether we are learned, rich, or mighty—but reminds us, Beloved, whence did you get all you possess and are? Did you get it from yourself? No! From where, then? Is it not My gift? Yes, Lord, Yours it is. So, why are you vaunting yourself, then? If anyone should boast, it is I, for I am the one who gave you everything; certainly you should not vaunt yourself, but rather say, If I am rich, I know all too well that within an hour You may make me poor; if I am wise and learned, with one word You can make me a fool. That is humility, when you do not brag about yourself or despise others, because you are more attractive, more pious, and richer than they.

11. It would be very much in order were we to employ such arrogance when addressing the devil and say, I have God's Word and I know that with it I have accomplished much good—some I have instructed, others I have admonished, here I have helped some with charitable gifts; I know these to be good works in spite of the devil's slander. I say, we may boast before the devil, because we have received nothing from him. But toward God, from whom we have everything, we may not boast; rather we must humble ourselves.

12. One ought not despise his neighbor, but rather think that since all gifts are God's and come from Him, even though I may have more than my neighbor, God could still decide to give my

neighbor, who may not have a tenth of what I have, to have more than what I have because of his virtue. Why should I then boast or be presumptuous? I should rather be concerned that if I possess much I do not misuse the same. Moreover, I should think God acts according to His own good pleasure, giving much to one, and little to another. It could well be that He is more gracious to the one who has little. Why? The one with much has the greater need to give an accounting, while the one with little has less responsibility.

13. Not so the Pharisee! He blusters arrogantly, I am not like other people. I am not like this tax collector. I give a tithe, while the tax collector robs everyone; I cheat no one, while this man burdens and bleeds everybody. In short, the Pharisee carries on as though he's number one, one who has everything, while the tax collector is nothing and has nothing. O, you double-dipped rogue! Ought you not rather say, True, I give my tithe, I fast, I do as much as I am able, but I don't know how to build on that. Dear God, it is Your gift, and it is evident that this tax collector pleases You more than I do. The Pharisee should have esteemed the tax collector above himself, or at least allowed him to walk at his side, assuring him that it matters not at all whether he has much or little, but only that he has a gracious God. It is the same God who loves one as much as another, the little fellow as much as the bigwig. Why would anyone be uppity and despise others, when all depends on God's mercy and not on how important or how wealthy one might be? The Pharisee knows only how to flaunt his holiness as he stands before God and prays.

14. The Lord has forbidden us to be presumptuous because of our piety or our talents; on the other hand, no one should despair because he is a sinner and has few talents. For we all have one God, who spreads His grace over us like a cloak, over the pious and sinners alike, over learned and ignorant, over rich and poor. In short, He is God over all; there is none beside Him, and no one, rich or poor, can have another God. For this reason we should not be presumptuous, but humble, not looking about to see whether we have more and others less. For God may be more graciously and kindly disposed toward the man to whom He has given little than to whom He has given much. After all, God can strip you bare and clothe him who is naked with finer clothing

than yours. Why, then, would you despise others and try to promote yourself?

15. In everyday life there will be differences between people,
differing stations in life, and some with more earthly possessions
than others. But before God such differences don't count. Only His
grace matters. Before Him no person can boast or praise himself.
We can only humble ourselves, realizing that although we differ
among ourselves, God does not differentiate. He looks no differently at the one who has much than at the one who has little. We
must all learn to hold fast to His grace and mercy, for everyone, the
righteous and sinner alike, rich and poor, strong and weak, belong
to the Lord. What each has, he has from God. On his part each
person has nothing but sin. For that reason no one should exalt
himself over another, but rather humble himself. Whatever good
he has is a gift of God, and he should be praised, not you. His gifts
should be used with thanksgiving and reverence for the Lord. For
God cannot tolerate arrogance, pride, or vaunting of self.

16. Just as God wants no one to flaunt his piety or talents, He
likewise wants no one to despair when he realizes what a miserable
sinner he is. Rather, one should trust in God's mercy, that even
though he does not have as much as another, nevertheless he has the
same merciful God. For this reason I will be content. I will carry
out my duty and fulfill my obligations even as God has blessed me. I
will despise no one, nor will I be presumptuous as regards my abili-
ties, nor be concerned that others have more than I. For me it will
suffice to have the same God as they, and to know that God is never
unjust, even though men are unequal among themselves. That is
what Christ meant when He concludes the parable with the words
"For everyone that exalteth himself shall be abased; and he that
humbleth himself shall be exalted." It is as though Christ were saying, If I find pious people who are content with what I give them, I
am minded to give them more, because they think little of themselves. On the other hand, from the person who has been blessed,
but now is arrogant and haughty, I will take one thing after
another, until finally in disgrace I push him into the abyss of hell.

17. If the Pharisee hadn't been so arrogant, but in humility had
offered his gifts to God and said, Lord You have shown me much

mercy in that You so graciously have kept me from this and other sins; this is a gift from You and I will rejoice in it; I will not be presumptuous because of it, nor despise anyone, for You could recall the gift if You wished—if he had reacted thus, God would have from day to day bestowed greater gifts and would not have been inimical toward him. But because he was self-righteous and disdainfully judged others, boasting, I am everything while the tax collector is nothing, our Lord Jesus completely denounced him so that there was nothing left to praise. It was Christ's verdict that the tax collector returned home justified, while the Pharisee, who is unjust, is consigned to hell with the devil. In contrast, the tax collector, who prays, "God be merciful to me," will be a saint in the Church, for he has a merciful God.

18. Christ wants us daily to learn who we are and what we have. If you possess money, health, home, and property, appreciate these things. God gladly grants them to you and wants to give you more, but do not extol yourself or despise a single other person. Remember that the next person, who does not have what you have, has just as gracious a God as you have. Therefore, do not despise him, but allow him to walk beside you. Then both of you may praise God duly. In contrast the would-be Christians dishonor and defame God, even though they may not do it with their mouths.

19. If we were to judge the Pharisee on the basis of his words, "God, I thank You," we could find nothing amiss. The same words are used by true saints in their prayers, but with a different heart. When they thank God for something, they acknowledge that it is His work and grace, not their own doing. But that is not the attitude of the Pharisee; otherwise he would have said, The fact that I am not an adulterer, a robber, or an unjust person, for this I have no one to thank but You, Lord; in my case if it were not for Your grace I would be in the same position as other people, for we are all the same, and no one should extol himself above another. But the Pharisee did not think thus, but turned things right around, "I thank Thee, that I am not as other men are." He indicates that all his virtue is his own and not from God, else he would have said, You have given it. Instead he acts as though he were so rich that he could give to God. He does not exult in God, but rather in himself,

his intellect, his free will, and power, that he has been able to do so much.

20. Now it is true, if God gives a special gift, we should recognize and greatly appreciate it. We certainly would not want to deny that we are blessed with faculties above those of a donkey or other animals. When God has blessed a person with money and possessions, he certainly ought not foolishly think of himself as a poor beggar. If we have helped the needy with good counsel or gifts, we certainly should not deny this by saying that we have done nothing good. No, that would not be true. One should recognize God's gifts, praise Him for receiving them, and do it gratefully. But in addition one should humbly say, My God, it is Yours and not mine; You have given it; I thank You for the same. That would be the right and humble way to receive them. We must not consider God's gifts insignificant or of little value, but recognize them and esteem them, never becoming arrogant and despising others. Rather, as we have said repeatedly, one should say, Dear God, it is Your gift which You have given me; if another person does not have the same, that is of no count, for he has the same gracious God as I; so why should I despise him?

21. In today's gospel lesson, therefore, our Lord Jesus Christ wants to teach us such humility and warn us against self-righteousness and pride. It is a forgone conclusion that the person who elevates himself will be brought down. Because of arrogance God destroyed His chosen people Israel. Other great kingdoms and empires were likewise destroyed, and for the same reason Lucifer was ousted from heaven, and Adam and Eve from paradise.

22. Therefore, learn to say, Lord what I have is Yours; You gave it to me; You can again take it away. This will keep the self-righteous attitude in check. For who wants to tempt God? The person who acts as though all he possesses comes from his own effort will find himself under this judgment, that God will dispossess him of everything, so that he finally has nothing, because he is evil and has become the devil's property. God give us grace that we heed this teaching well! Amen.

TWENTY-THIRD SUNDAY AFTER TRINITY*

The most important thing our Lord Jesus Christ teaches us in this gospel lesson is the distinction between the two kingdoms, that is, the kingdom of God and the kingdom of the world. . . . The kingdom of God, which is the greatest and most sublime of the two, often finds itself opposed by its adversaries. But so also the kingdom of the world. The devil is always working through his lackeys to destroy both kingdoms on earth.

MATTHEW 22:15–22

Then went the Pharisees, and took counsel how they might entangle Him in His talk. And they sent out unto Him their disciples with the Herodians, saying, Master, we know that Thou art true, and teachest the way of God in truth, neither carest Thou for any man: for Thou regardest not the person of men. Tell us therefore, what thinkest Thou? Is it lawful to give tribute unto Caesar, or not? But Jesus perceived their wickedness, and said, Why tempt ye Me, ye hypocrites? Shew Me the tribute money. And they brought unto Him a penny. And He saith unto them, Whose is this image and superscription? They say unto Him, Caesar's. Then saith He unto them, Render therefore unto Caesar the things which are Caesar's; and unto God the things that are God's. When they had heard these words, they marveled, and left Him, and went their way.

1. The most important thing our Lord Jesus Christ teaches us in this gospel lesson is the distinction between the two kingdoms, that is, the kingdom of God and the kingdom of the world. We must carefully differentiate between the two, allowing each its own purpose and function, so that neither infringes upon the other, as happens regularly in the case of the factious spirits. The kingdom of God, which is the greatest and most sublime of the two,

*Preached at the parish church, 1529.

often finds itself opposed by its adversaries. But so also the kingdom of the world. The devil is always working through his lackeys to destroy both kingdoms on earth.

2. However, God has ordained and established them both, and has built a wall around them to protect them against all fanatics. What this wall is, Christ tells us in the words "Render unto Caesar the things which are Caesar's, and unto God the things which are God's." This is addressed to all people, so that they pay attention to it and do it. If they do it willingly, well and good. If not willingly and gladly, they will have to do it anyway. Whoever gives God what is God's and Caesar what is Caesar's does so willingly and receives special commendation. If he does it grudgingly, he still has to do it. For since the word "give" is appended to each kingdom, it becomes the kind of moat, wall, and buttress that compels all people to give.

3. The devil would like to stop this. He gives rise to many factious spirits and sects within the Church in order to check this giving to God what is God's. But to no avail. The more the devil rages and fumes against God's kingdom and the Church, the stronger it becomes. And the more that Christian blood is shed, the more martyrs there will be. In the secular realm, or kingdom, this is what happens: the more vigorously the devil plants himself against it, the more firmly God asserts His ordinance; and historians attest to the fact that God never lets rebellion go unpunished.

4. With the words, Give Caesar what is Caesar's, Christ validates and establishes the civil state. If civil government were not warranted and ordained by God, Christ would not say, Give Caesar what is Caesar's. For He is a preacher and teacher of truth; He cannot lie and always speaks absolute truth. So, if we are to give to Caesar, we must consider him to be a man of authority and power. Now, at that time Caesar was a gentile, knowing nothing of Christ. His kingdom was founded on principles of common sense and good order, and governed according to the dictates of human reason. Accordingly, Christ says here that because Caesar has the authority, he is to be obeyed. And even if persons were to disagree with him, they still were obligated to obey him.

5. This word, Give Caesar what is Caesar's, Christians gladly and gratefully accept, yielding Caesar what is his without com-

plaint. For they are taught and enlightened by God's Word to understand the value of the political state. This is the reason they are not ungrateful as are the Anabaptists, who disdain the civil state. A Christian, first of all, looks at the word "give" and willingly acknowledges the implications of the word because Christ Himself has spoken it. He carefully notes that scripture calls the civil state God's ordinance and considers the purpose which the political state serves on earth. For as long as God upholds it, there is peace on earth and wicked scoundrels do not, by and large, get away with murder. This peace is such a great treasure that no one, except the Christian, is able to grasp its true significance. Furthermore, a Christian looks at the obligation involved, realizing that everything he possesses has been received from God and belongs to Caesar, or to the magistrate to whom Caesar has delegated authority. When swearing allegiance, each citizen pledges wholeheartedly to obey the existing authorities as required.

6. So the Word, Give unto Caesar what is Caesar's, also signifies that life and property are removed from the citizen and given to Caesar. First Sam. 8 clearly states what the king's right is. Samuel says to the people who were requesting a king [vv. 11–17]: "This will be the manner of the king that shall reign over you: He will take your sons, and appoint them for himself, for his chariots, and to be his horsemen; and some shall run before his chariots. And he will appoint him captains over thousands, and captains over fifties; and will set them to cultivate his ground, and to reap his harvest, and to make his instruments of war, and instruments of his chariots. And he will take your daughters to be confectioneries, and to be cooks, and to be bakers. And he will take your fields, and your vineyards, and your olive yards, even the best of them, and give them to his servants. And he will take the tenth of your seed, and of your vineyards, and give to his officers, and to his servants. And he will take your menservants, and your maidservants, and your goodliest young men, and your asses, and put them to his work. He will take the tenth of your sheep: and ye shall be his servants." And to Nebuchadnezzar, the king of Babylon, the prophet Daniel says [2:37–38]: "Thou, O king, art a king of kings: for the God of heaven hath given thee a kingdom, power, and strength, and glory. And wheresoever the children of men dwell, the beasts of the field and

the fowls of the heaven hath He given into thine hand, and hath made thee ruler over them all."

7. Christians know this from holy scripture. They are provided with spiritual understanding. So that peace may continue on earth, they are content with the political state. They are ready to do Caesar's bidding. They serve him even if it means life and property. Because of this they will have approval. As St. Paul says [Rom. 13:3]: "Wilt thou then not be afraid of the power? Do that which is good, and thou shalt have praise of the same." It is this minority, made up of true Christians, which is cognizant of this word, Give Caesar what is Caesar's, and consequently think: Because God has commanded and so wants it, thus shall it be. These are the ones who uphold the civil government. If Christians did not engage in prayer, there would be no civil state on earth to maintain peace. Only Christians take up the challenge of this word, Give unto Caesar, and on account of their obedience they are approved of God and men.

8. But the majority, the restless rabble, do not do this. Though they have been told, they do not believe that the secular state and government officials are instituted by God. They do not believe that God's Word rightly teaches that the state is an ordinance of God. They look upon civil government as an affliction, a yoke around their neck. The godless do not set store by God's ordinance, ordering, and command. Their only thought is to fill their purses and have a good feast time, regardless of whom God constitutes as head of state, and whether peace or unrest prevail.

9. Ah, dear friend, were our Lord God always to allow peace to reign in the land, to let you dance and frolic, and you were not obligated to thank Him for it and pay taxes, you would rejoice. You do not believe that your possessions belong to Caesar and the state. You think they are yours, and you forget that you have sworn to obey your country with life and property. This is the way the wicked think. They give no thought to prayer in behalf of their government, nor that peace is a precious treasure. Still less do they think of the homage they have pledged their country. People today generally raise their voices against the state because they have to pay taxes. This happens because they do not believe that God has

said or commanded anything as regards Caesar. They think that what they possess is theirs, even though the Lord says here, Give Caesar what is Caesar's. What is Caesar's? The life and property which you swore to him when you made your vow of allegiance. However, you oppose your head of state as if you yourself were he, and the head of state had sworn allegiance to you.

10. This is the group of people who do not understand this Word, Give unto Caesar, and so on. Nor do they understand what a needful, precious thing earthly peace is, but are like swine that think everything is theirs. These constitute the majority of the people; they are ready to destroy the state were they not walled in on all sides by God's Word and command. That Word compels the godless masses; for it says, You will have to obey your government whether you want to or not; and Master Hans will teach you in due time. If you were unwilling to obey government, you should never have pledged allegiance, but should have said instead, I refuse to render obedience with life and property. But face up to it, you swore allegiance and vowed obedience; and despite this you would endanger yourself by contesting whether you are going to obey and give Caesar what is his, or not.

11. And as we read in this gospel lesson, that is exactly what the Jews did. They allowed Caesar to come in; they paid him homage and vowed obedience. And now, first, they ask Christ whether they ought to obey Caesar. The Lord replies, This coin is used to pay taxes due Caesar, and you have sworn loyalty to him; so bear this in mind and give him what is his. Let Me also say, Why did you accept Caesar as your ruler if you do not want to obey him? Hence, I tell you: If you have sworn obedience to the state, you must render that obedience; and if the government is tottery and unstable, Master Hans and the Turk will teach you soon enough. At the moment you have peace and are confident that body and possessions are yours; the thought never enters your mind that just maybe you have these things because God and Caesar gave them to you. God tells you in His Word, Give Caesar what is Caesar's, but you respond, Not so! It is I who tell Caesar what is his. And so you mock God. And He will in consequence send you the Turk to be a noose around your neck, who will not leave your wife, child, home, or possessions untouched for long, just as recently hap-

pened to the Viennese peasants. The Turks despoiled them and in two days carried off ninety thousand women and children. Thus our Lord God taught those poor people that neither house nor home, neither wife nor child are yours but Caesar's, through whom God gives them.

12. We Christians should not be influenced by how the godless world thinks. We should willingly and gladly yield to Caesar what is his. I have nothing of value but four or six goblets. Yet, if necessary, I would gladly let him have them and my life as well. No matter what you think, you will never tear down this wall whereby Christ firmly establishes Caesar in his position. If you are unwilling to give Caesar his due in God's name, be assured you will have to give to some tyrant in the devil's name.

13. Many revile us because we obey the state, but we do not give a rap about their slanderous words. Whoever wants to be a Christian knows that he is not living in paradise, where only good prevails. He knows that he is living in the midst of Sodom and Gomorrah, where there are people who neither know nor understand, nor do they want to know and understand, what God has commanded. We are not saying these things for their sakes; but we do not want them to be left unsaid either. If they demure and refuse to obey God, the Lord will nonetheless have His way. Meanwhile, we will have to live with their sins, and for ourselves with ready heart and spirit do what God has commanded, not looking at their disobedience, but at God's command. For the sake of a righteous man, God often tolerates a whole country's sinfulness, as in the case of Lot, who pleaded in behalf of his countrymen and by his prayer succeeded in forestalling the destruction of the cities. However, no sooner was he gone from Sodom than it was destroyed. So, while we are living on earth, let us, as obedient people, pray that God will not impute their sins to the ungodly. However, once we have departed, they will come into hell in the name of the devil. The die is cast; they will not escape. I say this to those who love the gospel. The rest are not worthy to hear a single word of what I am saying.

14. This, then, is the reason why we are to know that God has commanded to give Caesar what is Caesar's. But what is Caesar's?

Let's talk about duty. You pledge loyalty to the civil magistrates and the prince, and he in turn pledges with life and property to serve the emperor. When the time comes that you are approached by the state, then remember your pledge. If you do not want to do what is asked, then go to your civil authority, to Caesar, and say, Dear sir, gracious prince, benevolent emperor, in times past I have sworn and pledged allegiance to you, but I do not wish to obey you any longer; for this reason I am now retracting my vow. You will hear soon enough what your magistrate, prince, or Caesar will have to say about this! On the other hand, if you want to keep your pledge of loyalty, then with heart and soul do what you promised when you publicly vowed allegiance, and be on guard against those who refuse to give what they owe, for in the end it will cost them their life.

15. Pious Christians heed the words, Give unto Caesar, and give Caesar what is his. In turn, a just government accepts what subjects give, not only that it might enjoy esteem, but that citizens may live in peace, sleep securely in their homes, and the world be kept in line. We should recognize blessings like these and be thankful for them. God will visit the ungrateful in His own time. This is Christ's meaning in Matt. 21, the parable of the landowner. A landowner planted a vineyard, let it out to tenants, and then went abroad. But the tenants greedily grabbed the fruits of the vineyard for themselves, as if the vineyard was theirs. They forgot that the vineyard was leased to them, that in due course they would have to account for the fruits thereof. In short, they dealt with the vineyard as if it were their own property. And when the landowner demanded his share of the vineyard's produce, the tenants killed not only the servants, but also the son of the landowner so that they might get his inheritance. How do you think, says Christ, the owner of the vineyard will deal with these tenants? He will bring those scoundrels to a sorry end and lease his vineyard out to other tenants, who will give him his share of the crop at harvest time.

16. I wonder whether you could tolerate such mischief on your estate. If you would cultivate your land and entrust your property to a servant who swore that he would take care of everything for you, but then, while you were gone he would break to pieces everything in the house, what would you do about it? Verily, you would deal with the servant just as the gospel lesson says the

landowner will deal with his tenants. Why shouldn't our Lord God do the same? Who can fault our Lord when He sent the Turks to plague the ungrateful and disobedient?

17. Our Lord God has given you possessions through Caesar, and you have sworn loyalty to Caesar. And now you are disavowing your allegiance and acting as if the possessions were yours and not Caesar's. For this reason you need someone like this tyrant, the Turk, to threaten and give you a thrashing. Something of this sort is going to happen. Whoever will not accept this word, Give unto Caesar, by fair means will have to accept it by foul. That's what happened to the Jews: They had accepted Caesar as Caesar, as they themselves admitted, We have no king but Caesar. While wanting nothing to do with Caesar, they had to accept him. Emperor Titus came and taught them this to their destruction, for he smashed them completely.

18. On the other hand, when Christ adds the words, Give God what is God's, He establishes and confirms the spiritual polity, called the kingdom of God. There is not the same and immediate urgency to establish and confirm this kingdom as for the civil state, for God is Lord over the whole world, whether it acknowledges this voluntarily or involuntarily. Moreover, this kingdom endures forever, even though there are many who defy it. Just the same, it requires as much explanation as does the worldly kingdom, if we are properly to understand it. Human reason grasps and comprehends the political kingdom, but this spiritual realm or kingdom lies beyond human reason's competence.

19. This spiritual kingdom is a realm in which those are gathered whose hearts are united in trust of God. For the citizens of this kingdom have sworn allegiance to God in baptism. Just as a citizen and subject swears allegiance before the bench of the civil state, so all Christians solemnly pledge and promise fealty in baptism, that Christ is their Lord and God. Is not this exactly what we do prior to our baptism when we disavow the devil, all his works and all his ways, and say that we believe in God the Father, Son, and Holy Spirit, pledging with all our hearts to believe in the one true God and in none other, and to bring forth good works, to be patient, meek, and loving toward our neighbor? Our Lord God

requires of us the vow to cling to Christ alone, to listen to no other word, and to accept no other belief than the gospel of Christ and believe in Him. This is what is meant when Christ says, Give God what is God's. What is God's? Nothing other than faith in God and love of the neighbor.

20. Many contend against this faith in one way or another. Some give God what is God's; many do not. Just as in the civil state there are some obedient citizens, so also in the spiritual realm there are some upright, righteous Christians, even though others may merely bear His name and be intermingled in the external fellowship. A handful willingly give God what is His. Pious hearts call and cry unceasingly to God to have their faith made stronger and to produce fruits commensurate with their faith. These are the righteous Christians. God does not look for our money, life, and property. These He has given to Caesar, and to us through Caesar. But the heart, the greatest and best that man has, God has reserved for Himself. We owe this to God in faith.

21. However, the majority of people in the world—by far the greatest throng—do not give God what is His. The mass of humanity is constituted by so many factious spirits and sects that we are unable to count them. In each of these the devil attempts to create new and strange beliefs, as those spawned by the enthusiasts, Anabaptists, and Sacramentarians. Just like the papacy, they, too, have torn holy scripture to shreds and robbed the people of God's Word. One and all, they are guilty of subversion within the kingdom of God. Like those within the civil state who are rebellious and think that everything belongs to them and do not give Caesar what is Caesar's, rebellious people exist within the spiritual realm. They think that spiritual blessings and God's Word belong only to them. They feel that these things are theirs to adapt, bend, and pervert to suit themselves, to adulterate Christian belief, and design good works according to their way of thinking. In short, they wish to be masters of their faith and lords over all of holy scripture, even though in baptism they have sworn allegiance to remain true to the Christian faith and to the pure Word.

22. Pious Christians, however, who pledge loyalty to the true faith and pure doctrine, meanwhile, continue to pray, and bear

with such rebellion, thereby staving off God's anger, until God, once He has threshed out and gathered the wheat into the heavenly granaries, finally eliminates them from this earth and sets fire to the granaries along with the chaff. If the ungodly will not with heart and soul give God what is His, they must suffer the penalty. So God upholds His Word and the faith, despite the obstacles created by factious spirits. He will purge His threshing floor and burn up the chaff. Christians and those who fear God are mindful of such divine vengeance and punishment, and for that reason pray and stave off God's anger as long as possible. A righteous Christian must be like Lot in this world. Because of such people the Word remains pure and unadulterated. But as for the rest, the Word does not stay pure and unadulterated for even a moment. Yes, as indicated, they do much to impede God and His Word and strive to obliterate it quickly and completely.

23. Therefore, it is Christians alone who by their prayers sustain these two kingdoms on earth, God's and Caesar's. Were it not for the Christians and their prayers on behalf of these two realms, it would be impossible for them to continue to exist. In short, it is for the sake of the Christians that God spares the world. For His thoughts are these: My Christians give Me what is Mine and give Caesar what is Caesar's, and for this reason they must have peace, peace which it is Mine to provide and bestow. When God now grants Christians peace, this same peace also spreads over the ungrateful, who benefit from what Christians enjoy.

24. That fruits now spring forth and peace reigns on earth does not happen for the sake of the godless masses, but for the sake of pious Christians; and often it is true that the godless have more peace than the Christians. God is a Lord who abounds in mercy and goodness. He scatters His blessings throughout the world, even among the ungodly, as Christ Himself says [Matt. 5:45]: "He maketh His sun to rise on the evil and on the good, and sendeth rain on the just and on the unjust." Nevertheless, all this occurs for the sake of the upright and the grateful, even though the wicked and the ungrateful also enjoy the blessings, until ultimately the upright have all entered heaven and the chaff is set ablaze and consumed. This is what happened in Jerusalem. Once the apostles and the Christians were gone, along with them went grain, wine,

bread, and meat. And upon the multitudinous mass of Jews came pestilence, hunger, and sword, to the point that they killed and devoured one another. For what was left was chaff; the wheat was gone. This is the way it ultimately ends. As long as there are upright Christians living in the world, so long will there be peace and abundant blessing. But once the faithful depart this world, they take all blessings with them—food, life, and property. As with the Jews, all will be gone.

25. We must, therefore, be aware of this distinction between these two kingdoms, God's kingdom and Caesar's. When a person hears the Word, Give God what is God's, he should call to mind the vow he made to God in baptism and be on his guard against alien and false belief, heeding God's Word so as not to be deceived and led astray. When he hears the Word, Give Caesar what is Caesar's, he should be thinking of the magistrates and the ruling prince, and should recall the pledge and the oath he made to the civil authorities. In this way he will give each his due, as St. Paul says in Rom. 13:6–7. The one who does this with heart and soul will be repaid by God many times over and, in addition, will receive honor and praise from the civil authorities. The one who does not do so will run headlong into the verdict: In the name of a thousand devils hand it over!

26. Solomon says [Eccles. 3:1]: "To everything there is a season." Up till now it has been a time for peace; but now it is time for conflict. Up till now a time for laughing and dancing; now it is time for crying and lamentation. For so long a time God graciously granted His mercy and a day of salvation, time during which to hear and learn His Word. But the time of His fury and wrath is now here. The time of gathering now gives way to scattering. If until now you have scorned God and Caesar, for this you will now shed tears in captivity. If before you have reveled and lived in abundance, you must now take up arms and march against the foes. For this reason I pray that you will give God what is God's and Caesar what is Caesar's. And do this not for my sake, but for the sake of Him who has so commanded. If you do it with thanks, you do well. But if you do not do it with thanks, you will have to do it with ingratitude, and as a result suffer not only shame and disgrace, but also harm to body, possessions, and soul.

TWENTY-FOURTH SUNDAY AFTER TRINITY

In the raising of the little girl to life, we have evidence and the proof that He can and will resurrect us. In this conviction I can die and permit myself to be buried, saying: Now I must pass away, but at the appointed time I will be raised to life, because God has told me that He is my Lord who promises to rescue me from death.

On Sunday we ought to listen to God's Word as He commands in the Third Commandment, "Remember the sabbath day to keep it holy," that is, honoring it and thus keeping it holy. Now, that happens when we hear and learn from God's Word, how we are to believe and trust in Him. Accordingly, St. Mark writes as follows:

MARK 5:21–43

And when Jesus was passed over again by ship unto the other side, much people gathered unto Him: and He was nigh unto the sea. And, behold, there cometh one of the rulers of the synagogue, Jairus by name; and when he saw Him, he fell at His feet, and besought Him greatly, saying, My little daughter lieth at the point of death: I pray Thee, come and lay Thy hands on her, that she may be healed; and she shall live. And Jesus went with him; and much people followed Him, and thronged Him. And a certain woman, which had an issue of blood twelve years, and had suffered many things of many physicians, and had spent all that she had, and was nothing bettered, but rather grew worse, when she had heard of Jesus, came in the press behind, and touched His garment. For she said, If I may touch but His clothes, I shall be whole. And straightway the fountain of her blood was dried up; and she felt in her body that she was healed of that plague. And Jesus, immediately knowing in Himself that virtue had gone out of Him, turned Him about in the press, and said, Who touched My clothes? And His disciples said unto Him, Thou seest the multitude thronging Thee, and sayest Thou, Who touched Me? And He looked round about to see her that had done this thing. But the woman fearing and trembling, knowing what was done in her, came and fell down before

Him, and told Him all the truth. And He said unto her, Daughter, thy faith hath made thee whole; go in peace, and be whole of thy plague. While He yet spake, there came from the ruler of the synagogue's house certain which said, Thy daughter is dead: why troublest thou the Master any further? As soon as Jesus heard the word that was spoken, He saith unto the ruler of the synagogue, Be not afraid, only believe. And He suffered no man to follow Him, save Peter, and James, and John the brother of James. And He cometh to the house of the ruler of the synagogue, and seeth the tumult, and them that wept and wailed greatly. And when He was come in, He saith unto them, Why make ye this ado, and weep? The damsel is not dead, but sleepeth. And they laughed Him to scorn. But when He had put them all out, He taketh the father and the mother of the damsel, and them that were with Him, and entereth in where the damsel was lying. And He took the damsel by the hand, and said unto her, Talitha cumi; *which is, being interpreted, Damsel, I say unto thee, arise. And straightway the damsel arose, and walked; for she was of the age of twelve years. And they were astonished with a great astonishment. And He charged them straitly that no man should know it; and commanded that something should be given her to eat.*

1. This incident teaches us that our Lord Jesus Christ is a helper and rescuer from life's worst extremity, death. We are aware that all men must die, from the first human being, Adam, to the last; from the beginning of the world until its end. One individual drowns, another loses his life in a fire, or in an epidemic, or some other illness; and those presently alive can anticipate nothing more certain than death. The question presses: What must be done to overcome death? Or if it's inevitable, how can we learn the magic of restoring life again? Christ teaches us this art here, not how to become rich, but rather how to be rescued from death.

2. While death is an ever present threat to all mankind, mankind nonetheless despises what scripture teaches about death, and in particular about the Lord who can rescue from death. This is no mere human frailty, but a devilish maliciousness, since young and old know that they must die. Yet they march along in bold security, bucking the wind, despising Him who wants to rescue

mankind from death. For less urgent needs and lesser harm, everyone seeks help. If someone has an injury, he seeks a medical doctor, incurring whatever it costs to obtain relief. If one has nothing to eat, he will go over land and water, through fire and hazard, to fill his belly. In any distress and misery, people race and run to be rid of the burden. Now, people know that death is the greatest evil of all, greater than all the rest, simply because if there is no help, we die not only in this life, but eternally.

3. Now comes Jesus, our dear Lord, the true physician and trusted helper, who says, Listen, dear man, to what I wish to do for you. You are saddled with death and there's no way you can outrun it. No one else can help you. But I can, and not only will I rescue you from death, but I will also give you eternal life. Only cling to Me and believe My Word; then you will be freed from death. Just as I live, you too shall live. Such a message, however, should be preached only to those who see their need, who confess, feel, and know that they must die. The rest, who do not feel that death is inevitable, go their merry way, bucking the wind, just as peasants, burghers, and nobles do today, having more regard for a blade of straw than for this sermon in which we learn how to escape death and come to eternal life.

4. It is an especially abominable and atrocious situation that the Lord, who can and wants to rescue from death, is so despised, and that individuals become vexed at hearing God's Word, as though it were a great burden. Imagine, if an experienced and highly esteemed physician came to a sick person suffering from a throat infection and said, I will give you a specific medication for your ailment if you will listen to me, and the sick person responded, Stay away from me; I don't like your medicine; I'd rather die than take your medicine. Everyone would consider such a sick person out of his mind, and would tell him, Very well, go ahead and die, in the devil's name, because you have refused to listen to the physician. Similarly, in this situation, if you opt for death rather than our Lord God's help, then go ahead, into hellfire as well. Death marches on. Today it tears this one from life, tomorrow another. People see this right and left, and yet pay no attention, and feel no fear. Even though men know that they must die, they refuse to mobilize against death that they might escape it.

5. Christians, who desire comfort and help, and who anticipate living eternally, have in this lesson a good picture of what sort of man Christ is and how He seeks to help mankind at the hour of greatest need, as a man faces death. Then, when everything comes to an end, when friends forsake, and the whole world cannot help, there still is a helper, namely, Jesus Christ, who can trample death before our eyes and rescue us from death's power.

6. Christ's words and deeds bear this out. He states that the maiden is not dead but is sleeping, takes her by the hand, and raises her up. It is as though He said, To you the maiden is dead, but to Me she is not dead, but rather sleeps. Therefore, if you truly wish to know Me, you must realize that I am master over death and that the dead for Me are not dead, but asleep. What He says, He proves with His deed. It is impossible for the entire world to raise anyone from the dead. For the Lord Christ, however, it is not only possible, but a light and easy task, hardly more than rousing a sleeping individual by thumping his bed and saying, Hey, get up! So Christ does here. As a matter of fact, it is easier for Christ to awaken someone from death than for us to arouse someone from sleep.

7. The Lord here solicits our faith and does not want us to coast along thoughtlessly like swine, like careless clods who spend their Sundays and workdays sitting in the beer halls guzzling beer like cattle drink water. They say, Heck, what do I care about God, or about death? Miserable swine! They will reap what they sow. They will die and go straight into hell. Because they despise the Lord God, who not only created them but also wants to give them eternal life, they will be punished with hellfire. Nor will this in any way be an injustice.

8. If we wish to be Christians, we must be circumspect, guarding against false security and despising of God. We realize that we must die and that we will have to suffer shame and death, with no one to help us. Therefore, we should learn that God is our Lord and that He wishes to help us and rescue us from death. The First Commandment teaches us: "I am the Lord your God who led you from Egypt." That is to say, I am your God who guides you and rescues you from every distress, will resurrect you from death, give you good health, and heal all your diseases, and who will

finally draw you out of the earth to make you alive. That is all summed up in the First Commandment. In Matt. 22:32, Christ states: "God is not the God of the dead, but of the living." Because God states in the First Commandment that He wants to be our God, it follows that He wants to help and rescue us from death. It is tantamount to His saying, Only believe in Me; I will lead you out of your Egypt; I do not look for My advantage, but your advantage. Why else would I ask about you! For I was God long before you came into existence and will be God long after you have died. Whatever I do, I do for your benefit. Therefore, you should learn to have faith that I can and want to help where no one can help, namely, to lead you out of your Egypt, that is, sin and death. On judgment day I will knock on your grave, in order that you need no longer remain there, but come forth to eternal life.

9. This is what we should learn. That's the purpose for preaching, that listeners may understand God's Word, especially the First Commandment: "I am the Lord your God." God wants to be our God, just as Christ here for the maiden. The little girl was near death when the father came to Jesus and said, O Lord come, prove the First Commandment, lay Your hands on her that she may be well and live. The Lord Christ recognized His office, under the promise of the First Commandment; gets up and follows the father, that we might learn that the First Commandment is true. He resurrects the maiden, takes her by the hand, and says to her, Little girl, I say to you, get up! Immediately the little girl responded, moving about as though she had just awakened from sleep.

10. Christ thereby demonstrated that He can and wishes to rescue us from death. He doesn't do it at all times and for everyone, for then no man would lie in the grave, but all who die would immediately arise and live. It is sufficient that He has done it for some; the rest He saves for the day of judgment. That He did it in this and other instances is a mighty proof of the First Commandment. We learn thereby that He has the power to resurrect from the dead. What He did for this maiden should be proof for me that I might believe that He will do the same for me on judgment day. In the meantime, I will rest content in God's grace, until I am resurrected on the last day.

11. We are, therefore, to differentiate between the general exodus out of Egypt on judgment day, that appertains to all mankind, and the miracles which were performed and which, if He deemed necessary, could happen today to bring about understanding of, and faith in, the First Commandment, namely, that God is our Lord who will rescue us from death. As yet we have not witnessed the general resurrection, but His Word stands true, which God Himself affirms: "I am the Lord your God." In the raising of the little girl to life, we have the evidence and the proof that He can and will resurrect us. In this conviction I can die and permit myself to be buried, saying: Now I must pass away, but at the appointed time I will be raised to life, because God has told me that He is my Lord who promises to rescue me from death. I have His Word for this and, to verify His Word, proof in the resurrection of the nobleman's daughter. Just as He did with this maiden, so He also did for Lazarus, who had been in the grave for four days, whose body, no doubt, had already begun to decompose.

12. You might ask, Why doesn't He awaken all the others from death as He awakened the maiden? The answer is that He spares the rest until His appointed time. Meanwhile, He awakens a few to undergird our understanding of the First Commandment. If no one had ever been raised from the dead, the First Commandment would be hard to believe. But because this maiden, as well as Lazarus and the son of the widow at Nain were awakened from death, this should be evidence for us to learn, understand, and believe the First Commandment. That is why God states in Exod. 3:6: "I am the God of thy father, the God of Abraham, the God of Isaac, and the God of Jacob." That is as much as to say (as Christ explains in Matt. 22): Abraham, Isaac, and Jacob live; though they are dead to the world, they are alive to Me. That is how one should speak of the dead, that they are not dead to our Lord even though they are dead to us. This God will make clear on the day of judgment. Just as here Christ brought forth the maiden from death, so God will bring forth Abraham, Isaac, Jacob, and all of us. For there stands His Word: "I am the Lord, your God." And here are the miracles accompanying His Word, by which we may learn to believe and say: If Christ has resurrected so many who were dead,

it is evident that He is able and will do it, as He states in the First Commandment, "I am the Lord, your God." In other words, He will help in every need, and if you die, nevertheless you shall live again. Thus you learn to know who I am, Christ says.

13. It is God's command to preach, so that people believe in Him and cry out for His help: O Lord, preserve me from death! Be my Lord and God as the First Commandment promises! The Sunday sermons are intended to proclaim this so that we might learn these truths. Moreover, that would be serving God acceptably when we laud and praise Him, when we learn to have faith in Him and speak of Him according to the First Commandment. We ought not act like thoughtless, brutish clods, like the peasants, burghers, and nobility of today who, though they see that they must die, nevertheless despise God and His Word, and succumb to death like cattle.

14. Surely an alarming attitude in the face of death's reality! They brashly despise God, who offers them His grace. What? say these knaves, should I listen to the parson? Pass the beer, let us have a drink! O you shameful, miserable swine! Can you thus despise your Lord and God, who so kindly invites you? You are impressed when your servant does something special for you, when your cow gives milk, when your horse gives you a ride, when your needs are met. But when your God and Lord wants to give you life, you despise and reject Him, and try to keep Him from speaking any longer to you in sermons; you have no desire to learn how to call upon Him in time of need. I say it is disgraceful that our Lord God offers His help uselessly to people who beat against the wind but have no other source of help. The result of such false security and despising of God will be that they coast along in the devil's name, until they come into hell and are lost eternally.

15. For this reason, you young people, you children, you servants, you boys and girls should diligently learn to fear our Lord God from early youth, to learn to love His Word. You do have recourse in every need, especially for the terrors of death, namely, by the assurance that God is our Lord who wants to rescue us from death. This is the first and paramount lesson in today's gospel.

16. The other part of the lesson has to do with the fife players and wailers, and how we ought rather act at such time. The pro-

fessional pipers at a funeral were the Jew's bells. They went to the door of the deceased and wailed songs of sorrow, of mourning, and of lamentation. They stood at the bier and bewailed death. Here now Christ asked that they be removed, saying, Why all this commotion and wailing? The child is not dead, but asleep. They laughed at Him, just as today the world considers our dear Lord Jesus a fool. But even though they mocked Him, He persisted and drove out the fife players. The same thing will happen to all those who foolishly pipe lamentations over death, whether they are false teachers or those who live an un-Christian life. So, also, all preaching that is not Christ-centered is tantamount to piping unto death, as is also a life of despising and disobeying God.

17. Jesus wants to get rid of all this. He drives them all out, as though to say, Away with all false teaching and all un-Christian living; take note of what I have to say and do as I bid you. I will pipe the right tune for death. And what is that tune? "Little girl, I say unto you, get up!" Just as the First Commandment states, "I am the Lord your God!" If you are a Christian, you should know that you are to believe in God, trust in Him, call upon Him in every need, also at death. Then He also said to the maiden that she should eat, drink, and be an obedient girl. He asks nothing of her but obedience. Life is a sheer gift, not a reward. It is Christ's gift to the little girl, out of grace, freely, that she may know that He is her God. After that He commands her to eat, drink, be pious, and obedient. That is to pipe a tune for death!

18. Christ is our helper and our rescuer, as He states in Ps. 68:20: "Our God is the God of salvation; and unto God the Lord belong the issue from death." Therefore, we should recognize Him, call upon Him, and do what is our duty to do. He didn't suggest that the maiden enter a cloister, but told her to eat, drink, and help about the house, as requested by her father and mother. If Christ is our personal Savior and we have faith in Him, we demonstrate this sufficiently by our personal attention to duty. We are God's people for eternity.

19. When the hour comes for us to die, we proceed, assured of our salvation and that, once placed in the grave, we will be awakened in eternity. A thousand years will be no longer than if we had

slept in the grave for half an hour. This is how it seems in sleep. Even more so, that will be our experience in death! A thousand years will pass as a night's sleep. Before we realize it, we will be like beautiful angels and soar with Christ in the heavens.

20. This is what our dear Lord Jesus wishes to picture for us here. It is as though He said, My dear people, learn from Me who I am, so that you may know what a powerful God you have in Me who can raise you from the dead. In the meantime, be pious and obedient. When death comes, cheerfully rely on Me; then you may be assured of eternal life, for I was your aid in the exodus from Egypt and I am your rescuer from death. May God give us His grace that we believe. Amen.

THE DAY OF ST. MARY MAGDALENE

1536

So this is the office of our Lord which He introduces into the world, namely, that of rebuking sin and forgiving sin. He rebukes the sins of those who do not recognize their sin, and in particular those who claim not to be sinners but presume to be righteous, as this Pharisee did. He forgives the sins of those who perceive their sin and desire forgiveness; the woman was this type of sinner.

LUKE 7:36–50

And one of the Pharisees desired Him that He would eat with him. And He went into the Pharisee's house, and sat down to meat. And, behold, a woman in the city, which was a sinner, when she knew that Jesus sat at meat in the Pharisee's house, brought an alabaster box of ointment, and stood at His feet behind Him weeping, and began to wash His feet with tears, and did wipe them with the hairs of her head, and kissed His feet, and anointed them with the ointment. Now when the Pharisee which had bidden Him saw it, he spake within himself, saying, This man, if He were a prophet, would have known who and what manner of woman this is that toucheth Him: for she is a sinner. And Jesus answering said unto him, Simon, I have somewhat to say unto thee. And he saith, Master, say on. There was a certain creditor which had two debtors: the one owed five hundred pence, and the other fifty. And when they had nothing to pay, he frankly forgave them both. Tell me, therefore, which of them will love him most? Simon answered and said, I suppose that he to whom he forgave most. And He said unto him, Thou hast rightly judged. And He turned to the woman, and said unto Simon, Seest thou this woman? I entered into thine house, thou gavest Me no water for My feet: but she hath washed My feet with tears, and wiped them with the hairs of her head. Thou gavest Me no kiss: but this woman since the time I came in hath not ceased to kiss My feet. My head with oil thou didst not anoint: but this woman hath anointed My feet with ointment. Wherefore I say unto thee, Her sins, which are many, are forgiven; for she loved much: but to whom little is forgiven, the same loveth little. And He said unto her, Thy sins are forgiven. And they that sat at meat with Him began to say within themselves, Who is this that forgiveth sins also? And He said to the woman, Thy faith hath saved thee; go in peace.

1. This is a beautiful gospel text, well worth an in-depth treatment. But even though there is not enough time to do this in a single session, we do want to speak a few words about it. Our beloved Lord Jesus Christ models the office He has entrusted to His apostles and preachers. In other places He decrees and testifies verbally; but here He confirms it with deed. Moreover, the office and the command is to do as He does, not in order to please mankind. For His office is to rebuke sin and to forgive sin. If He rebukes sin, the world won't stand for it, saying that He ought to preach only gospel and grace. If He forgives sin, then the Pharisees and the holier than thou turn up their noses and say that He prohibits good works and preaches only grace without reproving sin.

2. In this office we preachers are to help our Lord God, also rebuking and forgiving sin for His sake. Those preachers who do not rebuke sin open the gates of hell and close heaven. On their part, those who refuse to forgive sins likewise open the gates of hell

and close heaven. Therefore, both must be proclaimed, reproof and pardon of sin.

3. But as we said above, the world wants no part of this. To reprove and punish sin is wrong; to offer comfort and pardon is also wrong. Whatever you do, it makes no difference. What Christ experienced here is exactly what we experience today. He was wrong to forgive Mary Magdalene, and the Pharisees said He was shutting up hell, He was giving people the opportunity and the desire to sin without restraint, and He was blaspheming God. But when He opened to Simon a festering wound and revealed to him the sin of which he had been unaware, who had been flattering himself that he was righteous, it did no good. So the Lord is not complaining in vain or without cause about this sort of evil in the world when He says [Matt. 11:16–19]: "But whereunto shall I liken this generation? It is like unto children sitting in the markets, and calling unto their fellows, and saying, We have piped unto you, and ye have not danced; we have mourned unto you, and ye have not lamented. For John came neither eating nor drinking, and they say, He hath a devil. The Son of Man came eating and drinking, and they say, Behold a man gluttonous, and a wine bibber, a friend of publicans and sinners!" John preached repentance, rebuked sins, lived a disciplined life, and they said, He keeps himself from the people; he is a devil; who would want to listen to what he says? Christ preached forgiveness of sins, accepted sinners, and they said, He keeps company with harlots and miscreants, makes them insolent and secure; how can He be a true prophet?

4. This is without doubt a very good rule, from the point of view of reason, which Christ has enjoined upon us, to have to endure reproach as blasphemers and heretics before God, like John was, or be labeled an associate of harlots and ne'er-do-wells, as Christ was. But what can we do? If Christ experienced this, we will fare no better. So we may as well accept it, and get used to the fact that people do not like it, especially from us who hold the office. If we did not do this, neither rebuking nor forgiving sin, who would be saved?

5. The Pharisee Simon does not realize that he lacks the essential thing. He imagines that he is doing a good work and considers

it a great favor to invite Christ, the prophet, to be his guest, to give Him a seat among the Pharisees as a distinguished rabbi. But something needs to be done; he continues to be oblivious of his own sin, and does not desire to have his sins forgiven. So our Lord must rebuke him, and makes this magnanimous work of his, of which he is proud, a sin and a shame to him. You invited Me, He says, but in so doing you have only your own pride and benefit in mind. You did not give Me water for My feet, and even if you had, it would have been a meager service in comparison with that which this woman has just shown Me. For this sinner provided not water, but the tears from her own eyes, and sprinkled neither My hands, nor My head, nor My face, but the lowliest of My members, My feet, which are soiled by the dust of the earth; and she did it from behind. What do you think of this work which the sinner did to Me, in comparison with your work, of which you are so proud, and yet you gave Me no water to wash either My face, My hands, or My feet?

6. You gave Me no wipe or towel to dry My face, hands, or feet. But she gave Me not a silk kerchief, but her hair, her tresses, the most glorious ornament she possesses (for her hair is a woman's greatest glory, 1 Cor. 11:15). With this she dried not My face, not My neck, but My feet. You gave Me no kiss, neither on My hand, nor My cheek, nor My mouth. For in the land of Israel this was the common custom for one to kiss another, as is still the custom in the Netherlands and elsewhere. Therefore Christ says, You might have given Me a kiss, in keeping with the customs of this people and country; but you did not do this, you proud, haughty ass. But this woman accounted herself unworthy to kiss My hand, or cheek, or mouth; so she fell to her knees, and has not ceased from kissing My feet, however disreputable this might seem to you.

7. You did not anoint My head with oil, or as we might say, with perfume, as we customarily honor guests with oil of spikenard or rose water. You dispensed with this and did not do it. But she poured a costly perfume, balsam, oil of spikenard, which is of exquisite quality and expensive, on My dusty feet. You did not perceive at all what this woman graciously did for Me. And as for you, you have not perceived this sin in yourself, which is a very great burden of sin indeed, and a great and deadly corruption, if you must come before God for judgment still encumbered with it. And

so the Lord rebukes the Pharisee for his sin and, in contradistinction, forgives the woman her sins, saying, "Thy sins are forgiven."

8. So this is the office of our Lord which He introduces into the world, namely, that of rebuking sin and forgiving sin. He rebukes the sins of those who do not recognize their sin, and in particular those who claim not be sinners but presume to be righteous, as this Pharisee did. He forgives the sins of those who perceive their sin and desire forgiveness; the woman was this type of sinner. For rebukes He receives small gratitude; for pardoning sins He elicits accusations of heresy and blasphemy against His doctrine. We must suffer this to happen. If the Lord Himself could not be exempt from this, but voices His complaint, as it is written in Matt. 11, then we shall not fare any better. If we wish to be Christians, and especially preachers, then we must have patience, and consider the saying of Paul [2 Cor. 6:4, 7–8]: "But in all things approving ourselves as the ministers of God, in much patience, in afflictions, in necessities, in distresses. . . . By the word of truth, by the power of God, by the armor of righteousness on the right hand and on the left, by honor and dishonor, by evil report and good report: as deceivers, and yet true." When the Lord reproves the Pharisees, they become resentful and do not want to hear it. Although the text at this place is silent on this point, it is clearly evident at other places how they received His reproofs. When He says to the woman, "Thy sins are forgiven," they reply, Did the devil send this prophet? Who is this that claims to forgive sins? This is the kind of thing the Lord had to put up with. So He says not a word until the proud asses have spoken condemnation and judgment upon Him, and when they have said their piece and quieted down, He turns to the woman and says, "Thy faith hath saved thee; go in peace."

9. We do the very same thing: we rebuke sin and forgive sin, and have our opponents, the papists, maligning us as heretics. They accuse us of forbidding good works and offering them a pretext to sin, although we rebuke sin more severely than they do. For though they rebuke sins till the end of the age, they stick to the second table, rebuking only the gross, open sins, as does this Pharisee. He thinks: I am a holy man; I am not a sinner as this woman is. He is fairly well acquainted with the second table. He sees as well as understands that prostitution is wrong and a sin. But he under-

stands the first table not a whit; he has no idea that he lacks faith in God's goodness and mercy, nor does he recognize that he is worse than a pagan, having no love for God or for his neighbor, but instead is full of pride, arrogance, and presumption. And yet, for all that, he goes along blindly and obstinately, unaware of these sins. So Christ must lance his festering boil, expose the sin, and point out the source of the trouble. True, you did invite Me here to eat with you, He says, but what do you mean by being so puffed up and heady about this work of yours? You are, no doubt, a reasonable and intelligent man, and judged correctly that he who receives much loves much. You are also a pious man in the eyes of the world, not an adulterer, not a thief, not a lawbreaker; but you are an unbelieving, godless man; for you are presumptuous, you have neither God, nor grace, nor His mercy, no forgiveness of sins, and you are arrogant and covetous toward your neighbor. Yes, indeed, I mean proud, Simon, vain and self-canonized.

10. This is what needs to be done; that is our office. Sins are not to be pardoned without first being rebuked and brought to the sinner's attention, particularly sins of the first table, such as unbelief, idolatry, no fear of God, presumption, no knowledge of God or respect for Him and others. But on the other side, forgiveness is not to be excluded either. They are operative together, as a pendulum swings from one side to the other: to rebuke sin and to forgive sin, the exhortation to repentance and the declaration of pardon. If sins are not rebuked, the soul is not humbled, and the preaching of grace remains unfruitful. But the soul which is smitten by a rebuke or the preaching of the law, as this poor harlot, needs a proclamation of grace and forgiveness, or it must be overcome with despondency and despair. The poor woman is not so self-assured as the proud Pharisee, Simon: he is presumptuous and proud, flattering himself to be quite pure, not only outwardly, but also his heart and everything about him. Therefore, he must be reproved and his sins exposed. But this poor woman has recognized and felt her sinfulness; she is sorrowful and humble, so she needs forgiveness.

11. Neither of these can be neglected. The call to repentance and the rebuke are both necessary to bring people face-to-face with their sins and humble them. The proclamation of grace and

forgiveness are necessary too, lest the people lose all hope. There-fore, the office of preaching must walk the middle way between presumption and despair, to preach so that the people become nei-ther proud nor despairing. Both of these sins are proscribed by God in the First Commandment: "I am the Lord, thy God," as if to say, You are not to be proud; if you are, I am not the Lord your God; likewise, you are not to despair; if you do I am not the Lord your God. Reprove the sin of the presumptuous and comfortable people who are not aware of their sin; not merely blatant sins of the flesh, but also, and foremost, the subtle, underlying, spiritual sins. As for the others who know their sins and fear death, comfort them and say, Dear brother, you have had enough terrors, I may not frighten you anymore. Before you had no God because of your presumption, but now the devil wants to lure you away from God on the other side by despair. God has forbidden both of these, and He has ordained the office of preaching to restrain both: presump-tion, by the call to repentance and the rebuke; despair, by the preaching of grace and forgiveness of sins.

12. That is the sum total of this gospel, which teaches of Christ's office—reprove sins and forgive sins—in which office He is either reproached as a devil or a blasphemer in the world. If He preaches repentance, rebuking the people's sins as John the Baptist did, then He is a devil; if He preaches grace and pardons sins, then He is a glutton and wine bibber, a friend of harlots and outcasts. Whatever he does, it's wrong. If He takes a hard line against the obstinate and the haughty, that's not right; if He is gentle, mild, and kindly toward the poor sinners, that's not right either. If He plays the pipe, it's no good; if He sings a dirge, it's not good either.

13. Now this office and twofold preaching are vital to Chris-tianity if anyone is to be saved at all. As Christ commanded, preach in His name repentance and forgiveness of sins, come what may. Moreover, each part is to be rightly distinguished and admin-istered. Therefore, also, St. Paul commands Timothy his disciple [2 Tim. 2:15]: "Study to shew thyself approved unto God, a work-man that needeth not to be ashamed, rightly dividing the word of truth"; as if to say, hold firmly to the word of truth, but take care that you divide one part from the other, and administer it prop-erly. It is a sharp two-edged sword. Keep the word of reproof, so

that all sins, both the inward and the outward, the fleshly and the spiritual, which people commit against us may be reproved. Keep the word of grace, so that we and others may have a true and certain consolation against sin. Both are necessary, the preaching of reproof and the preaching of grace, to keep people on the middle way, falling neither to the right into presumption and complacency, nor to the left into despair. Where there is despair, a man is swept over the brink into hell and where there is presumption, a man rushes into hell full speed ahead.

14. So take careful note of this gospel; and would to God that everyone would take to heart this example of our Lord Jesus Christ, how He behaved toward the proud Pharisee and toward the poor sinner. To Simon, the Pharisee, He is a strict judge and preaches a severe word, making it especially disagreeable and unpalatable. On the other hand, He is a gracious confessor and a consoling preacher. He pronounces over the woman a merciful remission of sins and makes her a saint; but He commits Simon, the Pharisee, to the devil. That is preaching reproof and grace. The miserable harlot He frees from sin and clothes her with heavenly grace. He shows the proud Pharisee his sin and burdens his conscience; yet He means him no evil, but seeks his salvation, revealing his sin to him so that he would recognize it, seek counsel, and escape damnation with the other presumptuous hypocrites, if he would only obey.

15. You hear such things preached by us all the time. And this is how we should preach, so that we always find ourselves there with those sinners who know their sinfulness and are fearful because of it, as Magdalene acknowledges her sins and is frightened by them. Let us not be found in the number of those who are without sin and imagine themselves holy, or justify their sins and refuse to be corrected. God grant that we not be found among sinners who refuse to be sinners. If He permits us to fall, let us fall into sins which we acknowledge and that He will pardon; let us not fall into sin which He cannot pardon because it claims to be not sin, but righteousness.

16. A Christian is in this state as long as he is on earth, even if he is no adulterer, or murderer, or thief; even if he does not have

the sins which war against the soul, as St. Peter calls them [1 Pet. 2:11], that is, against faith and a good conscience; nevertheless he is and remains a sinner in the eyes of God, with a heart full of sins, not just in violation of the First Commandment, but against all the commandments of both tables. He does not love God with his whole heart, he does not delight in God's Word and work as he should, and he does not have a fervent love for his neighbor. In sum, he experiences a whole range of evil inclinations, lusts, and desires contrary to God's commandments, although he resists them through the Spirit of God in faith, and does not yield to them. This defilement is with us until we die. St. Paul mortifies his body and keeps it tightly reined up [1 Cor. 9:27]. Yet for all that, he grieves that he has still not gotten a firm grip on it, neither shall he completely [Phil. 3:12]; and in Rom. 7, he says that he longs to be godly, he would only too gladly be ablaze with love toward God and his neighbor; but he has a demon in his heart, drawing him back, that is, his sinful nature. "For I delight in the law of God after the inward man: but I see another law in my members, warring against the law of my mind, and bringing me into captivity to the law of sin which is in my members. O wretched man that I am! who shall deliver me from the body of this death? I thank God through Jesus Christ our Lord" [vv. 22–25].

17. This is the case with all Christians: they both possess and feel the sinful nature. But they do not let it rule over them, or even hold the upper hand; they do not allow the sinful nature to rage against the hope which they have or drive them to despair; neither do they allow it to rage against fear and humility, or drive them to presumption, pride, and arrogance against God and their neighbor. They are, therefore, in a continual struggle, battling against their sins, and praying to God to redeem them from the accursed, sinful body. Everyone who so proceeds is on the right path to salvation. Although he be a sinner, still feeling his sins, they shall not destroy him. He who confesses his sin, submits to discipline, and bestirs himself to resist can be confident that his sins are forgiven. But if he does not confess his sins, but on the contrary defends them, refusing correction, he has no such hope.

18. This is enough for now about the office of our Lord Jesus Christ, which we execute in His name, both to rebuke sins and for-

give them, as He commanded us. This is an indispensable office for us, for all time, until the last day. For we will never achieve in this life absolute purity and sinless perfection. The old leaven has spread too far beyond all reasonable bounds, that we will never be free from it until we die to it, bodily as well as spiritually. So we will always be in need of reproof and forgiveness, in order to resist and harness the sinful nature. May God grant us His grace to remain godly sinners rather than holy blasphemers, that is, that we would let God be just and His words be right, so that He might justify us. Amen.

IV

Teachings

THE ESTATE OF MARRIAGE

Part Three

Though he did not marry for love, Luther soon came to greatly esteem his wife, Katharina von Bora, bearing deep affection for her and for their six children. Contrary to the common opinion held in the Middle Ages that sex was a debased act, Luther found justification in Genesis to teach that passion in marriage is an expression of God's creative power and vitality. God Himself, Luther held, constitutes the union of man and wife. He resisted the spiritualization of the human being, by which the life of the body was despised, and condemned the glorification of virginity and celibacy as the work of the devil, who tries to wreak havoc on the world by undermining the marital state with a perverted sense of holiness.

Luther appreciated marriage as a great school for virtue wherein one will learn patience, charity, fortitude, and humility. Parents must be provident and affectionate, accepting their children as gifts from God Himself. Husband and wife should be loyal and loving friends to each other. He was vehement in regarding divorce as evil because it left women in an unprotected state, and he was of the opinion that adulterers should suffer the death penalty. Luther's high estimate of marriage and his compassionate concern for women and for their well-being were progressive views for his times.

In order that we may say something about the estate of marriage which will be conducive toward the soul's salvation, we shall now consider how to live a Christian and godly life in that estate. I will pass over in silence the matter of the conjugal duty, the granting and the withholding of it, since some filth-preachers have been shameless enough in this matter to rouse our disgust. Some of them designate special times for this, and exclude holy nights and women who are pregnant. I will leave this as St. Paul left it when he said in 1 Cor. 7 [9], "It is better to marry than to burn"; and again [in v. 2], "To avoid immorality, each man should have his own wife, and each woman her own husband." Although Christian married folk should not permit themselves to be governed by their bodies in the passion of lust, as Paul writes to the Thessalonians [I Thess. 4:5], nevertheless each one must examine himself so that by his abstention he does not expose himself to the danger of fornication and other sins. Neither should he pay any attention to holy days or workdays, or other physical considerations.

What we would speak most of is the fact that the estate of marriage has universally fallen into such awful disrepute. There are many pagan books which treat of nothing but the depravity of womankind and the unhappiness of the estate of marriage, such that some have thought that even if Wisdom itself were a woman one should not marry. A Roman official was once supposed to encourage young men to take wives (because the country was in need of a large population on account of its incessant wars). Among other things he said to them, "My dear young men, if we could only live without women we would be spared a great deal of annoyance; but since we cannot do without them, take to yourselves wives," etc. He was criticized by some on the ground that his words were ill-considered and would only serve to discourage the young men. Others, on the contrary, said that because Metellus was a brave man he had spoken rightly, for an honorable man should speak the truth without fear or hypocrisy.[44]

So they concluded that woman is a necessary evil, and that no household can be without such an evil. These are the words of blind heathen, who are ignorant of the fact that man and woman are God's creation. They blaspheme His work, as if man and woman just came into being spontaneously! I imagine that if women were to write books they would say exactly the same thing about men. What they have failed to set down in writing, however, they express with their grumbling and complaining whenever they get together.

Every day one encounters parents who forget their former misery because, like the mouse, they have now had their fill.[45] They deter their children from marriage but entice them into priesthood and nunnery, citing the trials and troubles of married life.

[44]This story, referred to frequently by Luther, is from the *Attic Nights* of Aulus Gellius I.vi.1–6. Metellus Numidieus was a Roman censor in 102 B.C.
[45]Luther's variation of the old proverb about the sated mouse may be paraphrased in English, "To a full belly all meat is bad."

Thus do they bring their own children home to the devil, as we daily observe; they provide them with ease for the body and hell for the soul.

Since God had to suffer such disdain of His work from the pagans, He therefore also gave them their reward, of which Paul writes in Rom. 1 [:24–28], and allowed them to fall into immorality and a stream of uncleanness until they henceforth carnally abused not women but boys and dumb beasts. Even their women carnally abused themselves and each other. Because they blasphemed the work of God, He gave them up to a base mind, of which the books of the pagans are full, most shamelessly crammed full.

In order that we may not proceed as blindly, but rather conduct ourselves in a Christian manner, hold fast first of all to this, that man and woman are the work of God. Keep a tight rein on your heart and your lips; do not criticize His work, or call that evil which He Himself has called good. He knows better than you yourself what is good and to your benefit, as He says in Gen. 1 [2:18], "It is not good that the man should be alone; I will make him a helper fit for him." There you see that He calls the woman good, a helper. If you deem it otherwise, it is certainly your own fault, you neither understand nor believe God's Word and work. See, with this statement of God one stops the mouths of all those who criticize and censure marriage.

For this reason young men should be on their guard when they read pagan books and hear the common complaints about marriage, lest they inhale poison. For the estate of marriage does not set well with the devil, because it is God's goodwill and work. This is why the devil has contrived to have so much shouted and written in the world against the institution of marriage, to frighten men away from this godly life and entangle them in a web of fornication and secret sins. Indeed, it seems to me that even Solomon, although he amply censures evil women, was speaking against just such blasphemers when he said in Prov. 18 [:22], "He who finds a wife finds a good thing, and obtains favor from the Lord." What is this good thing and this favor? Let us see.

The world says of marriage, "Brief is the joy, lasting the bitterness." Let them say what they please; what God wills and creates is bound to be a laughingstock to them. The kind of joy and pleasure they have outside of wedlock they will be most acutely aware of, I suspect, in their consciences. To recognize the estate of marriage is something quite different from merely being married. He who is married but does not recognize the estate of marriage cannot continue in wedlock without bitterness, drudgery, and anguish; he will inevitably complain and blaspheme like the pagans and blind, irrational men. But he who recognizes the estate of marriage will find therein delight, love, and joy without end; as Solomon says, "He who finds a wife finds a good thing," etc. [Prov. 18:22].

Now the ones who recognize the estate of marriage are those who firmly believe that God Himself instituted it, brought husband and wife together, and ordained that they should beget children and care for them. For this they have God's Word, Gen. 1 [:28], and they can be certain that He does not lie. They can therefore also be certain that the estate of marriage and everything that goes with it in the way of conduct, works, and suffering is pleasing to God. Now tell me, how can the heart have greater good, joy, and delight than in God, when one is certain that his estate, conduct, and work is pleasing to God?

That is what it means to find a wife. Many *have* wives, but few *find* wives. Why? They are blind; they fail to see that their life and conduct with their wives is the work of God and pleasing in His sight. Could they but find that, then no wife would be so hateful, so ill-tempered, so ill-mannered, so poor, so sick that they would fail to find in her their heart's delight and would always be reproaching God for His work, creation, and will. And because they see that it is the good pleasure of their beloved Lord, they would be able to have peace in grief, joy in the midst of bitterness, happiness in the midst of tribulations, as the martyrs have in suffering.

We err in that we judge the work of God according to our own feelings, and regard not His will but our own desire. This is why we are unable to recognize His works and persist in making evil that which is good, and regarding as bitter that which is pleasant. Nothing is so bad, not even death itself, but what it becomes sweet and tolerable if only I know and am certain that it is pleasing to God. Then there follows immediately that of which Solomon speaks, "He obtains favor from the Lord" [Prov. 18:22].

Now observe that when that clever harlot, our natural reason (which the pagans followed in trying to be most clever), takes a look at married life, she turns up her nose and says, "Alas, must I rock the baby, wash its diapers, make its bed, smell its stench, stay up nights with it, take care of it when it cries, heal its rashes and sores, and on top of that care for my wife, provide for her, labor at my trade, take care of this and take care of that, do this and do that, endure this and endure that, and whatever else of bitterness and drudgery married life involves? What, should I make such a prisoner of myself? O you poor, wretched fellow, have you taken a wife? Fie, fie upon such wretchedness and bitterness! It is better to remain free and lead a peaceful, carefree life; I will become a priest or a nun and compel my children to do likewise."

What then does Christian faith say to this? It opens its eyes, looks upon all these insignificant, distasteful, and despised duties in the Spirit, and is aware that they are all adorned with divine approval as with the costliest gold and jewels. It says, "O God, because I am certain that Thou hast created me as a man and hast from my body begotten this child, I also know for a certainty that it meets with Thy perfect pleasure. I confess to Thee that I am not worthy to rock the little babe or wash its diapers, or to be entrusted with the care of the child and its mother. How is it that I, without any merit, have come to this distinction of being certain that I am serving Thy creature and Thy most precious will? O how gladly will I do so, though the duties should be even more insignificant and despised. Neither frost nor heat, neither drudgery nor labor will distress or dissuade me, for I am certain that it is thus pleasing in Thy sight."

A wife too should regard her duties in the same light, as she suckles the child, rocks and bathes it, and cares for it in other ways, and as she busies herself with other duties and renders help and obedience to her husband. These are truly golden and noble works. This is also how to comfort and encourage a woman in the pangs of childbirth, not be repeating St. Margaret[46] legends and other silly old wives' tales but by speaking thus, "Dear Grete,

---

[46]For centuries Margaret of Pisidian Antioch was widely venerated as the patron saint of pregnant women. According to tradition, she suffered torture and martyrdom for refusing to renounce her faith and marry the Roman prefect Olybrius. Her dates are uncertain though she may have died about the time of the Diocletian persecution (c. 303–5). Among the legends of her martyrdom is the story of her prayer, just before being beheaded, that "whenever a woman in labor should call upon her name, the child might be brought forth without harm."

remember that you are a woman, and that this work of God in you is pleasing to Him. Trust joyfully in His will, and let Him have His way with you. Work with all your might to bring forth the child. Should it mean your death, then depart happily, for you will die in a noble deed and in subservience to God. If you were not a woman you should now wish to be one for the sake of this very work alone, that you might thus gloriously suffer and even die in the performance of God's work and will. For here you have the Word of God, who so created you and implanted within you this extremity." Tell me, is not this indeed, as Solomon says [Prov. 18:22], "to obtain favor from the Lord," even in the midst of such extremity?

Now you tell me, when a father goes ahead and washes diapers or performs some other mean task for his child, and someone ridicules him as an effeminate fool—though that father is acting in the spirit just described and in Christian faith—my dear fellow, you tell me, which of the two is most keenly ridiculing the other? God, with all His angels and creatures, is smiling—not because that father is washing diapers, but because he is doing so in Christian faith. Those who sneer at him and see only the task but not the faith are ridiculing God with all His creatures, as the biggest fool on earth. Indeed, they are only ridiculing themselves; with all their cleverness they are nothing but devil's fools.

St. Cyprian, that great and admirable man and holy martyr, wrote that one should kiss the newborn infant, even before it is baptized, in honor of the hands of God here engaged in a brand new deed.[47] What do you suppose he would have said about a baptized infant? There was a true Christian, who correctly recognized and regarded God's work and creature. Therefore, I say that all nuns and monks who lack faith, and who trust in their own chastity and in their order, are not worthy of rocking a baptized child or preparing its pap, even if it were the child of a harlot. This is because their order and manner of life has no Word of God as its warrant. They

[47]Cyprian, bishop of Carthage, martyred in A.D. 258, was the author of numerous letters, to one of which Luther is referring. In his letter to Fidus on the baptizing of infants [Ep. LXIV.4] Cyprian writes, "In the kiss of an infant, each of us should, for very piety, think of the recent hands of God, which we in a manner kiss, in the lately formed and recently born man, when we embrace that which God has made."

cannot boast that what they do is pleasing in God's sight, as can the woman in childbirth, even if her child is born out of wedlock.

I say these things in order that we may learn how honorable a thing it is to live in that estate which God has ordained. In it we find God's Word and good pleasure, by which all the works, conduct, and sufferings of that estate become holy, godly, and precious so that Solomon even congratulates such a man and says in Prov. 5 [:18], "Rejoice in the wife of your youth," and again in Eccles. 11 [9:9], "Enjoy life with the wife whom you love all the days of your vain life." Doubtless, Solomon is not speaking here of carnal pleasure, since it is the Holy Spirit who speaks through him. He is rather offering godly comfort to those who find much drudgery in married life. This he does by way of defense against those who scoff at the divine ordinance and, like the pagans, seek but fail to find in marriage anything beyond a carnal and fleeting sensual pleasure.

Conversely, we learn how wretched is the spiritual estate of monks and nuns by its very nature, for it lacks the Word and pleasure of God. All its works, conduct, and sufferings are unchristian, vain, and pernicious, so that Christ even says to their warning in Matt. 15 [:9], "In vain do they worship Me according to the commandments of men." There is therefore no comparison between a married woman who lives in faith and in the recognition of her estate, and a cloistered nun who lives in unbelief and in the presumptuousness of her ecclesiastical estate, just as God's ways and man's ways are beyond compare, as He says in Isa. 55 [:9], "As the heavens are higher than the earth, so are My ways higher than your ways." It is a great blessing for one to have God's word as his warrant, so that he can speak right up and say to God, "See, this Thou hast spoken, it is Thy good pleasure." What does such a man care if it seems to be displeasing and ridiculous to the whole world?

Small wonder that married folk for the most part experience little but bitterness and anguish. They have no knowledge of God's Word and will concerning their estate, and are therefore just as wretched as monks and nuns since both lack the comfort and assurance of God's good pleasure. This is why it is impossible for them to endure outward bitterness and drudgery, for it is too much for a man to have to suffer both inward and outward bitterness. If they inwardly fail to realize that their estate is pleasing in the sight of God, bitterness is already there; if they then seek an outward pleasure therein, they fail to find it. Bitterness is joined with bitterness, and thence arises of necessity the loud outcry and the writings against women and the estate of marriage.

God's work and ordinance must and will be accepted and borne on the strength of God's Word and assurance; otherwise they do damage and become unbearable. Therefore, St. Paul tempers his words nicely when he says, 1 Cor. 7 [:28], "Those who marry will have worldly troubles," that is, outward bitterness. He is silent on the inner, spiritual delight, however, because outward bitterness is common to both believers and unbelievers; indeed, it is characteristic of the estate of marriage. No one can have real happiness in marriage who does not recognize in firm faith that this estate together with all its works, however insignificant, is pleasing to God and precious in His sight. These works are indeed insignificant and mean; yet it is from them that we all trace our origin, we have all had need of them. Without them no man would exist. For this reason they are pleasing to God, who has so ordained them and thereby graciously cares for us like a kind and loving mother.

Observe that thus far I have told you nothing of the estate of marriage except that which the world and reason in their blindness shrink from and sneer at as a mean, unhappy, troublesome mode of life. We have seen how all these shortcomings in fact comprise noble virtues and true delight if one but looks at God's Word and will, and thereby recognizes its true nature. I will not mention the other advantages and delights implicit in a marriage that goes well—that husband and wife cherish each other, become one, serve each other, and other attendant blessings—lest somebody shut me up by saying that I am speaking about something I have not experienced,[48] and that there is more gall than honey in marriage. I base my remarks on scripture, which to me is surer than all experience and cannot lie to me. He who finds still other good things in marriage profits all the more, and should give thanks to God. Whatever God calls good must of necessity always be good, unless men do not recognize it or perversely misuse it.

I therefore pass over the good or evil which experience offers, and confine myself to such good as scripture and truth ascribe to marriage. It is no slight boon that in wedlock fornication and

---

[48]Luther was not yet married.

unchastity are checked and eliminated. This in itself is so great a good that it alone should be enough to induce men to marry forthwith, and for many reasons.

The first reason is that fornication destroys not only the soul but also body, property, honor, and family as well. For we see how a licentious and wicked life not only brings great disgrace but is also a spendthrift life, more costly than wedlock, and that illicit partners necessarily occasion greater suffering for each other than do married folk. Beyond that it consumes the body, corrupts flesh and blood, nature, and physical constitution. Through such a variety of evil consequences God takes a rigid position, as though He would actually drive people away from fornication and into marriage. However, few are thereby convinced or converted.

Some, however, have given the matter thought and so learned from their own experience that they have coined an excellent proverb, "Early to rise and early to wed; that should no one ever regret." Why? Well because from that there come people who retain a sound body, a good conscience, property, and honor and family, all of which are so ruined and dissipated by fornication that, once lost, it is well-nigh impossible to regain them—scarcely one in a hundred succeeds. This was the benefit cited by Paul in 1 Cor. 7 [:2], "To avoid immorality, each man should have his own wife, and each woman her own husband."

The estate of marriage, however, redounds to the benefit not alone of the body, property, honor, and soul of an individual, but also to the benefit of whole cities and countries, in that they remain exempt from the plagues imposed by God. We know only too well that the most terrible plagues have befallen lands and people because of fornication. This was the sin cited as the reason why the world was drowned in the deluge, Gen. 6 [:1–13], and Sodom and Gomorrah were buried in flames, Gen. 19 [:1–24]. Scripture also cites many other plagues, even in the case of holy men such as David [2 Sam. 11–12], Solomon [1 Kings 11:1–13], and Samson [Judg. 16:1–21]. We see before our very eyes that God even now sends more new plagues.[49]

---

[49]Syphilis was widespread in Luther's day. Its sudden upsurge late in the fifteenth century gave rise to the legend that it was brought from the New World by the sailors of Columbus.

Many think they can evade marriage by having their fling for a time and then becoming righteous. My dear fellow, if one in a thousand succeeds in this, that would be doing very well. He who intends to lead a chaste life had better begin early, and attain it not with but without fornication, either by the grace of God or through marriage. We see only too well how they make out every day. It might well be called plunging into immorality rather than growing to maturity. It is the devil who has brought this about, and coined such damnable sayings as "One has to play the fool at least once"; or "He who does it not in his youth does it in his old age"; or "A young saint, an old devil." Such are the sentiments of the poet Terence[50] and other pagans. This is heathenish; they speak like heathens, yea, like devils.

It is certainly a fact that he who refuses to marry must fall into immorality. How could it be otherwise, since God has created man and woman to produce seed and to multiply? Why should one not forestall immorality by means of marriage? For if special grace does not exempt a person, his nature must and will compel him to produce seed and to multiply. If this does not occur within marriage, how else can it occur except in fornication or secret sins? But, they say, suppose I am neither married nor immoral, and force myself to remain continent? Do you not hear that restraint is impossible without the special grace? For God's Word does not admit of restraint; neither does it lie when it says, "Be fruitful and multiply" [Gen. 1:28]. You can neither escape nor restrain yourself from being fruitful and multiplying; it is God's ordinance and takes its course.

Physicians are not amiss when they say: If this natural function is forcibly restrained it necessarily strikes into the flesh and blood and becomes a poison, whence the body becomes unhealthy, enervated, sweaty, and foul-smelling. That which should have issued in fruitfulness and propagation has to be absorbed within the body itself. Unless there is terrific hunger or immense labor or the supreme grace, the body cannot take it; it necessarily becomes unhealthy and sickly. Hence, we see how weak and sickly barren

---

[50]Luther frequently cited this line from the Roman comic poet Terence (*c.* 190–*c.* 159 B.C.), "It is no crime, believe me, that a youth wenches" (*The Brothers* I.ii.21–22).

women are. Those who are fruitful, however, are healthier, clean-
lier, and happier. And even if they bear themselves weary—or
ultimately bear themselves out—that does not hurt. Let them bear
themselves out. This is the purpose for which they exist. It is better
to have a brief life with good health than a long life in ill health.

But the greatest good in married life, that which makes all suffering and labor worthwhile, is that God grants offspring and commands that they be brought up to worship and serve Him. In all the
world this is the noblest and most precious work, because to God
there can be nothing dearer than the salvation of souls. Now since
we are all duty bound to suffer death, if need be, that we might
bring a single soul to God, you can see how rich the estate of marriage is in good works. God has entrusted to its bosom souls begotten of its own body, on whom it can lavish all manner of Christian
works. Most certainly father and mother are apostles, bishops, and
priests to their children, for it is they who make them acquainted
with the gospel. In short, there is no greater or nobler authority on
earth than that of parents over their children, for this authority
is both spiritual and temporal. Whoever teaches the gospel to
another is truly his apostle and bishop. Miter and staff and great
estates indeed produce idols, but teaching the gospel produces
apostles and bishops. See therefore how good and great is God's
work and ordinance!

Here I will let the matter rest and leave to others the task of
searching out further benefits and advantages of the estate of marriage. My purpose was only to enumerate those which a Christian
can have for conducting his married life in a Christian way, so
that, as Solomon says, he may find his wife in the sight of God and
obtain favor from the Lord [Prov. 18:22]. In saying this I do not
wish to disparage virginity, or entice anyone away from virginity
into marriage. Let each one act as he is able, and as he feels it has
been given to him by God. I simply wanted to check those scandal-
mongers who place marriage so far beneath virginity that they
dare to say: Even if the children should become holy [1 Cor. 7:14],
celibacy would still be better. One should not regard any estate as
better in the sight of God than the estate of marriage. In a worldly
sense celibacy is probably better, since it has fewer cares and anxieties. This is true, however, not for its own sake but in order that
the celibate may better be able to preach and care for God's word,

as St. Paul says in 1 Cor. 7 [:32–34]. It is God's Word and the preaching which make celibacy—such as that of Christ and of Paul—better than the estate of marriage. In itself, however, the celibate life is far inferior.

Finally, we have before us one big, strong objection to answer. Yes, they say, it would be a fine thing to be married, but how will I support myself? I have nothing; take a wife and live on that, etc. Undoubtedly, this is the great obstacle to marriage; it is this above all which prevents and breaks up marriage and is the chief excuse for fornication. What shall I say to this objection? It shows lack of faith and doubt of God's goodness and truth. It is therefore no wonder that where faith is lacking, nothing but fornication and all manner of misfortune follow. They are lacking in this, that they want to be sure first of their material resources, where they are to get their food, drink, and clothing [Matt. 6:31]. Yes, they want to pull their head out of the noose of Gen. 3 [:19], "In the sweat of your face you shall eat bread." They want to be lazy, greedy rascals who do not need to work. Therefore, they will get married only if they can get wives who are rich, beautiful, pious, kind—indeed, wait, we'll have a picture of them drawn for you.

Let such heathen go their way; we will not argue with them. If they should be lucky enough to obtain such wives the marriages would still be unchristian and without faith. They trust in God as long as they know that they do not need Him and that they are well supplied. He who would enter into wedlock as a Christian must not be ashamed of being poor and despised, and doing insignificant work. He should take satisfaction in this: first, that his status and occupation are pleasing to God; second, that God will most certainly provide for him if only he does his job to the best of his ability, and that, if he cannot be a squire or a prince, he is a manservant or a maidservant.

God has promised in Matt. 6 [:25, 33], "Do not be anxious about what you shall eat, drink, and put on; seek first the kingdom of God and His righteousness, and all these things shall be yours as well." Again, Psalm 37 says, "I have been young and now am old, yet I have not seen the righteous forsaken, or his children begging bread." If a man does not believe this, is it any wonder that he suffers hunger, thirst, and cold, and begs for bread? Look at Jacob, the holy patriarch, who in Syria had nothing and simply tended sheep; he received such possessions that he supported four wives with a large number of servants and children, and yet he had enough.[51] Abraham, Isaac, and Lot also became rich, as did many other holy men in the Old Testament.

Indeed, God has shown sufficiently in the first chapter of Genesis how He provides for us. He first created and prepared all things in heaven and on earth, together with the beasts and all growing things, before He created man. Thereby He demonstrated how He has laid up for us at all times a sufficient store of food and clothing, even before we ask Him for it. All we need to do is to work and avoid idleness; then we shall certainly be fed and clothed. But a pitiful unbelief refuses to admit this. The unbeliever sees, comprehends, and feels all the same that even if he worries himself to death over it, he can neither produce nor maintain a single grain of wheat in the field. He knows too that even though all his storehouses were full to overflowing, he could not make use of a single morsel or thread unless God sustains him in life and health and preserves to him his possessions. Yet this has no effect upon him.

To sum the matter up: whoever finds himself unsuited to the celibate life should see to it right away that he has something to do and to work at; then let him strike out in God's name and get married. A young man should marry at the age of twenty at the latest, a young woman at fifteen to eighteen; that's when they are still in good health and best suited for marriage. Let God worry about how they and their children are to be fed. God makes children; He will surely also feed them. Should He fail to exalt you and them here on earth, then take satisfaction in the fact that He has granted you a Christian marriage, and know that He will exalt you there; and be thankful to Him for His gifts and favors.

With all this extolling of married life, however, I have not meant to ascribe to nature a condition of sinlessness. On the contrary, I say that flesh and blood, corrupted through Adam, is conceived and born in sin, as Psalm 51 [:5] says. Intercourse is never without sin; but God excuses it by His grace because the estate of marriage is His work, and He preserves in and through the sin all that good which He has implanted and blessed in marriage.

[51]Gen. 28–33, especially 32:10.

THAT JESUS CHRIST WAS BORN A JEW

Luther's tract was written in 1523, a year after he translated the New Testament into German. He was motivated, first of all, to defend himself against accusations by some Catholics that he denied the virgin birth of Christ. In the second place, he wanted to reprimand his Catholic foes by asserting that if scripture were properly preached, the Jews, whose own religion is anchored in the Bible, would convert. But if Christians treat Jews with malice (and Luther felt himself to be a victim of Christian cruelty), how can they then be drawn to Christ? In response to the messianism of his times, Luther hoped to convince the Jews that the Messiah they longed for had indeed already come in the person of Jesus. He determined to prove that the Old Testament is fulfilled in the Christ of the New Testament. He saw an eschatological alignment between the conversion of the Jews and the Second Coming of Jesus. As the years went by, Luther was to become obsessed with their conversion, and his fury against them built, along with their resistance, until it reached titanic proportions. The whole of scripture, the subject of Luther's entire life work, spoke to him of Christ. In his view, for the Jews to reject Christ was to reject their very flesh and blood. In the end, they became scapegoats for Luther's wrath toward all who resisted him and the theology he preached.

A new lie about me is being circulated. I am supposed to have preached and written that Mary, the mother of God, was not a virgin either before or after the birth of Christ, but that she conceived Christ through Joseph and had more children after that. Above and beyond all this, I am supposed to have preached a new heresy, namely, that Christ was [through Joseph] the seed of Abraham. How these lies tickle my good friends the papists! Indeed, because they condemn the gospel, it serves them right that they should have to satisfy and feed their heart's delight and joy with lies. I would venture to wager my neck that none of those very liars who allege such great things in honor of the mother of God believes in his heart a single one of these articles. Yet with their lies they pretend that they are greatly concerned about the Christian faith.

But after all, it is such a poor miserable lie that I despise it and would rather not reply to it. In these past three years I have grown quite accustomed to hearing lies, even from our nearest neighbors.[52] And they in turn have grown accustomed to the noble virtue of neither blushing nor feeling ashamed when they are publicly convicted of lying. They let themselves be chided as liars, yet continue their lying. Still they are the best Christians, striving with all that they have and are to devour the Turk and to extirpate all heresy.

Since for the sake of others, however, I am compelled to answer these lies, I thought I would also write something useful in addition, so that I do not vainly steal the reader's time with such dirty rotten business. Therefore, I will cite from scripture the reasons that move me to believe that Christ was a Jew born of a virgin, that I might perhaps also win some Jews to the Christian faith. Our fools, the popes, bishops, sophists, and monks—the crude asses' heads—have hitherto so treated the Jews that anyone who wished to be a good Christian would almost have had to become a Jew. If I had been a Jew and had seen such dolts and blockheads govern and teach the Christian faith, I would sooner have become a hog than a Christian.

They have dealt with the Jews as if they were dogs rather than human beings; they have done little else than deride them and seize their property. When they baptize them they show them nothing of Christian doctrine or life, but only subject them to popishness and monkery. When the Jews then see that Judaism has such strong support in scripture, and that Christianity has become a mere babble without reliance on scripture, how can they possibly compose themselves and become right good Christians? I have myself heard from pious baptized Jews that if they had not in our day heard the gospel they would have remained Jews under the cloak of Christianity for the rest of their days. For they acknowledge that they have never yet heard anything about Christ from those who baptized and taught them.

I hope that if one deals in a kindly way with the Jews and instructs them carefully from holy scripture, many of them will become genuine Christians and turn again to the faith of their

---

[52]This is probably an allusion to Duke George of Saxony, a consistent opponent of Luther.

fathers, the prophets and patriarchs.[53] They will only be frightened further away from it if their Judaism is so utterly rejected that nothing is allowed to remain and they are treated only with arrogance and scorn. If the apostles, who also were Jews, had dealt with us gentiles as we gentiles deal with the Jews, there would never have been a Christian among the gentiles. Since they dealt with us gentiles in such brotherly fashion, we in our turn ought to treat the Jews in a brotherly manner in order that we might convert some of them.[54] For even we ourselves are not yet all very far along, not to speak of having arrived.[55]

When we are inclined to boast of our position we should remember that we are but gentiles, while the Jews are of the lineage of Christ. We are aliens and in-laws; they are blood relatives, cousins, and brothers of our Lord. Therefore, if one is to boast of flesh and blood, the Jews are actually nearer to Christ than we are, as St. Paul says in Rom. 9 [:5]. God has also demonstrated this by His acts, for to no nation among the gentiles has He granted so high an honor as He has to the Jews. For from among the gentiles there have been raised up no patriarchs, no apostles, no prophets, indeed, very few genuine Christians either. And although the gospel has been proclaimed to all the world, yet He committed the holy scriptures, that is, the law and the prophets, to no nation except the Jews, as Paul says in Rom. 3 [:2] and Psalm 147 [:19–20], "He declares His word to Jacob, His statues and ordinances to Israel. He has not dealt thus with any other nation; nor revealed His ordinances to them."

Accordingly, I beg my dear papists, should they be growing weary of denouncing me as a heretic, to seize the opportunity of denouncing me as a Jew. Perhaps I may yet turn out to be also a Turk, or whatever else my fine gentlemen may wish.

Christ is promised for the first time soon after Adam's fall, when God said to the serpent, "I will put enmity between you and the woman, and between your seed and her seed; he shall crush your head, and you shall bruise his heel" [Gen. 3:15]. Here I defer

---

[53]Luther invariably refers to the righteous believers of the Old Testament as Christians.
[54]Cf. 1 Cor. 9:19–22.
[55]Cf. Phil. 3:12–14.

demonstrating that the serpent spoke possessed of the devil, for no dumb beast is so clever that it can utter or comprehend human speech, much less speak or inquire about such exalted matters as the commandment of God, as the serpent does here. Therefore, it must certainly have been a rational, highly intelligent, and mighty spirit which was able to utter human speech, deal so masterfully with God's commandments, and seize and employ human reason.

Since it is certain that a spirit is something higher than a man, it is also certain that this is an evil spirit and an enemy of God, for it breaks God's commandment and acts contrary to His will. Therefore, it is undoubtedly the devil. And so the Word of God which speaks of crushing the head must refer also to the devil's head; though not to the exclusion of the natural head of the serpent, for with a single word He speaks of both devil and serpent as of one thing. Therefore, He means both heads. But the devil's head is that power by which the devil rules, that is, sin and death, by means of which he has brought Adam and all Adam's descendants under his control.

This seed of the woman, therefore, because He is to crush the devil's power, that is, sin and death, must not be an ordinary man, since all men have been brought under the devil through sin and death. So He must certainly be without sin. Now human nature does not produce such seed or fruit, as has been said, for with their sin they are all under the devil. How, then, can this be? The seed must be the natural child of a woman; otherwise it could not be or be called the seed of the woman. On the other hand, as has been pointed out, human nature and birth does not produce such seed. Therefore, the solution must ultimately be that this seed is a true natural son of the woman; derived from the woman, however, not in the normal way but through a special act of God, in order that the scripture might stand, that He is the seed only of a woman and not of a man. For the text [Gen. 3:15] clearly states that He will be the seed of woman.

This is thus the first passage in which the mother of this child is described as a virgin. She is His true natural mother; yet she is to conceive and bear supernaturally, by God, without a man, in order that her child may be a distinctive man, without sin, yet having ordinary flesh and blood like other men. This could not have been the case had He been begotten by a man like other men because the flesh is consumed and corrupted by evil lust, so that its natural act of procreation cannot occur without sin. Whatever conceives and bears through an act of the flesh produces also a carnal and sinful fruit. This is why St. Paul says in Eph. 1 [2:3] that we are all by nature children of wrath.

Now this passage [Gen. 3:15] was the very first gospel message on earth. For when Adam and Eve, seduced by the devil, had fallen and were summoned for judgment before God, Gen. 3 [:9], they were in peril of death and the anguish of hell, for they saw that God was against them and condemned them; they would gladly have fled from Him, but could not. Had God let them remain in their anguish, they would soon have despaired and perished. But when, after their terrible punishment, He let them hear His comforting promise to raise up from the woman's seed one who would tread upon the serpent's head, their spirits were quickened again. From that promise they drew comfort, believing firmly in that blessed seed of the woman which would come and crush the serpent's head, that is, sin and death, by which they had been crushed and corrupted.

The fathers, from Adam on, preached and inculcated this gospel, through which they acknowledged the promised seed of this woman and believed in Him. And so they were sustained through faith in Christ just as we are; they were true Christians like ourselves. Only, in their day this gospel was not proclaimed publicly throughout the world, as it would be after the coming of Christ, but remained solely in the possession of the holy fathers and their descendants down to the time of Abraham.

The second promise of Christ was to Abraham, Gen. 22 [:18], where God said, "In your seed shall all the gentiles be blessed." If all the gentiles are to be blessed, then it is certain that otherwise, apart from this seed of Abraham, they were all unblessed and under a curse. From this it follows that human nature has nothing but cursed seed and bears nothing but unblessed fruit; otherwise, there would be no need for all of them to be blessed through this seed of Abraham. Whoever says "all" excludes no one; therefore, apart from Christ, all who are born of man must be under the devil, cursed in sin and death.

Here again the Mother of God is proven to be a pure virgin. For since God cannot lie, it was inevitable that Christ should be the seed of Abraham, that is, his natural flesh and blood, like all of Abraham's descendants. On the other hand, because He was to be the blessed seed which should bless all others, He could not be begotten by man, since such children, as has been said, cannot be conceived without sin because of the corrupt and tainted flesh, which cannot perform its function without taint and sin.

Thus the word by which God promises that Christ will be the seed of Abraham requires that Christ be born of a woman and be her natural child. He does not come from the earth like Adam [Gen. 2:7]; neither is He from Adam's rib, like Eve [Gen. 2:21–22]. He comes rather like any woman's child, from her seed. The earth was not the natural seed for Adam's body; neither was Adam's rib the natural seed for Eve's body. But the virgin's flesh and blood, from which children come in the case of all other women, was the natural seed of Christ's body. And she too was of the seed of Abraham.[56]

On the other hand, this word by which God promises His blessing upon all gentiles in Christ requires that Christ may not come from a man, or by the act of a man; for work of the flesh (which is cursed) is incompatible with that which is blessed and is pure blessing. Therefore, this blessed fruit had to be the fruit of a woman's body only, not of a man, even though that very woman's body came from man, indeed, even from Abraham and Adam. So this mother is a virgin, and yet a true natural mother; not, however, by natural capacity or power, but solely through the Holy Spirit and divine power.

Now this passage [Gen. 22:18] was the gospel from the time of Abraham down to the time of David, even to the time of Christ. It is a short saying, to be sure, but a rich gospel, subsequently inculcated and used in marvelous fashion by the fathers both in writing and in preaching. Many thousands of sermons have been preached from this passage, and countless souls saved. For it is the living Word of God, in which Abraham and his descendants believed and by which they were redeemed and preserved from sin and death and the power of the devil. However, it too was not yet pro-

---

[56]In his 1543 *Vom Schem Hamphoras und vom Geschlecht Christi*, Luther dealt at length with the problem of the New Testament genealogies which seem to trace Jesus' lineage through Joseph rather than Mary.

claimed publicly to all the world, as happened after the coming of Christ, but remained solely in the possession of the fathers and their descendants.

Now just take a look at the perverse lauders of the mother of God. If you ask them why they hold so strongly to the virginity of Mary, they truly could not say. These stupid idolaters do nothing more than to glorify only the mother of God; they extol her for her virginity and practically make a false deity of her. But scripture does not praise this virginity at all for the sake of the mother; neither was she saved on account of her virginity. Indeed, cursed be this and every other virginity if it exists for its own sake, and accomplishes nothing better than its own profit and praise.

The Spirit extols this virginity, however, because it was needful for the conceiving and bearing of this blessed fruit. Because of the corruption of our flesh, such blessed fruit could not come, except through a virgin. Thus this tender virginity existed in the service of others to the glory of God, not to its own glory. If it had been possible for Him to have come from a [married] woman, He would not have selected a virgin for this, since virginity is contrary to the physical nature within us, was condemned of old in the law,[57] and is extolled here solely because the flesh is tainted and its built-in physical nature cannot bestow her fruit except by means of an accursed act.

Hence we see that St. Paul nowhere calls the mother of God a virgin, but only a woman, as he says in Gal. 3 [4:4], "The Son of God was born of a woman." He did not mean to say she was not a virgin, but to extol her virginity to the highest with the praise that is proper to it, as much as to say: In this birth none but a woman was involved, no man participated; that is, everything connected with it was reserved to the woman; the conceiving, bearing, suckling, and nourishing of the child were functions no man can perform. It is therefore the child of a woman only; hence, she must certainly be a virgin. But a virgin may also be a man; a mother can be none other than a woman.

For this reason, too, scripture does not quibble or speak about the virginity of Mary after the birth of Christ, a matter about which the hypocrites are greatly concerned, as if it were something

---

[57]Cf., e.g., Isa. 4:1; Judg. 11:37–38.

of the utmost importance, on which our whole salvation depended. Actually we should be satisfied simply to hold that she remained a virgin after the birth of Christ because scripture does not state or indicate that she later lost her virginity. We certainly need not be so terribly afraid that someone will demonstrate, out of his own head apart from scripture, that she did not remain a virgin. But the scripture stops with this, that she was a virgin before and at the birth of Christ; for up to this point God had need of her virginity in order to give us the promised blessed seed without sin.

The third passage is addressed to David, 2 Samuel 7 [:12–14], "When your days are fulfilled, and you sleep with your fathers, I will raise up your seed after you, who shall come forth from your body, and I will establish his kingdom forever. He shall build a house for My name, and I will establish the throne of His kingdom forever. I will be His father, and He shall be My Son." These words cannot have been spoken of Solomon, for Solomon was not a posthumous son of David raised up after his death. Neither did God after Solomon (who during David's lifetime was born and became king) ever designate anyone as His son, give Him an ever-lasting kingdom, or have Him build such a house. Consequently, the whole passage must refer to Christ. We will let this passage go for the present because it is too broad and requires so much in the way of exegesis; for one would have to show here that Christ accordingly had to be the son of a woman only in order to be called here God's child, who neither should nor could come out of an accursed act.

The fourth passage is Isaiah 7 [:14], "God Himself will give you a sign. Behold, a virgin is with child, and shall bear a son." This could not have been said of a virgin who was about to be married. For what sort of a marvelous sign would that be if someone who is presently a virgin should bear a child within a year? Such is the ordinary course of nature, occurring daily before our eyes. If it is to be a sign from God, therefore, it must be something remarkable and marvelous not given by the ordinary course of nature, as is commonly the case with all God's signs.

It is of no help for the Jews either to try to evade the issue here and come up with this way of getting around it, namely: the sign consists in the fact that Isaiah says flatly that the child shall be a son and not a daughter. By such an interpretation the sign would have nothing to do with the virgin but only with the prophet Isaiah, as the one who had divined so precisely that it would not be a daughter. The text would then have to speak of Isaiah thus, "Behold, God Himself will give you a sign, namely, that I, Isaiah, will divine that a young woman is carrying a son, and not a daughter." Such an interpretation is disgraceful and childish.

Now the text forcefully refers the sign to the woman, and states clearly that it shall be a sign when a woman bears a son. Now it certainly is no sign when a woman who is no longer virgin bears a child, be it the mother of Hezekiah or whatever woman the Jews may point to.[58] The sign must be something new and different, a marvelous and unique work of God, that this woman is with child; her pregnancy is to be the sign. Now I do not deem any Jew so dense that he would not grant God sufficient power to create a child from a virgin, since they are compelled to acknowledge that He created Adam from the earth [Gen. 2:7] and Eve from Adam [Gen. 2:21–22], acts which require no less power.

But then they contend that the Hebrew text does not read, "A virgin is with child," but, "Behold, an *almah* is with child." *Almah*, they say, does not denote a virgin; the word for virgin is *bethulah*, while *almah* is the term for young damsel. Presumably, a young damsel might very well have had intercourse and be the mother of a child.

Christians can readily answer this from St. Matthew and St. Luke, both of whom apply the passage from Isaiah [7:14] to Mary, and translate the word *almah* as "virgin."[59] They are more to be believed than the whole world, let alone the Jews. Even though an angel from heaven [Gal. 1:8] were to say that *almah* does not mean virgin, we should not believe it. For God the Holy Spirit speaks through St. Matthew and St. Luke; we can be sure that He understands Hebrew speech and expressions perfectly well.

But because the Jews do not accept the evangelists, we must confront them with other evidence. In the first place, we can say, as

[58]The Jews interpreted the text to mean, "Behold, a young woman shall conceive and bear a son." The "woman" was frequently taken to be Abijah, mother of Hezekiah (2 Kings 18:1–2; 2 Chron. 28:27–29:1), and the prophecy thus to refer to the birth of Ahaz's successor on the throne of Judah.

[59]Matt. 1:23 and Luke 1:27, in referring to Mary, both use the Greek term *parthenos*, with which the Septuagint had rendered *almah* in Isa. 7:14.

above, that there is no marvel or sign in the fact that a young woman conceives, otherwise, we would have a perfect right to sneer at the prophet Isaiah, and say, "What women would you expect to conceive if not the young ones? Are you drunk? Or is it in your experience a rare event for a young woman to bear a son?" For this reason that strained and far-fetched answer of the Jews is just a vain and feeble excuse for not keeping silent altogether.

In the second place, grant that *bethulah* means virgin and not *almah*, and that Isaiah here uses *almah*, not *bethulah*. All this too is still nothing but a poor excuse. For they act as if they did not know that in all of scripture *almah* nowhere designates a woman who has had intercourse (a fact of which they are perfectly well aware). On the contrary, in every instance[60] *almah* signifies a young damsel who has never known a man carnally or had intercourse. Such a person is always called a virgin, just as St. Matthew and St. Luke here translate Isaiah.

Now since they are such literalists and like to argue about semantics, we will concede that *bethulah* is not the same word as *almah*. But the only point they have established thereby is that this young woman is not designated by the term "virgin." However, she is designated by another term which also means a young woman who has never had intercourse; call her by whatever term you please, in her person she is still a virgin. It is childish and disgraceful to take recourse to words when the meaning is one and the same.

Very well; to please the Jews we will not translate Isaiah thus: "Behold, a virgin is with child," lest they be confused by the word "virgin," but rather, "Behold, a maiden is with child." Now in German the word "maiden" denotes a woman who is still young, carries her crown[61] with honor, and wears her hair loose, so that it is said of her: She is still a maiden, not a wife (although "maiden" is not the same word as "virgin"). In like manner also, the Hebrew *elem* is a stripling who does not yet have a woman; and *almah* is a maiden

---

[60]The term *almah* occurs in the singular in Gen. 24:43, Exod. 2:8, Prov. 30:19, and Isa. 7:14; in the plural in Ps. 68:25, Song of Sol. 1:3 and 6:8. Luther's distinction covers both groups, though he does distinguish between them in his 1543 *Vom Schem Hamphoras und vom Geschlecht Christi*.

[61]The *krantz* was a decorative wreath or garland, worn on the head. Along with the flowing, unbound tresses of the hair, it was in the Middle Ages an emblem of a girl's virginity.

who does not yet have a man, not a servant girl[62] but one who still carries a crown. Thus the sister of Moses is called an *almah* in Exodus 3 (2:8) as is Rebekah in Genesis 24,[63] when they were still virgins.

Suppose I say in German, "Hans is engaged to a maiden," and someone should comment, "Well, then he is not engaged to a virgin." Why, everyone would laugh at him for vainly disputing about words if he thinks that "virgin" and "maiden" are not the same thing because they are different words. This is true also in the Hebrew, when the Jews argue with respect to this passage in Isaiah [7:14] and say, "Isaiah does not say *bethulah*, but *almah*." I submit that among themselves their own conscience tells them this is so. Therefore, let them say what they please, *bethulah* or *almah;* Isaiah means a damsel who is nubile but still wears her crown, whom in the truest German we call a maiden. Hence, the Mother of God is properly called the pure maiden, that is, the pure *almah*.

And if I should have had to tell Isaiah what to speak, I would have had him say exactly what he did say, not *bethulah*, but *almah*, for *almah* is even more appropriate here than *bethulah*. It is also more precise to say, "Behold, a maiden is with child," than to say, "A virgin is with child." For "virgin" is an all-embracing term which might also be applied to a woman of fifty or sixty who is no longer capable of childbearing. But "maiden" denotes specifically a young woman, nubile, capable of childbearing, but still a virgin; it includes not only the virginity but also the youthfulness and the potential for childbearing. Hence, in German too we commonly refer to young people as maidens or maidenfolk, not virginfolk.

Therefore, the text of Isaiah [7:14] is certainly most accurately translated, "Behold, a maiden is with child." No Jew who understands both German and Hebrew can deny that this is what is said in the Hebrew, for we Germans do not say "*concepit,* the woman has conceived"; the preachers have so rendered the Latin[64] into German. Rather, the German would say in his mother tongue, "The woman is with child" or "is heavy with child" or "is pregnant."

---

[62]The German word for a servant girl and for a young unmarried woman, as in English, is one and the same: "maid."

[63]Gen. 24:43 calles Rebekah an *almah*—rendered as *parthenos* in the Septuagint— after she had been designated a *bethulah* in Gen. 24:16.

[64]Jerome's Vulgate reads *concipiet,* which the Douay version renders as "shall conceive."

But here in the Hebrew it does not say, "Behold, a maiden shall be with child," as though she were not as yet. It says rather, "Behold, a maiden is with child," as though she has the fruit already in her womb and nevertheless is still a maiden, in order that you will have to notice how the prophet himself is amazed that there stands before him a maiden who is with child even before she knows a man carnally. She was, of course, going to have a husband, she was physically fit and mature enough for it; but even before she gets to that she is already a mother. This is indeed a rare and marvelous thing.

This is the way St. Matthew [1:18] construes this passage when he says, "When Mary the mother of Jesus had been betrothed to Joseph, before they came together she was found to be with child of the Holy Spirit," etc. What does this mean other than that she was a young maiden who had not yet known a man although she was capable of it, but before she knew the man she was with child, and that this was an amazing thing since no maiden becomes pregnant prior to intercourse with a man? Thus, the evangelist regarded her in the same light as did the prophet, and set her forth as the sign and wonder.

Now this refutes also the false interpretation which some have drawn from the words of Matthew, where he says, "Before they came together she was found to be with child." They interpret this as though the evangelist meant to say, "Later she came together with Joseph like any other wife and lay with him, but before this occurred she was with child apart from Joseph," etc. Again, when he says, "And Joseph knew her not until she brought forth her firstborn son" [Matt. 1:25], they interpret it as though the evangelist meant to say that he knew her, but not before she had brought forth her firstborn son. This was the view of Helvidius[65] which was refuted by Jerome.[66]

[65]Helvidius, disciple of the Arian bishop of Milan, Auxentius, was living in Rome at the time of Jerome's second sojourn there in 382–5. As a layman he wrote a treatise against the generally accepted view of Mary's perpetual virginity, in which he attacked primarily the practical consequences drawn from the doctrine in terms of monasticism as a higher kind of Christian life.

[66]The treatise of Helvidius is known only through its rebuttal by Jerome, who did not know him personally but who took up the debate at the urging of friends in order to promote and defend monasticism.

Such carnal interpretations miss the meaning and purpose of the evangelist. As we have said, the evangelist, like the prophet Isaiah, wishes to set before our eyes this mighty wonder, and point out what an unheard-of thing it is for a maiden to be with child before her husband brings her home and lies with her; and further, that he does not know her carnally until she first has a son, which she should have had after first having been known by him. Thus, the words of the evangelist do not refer to anything that occurred after the birth, but only to what took place before it. For the prophet and the evangelist, and St. Paul as well, do not treat of this virgin beyond the point where they have from her that fruit for whose sake she is a virgin and everything else. After the child is born they dismiss the mother and speak not about her, what became of her, but only about her offspring. Therefore, one cannot from these words [Matt. 1:18, 25] conclude that Mary, after the birth of Christ, became a wife in the usual sense; it is therefore neither to be asserted nor believed. All the words are merely indicative of the marvelous fact that she was with child and gave birth before she had lain with a man.

The form of expression used by Matthew is the common idiom, as if I were to say, "Pharoah believed not Moses, until he was drowned in the Red Sea." Here it does not follow that Pharoah believed later, after he had drowned; on the contrary, it means that he never did believe. Similarly when Matthew [1:25] says that Joseph did not know Mary carnally until she had brought forth her son, it does not follow that he knew her subsequently; on the contrary, it means that he never did know her. Again, the Red Sea overwhelmed Pharaoh before he got across. Here too it does not follow that Pharaoh got across later, after the Red Sea had overwhelmed him, but rather that he did not get across at all. In like manner, when Matthew [1:18] says, "She was found to be with child before they came together," it does not follow that Mary subsequently lay with Joseph, but rather that she did not lie with him.

Elsewhere in scripture the same manner of speech is employed. Psalm 110 [:1], reads, "God says to my Lord: 'Sit at My right hand, till I make Your enemies Your footstool.'" Here it does not follow that Christ does not continue to sit there after His enemies are placed beneath His feet. Again, in Genesis 28 [:15], "I will not leave you until I have done all that of which I have spoken to you."

Here God did not leave him after the fulfillment had taken place. Again, in Isaiah 42 [:4], "He shall not be sad, nor troublesome,[67] till He has established justice in the earth." There are many more similar expressions, so that this babble of Helvidius is without justification; in addition, he has neither noticed nor paid any attention to either scripture or the common idiom.

This is enough for the present to have sufficiently proved that Mary was a pure maiden, and that Christ was a genuine Jew of Abraham's seed. Although more scripture passages might be cited,[68] these are the clearest. Moreover, if anyone does not believe a clear saying of His Divine Majesty, it is reasonable to assume that he would not believe either any other more obscure passages. So certainly no one can doubt that it is possible for God to cause a maiden to be with child apart from a man, since He has also created all things from nothing. Therefore, the Jews have no ground for denying this, for they acknowledge God's omnipotence, and they have here the clear testimony of the prophet Isaiah.

[67]Douay version.
[68]In his 1543 *Vom Schem Hamphoras und vom Geschlecht Christi*, Luther treats these same passages plus Gen. 49:10, Luke 1:42, Ps. 22:10–11, Ps. 110:3, Jer. 31:22, and Luke 1:38 in discussing the virgin birth.

V

Letters, Table Talk

As his fame after the notoriety of the Ninety-five Theses of 1517 grew year by year, so did Martin Luther's correspondence. The new ideas that he was teaching and preaching prompted the admiration and piqued the curiosity of many in German ecclesiastical and academic circles, and well beyond. They also provoked the rage and censure of others, from the pope to Henry VIII in England. Soon Luther stood in the middle of a torrent of questions that demanded clarification and response.

Though he wearied of the effort, he was a faithful correspondent to clergy and students spreading the new Evangelical teaching, to friends and colleagues looking for direction and confirmation, even to opponents bent on refuting and pulling down all that his labors had accomplished. The subjects of his letters are numerous, to be sure, but Luther's vigorous, attentive focus informs them all, whether he was answering an inquiry about how to respond to a plague or expressing tender affection for the dying father who had once been so disappointed at his son's youthful decision to become a monk.

Luther lived the majority of his life in Wittenberg, from his posting to its new (as of 1502) university, through his years of danger and controversy, to his marriage and maturity. After its main building, the Black Cloister, ceased to house the monks of his Augustinian Eremite order, Luther was given it for a home and a place to receive and teach students and others who made continuous pilgrimage to see and sit at the feet of the great reformer.

Numerous accounts of his conversation have been preserved, but the best of such anecdotes are collected in his Table Talk. He knew well that at his own table his opinion was assured the greatest weight, and he granted his unspoken approval for anything of importance he said to be faithfully noted and repeated throughout the network of the faithful. Nonetheless, scattered amid the intense theological and polemical commentary he chose to expound so readily and so well, we also find moments of gentle expression, humor, and compassion.

TO HANS LUTHER

Informed by James, his brother in Mansfeld, of their father's serious illness, Luther wrote the following letter of spiritual counsel. Luther explains why he does not visit his father, and expresses his hope that both his father and mother can come to Wittenberg and stay in the Luther house, apparently for the rest of their days. He even dispatches his nephew (a certain Cyriac Kaufmann, who was then studying at Wittenberg) to Mansfeld to investigate this matter further. Strengthening his father in this time of illness, Luther emphasizes that his father's faith is a sign of God's gracious dealings with him; Luther stresses that God's promises are valid and true, and that in Jesus Christ man has the most faithful helper in the hour of death. Encouraging his father not to become disheartened, Luther admonishes him to hold firmly to God's word of promise. He further points out that death, on the one hand, means an end to man's pilgrimage through the vale of tears; on the other hand, the entrance into the peace of Christ and the certainty of a joyous reunion of all believers.

This letter is among the finest of Luther's writings. It throws a light on the relationship between father and son, a relationship which must have been different than is sometimes suggested. Copies of the letter were circulated among some of Luther's friends, and the text is available in several sixteenth-century manuscript copies; the letter can also be found in the earliest collection of Luther's writings of pastoral counsel. These facts seem to suggest that even Luther's contemporaries held the letter in high regard.

To my dear Father, Hans Luther, a citizen at Mansfeld in the valley: Grace and peace in Christ Jesus, our Lord and Saviour. Amen

Dear Father: James, my brother,[69] has written me that you are seriously ill. As the weather is now bad, and as there is danger everywhere, and because of the season, I am worried about you. For even though God has thus far given to and preserved for you a

---

[69]Luther's younger brother, James, was a city councilor in Mansfeld, and died in 1570. Luther was apparently very close to him.

strong, tough body, yet your age gives me anxious thoughts at this time—although regardless of this [worry], none of us is, or should be, sure of his life at any time. Therefore because of these circumstances I would have liked to come to you personally, but my good friends advised me against it, and have talked me out of it. I myself have to agree, for I did not dare to venture into danger at the risk of tempting God, since you know how lords and peasants feel toward me. It would be great joy for me, however, if it were possible for you and mother to be brought here to us; this my Katie, too, desires with tears, and we all [join her in this]. I hope we would be able to take care of you in the best way. Therefore I am sending Cyriac[70] to see whether your weakness [will allow you to be moved]. For if according to God's will your illness turns out to be one either to life or to death, it would be a heartfelt joy for me (as would be only right) to be around you in person and to show, with filial faithfulness and service, my gratitude to God and to you, according to the Fourth Commandment.

In the meantime I pray from the bottom of my heart that the Father, who has made you my father and given you to me, will strengthen you according to His immeasurable kindness, and enlighten and preserve you with His Spirit, so that you may perceive with joy and thanksgiving the blessed teaching concerning His son, our Lord Jesus Christ, to which you too have been called and have come out of the former terrible darkness and error.[71] I hope that His grace, which has given you such knowledge[72] and begun His work in you, will preserve and complete [His work] up to the arrival of the future life and the joyous return of our Lord Jesus Christ.[73] Amen. God has also sealed this teaching and faith in you and has confirmed them with marks;[74] that is, because of me, you, together with all of us, have suffered much slander, dis-

---

[70]Cyriac Kaufmann, son of Luther's sister, who was married to George Kaufmann, a Mansfeld citizen. This nephew had matriculated at Wittenberg on November 22, 1529. Apparently Cyriac's parents were dead by 1534, and Luther had an active part in guiding Cyriac and his younger brothers and sisters through their years of adolescence.

[71]See 1 Pet. 2:9.

[72]I.e., knowledge of redemption.

[73]See Phil. 1:6.

[74]See Gal. 6:17.

grace, scorn, mockery, contempt, hatred, hostility, and even danger. These are but the true marks with which we have to become identical to our Lord Christ, as St. Paul says,[75] so that we may also become identified with His future glory.

Therefore let your heart now be bold and confident in your illness, for we have there, in the life beyond, a true and faithful helper at God's side, Jesus Christ, who for us has strangled death, together with sin, and now sits [in heaven] for us; together with all the angels He is looking down on us, and awaiting us, so that when we are to depart, we dare not worry or fear that we might sink or fall to the ground. His power over death and sin is too great for them to harm us. He is so wholeheartedly faithful and righteous that He cannot forsake us, nor would He wish to do so; [He wishes] only that we desire [His help] without doubting His promise, for He has said, promised, and pledged [His help]. He will not and cannot lie to us, nor trick us; there is no doubt about this. "Ask," He says, "and it will be given you; seek, and you will find, knock, and it will be opened to you" [Matt. 7:7]. And elsewhere: "All who call on the name of the Lord shall be saved" [Acts 2:21]. The whole psalter is full of such comforting promises, especially Psalm 91, which is particularly good to be read by all who are sick.

I wished to talk this over with you in writing, because I am anxious about your illness (for we know not the hour), so that I might participate in your faith, temptation, consolation, and gratitude to God for His holy Word, which in these days He has given to us so richly, powerfully, and graciously. Should it be His divine will, however, for you to wait still longer for that better life, [and] to continue to suffer with us in this troubled and sorrowful vale of tears, and to see and hear sadness, or, together with all Christians, to assist [others] in enduring and overcoming [this sadness], then He will also give [you] the grace to accept all this willingly and obediently. This cursed life is nothing but a real vale of tears, in which the longer a man lives, the more sin, wickedness, torment, and sadness he sees and feels. Nor is there respite or cessation of all of this until we are buried; then, of course, [this sadness] has to stop and let us sleep contentedly in Christ's peace, until He comes again to wake us with joy. Amen.

[75]See Rom. 8:17; 6:5.

Herewith I commend you to Him who loves you more than you love yourself. He has proved His love by taking your sins upon Himself and by paying [for them] with His blood, and He has let you know this through the gospel, and has given it to you freely to believe this by His Spirit.[76] Consequently, He has prepared and sealed everything in the most certain way, so that you are not permitted to worry about or be concerned for anything except keeping your heart strong and reliant on His Word and faith. If you do this, then let Him care for the rest. He will see to it that everything turns out well.[77] Indeed, He has already accomplished this in the best way, better than we can understand. May He, our dear Lord and Savior, be with you and at your side, so that (may God grant it to happen either here or there)[78] we may joyfully see each other again. For our faith is certain, and we don't doubt that we shall shortly see each other again in the presence of Christ. For the departure from this life is a smaller thing to God than if I moved from you in Mansfeld to here, and or if you moved from me in Wittenberg to Mansfeld. This is certainly true; it is only a matter of an hour's sleep, and all will be different.

I hope that in these matters your pastor and preacher will abundantly demonstrate their faithful service to you, so that you will not need my words. Yet I could not refrain from excusing my physical absence, which (God knows) causes me heartfelt sorrow. My Katie, Hänschen,[79] Lenchen,[80] Aunt Lena,[81] and all my household send you greetings and pray for you faithfully. Greet my dear mother and all my relatives. God's grace and strength be and abide with you forever. Amen.

Your loving son,
MARTIN LUTHER

[Written] at Wittenberg,
February 15, 1530

[76]Another possible translation would be: "given grace through His Spirit to believe this."
[77]Ps. 37:5 (Luther Bible).
[78]I.e., either in this life or the life to come, or in Wittenberg or Mansfeld.
[79]John Luther.
[80]Magdalen Luther.
[81]Magdalene von Bora (an aunt of Luther's wife), a former nun who sometime after 1523 left the nunnery and lived with the Luther household until she died.

TO JOHN HESS

November 1527

Breslau, in Silesia, was hard hit by the plague during the late summer and fall of 1527, and the Evangelical clergymen there asked Luther, through John Hess, whether it is proper for Christians to flee in the face of such danger. After some delay and a repeated request, Luther responded, and because the plague was also raging in Wittenberg at the time, he thought it well to publish his reply as an open letter. It was reprinted again and again in time of epidemic elsewhere. On account of his leadership in the introduction of the Reformation there, John Hess (1490–1547) is commonly called the reformer of Silesia.

To the esteemed Dr. John Hess, pastor in Breslau, and to his fellow ministers in the gospel of Christ: grace and peace from God our Father and from the Lord Jesus Christ.

I have long since received the question (whether it is proper for a Christian to flee when in danger of death) that you sent to me here in Wittenberg, and it should long since have been answered if Almighty God had not been scourging and chastising me so hard that I was unable to do much reading or writing. Besides, I thought that inasmuch as God the Father has so richly endowed you with all manner of understanding and truth in Christ, you would yourself be able, with the aid of His Spirit and grace and without my help, to decide and answer such a question as this, and greater ones too.

Since you have not stopped insisting and have so humbly desired to know my opinion in this matter in order, as St. Paul teaches again and again, that we may all be found to have the same mind and judgment [Phil. 2:2; 1 Cor. 1:10; 2 Cor. 13:11.], I am here expressing my opinion in so far as God has enabled me and I may have understanding. I am offering this opinion in all humility in order that, as is proper, it may be weighed and judged by your insight and that of all godly Christians. Because there are rumors of fatal disease here among us and in many other places, I have had it printed in case others may also desire or use such instruction.

Some insist that one may not and should not flee under peril of death. They say that because death is a punishment which God has sent upon us on account of our sin, we should remain and patiently await God's punishment with true and firm faith. They regard flight as wrong and nothing short of unbelief in God. Others, however, hold that one may flee, especially if one is not encumbered with responsibilities.

I am unable to criticize the opinion of the first group, for they emphasize a good thing—strong faith—and are to be praised for desiring that all Christians have a strong, firm faith. It takes more than milk-fed [82] faith to await death, which terrified almost all the saints and still does so. Who would not praise those who are sincerely of a mind to despise death and willingly submit to the scourge of God insofar as this may be done without tempting God, as I shall mention below?

However, since there are few strong Christians and many weak ones, all cannot be expected to bear the same thing. One who is strong in faith can drink poison without suffering harm, as we read in the last chapter of Mark [Mark 16:18], but one who is weak in faith will die of it. Because he was strong in faith Peter could walk on the sea, but when he doubted and was weak in faith he sank and almost drowned [Matt. 14:29, 30]. When a strong man walks with a weak man he must be careful not to walk to the limit of his strength lest he walk the weak man to death. Christ does not wish His weak members to be cast away, as St. Paul teaches in Romans, chapter 15, and 1 Corinthians, chapter 12 [Rom. 15:1; 1 Cor. 12:22].

To put the matter briefly and precisely, there are two ways of dying and fleeing death. The first is to act contrary to God's Word and command, as when somebody who has been imprisoned for the sake of God's Word denies or recants God's Word in order to escape death. In such a case everyone has a clear order and command from Christ not to flee but rather to die, for He says, "Whosoever shall deny Me before men, him will I also deny before My Father which is in heaven" [Matt. 10:33]. And in Luke, chapter 12, "Be not afraid of them that kill the body and after that have no more that they can do" [Luke 12:4].

In like fashion those who are in the ministry, such as preachers

---

[82] Cf. 1 Cor. 3:2.

and pastors, are also obliged to stay and remain when there is peril of death, for there is a clear command of Christ, "The good shepherd giveth his life for the sheep, but he that is a hireling seeth the wolf coming and fleeth" [John 10:11, 12]. In time of death one is especially in need of the ministry, which can strengthen and comfort one's conscience with God's Word and Sacrament in order to overcome death with faith. However, where enough preachers are available and they come to an agreement among themselves that some of their number should move away because there is no necessity for their remaining in such danger, I do not count it a sin, because an adequate ministry is provided and, if need be, these would be ready and willing to stay. So we read that St. Athanasius fled from his church to save his life because there were many others there to perform the duties of the office.[83] In Damascus, St. Paul's disciples let him down by the wall in a basket so that he escaped (Acts, chapter 9) [Acts 9:25], and it is written in Acts, chapter 19, that his disciples suffered him not to face danger in the marketplace because it was not necessary [Acts 19:30].

Similarly all those who hold secular offices, such as burgomasters, judges, and the like, are obliged to remain. Here again there is a Word of God by which secular government was instituted and commanded in order to rule, protect, and preserve cities and lands. So St. Paul says in Romans, chapter 13, "Government is God's minister to keep the peace," etc.[84] It would be a great sin for somebody who has been commanded to take care of a whole community to leave it without head and government in time of danger (such as fire, murder, rebellion, and other calamities which the devil might prepare) because there is no order there. St. Paul says, "If any provide not for his own, he hath denied the faith, and is worse than an infidel" [1 Tim. 5:8]. If out of great weakness they flee, they must (as I have said above) see to it that a sufficient number of administrators are put in their places in order that the community may be well cared for and preserved, and they must also diligently inquire and insist that everything is done.

What I have now said about these two offices must be understood to apply to all other persons who are bound to others by

[83]Augustine in Migne, *P.L.*, XXX, 1017.
[84]Cf. Rom. 13:6.

duties and responsibilities. So a servant should not flee from his master, nor a maid from her mistress, unless it be with the knowledge and consent of the master or mistress. On the other hand, a master should not forsake his servant nor a mistress her maid unless these are sufficiently provided for in some other way or place. In all these cases it is God's command that servants and maids are bound to serve, and should be obedient, while masters and mistresses must care for their servants. Fathers and mothers are similarly bound by God's command to serve and help their children, while children are bound to serve and help their parents. Nor may the common people who are hired for wages or pay (such as town physician, town official, mercenary soldier, or whatever they may be) flee unless they put in their places enough other able persons who are acceptable to their superiors.

Where there are no parents, guardians and close relatives are obliged to take in those who are related to them, or at least be careful to see to it that others are provided in their places to care for their sick relatives. In fact, no one may flee from his neighbor unless there is somebody to take his place in waiting upon and nursing the sick. In all such cases these words of Christ are to be feared: "I was sick and ye visited Me not" [Matt. 25:43]. These words of Christ bind each of us to the other. No one may forsake his neighbor when he is in trouble. Everybody is under obligation to help and support his neighbor as he would himself like to be helped.[85]

When no such need exists, when there are enough other people to do the nursing and helping (whether because it is their own duty or desire or whether because they have been commissioned by arrangement of those who are weak in faith), and when the sick do not want them to stay but rather object to this, I believe that they are free either to flee or to remain. Let him who is bold and strong in faith stay in God's name; he does not sin by doing so. On the other hand, let him who is weak and fearful flee in God's name so long as he does so without prejudice to his duty to his neighbor and after providing and arranging for adequate substitutes. The instinct to flee death and save one's life is implanted by God and is not forbidden, provided it is not opposed to God and neighbor. It is as St. Paul says in Ephesians, chapter 4, "No man ever yet hated

[85]Cf. Matt. 7:12.

his own flesh; but nourisheth and cherisheth it" [Eph. 5:29]. Indeed, we are commanded to preserve our bodies and lives as well as we can and not neglect them. St. Paul says in 1 Corinthians, chapter 12, that God has provided our bodies with members that one member may always have care and work for the other.[86]

It is not forbidden but rather commanded that we seek our daily bread, clothing, and all the necessities of life in the sweat of our face[87] and avoid harm and trouble where we can, provided this can be done without prejudice or injury to the love we are to bear and the duty we are to perform toward our neighbor. How proper it is, then, to try to preserve life and escape death where this can be done without disadvantage to neighbor! For behold, body and life are more than meat and raiment, as Christ Himself says in Matthew, chapter 5.[88] If anyone is so strong in faith that he can willingly endure nakedness, hunger, and want without tempting God and without attempting to extricate himself from the situation in which he finds himself, let him do so without condemning those who do not or cannot do likewise.

There are plenty of examples in the scriptures to prove that fleeing from death is not wrong in itself. Abraham was a great saint, yet he feared death and fled from it when he gave his wife, Sarah, out to be his sister,[89] but because he did this without harming or neglecting his neighbor it was not reckoned against him as sin. His son Isaac did likewise.[90] Jacob also fled from his brother, Esau, to escape being killed.[91] David also fled before Saul and Absalom,[92] and the prophet Urijah fled into Egypt before King Jehoiakim [Jer. 26:21]. The thirsty prophet Elijah too, when Queen Jezebel threatened him after he had slain the prophets of Baal in his great faith, was afraid and fled into the wilderness.[93] And before him Moses, when the king of Egypt sought him, fled into the land of Midian.[94]

---

[86]Cf. 1 Cor. 12:21–26.
[87]Cf. Gen. 3:19.
[88]Cf. Matt. 6:25.
[89]Cf. Gen. 12:13.
[90]Cf. Gen. 26:7.
[91]Cf. Gen. 27:43–45.
[92]Cf. 1 Sam. 19:10–17; 2 Sam. 15:14.
[93]Cf. 1 Kings 19:3.
[94]Cf. Exod. 2:15.

There are many other examples. All of these fled from death as they were able in order to save their lives, but without thereby depriving their neighbors of anything and only after first fulfilling their obligations.

"Yes," you will say, "but these are not examples of dying in pestilence but of being killed as a result of persecution." Answer: death is death, no matter by what means it comes. So God refers in the scriptures to the four plagues, or punishments, as the pestilence, the famine, the sword, and the noisome beast [Ezek. 14:21]. If one may with good conscience and God's permission flee from one or several of these, why not from all four? The above examples show how the dear patriarchs fled from the sword, and it is clear enough that Abraham, Isaac, Jacob, and his sons fled from the second plague—that is, from famine or hunger—when they fled into Egypt on account of the famine, as we read in Genesis [Gen., chs. 40–47]. Why, then, should one not flee from the noisome beasts? Am I to suppose that if a war or the Turk comes, no one should flee from a village or town but must await God's punishment there at the hand of the sword? Very well. Let him who is so strong in faith stay, but let him not condemn those who flee.

Am I to suppose that if a house is on fire, no one must run out of it and no one must attempt to rescue those inside because fire is a punishment of God? Or that if somebody falls into a lake, he should not swim out but allow himself to drown as a punishment from God? Well, if you are able, do so without tempting God, but let others do what they are able to do. Again, if a person breaks a leg or is wounded or bitten, must he avoid medical aid and say, "It is God's punishment, and so I shall endure it until it heals itself"? Cold and frost are also God's punishment, and one could die of them. Why do you run to a fire or into the house when it is cold? Be strong and stay out in the cold until it becomes warm again. According to this opinion there would be no need for apothecary shops, medicine, and physicians, for all sicknesses are punishments of God. Hunger and thirst are also great punishments and forms of martyrdom. Why, then, do you eat and drink and not allow yourself to be punished by these until they stop of their own accord? This notion will finally carry us so far that we will abolish the Lord's Prayer and cease praying: "Deliver us from evil, Amen [Luke 11:4]," inasmuch as all kinds of evil are God's punishments and we could henceforth no longer pray to be delivered from hell and could not avoid it because it too is God's punishment. What would this lead to?

From all this we can conclude that we should pray against all manner of evil and should also defend ourselves against evil insofar as we are able, provided that in doing so we do not act against God, as I have said above. If God desires that we suffer evil and be overcome by it, our defense will not help us. Accordingly let everyone be guided by this. If anyone is bound to remain in peril of death in order to serve his neighbor, let him commit himself to God's keeping and say: "Lord, I am in Thy hands. Thou has obligated me to serve here. Thy will be done [Luke 11:2], for I am Thy poor creature. Thou canst slay or preserve me here as well as if I were in duty bound to suffer fire, water, thirst, or some other danger." On the other hand, if anyone is not bound to serve his neighbor and is in a position to flee, let him also commit himself to God's keeping and say: "Dear God, I am weak and afraid; I am therefore fleeing from this evil and am doing all that I can to defend myself against it. Nevertheless, I am in Thy hands, whether in this or some other evil which may befall me. Thy will be done. My flight will not save me, for evils and misfortunes will assail me everywhere, and the devil, who is a murderer from the beginning and tries to commit murder and cause misfortune everywhere, does not sleep or take a holiday."

In like fashion we are obliged to treat our neighbor in all other troubles and perils too. If his house is on fire, love requires that I run there and help put out the fire. If there are enough other people there to extinguish the flames, I may either go home or stay. If he falls into a pit or into water, I must not go away but must hurry to his side as well as I can to help him. But if others are there who are rescuing him, I am free to depart. If I see that he is hungry or thirsty, I must not forsake him but give him to eat and drink without regard to the danger that I might thereby become poorer. If we are not to help and support our neighbor unless we can do so without danger and harm to our bodies and goods, we shall never help our neighbor, for it will always appear as if this will involve us in interruption, peril, loss, or neglect of our interests. We would rather take the risk of having the fire or other misfortune spread from our neighbor's house and destroy us, our bodies, goods, wife, child, and all that we have.

Anyone who refuses to help his neighbor, who allows him to remain in need, and who flees from him is a murderer in God's sight, as St. John says in his epistle, "He that loveth not his brother is a murderer," and again, "Whoso hath this world's good and seeth his brother have need, how dwelleth the love of God in him?"[95] This was one of the sins that God reckoned to the account of the city of Sodom when He said through the prophet Ezekiel, "Behold, this was the iniquity of thy sister Sodom: pride and fullness of bread, yet she did not strengthen the hand of the poor and needy" [Ezek. 16:49]. On the last day Christ will damn them as murderers and will say, "I was sick and ye visited Me not."[96] If those who do not go to the poor and sick and offer help are to be judged so, what will happen to those who run away and let them die like dogs and pigs? Yes, what will happen to those who go beyond this, take from them what they have, and add to their troubles—as the tyrants are now doing to the poor people who are accepting the gospel? But let them go. They will have their reward.[97]

To be sure, it would be good, praiseworthy, and Christian for towns and lands that can do so to make provision for the maintenance of community houses and hospitals and for people to minister in them so that all the sick can be gathered from all homes and committed there. This is what our forefathers desired and intended when they established so many foundations, hospitals, and infirmaries in order that every citizen would not have to maintain a hospital in his own home. Where these exist it is altogether proper that everyone should help and contribute liberally to their support, especially the government. But where there are no such institutions (and there are few of them), each of us must be his neighbor's nurse and hospital director in time of need, at the risk of losing salvation and God's favor. Here we have a word and commandment of God: "Love thy neighbor as thyself" [Matt. 22:39], and Matthew, chapter 7, "All things whatsoever ye would that men should do to you, do ye even so to them" [Matt. 7:12].

When people are beginning to die [in a time of pestilence], we should stay with them, make preparations to counteract the dis-

---

[95]Cf. 1 John 3:14, 15, 17.
[96]Cf. Matt. 25:43.
[97]Cf. Matt. 6:2.

ease, and assure ourselves, especially those of us who have such
responsibilities toward others (as I mentioned above), that we cannot leave or flee. We should be comforted by our certainty that it is
God's punishment sent upon us not only to punish sin but also to
test our faith and love—our faith in order that we may see and
know what our attitude is toward God, and our love in order that
we may see what our attitude is toward our neighbor. Although I
believe that every pestilence, like other plagues, is spread among
the people by evil spirits who poison the air or somehow exhale a
noisome breath and inject deadly poison into men's bodies, nevertheless it is also God's will and punishment. Accordingly we
should submit to it patiently and risk our lives in the service of our
neighbor, as St. John teaches: "Because Christ laid down His life for
us, we ought to lay down our lives for the brethren" [1 John 3:16].

If the sick strike fear and terror into anyone's heart, let such a
person be of good courage and so strengthen and comfort himself
that he has no doubt that it is the devil who is responsible for this
fear, terror, and horror. The devil is so very evil that he not only
tries constantly to kill and murder but also gives vent to his spleen
by making us fearful, afraid, and timid about death in order that
death might appear to us to be the worst possible thing, that we
might have neither rest nor peace in this life, and that we might
despair of our life. In this way he tries to bring it about that we
despair of God, become unwilling and unprepared to die, become
so enveloped in the dark clouds of fear and worry that we forget
and lose sight of Christ, our light and life, forsake our neighbor in
his need, and so sin against God and man. This is the devil's desire
and purpose. Because we know that such fear and terror are the
devil's game, we should be the more unwilling to be affected by it,
gather up our courage in defiance of him and to vex him, and
throw off his terror and cast it back at him. We should defend ourselves with such weapons and say:

"Away with you and your fears, devil! Because it will vex you, I
shall defy you by going at once to my sick neighbor to help him. I
shall pay no attention to you but shall attack you on two points.
The first is that I know for certain that this work is pleasing to
God and all angels when I do it in obedience to His will and as a
divine service. It must indeed be especially pleasing to God
because it displeases you so much and you so vigorously oppose it.

How willingly and gladly I would do it if it pleased only one angel and he watched me and rejoiced over what I did! However, since it pleases my Lord Jesus Christ and all the heavenly hosts, and is at the same time the will and command of God my Father, why should I be so influenced by your terror as to prevent such joy in heaven, obstruct the desire of my Lord, and provide you and your demons in hell with an occasion to be gay, to laugh, and to mock me? Not so! You are not to have your way. If Christ shed His blood for me and died in my behalf, why should I not place myself in a little danger for His sake and face the effects of a powerless pestilence? If you can terrify, my Christ can strengthen. If you can slay, Christ can give life. If you have poison on your breath, Christ has more potent medicine. If my dear Christ with His command, His benefaction, and all His comfort would not mean more to my spirit than you, cursed devil, can do to my frail flesh with your false terrors, God would surely be displeased. Get thee behind me, Satan![98] Christ is here, and I am His servant in this work. He shall prevail. Amen."

The other point on which to attack the devil is the sure promise of God with which He comforts all those who consider the poor and needy. He says in Psalm 41: "Blessed is he that considereth the poor: the Lord will deliver him in time of trouble. The Lord will preserve him, and keep him alive; and he shall be blessed upon the earth: and thou wilt not deliver him unto the will of his enemies. The Lord will strengthen him upon the bed of languishing: Thou wilt transform his whole bed in his sickness" [Ps. 41:1–3]. Are not these great and glorious promises of God, showered in abundance on those who consider the poor and needy? What is there that can frighten us or move us to act contrary to this great comfort of God? To be sure, the service that we may render to those in need is a small thing in comparison with these promises and rewards of God. St. Paul does well to say to Timothy, "Godliness is profitable unto all things, having promise of the life that now is, and of that which is to come" [1 Tim. 4:8]. Godliness is nothing but divine service, and divine service is service to one's neighbor. Experience teaches us that those who minister to the sick with love, devotion, and earnestness

[98]Cf. Matt. 16:23.

are generally preserved. Even if they too should be infected, it does not matter, for this psalm says, "Thou wilt transform his whole bed in his sickness," that is, God will turn his sickbed into a bed for the well. But it is not surprising if one who nurses a sick person for the sake of greed or inheritance, seeking his own good in what he does, is finally infected and defiled and afterward dies before he comes into possession of the property or inheritance.

Whoever ministers to the sick on the strength of these comforting promises (even if, needing them, he accepts fairly large wages for his services inasmuch as the laborer is worthy of his hire) [Luke 10:7] has another great comfort, namely, that he will be ministered unto. God Himself will nurse him, and will be his physician as well. What a nurse God is! What a physician He is! Or rather, what are all physicians, apothecaries, and nurses in comparison with God? Should not this give a person the courage to go to the sick and minister to their needs—even if they have as many pestilential boils as they have hairs on their whole bodies and they cough up enough pestilential poison to infect a hundred people? What are all pestilences and devils in comparison with God, who here promises to be your nurse and physician? Shame on you, and again I say, shame on you, O cursed unbelief, that you should despise such rich comfort and allow a small boil and uncertain danger to frighten you more than these certain, faithful promises of God strengthen you. What would it help if all physicians were there and all the world were attending you if God were not present? On the other hand, what harm would it do if all the world forsook you and no physician stayed with you as long as God remained with you with His promises? Do you not realize that you would be surrounded by thousands of angels who would help you to trample the pestilence underfoot? It is written in Psalm 91, "He shall give His angels charge over thee, to keep thee in all thy ways. They shall bear thee up in their hands, lest thou dash thy foot against a stone. Thou shalt tread upon the lion and adder: the young lion and the dragon shalt thou trample underfeet" [Ps. 91:11–13].

Therefore, dear friends, let us not be so fearful as to forsake those to whom we have obligations and shamefully flee before the devil's terror, whereby we would give him pleasure and occasion to mock us while God and all His angels would undoubtedly be displeased and disgusted. It is certainly true that anyone who despises the abundant promises and commands of God and leaves his neighbors in the lurch will be guilty of breaking all the divine commandments and will be regarded as a murderer of his forsaken neighbors. Then, I fear, the promises will be turned about and transformed into terrible threats, so that the psalm will be directed against such a person: "Cursed is he that considereth not the poor but fleeth and forsaketh them. The Lord will not deliver him in time of trouble, but will also flee from him and forsake him. The Lord will not preserve him and keep him alive, nor will He bless him upon the earth, but will deliver him into the hands of His enemies. The Lord will not strengthen him upon the bed of languishing, nor transform his bed in his sickness."[99] "For with what measure ye mete, it shall be measured to you again" [Matt. 7:2]. It cannot be otherwise. This is terrible to hear, more terrible to expect, most terrible to experience. If God takes away His hand and flees, what can you expect other than sheer devilishness and all evil? It cannot be otherwise if neighbors are forsaken contrary to God's Word and command. This will most assuredly happen to each and every one unless he honestly repents what he has done.

I know very well that if Christ Himself or his mother were now ill, everybody would be so devoted as to wish to help and serve. Everybody would try to be bold and brace. No one would want to run away. Everybody would come running. Yet they do not hear what He Himself says: "Inasmuch as ye have done it unto one of the least of these My brethren, ye have done it unto Me" [Matt. 25:40]. And when He spoke of the First Commandment he added, "The Second is like unto it, Thou shalt love thy neighbor as thyself" [Matt. 22:39]. Here you hear that the command to love your neighbor is like unto the First Commandment, that we should love God. And what you do or omit doing to your neighbor means as much as that you have done or failed to do it to God Himself. If, then, you would minister to and wait upon Christ, behold, you have a sick neighbor before you. Go to him and minister to him and you will assuredly find Christ in him, not according to the person, but in His Word. If you are unwilling to minister to your neighbor, you may be sure that if Christ Himself were there, you would do the same

[99] Cf. Ps. 41:1–3.

thing—run away, and let Him lie there. You would have nothing but false notions (which leave you in unprofitable ignorance) as to how you would minister to Christ if He were there. They are nothing but lies, for anyone who would minister to Christ in the body would also minister to his neighbor's needs. Let this be said as a warning and admonition against shameful flight and the terror with which the devil tempts us to act against God's Word and command with respect to our neighbor and to sin too much on the left hand.

On the other hand, some sin too much on the right hand and are too daring and foolhardy. They tempt God, neglect all the things with which they ought to protect themselves against pestilence or death, scorn the use of medicine, and do not avoid the places where there has been pestilence and the persons who have had it. On the contrary, they drink and play with such persons, try in this way to demonstrate their good cheer, and say: "It is God's punishment. If He wishes to protect me from it, He will do so without medicine and any effort on my part." This is not trusting in God but tempting God, for God created medicine and gave us our reason in order that we may so manage and care for our bodies as to be well and live. Whoever does not use medicine when he has it and can make use of it without injury to his neighbor neglects his body and runs the risk of being a suicide in God's sight. One might in similar fashion neglect food and drink and clothing and shelter, be foolhardy in one's faith, and say, "If God wishes to protect me from hunger and cold, He will do so without food and clothing." Such a man would really be a suicide. As a matter of fact, it would be worse for him to neglect his body in this way and not to employ such protection against the pestilence as is available because he might infect and defile others, who would have remained alive if he had taken care of his body as he ought. So he would be responsible for his neighbor's death and would be a murderer many times over in God's sight. Indeed, such a person would be like a man who, when a house is on fire in a town, will not help put it out but lets it burn until the whole town is on fire, and says, "If God wishes, He can preserve the town without water and without quenching the flames."

Not so, my dear friend. That would not be well done. Use medicine. Take whatever may be helpful to you. Fumigate your house, yard, and street. Avoid persons and places where you are not needed or where your neighbor has recovered. Act as one who would like to help put out a general fire. What is the pestilence, after all, but a fire which consumes body and life instead of wood and straw? Meanwhile think thus: "With God's permission the enemy has sent poison and deadly dung among us, and so I will pray to God that He may be gracious and preserve us. Then I will fumigate to purify the air, give and take medicine, and avoid places and persons where I am not needed in order that I may not abuse myself and that through me others may not be infected and inflamed with the result that I become the cause of their death through my negligence. If God wishes to take me, He will be able to find me. At least I have done what He gave me to do and am responsible neither for my own death nor for the death of others. But if my neighbor needs me, I shall avoid neither person nor place but feel free to visit and help him," as has already been said. Behold, this is a true and God-fearing faith, which is neither foolhardy nor rash and does not tempt God.

Whoever has succumbed to the pestilence and has recovered should likewise avoid people and be reluctant to have them near without necessity. Although he is to be helped and not forsaken in his need, as has been said, when he has recovered from his illness he must so conduct himself in his relations with others that no one is unnecessarily endangered on his account and dies because of him. "He that loveth danger," says the wise man, "shall perish therein" [Ecclus. 3:26]. If the people in a town so conducted themselves that they were bold in their faith when the need of neighbors required it, careful when there was no need, and helpful to one another in counteracting the poison wherever possible, death would indeed be light in such a town. But when it happens that some of the people are too fearful and flee from their neighbors in time of need, while others are so foolhardy that they do not help to counteract the disease but rather spread it, the devil will take advantage of the situation and the mortality will certainly be high. Both are very injurious to God and man, the former by fearfulness and the latter by tempting God. So the devil chases the people who flee and restrains the people who stay, and no one escapes his clutches.

Some people are even worse. When they contract the pestilential disease they keep it secret, go out among other people, and think that if they can infect and defile others with the sickness they will themselves get rid of it and become well. With this notion they frequent streets and houses in the hope of saddling others or their children and servants with the pestilence and thus saving themselves. I can well believe that the devil obliges and helps to further this notion so that it actually comes to pass. I am also told that some individuals are so desperately wicked that they carry the pestilence among the people and into houses for no other reason than that they regret that the disease has not struck there, and so they spread the pestilence as if this were a great joke, like slyly putting lice in somebody's clothes or gnats in somebody's room. I do not know whether I should believe this or not. If it is true, I do not know whether we Germans are human beings or devils. To be sure, there are immoderately coarse and wicked people, and the devil is not inactive. If such people are found, it would be my suggestion that the judge should seize them by the hair and turn them over to the hangman as real, malicious murderers and scoundrels. What are they but assassins in a town? They are like assassins who plunge a knife into a person so stealthily that it cannot be determined who did it. So these people infect a child here and a woman there and nobody knows how it happened. Meanwhile they go away laughing, as if they had done a good deed. It would be better to live among wild beasts than among such murderers. I do not know how to counsel these murderers, for they pay no attention. I commend them to the government, which must take care of them with the help and counsel not of physicians, but of the hangman. God Himself commanded in the Old Testament that lepers be removed from a community and be required to live outside of a town in order to prevent infection [Lev., chs. 13; 14]. We have even more reason to do this in the present dangerous sickness. Whoever gets it should at once remove himself or be removed from contact with other people and should quickly seek help in the form of medicine. He should be aided and not forsaken in his need, as I have made sufficiently clear above, in order that the infection might in time be checked, for the benefit not only of the individual but of the whole community, which would become infected if the disease were allowed to break out and spread.

Our present pestilence here in Wittenberg had its origin in nothing else than such contagion. Thank God, the air is still fresh and pure. It is only through foolhardiness and neglect that some few have been infected. However, the devil has had his fun in spreading terror among us and causing flight. May God hold him in check. Amen.

This, then, is my understanding and opinion about fleeing when in peril of death. If you have another opinion, may God disclose it to you. Amen.

MARTIN LUTHER

Comfort for Women Who Have Had a Miscarriage

A final word—it often happens that devout parents, particularly the wives, have sought consolation from us because they have suffered such agony and heartbreak in child-bearing when, despite their best intentions and against their will, there was a premature birth or miscarriage and their child died at birth or was born dead.

One ought not to frighten or sadden such mothers by harsh words because it was not due to their carelessness or neglect that the birth of the child went off badly. One must make a distinction between them and those females who resent being pregnant, deliberately neglect their child, or go so far as to strangle or destroy it. This is how one ought to comfort them.

First, inasmuch as one cannot and ought not know the hidden judgment of God in such a case—why, after every possible care had been taken, God did not allow the child to be born alive and be baptized—these mothers should calm themselves and have faith that God's will is always better than ours, though it may seem otherwise to us from our human point of view. They should be confident that God is not angry with them or with others who are involved. Rather is this a test to develop patience. We well know that these cases have never been rare since the beginning and that scripture also cites them as examples, as in Psalm 58 [:8], and St. Paul calls himself an *abortivum,* a misbirth or one untimely born.[100]

Second, because the mother is a believing Christian it is to be hoped that her heartfelt cry and deep longing to bring her child to be baptized will be accepted by God as an effective prayer. It is true that a Christian in deepest despair does not dare to name,

---

[100]Cf. 1 Cor. 15:8.

wish, or hope for the help (as it seems to him) which he would wholeheartedly and gladly purchase with his own life were that possible, and in doing so thus find comfort. However, the words of Paul, Romans 8 [:26–27], properly apply here: "Likewise the Spirit helps us in our weakness; for we do not know how to pray as we ought (that is, as was said above, we dare not express our wishes), rather the Spirit Himself intercedes for us mightily with sighs too deep for words. And he who searches the heart knows what is the mind of the Spirit," etc. Also Ephesians 3 [:20], "Now to Him who by the power at work within us is able to do far more abundantly than all that we ask or think."

One should not despise a Christian person as if he were a Turk, a pagan, or a godless person. He is precious in God's sight and his prayer is powerful and great, for he has been sanctified by Christ's blood and anointed with the Spirit of God. Whatever he sincerely prays for, especially in the unexpressed yearning of his heart, becomes a great, unbearable cry in God's ears. God must listen, as He did to Moses, Exodus 14 [:15], "Why do you cry to Me?" even though Moses couldn't whisper, so great was his anxiety and trembling in the terrible troubles that beset him. His sighs and the deep cry of his heart divided the Red Sea and dried it up, led the children of Israel across, and drowned Pharaoh with all his army [Exod. 14:26–28] and so forth. This and even more can be accomplished by a true, spiritual longing. Even Moses did not know how or for what he should pray—not knowing how the deliverance would be accomplished—but his cry came from his heart.

Isaiah did the same against King Sennacherib [Isa. 37:4] and so did many other kings and prophets who accomplished inconceivable and impossible things by prayer, to their astonishment afterward. But before that they would not have dared to expect or wish so much of God. This means to receive things far higher and greater than we can understand or pray for, as St. Paul says, Ephesians 3 [:20], etc. Again, St. Augustine declared that his mother was praying, sighing, and weeping for him, but did not desire anything more than that he might be converted from the errors of the Manicheans and become a Christian. Thereupon God gave her not only what she desired but, as St. Augustine puts it, her "chiefest desire" (*cardinem desideriieius*), that is, what she longed for with unutterable sighs—that Augustine become not only a

Christian but also a teacher above all others in Christendom. Next to the apostles Christendom has none that is his equal.

Who can doubt that those Israelite children who died before they could be circumcised on the eighth day were yet saved by the prayers of their parents in view of the promise that God willed to be their God. God (they say) has not limited His power to the sacraments, but has made a covenant with us through His Word. Therefore we ought to speak differently and in a more consoling way with Christians than with pagans or wicked people (the two are the same), even in such cases where we do not know God's hidden judgment. For He says and is not lying, "All things are possible to him who believes" [Mark 9:23], even though they have not prayed, or expected, or hoped for what they would have wanted to see happen. Enough has been said about this. Therefore one must leave such situations to God and take comfort in the thought that He surely has heard our unspoken yearning and done all things better than we could have asked.

In summary, see to it that above all else you are a true Christian and that you teach a heartfelt yearning and praying to God in true faith, be it in this or any other trouble. Then do not be dismayed or grieved about your child or yourself, and know that your prayer is pleasing to God and that God will do everything much better than you can comprehend or desire. "Call upon Me," He says in Psalm 50 [:15], "in the day of trouble; I will deliver you, and you shall glorify Me." For this reason one ought not straightway condemn such infants for whom and concerning whom believers and Christians have devoted their longing and yearning and praying. Nor ought one to consider them the same as others for whom no faith, prayer, or yearning are expressed on the part of Christians and believers. God intends that His promise and our prayer or yearning which is grounded in that promise should not be disdained or rejected, but be highly valued and esteemed. I have said it before and preached it often enough: God accomplishes much through the faith and longing of another, even a stranger, even though there is still no personal faith. But this is given through the channel of another's intercession, as in the gospel Christ raised the widow's son at Nain because of the prayers of his mother apart from the faith of the son [Luke 7:11–17]. And He freed the little daughter of the Canaanite woman from the demon through the faith of the mother apart from the daughter's faith [Matt. 15:22–28]. The same was true of the king's son, John 4 [:46–53], and of the paralytic and many others of whom we need not say anything here.

THE LUTHER HOUSEHOLD AT TABLE

TABLE TALK

What It Takes to Understand the Scriptures

FALL 1531

"I wonder whether Peter, Paul, Moses, and all the saints fully and thoroughly understood a single Word of God so that they had nothing more to learn from it, for the understanding of God is beyond measure.[100] To be sure, the saints understood the Word of God and could also speak about it, but their practice did not keep

---

[100]Cf. Ps. 147:5.

pace with it. Here one forever remains a learner. The scholastics illustrated this with a ball, which only at one point touches the table on which it rests, although the whole weight of the ball is supported by the table.

"Though I am a great doctor, I haven't yet progressed beyond the instruction of children in the Ten Commandments, the Creed, and the Lord's Prayer. I still learn and pray these every day with my Hans and my little Lena.[101] Who understands in all of its ramifications even the opening words, [102] 'Our Father who art in heaven'? For if I understood these words in faith—that the God who holds heaven and earth in His hand is my Father—I would conclude that therefore I am lord of heaven and earth, therefore Christ is my brother, therefore all things are mine, Gabriel is my servant, Raphael is my coachman, and all the other angels are ministering spirits[103] sent forth by my Father in heaven to serve me in all my necessities, lest I strike my foot against a stone. In order that this faith should not remain untested, my Father comes along and allows me to be thrown into prison or to be drowned in water. Then it will finally become apparent how well we understand these words. Our faith wavers. Our weakness gives rise to the question 'Who knows if it is true?' So this one word 'your' or 'our' is the most difficult of all in the whole scripture. It's like the word 'your' is the First Commandment, 'I am the Lord your God' [Exod. 20:2]."

Recollection of an Accident in Student Days

BETWEEN NOVEMBER 9 AND 30, 1531

When he [Martin Luther] set out for home and was on the way, he accidentally struck his shin on his short sword and cut an artery in his leg. At the time he was alone in the open field except for one companion, and he was as far from Erfurt as Eutzsch is distant

---

[101]Luther's son John was born in 1526 and his daughter Magdalena was born in 1529.
[102]Of the Lord's Prayer. Cf. Matt. 6:9.
[103]Cf. Heb. 1:14.

from Wittenberg, that is, a half mile. The blood gushed from the wound and could not be stopped. When he pressed his finger on the wound, his leg became greatly swollen. Finally a surgeon was fetched from the town, and he bound up the wound. There he [Luther] was in danger of death and cried out, "Mary, help!" "I would have died," he now added, "with my trust in Mary." Afterward, during the night, while he was in bed, the wound broke open. He almost bled to death and again prayed to Mary. This happened on the Tuesday after Easter. [104]

God Must Be a Devout Man

BETWEEN APRIL 7 AND 15, 1532

"Our Lord God must be a devout man to be able to love knaves. I can't do it, although I am myself a knave."

Dog Provides Example of Concentration

MAY 18, 1532

When Luther's puppy[105] happened to be at the table, looked for a morsel from his master, and watched with open mouth and motionless eyes, he [Martin Luther] said, "Oh, if I could only pray the way this dog watches the meat! All his thoughts are concentrated on the piece of meat. Otherwise he has no thought, wish, or hope."

Behold, the heart of the pious dog was also lacking in this, that he could not pray without thoughts.[106]

---

[104]Probably April 16, 1503.
[105]Luther's dog Tölpel is mentioned again and again in the *Table Talk*.
[106]The last sentence probably represents the writer's (i.e., Veit Dietrich's) observation.

Luther Explains His Vehement Writing

DECEMBER 1532

When asked by the younger margrave[107] why he wrote with such vehemence, he [Martin Luther] said, "Our Lord God must precede a heavy shower with thunder and then let it rain in a very gentle fashion so that the ground becomes soaked through. To put it differently, I can cut through a willow branch with a [bread] knife, but to cut through tough oak requires an axe and wedge, and even with these one can hardly split it."

Do Not Debate with Satan When Alone

SPRING 1533

"Almost every night when I wake up the devil is there and wants to dispute with me. I have come to this conclusion: when the argument that the Christian is without the law and above the law doesn't help, I instantly chase him away with a fart. The rogue wants to dispute about righteousness although he is himself a knave, for he kicked God out of heaven and crucified His Son. No man should be alone when he opposes Satan. The Church and the ministry of the Word were instituted for this purpose, that hands may be joined together and one may help another. If the prayer of one doesn't help, the prayer of another will."

As a Monk Luther Observed Prayers Strictly

SPRING 1533

"When I was a monk I was unwilling to omit any of the prayers,[108] but when I was busy with public lecturing and writing I often accumulated my appointed prayers for a whole week, or even two or three weeks. Then I would take a Saturday off, or shut myself in for as long as three days without food and drink, until I had said the prescribed prayers. This made my head split, and as a conse-

---

[107]Luther was with Elector Joachim II of Brandenburg (1538–71) in November 1532.

[108]Horary prayers, or prayers prescribed for monks at certain hours of the day.

quence I couldn't close my eyes for five nights, lay sick unto death, and went out of my senses. Even after I had quickly recovered and I tried again to read, my head went round and round. Thus our Lord God drew me, as if by force, from that torment of prayers. To such an extent had I been captive [to human traditions]! Therefore I readily forgive those who can't at once assent to my teaching. You young fellows know nothing about such outrages. What is written applies to you: 'Others have labored and you have entered into their labor' [John 4:38].

"In the *Dialogues* of St. Gregory there is a story to the effect that he had a very faithful steward who, because he had laid aside three gold coins without telling his brethren about them, was condemned. So it is here. When Christ is away the devil is present and says, 'You must do it to the very last detail.' But Christ overlooks all sins. God gives so that we may be thankful. He never bothers me about my having done wrong in my teaching, but this is unknown to those who were in monasteries a long time. Münzer,[109] Oecolampadius,[110] and Zwingli[111] escaped early, but they didn't stand up very long. For the devil can find a person quickly, especially if Christ is not in his heart. The devil leads such a person into the holy scriptures without Christ, that is, to the law and to works. So it takes toil and trouble before Christ Himself helps again."

Counsel for a Man Overtaken by Melancholy

SPRING 1533

I[112] asked him [Martin Luther] about a certain man who, when he had a stomachache for several days and as a consequence had pain in his head and was confused in his thoughts, got the notion and was afraid that he was falling into a state of melancholy. He disclosed his anxiety to me and asked that I notify the doctor, whereupon he [Martin Luther] responded with these words: "When the

[109]For a short time Thomas Münzer had been confessor in a monastery.
[110]John Oecolampadius held several ecclesiastical positions before he adopted Reformation views.
[111]Huldrych Zwingli was a parish priest when he came to his new understanding of the Christian faith.
[112]Veit Dietrich, the recorder of this conversation.

devil can bring this about, it means that imagination has produced the effect. On this account his thoughts ought to be changed. He ought to think about Christ. You should say to him, 'Christ lives. You have been baptized. God is not a God of sadness, death, etc., but the devil is. Christ is a God of joy, and so the scriptures often say that we should rejoice, be glad, etc. This is Christ. Because you have a gracious God, He won't take you by the throat.'

"A Christian should and must be a cheerful person. If he isn't, the devil is tempting him. I have sometimes been grievously tempted while bathing in my garden, and then I have sung the hymn 'Let us now praise Christ.' Otherwise I would have been lost then and there. Accordingly, when you notice that you have some such thoughts, say, 'This isn't Christ.' To be sure, he can hear the name of Christ, but it's a lie because Christ says, 'Let not your hearts be troubled [John 14:27]. Trust in Me,' etc. This is a command of God: 'Rejoice!'[113] I now preach this, and I also write it, but I haven't as yet learned it. But it happens that we learn as we're tempted. If we were always glad, the devil would befoul us.[114] Christ knows that our hearts are troubled, and it is for this reason that He says and commands, 'Let not your hearts be troubled.'

"Thus we are like the holy fathers in our faith. The weaker we are than the fathers, the greater the victory Christ obtains for us. We are very inexperienced, very weak, and very proud over against the devil; he has a great advantage over us, for our wisdom, power, and holiness are not so great as our fathers' were. But our Lord God wants to put an end to the devil's extreme arrogance. Paul had to say, 'I alone have resisted all the derision of Satan.'"

Father Criticizes Luther for Becoming Monk

FALL 1533

He [Martin Luther] became a monk against the will of his father. When he celebrated his first Mass and asked his father why he was angry about the step he took, the father replied reproachfully,

---

[113]Cf. Matt. 5:12.
[114]'That is, it would be more than we could bear.

"Don't you know that it's written, Honor your father and your mother" [Exod. 20:12]? When he excused himself by saying that he was so frightened by a storm that he was compelled to become a monk, his father answered, "Just so it wasn't a phantom you saw!" Afterward it was his father who advised him to get married.

He [Martin Luther] was born in Eisleben and is a native of the district of Möhra, near Eisenach. His grandfather was Henricus Luder, and his father was Johannes Luder.

The World Is Like a Drunken Peasant

FALL 1533

"The world is like a drunken peasant. If you lift him into the saddle on one side, he will fall off on the other side. One can't help him, no matter how one tries. He wants to be the devil's."

God Is Friendlier to Us Than Katie to Her Child

BEFORE DECEMBER 14, 1531

"God must be much friendlier to me and speak to me in friendlier fashion than my Katie to little Martin.[115] Neither Katie nor I could intentionally gouge out the eye or tear off the head of our child. Nor could God. God must have patience with us. He has given evidence of it, and therefore He sent His Son into our flesh in order that we may look to Him for the best.

"I think Paul himself was hostile to God because he couldn't believe as he wished he could.

"When I reflect on the magnitude of God's mercy and majesty, I am myself horrified at how far God has humbled Himself."

The Gospel Is Preached Through Music

BEFORE DECEMBER 14, 1531

"What is law doesn't make progress, but what is gospel does. God has preached the gospel through music, too, as may be seen in

[115]The son of Luther and his wife Katie was about a month old at this time.

Josquin,[116] all of whose compositions flow freely, gently, and cheerfully, are not forced or cramped by rules, and are like the song of the finch."

Death Is Caused by Satan, Not by God

BETWEEN JANUARY 8 AND MARCH 23, 1532

"The devil slays us all, for the scripture states that he causes death and is the author of death [John 8:44]. Satan put God's Son to death."

The doctor's wife[117] said, "Oh, no, my dear doctor! I don't believe it!"

Then the doctor said, "Who would love our Lord God if He Himself had a mind to kill us? He won't be a murderer because He commanded, 'You shall not kill' [Exod. 20:13]. If our Lord God wanted to kill me, it wouldn't matter inasmuch as I can expect good neither in heaven nor on earth. Besides, snakes, adders, toads, wolves, bears, lions—they all kill. What am I to expect?

"Everything that God makes He creates for life. He created things that they might be, and He called into being things that didn't exist, as if they did [Rom. 4:17]. This means that life belongs to God's purpose. But death has been introduced into the world through the devil's envy, and on this account the devil is called the author of death. For what else does Satan do then seduce from true religion, provoke sedition, cause wars, pestilence, etc., and bring about every evil?"

Luther Admonishes His Son Not to Be a Lawyer

BETWEEN APRIL 7 AND MAY 1, 1532

The doctor took his child[118] in his hands and said, "If you should become a lawyer, I'd hang you on the gallows. You must be a

---

[116]Josquin des Prez (d. 1521), a church musician on the eve of the Reformation whose compositions were prized by Luther and often sung at his table. See Paul Nettl, *Luther and Music* (Philadelphia: Muhlenberg, 1948), 1–104.

[117]The wife of Martin Luther.

[118]Luther's son Martin, who eventually studied theology but never occupied a pulpit.

preacher and must baptize, preach, administer the sacrament, visit the sick, and comfort the sorrowful."

Severe Whipping Makes Children Resentful
BETWEEN MAY 20 AND 27, 1532

"One shouldn't whip children too hard. My father once whipped me so severely that I ran away from him, and he was worried that he might not win me back again. I wouldn't like to strike my little Hans[119] very much, lest he should become shy and hate me. I know nothing that would give me greater sorrow. God acts like this [for He says], 'I'll chastise you, my children, but through another—through Satan or the world—but if you cry out and run to Me, I'll rescue you and raise you up again.' For God doesn't want us to hate Him."

We Must Often Try God's Patience
BETWEEN MAY 27 AND 31, 1532

The doctor took his son[120] on his lap, and the child befouled him. Thereupon he [Martin Luther] said, "How our Lord God has to put up with many a murmur and stink from us, worse than a mother must endure from her child!"

Luther Reads Through the Bible Twice a Year
OCTOBER 21, 1532

"For some years now," the doctor said, "I have read through the Bible twice every year. If you picture the Bible to be a mighty tree and every word a little branch, I have shaken every one of these branches because I wanted to know what it was and what it meant."

---

[119]John Luther was almost six years old at this time.
[120]Presumably Martin, then six months old.

Adam Must Have Lived a Simple Life

BETWEEN NOVEMBER 24 AND DECEMBER 8, 1532

"Adam was a very simple and unassuming man [said Luther]. I don't think he lighted candles. He didn't know that the ox has suet in his body, for he wasn't as yet slaughtering cattle. I wonder where he got the hides. Beyond this, Adam was undoubtedly a handsome man. He lived so long that he saw the eighth generation of his descendants, up to the time of Noah. No doubt he was a very sensible man and well practiced in a variety of trials. He lived most temperately and drank neither wine nor beer.

"I wish the brewing of beer had never been invented, for a great deal of grain is consumed to make it, and nothing good is brewed."

A Dog Suggests a Topic for Comment

BETWEEN DECEMBER 11, 1532, AND JANUARY 2, 1533

Dr. Martin Luther played with his dog[121] and said, "The dog is a very faithful animal and is held in high esteem if he isn't too ordinary. Our Lord God has made the best gifts most common. The preeminent gift given to all living things is the eye. Small birds have very bright eyes, like little stars, and can see a fly a room length away. But we don't acknowledge such everyday gifts. We are stupid clods. In the future life we'll see them, however; there we ourselves will make birds with pretty, shining eyes."

A Suggestion for Students on Reading

BETWEEN JANUARY 2 AND 26, 1533

"A student who doesn't want his work to go for nothing ought to read and reread some good author until the author becomes part, as it were, of his flesh and blood. Scattered reading confuses more than it teaches. Many books, even good ones, have the same effect on the student. So he is like the man who dwells everywhere and

---

[121]This dog may have been the one referred to elsewhere as Tölpel.

therefore dwells nowhere. Just as in human society we don't enjoy the fellowship of every friend every day, but only of a few chosen ones, so we ought to do in our studies."

Description of Luther's "Tower Experience"

BETWEEN JUNE 9 AND JULY 21, 1532

"The words 'righteous' and 'righteousness of God' struck my conscience like lightning. When I heard them I was exceedingly terrified. If God is righteous[122] [I thought], He must punish. But when by God's grace I pondered, in the tower and heated room of this building,[123] over the words 'He who through faith is righteous shall live' [Rome. 1:17] and 'the righteousness of God' [Rom. 3:21], I soon came to the conclusion that if we, as righteous men, ought to live from faith and if the righteousness of God should contribute to the salvation of all who believe, then salvation won't be our merit but God's mercy. My spirit was thereby cheered. For it's by the righteousness of God that we're justified and saved through Christ. These words [which had before terrified me] now became more pleasing to me. The Holy Spirit unveiled the scriptures for me in this tower."

Fishing and Eating Fish with Pleasure

FALL 1533

Dr. Luther went out with his wife into the garden to fish in the pond and on the bank of the river. There they caught pike, loach, trout, blacktail, carp. Some of them we ate at the table with great

---

[122]The Latin word *iustus* can be translated either by "righteous" or by "just."

[123]The "tower experience" of Luther is so called because it occurred in the tower of the Black Cloister in Wittenberg (later Luther's home), at an undetermined date between 1508 and 1518. This report of a conversation at table also indicates that Luther's exegetical discovery took place in a heated room *(hypocaustum),* which a variant calls "the secret place of the monks" and other variants appear to call the lavatory *(cloaca).* Here the meaning of the abbreviation *cl.* has been the subject of debate, some arguing that it meant "cell" or "chapter" rather than *cloaca.* Roman Catholic and Protestant historians who have debated about these accounts have hardly been warranted in their glee or their outrage at the place where Luther's experience may have occurred.

delight and thanksgiving. The doctor said, "Katie, you are more pleased over these few fish than many a nobleman when he fishes in several large ponds and catches thousands of fish. Alas, greed and ambition prevent us from enjoying things. Many a skinflint sits in the midst of the greatest luxuries and yet can't enjoy them with pleasure. It's said that the ungodly won't see the glory of God; in fact, they can't even recognize present gifts because God overwhelms us so much with them. If they were rare, we might esteem them more highly. But we can't reflect on the pleasure which the creatures give.

"See how well a little fish multiplies, for one produces probably a thousand! It happens this way, that the male strikes with his tail, deposits sperm in the water, and from it the female conceives. Consider the birds, how chastely their reproduction takes place! The rooster pecks the hen's head, the hen lays a little egg nicely in the nest, sits on it, and soon the young chick peeps out. Look how the little chick is hidden in the egg! If we had never seen such an egg and one were brought from Shangri-la,[124] we'd all be startled and amazed. And all the philosophers couldn't offer an explanation for these creatures. Only Moses gives an explanation: 'God said, and it was so' [Gen. 1:9]. He commanded, and they were made. 'Be fruitful and multiply' [Gen. 1:22]. And so it goes on."

Gravely Ill, Luther Prepares for His Death

FEBRUARY 1537

When[125] Philipp[126] looked at him [Martin Luther] he was dissolved in tears, and Luther said, "John Loeser[127] is accustomed to speak thus, 'It's no art to drink good wine, but to be able to drink bad wine is a real art.' So now you are thinking of teaching me to

---

[124]German: *Calekutte,* a legendary place far away.
[125]A variant inserts the date February 25, 1537. While in Schmalkalden to attend a meeting of the Schmalkalden League, Luther had become gravely ill with a kidney stone. This account is obviously not the record of a conversation at table; it is the report of an eyewitness in Schmalkalden, Veit Dietrich.
[126]Philipp Melanchthon.
[127]Hans Loeser was godfather of Luther's son Paul.

practice this art in order that I may be able to accept with resignation these pains of mine and this despair of life. If we accept good from the Lord's hands, why don't we submit to evil?[128] The Lord gave, and the Lord has taken away; blessed be the name of the Lord.[129] Long enough now have I played this game against the pope and the devil, and the Lord has wonderfully protected and comforted me. Why shouldn't I now bear with equanimity what He does with me according to His will? In any case our death is nothing compared with the death of the Son of God. Besides, so many very saintly men have been buried before us whose company we are not worthy of; if we desire to be with them, as we really do desire, it's necessary that we die. We ought to reach out for this with an eager spirit because our Lord is the Lord of life, who holds us in His hand.

"Of course, a great change has taken place as far as I am concerned: yesterday I was quite resolute in spirit and strong in body, while today, as you see, I am pitiably broken in my strength. How much I am changed from what I was yesterday! Yesterday I felt exuberant and light as a bird. But, O God, we are nothing, and all that is ours is nothing, even when we are everything! I might have prayed to our Lord God, or at least grumbled at Him, that He'd let me die in the land of my prince.[130] But if that's not to be, I'll be ready at whatever hour and place the Lord calls me. I'll be and I'll die an enemy of all the enemies of my Christ, and if I die under the excommunication of the pope, may he himself also die under the ban of my Christ."

The next day—that is, on February 26—he said when he vomited as a result of his sickness, "Ah, dear Father, take this dear soul into Thy hand. I give Thee thanks and bless Thee, and let all Thy creatures bless Thee. Grant that I may speedily be gathered to the fathers."

Later, when the vomiting ceased, he said, "Go, my dear soul, go in God's name. How poor and wretched we human beings are! I have almost no strength left, and yet how Satan troubles and dis-

[128]Cf. Job 2:10.
[129]Cf. Job 1:21.
[130]In the land of Elector John Frederick of Saxony.

turbs what little strength I have! Give me constancy and patience in Thy faithfulness, my Father, that I may overcome [Satan].

"To you, my dear Amsdorf,[131] I commend Katie, my wife. I have no doubt that Satan produces and sharpens these pains. There's an obstruction in my body that prevents the stone and urine from following their course. But by God's grace I'll have it better after this life. So nothing that I now suffer from the devil will hurt me. I'll gladly go to pieces; only let Satan not have his way in the Church after my death. I'm very much afraid of this because contempt of the gospel and ingratitude toward it are so great."

Hereupon he shed many bitter tears, sighed deeply, and folded his hands amid many sobs. "I'm concerned," he said, "lest the precious gospel may be lost, for it seems to me that I now observe some who first fall into strife and then yield to passions and forget that which is the chief thing in doctrine, with the result that the Word and the glory of God are lost to sight. How hard it became for us under the papacy! We read and did everything, and yet we found nothing. The more we looked, the further we were from our goal. I'm afraid the same thing will happen after I'm gone. The world doesn't care, but the pope knows that all his [utterances] are lies and trumpery."

At this point he again wept copiously [and continued], "Dear God, I am Thy little creature, and Thou art the Creator. I am Thy clay, and Thou art my potter.[132] If only the end will come for me and Thou mayest preserve the Word longer! But I have reason to fear the opposite. I observe that the more we are enlightened, the more we suffer."

Then he sipped some almond broth and said, "Dear God, may it be blest for me either in time or for eternity! If this illness lasts longer, I'll surely go mad. Even if this should happen, I know that my God remains skillful and wise. Good God, how subject to death this wretched little body is! Except that I have faith in Jesus Christ, it wouldn't be surprising if I took my own life with a sword. The devil hates me, and so he increases my pain. He's got me in his

[131]Nicholas Amsdorf.
[132]Cf. Isa. 29:16.

claws, and no doubt I've deserved this from him. But avenge Thyself, O Christ, against Thy foe! I've done right to pick the pope to pieces, and I must hold him in check now once more. If anything good is to come of it, this should be done not in order that my health may be restored but in order that the power of the devil may be smashed forever. It hurts us, but God doesn't forsake us; He renders to each according to his works. So let God only take me away, and pay the devil as he has deserved. Amen."

On the same day he [Martin Luther] spoke as follows in the presence of Ponikau,[133] a nobleman and chamberlain of the elector: "I'm obliged to be stoned to death like Stephen[134] and to give the pope an occasion for pleasure, but I hope he won't laugh very long. My epitaph shall remain true: 'While alive I was your plague, when dead I'll be your death, O pope.'"[135]

Afterward he gave thanks to God for preserving him in the faith and confession of God's Word and name. Finally he asked Ponikau to commend his [Luther's] wife and children to the prince[136] and to thank the prince for his kindness.

The next day he said the same to the prince himself. First he committed to him the care of the Church and afterward the care of his home. On that occasion the prince said that he hoped our Lord God would not do such a bad thing to His land and people [as to allow Luther to die], but if he did die, he promised to take care of the doctor's wife and children as if they were his own.

He [Martin Luther] ordered the ministers to report the following to the chancellor[137] of the duke of Saxony: "Tell my good friend the chancellor that I wish he might learn to know the pope as well as I know him. Then he'll be as hostile to him as I am."

He raised himself up and, after making the sign of the cross with his hand, he said to us who were standing around him, "The Lord fill you with His benediction and with hatred of the pope!"

---

[133]John von Ponikau, chamberlain of the elector of Saxony.
[134]Cf. Acts 7:54–60. Luther makes a play on words with the stones that struck and killed Stephen and the kidney stones that were causing him pain internally.
[135]Luther mentioned this "epitaph" several times.
[136]The elector of Saxony.
[137]Gregory Brück was a supporter of Luther and the Reformation at the court of the electors of Saxony.

Acknowledging God's Gifts in the Cherry Season

BETWEEN JUNE 18 AND JULY 28, 1537[138]

Dr. Justus Jonas praised the glorious blessing which God grants in fruit. "I have a branch with cherries on it hanging over my table," he said, "in order that when I look at it I may learn the article about divine creation."

Dr. Martin Luther responded, "Why don't you learn it daily by looking at your children, the fruit of your body? They're there every day, and surely they amount to much more than all the fruit of the trees! There you may see the providence of God, who created them from nothing. In half a year He gave them body, life, and limb, and He will also sustain them. Yet we overlook them, as if those gifts of God made us blind and greedy, as it usually happens that men become worse and more greedy when they have offspring; they don't realize that every child is apportioned his lot according to the saying. 'The more children the more luck.' Dear God, how great are the ignorance and the wickedness of man, who doesn't think about the best gifts of God but does just the opposite."

The Tyranny and Burden of Celibacy

FEBRUARY 24, 1538

Then he [Luther] spoke at length about the tyranny of celibacy, how great a burden celibacy was. "When he was quite old, Augustine[139] still complained about nocturnal pollutions. When he was goaded by desire, Jerome beat his breast with stones but was unable to drive the girl[140] out of his heart. Francis[141] made snowballs and Benedict[142] lay down on thorns. Bernard macerated his harassed body until it stank horribly. I believe that virgins also have temptations and enticements, but if there are fluxes and pollutions

---

[138]Some early manuscripts indicate that this entry belongs in the year 1536.
[139]Augustine, *Sermons* 292.5 ("Of Conjugal Chastity").
[140]A later version adds: "whom he had seen dancing in Rome."
[141]Francis of Assisi (1182–1226) was the founder of the Franciscan order.
[142]Benedict of Nursia (d. early in the sixth century) was the founder of the Benedictine order of monks.

the gift of virginity is no longer there; then the remedy of marriage which God has given should be taken hold of.

"People who occupied stations at least as high as ours lived in the estate of marriage. Peter had a mother-in-law,[143] and therefore had a wife too. So James, the brother of the Lord, and all the apostles were married, except John. Paul counted himself among the unmarried and widowers,[144] but it appears that he was married in his youth according to the custom of the Jews. Spyridion, bishop of Cyprus,[145] was married. Bishop Hilary had a wife, for when he was in exile he wrote a letter to his little daughter in which he urged her to be obedient and to learn to pray. He wrote that he had been at the home of a rich man who promised that if Hilary's daughter behaved he would send her a golden cloak. In such a childlike way Hilary wrote to his little daughter. I marvel that the holy fathers contended with such juvenile temptations and did not feel the loftier ones when they occupied such high offices."

What Will Occupy Us in Eternal Life

JUNE 27, 1538

Then they spoke about eternal life and the joy that will exist then. "I often think about it [said Luther] but I can't imagine what it's like, can't understand how we'll spend our time inasmuch as there will be no change, no work, no food and drink, and nothing to occupy us there. But I think we'll have enough to do with God. Accordingly Philip[146] put it well when he said, 'Lord show us the Father, and we shall be satisfied' [John 14:8]. This will be our very dear preoccupation."

---

[143]Cf. Mark 1:30.
[144]Cf. 1 Cor. 7:8.
[145]Spyridion, bishop of Trimithus, on Cyprus, in the fourth century.
[146]The disciple of Jesus.

Proposal to Publish Luther's Collected Works
SEPTEMBER 29, 1538

Men [printers] in Augsburg and Wittenberg urged Luther to allow them to publish his collected works. He replied, "I'll never consent to this proposal of yours. I'd rather that all my books would disappear and the Holy Scriptures alone would be read. Otherwise we'll rely on such writings and let the Bible go. Brenz wrote such a big commentary on twelve chapters of Luke[147] that it disgusts the reader to look into it. The same is true of my commentary on Galatians. I wonder who encourages this mania for writing! Who wants to buy such stout tomes? And if they're bought, who'll read them? And if they're read, who'll be edified by them?"

Discussion at Table About Mothers' Milk
NOVEMBER 14, 1538

Afterward there was talk about the excellence of mothers' milk, which is especially good and nourishing. In fact, calves are nourished more by milk than by other food. Infants also become stronger when they are nursed for a long time. Swiss children are said to go to cows as a rule in order to suckle.

Then there was discussion about breasts, which are an ornament to women if they are well proportioned. Large and flabby breasts cause unhappiness, it was said, because they promise much but produce little. Firm breasts, and even the small ones of tiny women, are fruitful and can provide milk for many children.

Then it was said that it is not good for a pregnant woman to nurse an infant because the fetus in her uterus always draws away the best stuff, takes the cream and leaves only skimmed milk for the guest outside. Accordingly it is the common judgment of all married women that it is better for the child to be weaned early.

---

[147]The commentary by John Brenz was published in 1537.

Some Field Mice Invade Luther's Home

MARCH 18, 1539

On March 18 some field mice broke into his [Martin Luther's] house and gnawed to pieces his best ornamental branches of fruit trees and laurels. He was quite annoyed. In a short time he caught a mouse in a mousetrap. It was almost as large as a dormouse, but with a bigger head, a shorter tail, and rather long teeth. When he had looked at it he said, "It looks like a beaver, which can also cut down trees. It has done me harm, but it has paid for it with the highest price."

That same day his wife drowned many mice in some holes in the garden. He [Martin Luther] said, "Mice also serve a useful purpose. For they make diligent house fathers. It's as Augustine said about heretics,[148] that they have the function of inciting and provoking Catholics and theologians not to be so cool toward the Word of God; when the opportunity is met, they begin to boil. It happened so to me. Unless the pope had challenged me with his abominations and false writings I'd never have come to this. Opportunities have taught me."

The Great Debt of Christians to the Jews

MARCH 20, 1539

Afterward he read in the psalter and spoke with admiration of David's genius: "Dear God, what people those were! This David was a husband, king, warlord, almost crushed by political affairs and submerged in public business, and yet he wrote such a book!

"In like fashion the New Testament was written by real Jews, for the apostles were Jews. Thus God indicates that we should honor the Word of God in the synagogue. We gentile Christians have no book that has such authority in the Church—except Augustine, who is the only doctor in the Church of the gentiles who stands out above others. Accordingly we gentiles are in no way equal to the Jews. Paul therefore makes an excellent distinc-

---

[148] Augustine, *Homilies on the Gospel of John,* Tractate 36.6.

tion between Sarai and Hagar and their two sons.[149] Hagar was a woman, too, but far from the equal of Sarai. It was therefore terrible temerity on the part of the pope to dare, as a man without Scripture, to oppose the Holy Scriptures."

Luther Rejects the Copernican Cosmology

JUNE 4, 1539

There was mention of a certain new astrologer[150] who wanted to prove that the earth moves and not the sky, the sun, and the moon. This would be as if somebody were riding on a cart or in a ship and imagined that he was standing still while the earth and the trees were moving. [Luther remarked,] "So it goes now. Whoever wants to be clever must agree with nothing that others esteem. He must do something of his own. This is what that fellow does who wishes to turn the whole of astronomy upside down. Even in these things that are thrown into disorder I believe the Holy Scriptures, for Joshua commanded the sun to stand still and not the earth [Josh. 10:12]."

Luther's Daughter Magdalene Placed in Coffin

SEPTEMBER 1542

When his dead daughter was placed in a coffin, he [Martin Luther] said, "You dear little Lena! How well it has turned out for you!"

He looked at her and said, "Ah, dear child, to think that you must be raised up and will shine like the stars, yes, like the sun!"

The coffin would not hold her, and he said, "The little bed is too small for her."

[Before this,] when she died, he said, "I am joyful in spirit but I am sad according to the flesh. The flesh doesn't take kindly to this. The separation [caused by death] troubles me above measure. It's

---

[149]Cf. Gal. 4:24–31.
[150]The reference is undoubtedly to Nicholas Copernicus (1473–1543). His revolutionary theory was finally set forth in his *Revolutions of the Celestial Spheres* (1543), but before this it was taught, among other places, in Wittenberg itself.

strange to know that she is surely at peace and that she is well off there, very well off, and yet to grieve so much!"

Luther's Last Observation, Left in a Note

FEBRUARY 16, 1546

"Nobody can understand Virgil in his *Bucolics* and *Georgics*[151] unless he has first been a shepherd or a farmer for five years.

"Nobody understands Cicero in his letters unless he has been engaged in public affairs of some consequence for twenty years.

"Let nobody suppose that he has tasted the Holy Scriptures sufficiently unless he has ruled over the churches with the prophets for a hundred years. Therefore there is something wonderful, first, about John the Baptist; second, about Christ; third, about the apostles. 'Lay not your hand on this divine *Aeneid,* but bow before it, adore its every trace.'[152]

"We are beggars. That is true."

These were the last thoughts of Dr. Martin Luther on the day before he died.

---

[151]Virgil was the greatest of the Latin poets (70–19 B.C.); his *Bucolics* are poems about the life of shepherds and his *Georgics* are poems about agriculture and farmers.

[152]Cf. Publius Papinius Statius, *Thebais* XII.816–17.

VI

Prayers, Devotions, and Hymns

Martin Luther, for all his mighty thundering against the decadence of the Church and the practices that led Christians away from God rather than to humble dependence on Him, was a man who knew fear and trembling. He lived in almost constant anguish that his faith in the mercy of Christ was insufficient to conquer his terror of death. As he labored over his Scripture translations and preached the Bible his entire life, Luther found a safe haven in the person of Christ revealed in Scripture. Christ was his beacon of light in a world otherwise shrouded in darkness, and he experienced in prayer the courage and consolation to live in trust that God's Word is true. The night of his death, February 18, 1546, Luther gasped out his final prayer, from Psalm 31, "Into Thy hands I commend my spirit. Thou hast redeemed me, Lord God of truth."

As an Augustinian monk, Luther had known the power of words wedded to music, and he could not have missed his patron St. Augustine's famous dictum "He who sings well prays twice." He understood well how music used in prayer gives expression to the deepest longings of the heart. As an educator he was familiar with the didactic dimension of music and prayer, for he and his brother monks memorized the Psalter by continuously chanting it, and he knew that the setting of text to music imprinted both on the listener's memory. However, it was as reformer that Martin Luther fully utilized the power of prayers and hymns to carry his message to the faithful.

Luther reformed the liturgy, composed prayers for use both morning and evening, and counseled people about what nowadays would be called spiritual matters. However, it is for his hymns that Luther is especially well remembered. He wrote more than three dozen. Their texts expressing his renewed theology and sung to the cadences of both sacred and secular German melodies, they were his best means of teaching, propelling the Reformation and reshaping the faith of generations of Christians.

THAT A CHRISTIAN SHOULD
BEAR HIS CROSS WITH PATIENCE

Some Excellent and Christian Thoughts of the Ancient
and Saintly Fathers and Theologians of the Church,
That a Christian Should Bear with Patience the
Cross Which God Places upon Him, Applied
and Elaborated by Luther

The ancient and saintly fathers and theologians have contrasted
the living wood with dead and have allegorized that contrast this
way: from the living wood[153] came sin and death; from the dead
wood,[154] righteousness and life. They conclude: do not eat from
that living tree or you will die, but eat of this dead tree; otherwise
you will remain in death.

You do indeed desire to eat and enjoy [the fruit] of some tree. I will
direct you to a tree so full that you can never eat it bare. But just as it
was difficult to stay away from that living tree, so it is difficult to
enjoy eating from the dead tree. The first was the image of life,
delight, and goodness, while the other is the image of death, suffering, and sorrow because one tree is living, the other dead. There is in
man's heart the deeply rooted desire to seek life where there is certain
death and to flee from death where one has the sure source of life.

Taking up the cross is by nature something that causes pain. It
must not be self-imposed (as the Anabaptists and all the work-
righteous teach); it is something that is imposed upon a person.

The Need for It

We must be conformed to the image of the Son of God, Rom. 8 [:29].

"All who desire to live a godly life in Christ Jesus will be persecuted," 2 Tim. 3 [:12].

"In the world you have tribulation" [John 16:33]. Likewise,

---

[153] The tree in the garden of Eden, Gen. 2:17.
[154] The tree of the cross on Golgotha.

"You will be sorrowful; you will weep and lament, but the world will rejoice," John 16 [:20].

"If we share in [Christ's] sufferings we shall also be glorified with Him," Rom. 8 [:17].

"If you are left without discipline, in which all have participated, then you are illegitimate children and not sons," Heb. 12 [:8]. Otherwise, what is the purpose of so many comforting passages of scripture?

The Source of It

Because the devil, a mighty, evil, deceitful spirit, hates the children of God. For them the holy cross serves for learning the faith, for [learning] the power of the Word, and for subduing whatever sin and pride remain. Indeed, a Christian can no more do without the cross than without food or drink.

The Entreaty

The touch of Christ sanctifies all the sufferings and sorrows of those who believe in Him. Whoever does not suffer shows that he does not believe that Christ has given him the gift of sharing in His own passion. But if anyone does not wish to bear the cross which God places upon him, he will not be compelled to do so by anyone—he is always free to deny Christ. But in so doing he must know that he cannot have fellowship with Christ or share in any of His gifts.

For example, a merchant, a hunter, a soldier risk so much pain for the sake of an uncertain gain and victory, while here, where it is certain that glory and blessedness will be the result, it is a disagreeable thing to suffer even for a bit, as Isa. 54 [:7], Christ in John 16 [:20–22], Peter in 1 Pet. 1 [:6], and Paul in 2 Cor. 4 [:17] usually put it, "for a little while," and momentarily.

Notice how our adversaries, those torturers from the devil, are torn and divided in their teachings in so many ways that they fail to realize their hopes, since they must be concerned with so much peril and misfortune that they can never act for a moment with certainty or confidence. And these penalties and punishments are only temporal! How can I comprehend their guilt, namely, that without God and through the devil's craftiness they, beset by an evil conscience, are eternally lost? Even though they are uncertain as to the outcome of their endeavor, they keep on rejoicing in a hope that is completely and absolutely lost, while we, on the other hand, have God's unfailing promises for our comfort.

In short, since God is the same and the cause is the same, in which He has upheld the faith of all the saints so that He might be vindicated, God will not now, just for our own sake, be found a liar; nor are we to make a liar of Him. God grant, whether we do or do not believe, that He will yet defend His Word and surely help [us]. This demands great effort and care so that, in the first place, we turn our eyes from the might [of this world] and second, hold fast to the Word. Eve disregarded the Word and relied on what was visible, but a Christian, in contrast, disregards what he can see and holds to the Word. The godless do not do so but rely upon the emperor to uphold them in this world, but because they neglect the Word, they will be ruined and lost to eternity. In the year 1530.

A SIMPLE WAY TO PRAY

A Simple Way to Pray
For a Good Friend

How One Should Pray,
For Peter, the Master Barber

Dear Master Peter: I will tell you as best I can what I do personally when I pray. May our dear Lord grant to you and to everybody to do it better than I! Amen.

First, when I feel that I have become cool and joyless in prayer because of other tasks or thoughts (for the flesh and the devil always impede and obstruct prayer), I take my little psalter, hurry to my room, or if it be the day and hour for it, to the church, where a congregation is assembled, and as time permits, I say quietly to myself and word for word the Ten Commandments, the Creed, and if I have time, some words of Christ or of Paul, or some psalms, just as a child might do.

It is a good thing to let prayer be the first business of the morning and the last at night. Guard yourself carefully against those false, deluding ideas which tell you, "Wait a little while. I will pray in an hour; first I must attend to this or that." Such thoughts get you away from prayer into other affairs, which so hold your attention and involve you that nothing comes of prayer for that day.

It may well be that you may have some tasks which are as good or better than prayer, especially in an emergency. There is a saying ascribed to St. Jerome that everything a believer does is prayer[155] and a proverb, "He who works faithfully prays twice." This can be said because a believer fears and honors God in his work and remembers the commandment not to wrong anyone or to try to steal, defraud, or cheat. Such thoughts and such faith undoubtedly transform his work into prayer and a sacrifice of praise.

On the other hand it is also true that the work of an unbeliever is outright cursing and so he who works faithlessly curses twice. While he does his work His thoughts are occupied with a neglect of God and violation of His law, how to take advantage of his neighbor, how to steal from him and defraud him. What else can such thoughts be but out-and-out curses against God and man, which makes one's work and effort a double curse by which a man curses himself. In the end they are beggars and bunglers. It is of such continual prayer that Christ says in Luke 11, "Pray without ceasing" [1 Thess. 5:17; cf. Luke 11:9–13], because one must unceasingly guard against sin and wrongdoing, something one cannot do unless one fears God and keeps His commandment in mind, as Psalm 1 [:1, 2] says, "Blessed is he who meditates upon His law day and night."

Yet we must be careful not to break the habit of true prayer and imagine other works to be necessary which, after all, are nothing of the kind. Thus at the end we become lax and lazy, cool and listless toward prayer. The devil who besets us is not lazy or careless, and our flesh is too ready and eager to sin and is disinclined to the spirit of prayer.

---

[155] Probably Jerome's *Commentary on Matthew,* book 4, under Matt. 25:11.

When your heart has been warmed by such recitation to your-self [of the Ten Commandments, the words of Christ, etc.] and is intent upon the matter, kneel or stand with your hands folded and your eyes toward heaven and speak or think as briefly as you can:

O Heavenly Father, dear God, I am a poor unworthy sinner. I do not deserve to raise my eyes or hands toward Thee or to pray. But because Thou hast commanded us all to pray and hast promised to hear us and through Thy dear Son Jesus Christ hast taught us both how and what to pray, I come to Thee in obedience to Thy word, trusting in Thy gracious promise. I pray in the name of my Lord Jesus Christ together with all Thy saints and Christians on earth as He has taught us: Our Father who art, etc., through the whole prayer, word for word.

Then repeat one part or as much as you wish, perhaps the first petition: "Hallowed be Thy name," and say: "Yes, Lord God, dear Father, hallowed be Thy name, both in us and throughout the whole world. Destroy and root out the abominations, idolatry, and heresy of the Turk, the pope, and all false teachers and fanatics who wrongly use Thy name and in scandalous ways take it in vain [Exod. 20:7] and horribly blaspheme it. They insistently boast that they teach Thy Word and the laws of the Church, though they really use the devil's deceit and trickery in Thy name to wretchedly seduce many poor souls throughout the world, even killing and shedding much innocent blood, and in such persecution they believe that they render Thee a divine service.

Dear Lord God, convert and restrain [them]. Convert those who are still to be converted that they with us and we with them may hallow and praise Thy name, both with true and pure doctrine and with a good and holy life. Restrain those who are unwilling to be converted so that they be forced to cease from misusing, defiling, and dishonoring Thy holy name and from misleading the poor people. Amen."

The second petition: "Thy kingdom come." Say: "O dear Lord, God and Father, Thou seest how worldly wisdom and reason not only profane Thy name and ascribe the honor due to Thee to lies and to the devil, but how they also take the power, might, wealth and glory Thou hast given them on earth for ruling the world and thus serving Thee, and use it in their own ambition to oppose Thy kingdom. They are many and mighty; they plague and hinder the tiny flock of Thy kingdom, who are weak, despised, and few. They will not tolerate Thy flock on earth and think that by plaguing them they render a great and godly service to Thee. Dear Lord, God and Father, convert them and defend us. Convert those who are still to become children and members of Thy kingdom so that they with us and we with them may serve Thee in Thy kingdom in true faith and unfeigned love and that from Thy kingdom, which has begun, we may enter into Thy eternal kingdom. Defend us against those who will not turn away their might and power from the destruction of Thy kingdom so that when they are cast down from their thrones and humbled, they will have to cease from their efforts. Amen."

The third petition. "Thy will be done on earth as it is in heaven." Say: "O dear Lord, God and Father, Thou knowest that the world, if it cannot destroy Thy name or root out Thy kingdom, is busy day and night with wicked tricks and schemes, strange conspiracies and intrigue, huddling together in secret counsel, giving mutual encouragement and support, raging and threatening and going about with every evil intention to destroy Thy name, Word, kingdom, and children. Therefore, dear Lord, God and Father, convert them and defend us. Convert those who have yet to acknowledge Thy goodwill that they with us and we with them may obey Thy will and for Thy sake gladly, patiently, and joyously bear every evil, cross, and adversity, and thereby acknowledge, test, and experience Thy benign, gracious, and perfect will. But defend us against those who in their rage, fury, hate, threats, and evil desires do not cease to do us harm. Make their wicked schemes, tricks, and devices to come to nothing so that these may be turned against them, as we sing in Ps. 7 [:16]."[156]

The fourth petition. "Give us this day our daily bread." Say: "Dear Lord, God and Father, grant us Thy blessing also in this temporal and physical life. Graciously grant us blessed peace. Protect us against war and disorder. Grant to our dear emperor fortune and success against his enemies. Grant him wisdom and understanding to rule over his earthly kingdom in peace and prosperity. Grant to all kings, princes, and rulers good counsel and the

---

[156] "His mischief returns upon his own head, and on his own pate his violence descends."

will to preserve their domains and their subjects in tranquillity and justice. Especially aid and guide our dear prince N., under whose protection and shelter Thou dost maintain us, so that he may be protected against all harm and reign blessedly, secure from evil tongues and disloyal people. Grant to all his subjects grace to serve him loyally and obediently. Grant to every estate—townsman or farmer—to be diligent and to display charity and loyalty toward each other. Give us favorable weather and good harvest. I commend to Thee my house and property, wife and child. Grant that I may manage them well, supporting and educating them as a Christian should. Defend us against the Destroyer and all his wicked angels who would do us harm and mischief in this life. Amen."

The fifth petition. "Forgive us our trespasses as we forgive those who trespass against us." Say: "O dear Lord, God and Father, enter not into judgment against us because no man living is justified before Thee. Do not count it against us as a sin that we are so unthankful for Thine ineffable goodness, spiritual and physical, or that we stray into sin many times every day, more often than we can know or recognize, Ps. 19 [:12]. Do not look upon how good or how wicked we have been but only upon the infinite compassion which Thou hast bestowed upon us in Christ, Thy dear Son. Grant forgiveness also to those who have harmed or wronged us, as we forgive them from our hearts. They inflict the greatest injury upon themselves by arousing Thy anger in their actions toward us. We are not helped by their ruin; we would much rather that they be saved with us. Amen." (Anyone who feels unable to forgive, let him ask for grace so that he can forgive; but that belongs in a sermon.)

The sixth petition. "And lead us not into temptation." Say: "O dear Lord, Father and God, keep us fit and alert, eager and diligent in Thy Word and service, so that we do not become complacent, lazy, and slothful as though we had already achieved everything. In that way the fearful devil cannot fall upon us, surprise us, and deprive us of Thy precious Word or stir up strife and factions among us and lead us into other sin and disgrace, both spiritually and physically. Rather grant us wisdom and strength through Thy Spirit that we may valiantly resist him and gain the victory. Amen."

The seventh petition. "But deliver us from evil." Say: "O dear Lord, God and Father, this wretched life is so full of misery and calamity, of danger and uncertainty, so full of malice and faithlessness (as St. Paul says, "The days are evil" [Eph. 5:16]) that we might rightfully grow weary of life and long for death. But Thou, dear Father, knowest our frailty; therefore help us to pass in safety through so much wickedness and villainy; and, when our last hour comes, in Thy mercy grant us a blessed departure from this vale of sorrows so that in the face of death we do not become fearful or despondent but in firm faith commit our souls into Thy hands. Amen."

Finally, mark this, that you must always speak the "Amen" firmly. Never doubt that God in His mercy will surely hear you and say "yes" to your prayers. Never think that you are kneeling or standing alone, rather think that the whole of Christendom, all devout Christians, are standing there beside you and you are standing among them in a common, united petition which God cannot disdain. Do not leave your prayer without having said or thought, "Very well, God has heard my prayer; this I know as a certainty and a truth." That is what "Amen" means.

You should also know that I do not want you to recite all these words in your prayer. That would make it nothing but idle chatter and prattle, read word for word out of a book, as were the rosaries by the laity and the prayers of the priests and monks. Rather do I want your heart to be stirred and guided concerning the thoughts which ought to be comprehended in the Lord's Prayer. These thoughts may be expressed, if your heart is rightly warmed and inclined toward prayer, in many different ways and with more words or fewer. I do not bind myself to such words or syllables, but say my prayers in one fashion today, in another tomorrow, depending upon my mood and feeling. I stay however, as nearly as I can, with the same general thoughts and ideas. It may happen occasionally that I may get lost among so many ideas in one petition that I forego the other six. If such an abundance of good thoughts comes to us we ought to disregard the other petitions, make room for such thoughts, listen to silence, and under no circumstances obstruct them. The Holy Spirit Himself preaches here, and one word of His sermon is far better than a thousand of our prayers. Many times I have learned more from one prayer than I might have learned from much reading and speculation.

It is of great importance that the heart be made ready and eager for prayer. As the Preacher says, "Prepare your heart for prayer, and do not tempt God" [Ecclus. 18:23]. What else is it but tempting God when your mouth babbles and the mind wanders to other thoughts? Like the priest who prayed, *"Deus, in adiutorium meum intende.*[157] Farmhand, did you unhitch the horses? *Domine ad adiuvandum me festina.*[158] Maid, go out and milk the cow. *Gloria Patri et Filio et Spiritui Sancto.*[159] Hurry up, boy, I wish the ague would take you!" I have heard many such prayers in my experience under the papacy; most of their prayers are of this sort. This is blasphemy and it would be better if they played at it if they cannot or do not care to do better. In my day I have prayed many such canonical hours myself, regrettably, and in such a manner that the psalm or the allotted time came to an end before I even realized whether I was at the beginning or in the middle.

Though not all of them blurt out the words as did the above-mentioned cleric and mix business and prayer, they do it by the thoughts in their hearts. They jump from one thing to another in their thoughts and when it is all over they do not know what they have done or what they talked about. They start with *Laudate*[160] and right away they are in a fool's paradise. It seems to me that if someone could see what arises as prayer from a cold and unattentive heart he would conclude that he had never seen a more ridiculous kind of buffoonery. But, praise God, it is now clear to me that a person who forgets what he has said has not prayed well. In a good prayer one fully remembers every word and thought from the beginning to the end of the prayer.

So, a good and attentive barber keeps his thoughts, attention, and eyes on the razor and hair and does not forget how far he has gotten with his shaving or cutting. If he wants to engage in too much conversation or let his mind wander or look somewhere else he is likely to cut his customer's mouth, nose, or even his throat. Thus if any-

---

[157] "Make haste, O God, to deliver me," Ps. 70:1.
[158] "Make haste to help me, O Lord."
[159] "Glory be to the Father and to the Son and to the Holy Spirit."
[160] "Praise."

thing is to be done well, it requires the full attention of all one's senses and members, as the proverb says, *"Pluribus intentus, minor est ad singula sensus"*—"He who thinks of many things, thinks of nothing and does nothing right." How much more does prayer call for concentration and singleness of heart if it is to be a good prayer!

This in short is the way I use the Lord's Prayer when I pray it. To this day I suckle at the Lord's Prayer like a child, and as an old man eat and drink from it and never get my fill. It is the very best prayer, even better than the psalter, which is so very dear to me. It is surely evident that a real master composed and taught it. What a great pity that the prayer of such a master is prattled and chattered so irreverently all over the world! How many pray the Lord's Prayer several thousand times in the course of a year, and if they were to keep on doing so for a thousand years they would not have tasted or prayed one iota, one dot,[161] of it! In a word, the Lord's Prayer is the greatest martyr on earth (as are the name and Word of God). Everybody tortures and abuses it; few take comfort and joy in its proper use.

If I have had time and opportunity to go through the Lord's Prayer, I do the same with the Ten Commandments. I take one part after another and free myself as much as possible from distractions in order to pray. I divide each commandment into four parts, thereby fashioning a garland of four strands. That is, I think of each commandment as, first, instruction, which is really what it is intended to be, and consider what the Lord God demands of me so earnestly. Second, I turn it into a thanksgiving; third, a confession; and fourth, a prayer. I do so in thoughts or words such as these:

"I am the Lord your God, etc. You shall have not other gods before Me," etc. Here I earnestly consider that God expects and teaches me to trust Him sincerely in all things and that it is His most earnest purpose to be my God. I must think of Him in this way at the risk of losing eternal salvation. My heart must not build upon anything else or trust in any other thing, be it wealth, prestige, wisdom, might, piety, or anything else. Second, I give thanks for His infinite compassion by which He has come to me in such a fatherly way and, unasked, unbidden, and unmerited, has offered

---

[161] "Jot and tittle," Matt. 5:18 (KJV).

to be my God, to care for me, and to be my comfort, guardian, help, and strength in every time of need. We poor mortals have sought so many gods and would have to seek them still if He did not enable us to hear Him openly tell us in our own language that He intends to be our God. How could we ever—in all eternity—thank Him enough! Third, I confess and acknowledge my great sin and ingratitude for having so shamefully despised such sublime teachings and such a precious gift throughout my whole life, and for having fearfully provoked His wrath by countless acts of idolatry. I repent of these and ask for His grace. Fourth, I pray and say: "O my God and Lord, help me by Thy grace to learn and understand Thy commandments more fully every day and to live by them in sincere confidence. Preserve my heart so that I shall never again become forgetful and ungrateful, that I may never seek after other gods or other consolation on earth or in any creature, but cling truly and solely to thee, my only God. Amen, dear Lord God and Father. Amen."

Afterward, if time and inclination permit, the Second Commandment likewise in four strands, like this: "You shall not take the name of the Lord your God in vain," etc. First I learn that I must keep God's name in honor, holiness, and beauty; not to swear, curse, nor to be boastful or seek honor and repute for myself, but humbly to invoke His name, to pray, praise, and extol it, and to let it be my only honor and glory that He is my God and that I am His lowly creature and unworthy servant. Second, I give thanks to Him for these precious gifts, that He has revealed His name to me and bestowed it upon me, that I can glory in His name and be called God's servant and creature, etc., that His name is my refuge like a mighty fortress to which the righteous man can flee and find protection, as Solomon says [Prov. 18:10]. Third, I confess and acknowledge that I have grievously and shamefully sinned against this commandment all my life. I have not only failed to invoke, extol, and honor His holy name, but have also been ungrateful for such gifts and have, by swearing, lying, and betraying, misused them in the pursuit of shame and sin. This I bitterly regret and ask grace and forgiveness, etc. Fourth, I ask for help and strength henceforth to learn [to obey] this commandment and to be preserved from such evil ingratitude, abuse, and sin against His name, and that I may be found grateful in revering and honoring His name.

I repeat here what I previously said in reference to the Lord's Prayer: if in the midst of such thoughts the Holy Spirit begins to preach in your heart with rich, enlightening thoughts, honor Him by letting go of this written scheme; be still and listen to Him who can do better than you can. Remember what He says and note it well and you will behold wondrous things in the law of God, as David says [Ps. 119:18].

The Third Commandment: "Remember the sabbath day, to keep it holy." I learn from this, first of all, that the sabbath day has not been instituted for the sake of being idle or indulging in worldly pleasures, but in order that we may keep it holy. However, it is not sanctified by our works and actions—our works are not holy—but by the Word of God, which alone is wholly pure and sacred and which sanctifies everything that comes in contact with it, be it time, place, person, labor, rest, etc. According to St. Paul, who says that every creature is consecrated by word and prayer, 1 Tim. 4 [:5], our works are consecrated through the Word. I realize therefore that on the sabbath I must, above all, hear and contemplate God's Word. Thereafter I should give thanks in my own words, praise God for all His benefits, and pray for myself and for the whole world. He who so conducts himself on the sabbath day keeps it holy. He who fails to do so is worse than the person who works on the sabbath.

Second, I thank God in this commandment for His great and beautiful goodness and grace, which He has given us in the preaching of His Word. And He has instructed us to make use of it, especially on the sabbath day, for the meditation of the human heart can never exhaust such a treasure. His Word is the only light in the darkness of this life, a Word of life, consolation, and supreme blessedness. Where this precious and saving Word is absent, nothing remains but a fearsome and terrifying darkness, error and faction, death and every calamity, and the tyranny of the devil himself, as we can see with our own eyes every day.

Third, I confess and acknowledge great sin and wicked ingratitude on my part because all my life I have made disgraceful use of the sabbath and have thereby despised His precious and dear Word in a wretched way. I have been too lazy, listless, and uninterested to listen to it, let alone to have desired it sincerely or to have been grateful for it. I have let my dear God proclaim His Word to me in vain, have dismissed the noble treasure, and have trampled it underfoot. He has tolerated this in His great and divine mercy and has not ceased in his fatherly, divine love and faithfulness to keep on preaching to me and calling me to the salvation of my soul. For this I repent and ask for grace and forgiveness.

Fourth, I pray for myself and for the whole world that the gracious Father may preserve us in His holy Word and not withdraw it from us because of our sin, ingratitude, and laziness. May He preserve us from factious spirits and false teachers, and may He send faithful and honest laborers into His harvest [Matt. 9:38], that is, devout pastors and preachers. May He grant us grace humbly to hear, accept, and honor their words as His own words and to offer our sincere thanks and praise.

The Fourth Commandment: "Honor your father and your mother." First, I learn to acknowledge God, my Creator; how wondrously He has created me, body and soul; and how He has given me life through my parents and has instilled in them the desire to care for me, the fruit of their bodies, with all their power. He has brought me into this world, has sustained and cared for me, nurtured and educated me with great diligence, carefulness, and concern, through danger, trouble, and hard work. To this moment He protects me, his creature, and helps me in countless dangers and troubles. It is as though He were creating me anew every moment. But the devil does not willingly concede us one single moment of life.

Second, I thank the rich and gracious Creator on behalf of myself and all the world that He has established and assured in the commandment the increase and preservation of the human race, that is, of households and of states. Without these two institutions or governments the world could not exist a single year, because without government there can be no peace, and where there is no peace there can be no family; without family, children cannot be begotten or raised, and fatherhood and motherhood would cease to be. It is the purpose of this commandment to guard and preserve both family and state, to admonish children and subjects to be obedient, and to enforce it, too, and to let no violation go unpunished—otherwise children would have disrupted the family long ago by their disobedience, and subjects would have disorganized the state and laid it to waste, for they outnumber parents and rulers. There are no words to fully describe the benefit of this commandment.

Third, I confess and lament my wicked disobedience and sin; in defiance of God's commandment I have not honored or obeyed my parents; I have often provoked and offended them, have been impatient with their parental discipline, have been resentful and scornful of their loving admonition and have rather gone along with loose company and evil companions. God Himself condemns such disobedient children and withholds from them a long life; many of them succumb and perish in disgrace before they reach adulthood. Whoever does not obey father and mother must obey the executioner or otherwise come, through God's wrath, to an evil end, etc. Of all this I repent and ask for grace and forgiveness.

Fourth, I pray for myself and for all the world that God would bestow His grace and pour His blessing richly upon the family and the state. Grant that from this time on we may be devout, honor our parents, obey our superiors, and resist the devil when he entices us to be disobedient and rebellious, and so may we help improve home and nation by our actions and thus preserve the peace, all to the praise and glory of God for our own benefit and for the prosperity of all. Grant that we may acknowledge these His gifts and be thankful for them.

At this point we should add a prayer for our parents and superiors, that God may grant them understanding and wisdom to govern and rule us in peace and happiness. May He preserve them from tyranny, from riot and fury, and turn them to honor God's Word and not oppress it, nor persecute anyone or do injustice. Such excellent gifts must be sought by prayer, as St. Paul teaches; otherwise the devil will reign in the palace and everything fall into chaos and confusion.

If you are a father or mother, you should at this point remember your children and the workers in your household. Pray earnestly to the dear Father, who has set you in an office of honor in His name and intends that you be honored by the name "father." Ask that He grant you grace and blessing to look after and support your wife, children, and servants in a godly and Christian manner. May He give you wisdom and strength to train them well in heart and will to follow your instruction with obedience. Both are God's gifts, your children and the way they flourish, that they turn out well and that they remain so. Otherwise the home is nothing but a pigsty and school for rascals, as one can see among the uncouth and godless.

The Fifth Commandment: "You shall not kill." Here I learn, first of all, that God desires me to love my neighbor, so that I do him no bodily harm, either by word or action, neither injure nor take revenge upon him in anger, vexation, envy, hatred, or for any evil reason, but realize that I am obliged to assist and counsel him in every bodily need. In this commandment God commands me to protect my own. As Sirach says, "He has committed to each of us his neighbor" [Ecclus. 9:14].

Second, I give thanks for such ineffable love, providence, and faithfulness toward me, by which He has placed this mighty shield and wall to protect my physical safety. All are obliged to care for me and protect me, and I, in turn, must behave likewise toward others. He upholds this command, and where it is not observed, He has established the sword as punishment for those who do not live up to it. Were it not for this excellent commandment and ordinance, the devil would instigate such a massacre among men that no one could live in safety for a single hour—as happens when God becomes angry and inflicts punishment upon a disobedient and ungrateful world.

Third, I confess and lament my own wickedness and that of the world, not only that we are so terribly ungrateful for such fatherly love and solicitude toward us—but what is especially scandalous, that we do not acknowledge this commandment and teaching, are unwilling to learn it, and neglect it as though it did not concern us or we had no part in it. We amble along complacently, feel no remorse that in defiance of this commandment we neglect our neighbor, and, yes, we desert him, persecute, injure, or even kill him in our thoughts. We indulge in anger, rage, and villainy as though we were doing a fine and noble thing. Really, it is high time that we started to deplore and bewail how much we have acted like rogues and like unseeing, unruly, and unfeeling persons who kick, scratch, tear, and devour one another like furious beasts and pay no heed to this serious and divine commandment, etc.

Fourth, I pray the dear Father to lead us to an understanding of this His sacred commandment and to help us keep it and live in accordance with it. May He preserve us from the murderer who is the master of every form of murder and violence. May He grant us His grace that we and all others may treat each other in kindly, gentle, charitable ways, forgiving one another from the heart, bearing each other's faults and shortcomings in a Christian and brotherly manner, and thus living together in true peace and concord, as the commandment teaches and requires us to do.

The Sixth Commandment: "You shall not commit adultery." Here I learn once more what God intends and expects me to do, namely, to live chastely, decently, and temperately, both in thoughts and in words and actions, and not to disgrace any man's wife, daughter, or maidservant. More than this, I ought to assist, save, protect, and guard marriage and decency to the best of my ability; I should silence the idle thoughts of those who want to destroy and slander their reputation. All this I am obliged to do, and God expects me not only to leave my neighbor's wife and family unmolested, but I owe it to my neighbor to preserve and protect his good character and honor, just as I would want my neighbor to do for me and mine in keeping with this commandment.

Second, I thank my faithful and dear Father for His grace and benevolence by which he accepts my husband, son, servant, wife, daughter, maidservant into His care and protection and forbids so sternly and firmly anything that would bring them into disrepute. He protects and upholds this commandment and does not leave violations unpunished, even though He Himself has to act if someone disregards and violates the commandment and precept. No one escapes him; he must either pay the penalty or eventually atone for such lust in the fires of hell. God desires chastity and will not tolerate adultery. That can be seen every day when the impenitent and profligate are overtaken by the wrath of God and perish miserably. Otherwise it would be impossible to guard one's wife, child, and servants against the devil's filthiness for a single hour or preserve them in honor and decency. What would happen would be unbridled immorality and beastliness, as happens when God in His wrath withdraws His hand and permits everything to go to wrack and ruin.

Third, I confess and acknowledge my sin, my own and that of all the world, how I have sinned against this commandment my whole life in thought, word, and action. Not only have I been ungrateful for these excellent teachings and gifts, but I have complained and rebelled against the divine requirement of such decency and chastity, that God has not permitted all sorts of fornication and rascality to go unchecked and unpunished. He will not allow marriage to be despised, ridiculed, or condemned, etc. Sins against this commandment are, above all others, the grossest and most conspicuous and cannot be covered up or whitewashed. For this I am sorry, etc.

Fourth, I pray for myself and all the world that God may grant us grace to keep this commandment gladly and cheerfully in order that we might ourselves live in chastity and also help and support others to do likewise.

Then I continue with the other commandments as I have time or opportunity or am in the mood for it. As I have said before, I do not want anyone to feel bound by my words or thoughts. I only want to offer an example for those who may wish to follow it; let anyone improve it who is able to do so and let him meditate either upon all commandments at one time or on as many as he may desire. For the mind, once it is seriously occupied with a matter, be it good or evil, can ponder more in one moment than the tongue can recite in ten hours or the pen write in ten days. There is something quick, subtle, and mighty about the mind and soul. It is able to review the Ten Commandments in their fourfold aspect very rapidly if it wants to do so and is in earnest.

The Seventh Commandment: "You shall not steal." First, I can learn here that I must not take my neighbor's property from him or possess it against his will, either in secret or openly. I must not be false or dishonest in business, service, or work, nor profit by fraud, but must support myself by the sweat of my brow[162] and eat my bread in honor. Furthermore, I must see to it that in any of the above-named ways my neighbor is not defrauded, just as I wish for myself. I also learn in this commandment that God, in His fatherly solicitude, sets a protective hedge around my goods and solemnly prohibits anyone to steal from me. Where that is ignored, He has imposed a penalty and has placed the gallows and the rope in the hands of Jack the hangman. Where that cannot be done, God Himself metes out punishment and they become beggars in the end, as the proverb says, "Who steals in his youth, goes begging in old age," or "Stolen gain goes down the drain."

In addition I give thanks for His steadfast goodness in that He

---

[162] Literally, "nose," the idiom in Luther's day.

has given such excellent teachings, assurance, and protection to me and to all the world. If it were not for His protection, not a penny or a crumb of bread would be left in the house.

Third, I confess my sins and ingratitude in such instances where I have wronged, deprived, or cheated anyone in my life.

Fourth, I ask that He grant to me and all the world grace to learn from this commandment, to ponder it, and to become better people, so that there may be less theft, robbery, usury, cheating, and injustice and that the judgment day, for which all saints and the whole creation pray, Rom. 8 [:20–23], shall soon bring this to an end. Amen.

The Eighth Commandment: "You shall not bear false witness." This teaches us, first of all, to be truthful to each other, to shun lies and calumnies, to be glad to speak well of each other, and to delight in hearing what is good about others. Thus a wall has been built around our good reputation and integrity to protect it against malicious gossip and deceitful tongues; God will not let that go unpunished, as He has said in the other commandments.

We owe Him thanks both for the teachings and the protection which He has graciously provided for us.

Third, we confess and ask forgiveness that we have spent our lives in ingratitude and sin and have maligned our neighbor with false and wicked talk, though we owe him the same preservation of honor and integrity which we desire for ourselves.

Fourth, we ask for help from now on to keep the commandment and for a healing tongue, etc.

The Ninth and Tenth Commandments: "You shall not covet your neighbor's house." Similarly, "his wife," etc.

This teaches us first that we shall not dispossess our neighbor of his goods under pretense of legal claims, or lure away, alienate, or extort what is his, but help him to keep what is his, just as we wish to be done for ourselves. It is also a protection against the subtleties and chicaneries of shrewd manipulators, who will receive their punishment in the end. Second, we should render thanks to Him. Third, we should repentantly and sorrowfully confess our sins. Fourth, we should ask for help and strength devoutly to keep such divine commandments.

These are the Ten Commandments in their fourfold aspect, namely, as a school text, songbook, penitential book, and prayer book. They are intended to help the heart come to itself and grow zealous in prayer. Take care, however, not to undertake all of this or so much that one becomes weary in spirit. Likewise, a good prayer should not be lengthy or drawn out, but frequent and ardent. It is enough to consider one section or half a section which kindles a fire in the heart. This the Spirit will grant us and continually instruct us in when, by God's Word, our hearts have been cleared and freed of outside thoughts and concerns.

Nothing can be said here about the part of faith and holy scriptures [in prayer] because there would be no end to what could be said. With practice one can take the Ten Commandments on one day, a psalm or chapter of Holy Scripture the next day, and use them as flint and steel to kindle a flame in the heart.

A Simple Exercise for Contemplating the Creed

If you have more time, or the inclination, you may treat the Creed in the same manner and make it into a garland of four strands. The Creed, however, consists of three main parts or articles, corresponding to the three Persons of the Divine Majesty, as it has been so divided in the catechism and elsewhere.

THE FIRST ARTICLE, OF CREATION

"I believe in God the Father Almighty, maker of heaven and earth."

Here, first of all, a great light shines into your heart if you permit it to and teaches you in a few words what all the languages of the world and a multitude of books cannot describe or fathom in words, namely, who you are, whence you came, whence came heaven and earth. You are God's creation, His handiwork, His workmanship. That is, of yourself and in yourself you are nothing, can do nothing, know nothing, are capable of nothing. What were you a thousand years ago? What were heaven and earth six thousand years ago? Nothing, just as that which will never be created is nothing. But what you are, know, can do, and can achieve is God's creation, as you confess [in the Creed] by word of mouth. Therefore you have nothing to boast of before God except that you are nothing and He is your Creator who can annihilate you at any moment. Reason knows nothing of such a light. Many great people have sought to know what heaven and earth, man and creatures are and have found no answer. But here it is declared and faith affirms that God has created everything out of nothing. Here is the soul's garden of pleasure, along whose paths we enjoy the works of God—but it would take too long to describe all that.

Furthermore, we should give thanks to God that in His kindness He has created us out of nothing and provides for our daily needs out of nothing—has made us to be such excellent beings with body and soul, intelligence, five senses, and has ordained us to be masters of earth, of fish, bird, and beast, etc. Here consider Genesis, chapters 1 to 3.

Third, we should confess and lament our lack of faith and gratitude in failing to take this to heart, or to believe, ponder, and acknowledge it, and having been more stupid than unthinking beasts.

Fourth, we pray for a true and confident faith that sincerely esteems and trusts God to be our Creator, as this article declares.

The Second Article, of Redemption

"And in Jesus Christ, His only Son, our Lord," etc.

Again a great light shines forth and teaches us how Christ, God's Son, has redeemed us from death, which, after the creation, had become our lot through Adam's fall and in which we would have perished eternally. Now think: just as in the first article you were to consider yourself one of God's creatures and not doubt it, now you must think of yourself as one of the redeemed and never doubt that. Emphasize one word above all others, for instance, Jesus Christ, *our* Lord. Likewise, suffered for *us,* died for *us,* arose for *us.* All this is ours and pertains to us; that "us" includes yourself, as the Word of God declares.

Second, you must be sincerely grateful for such grace and rejoice in your salvation.

Third, you must sorrowfully lament and confess your wicked unbelief and mistrust of such a gift. Oh, what thoughts will come to mind—the idolatry you have practiced repeatedly, how much you have made of praying to the saints and of innumerable good works of yours which have opposed such salvation.

Fourth, pray now that God will preserve you from this time forward to the end in true and pure faith in Christ our Lord.

THE THIRD ARTICLE, OF SANCTIFICATION

"I believe in the Holy Spirit," etc.

This is the third great light which teaches us where such a Creator and Redeemer may be found and plainly encountered in this world, and what this will all come to in the end. Much could be said about this, but here is a summary: Where the holy Christian Church exists, there we can find God the Creator, God the Redeemer, God the Holy Spirit, that is, Him who daily sanctifies us through the forgiveness of sins, etc. The Church exists where the Word of God concerning such faith is rightly preached and confessed.

Again you have occasion here to ponder long about everything that the Holy Spirit accomplishes in the Church every day, etc.

Therefore be thankful that you have been called and have come into such a Church.

Confess and lament your lack of faith and gratitude, that you have neglected all this, and pray for a true and steadfast faith that will remain and endure until you come to that place where all endures forever, that is, beyond the resurrection from the dead, in life eternal. Amen.

SAYINGS IN WHICH
LUTHER FOUND COMFORT

There are times when, for the sake of God's Word, we must endure the hardship, anguish, and persecution which the holy cross brings upon us. In such times we can rightfully bestir and strengthen ourselves with God's help in such a way that we can be bold, alert, and cheerful, committing our cause to God's gracious and fatherly will. Thus St. Paul says, 2 Tim. 3 [:12], "All who desire to live a godly life in Jesus Christ will be persecuted," and Acts 14 [:22], "Through many tribulations we must enter into the kingdom of God," and Philippians 2 [:12], "Work out your salvation with fear and trembling."

1

Our cause rests in the hand of Him who distinctly tells us, "No one can snatch them out of My hand," John 10 [:28]. Furthermore, the gates of hell shall not prevail against My church," Matt. 16 [:18]. And Isa. 46 [:4], "Even to your old age and to gray hairs I will bear you. I will do it, and I will bear; I will carry and will save."

2

It would be neither good nor prudent to take matters into our own hands because we could and would easily be defeated.

3

These comforting sayings are all true and surely do not deceive us: Psalm 46 [:1], "God is our refuge and strength, a great help in the trouble which besets us." Sirach [Ecclus. 2:10], that wise man, said, "What man who has put his trust in God has ever perished?" And 1 Macc. 2 [:61], None who puts his trust in Him will lack strength. Again, Psalm 9 [:10], "Lord, Thou hast not forsaken those who seek Thee."

4

In any case, it is true that God gave up His own Son for us all, Rom. 8 [:32]. If that be true, why do we falter, or worry, or hang our heads? If God gave up His own Son for us all, how could He ever intend to forsake us in less important things?

5

Truly God is very much stronger and more powerful than the devil, as 1 John 4 [:4] says, "He who is in you is greater than he who is in the world."

6

If we perish, then Christ the Almighty Ruler of the world Himself must suffer with us. Even if this cause[163] were to collapse, I would much rather be ruined with Christ than rule with Caesar.

7

Furthermore, this cause does not depend just on us, but there are many devout Christian people in other lands who make common cause with us and uphold us with heartfelt sighs and Christian prayer.

8

We possess God's many encouraging promises and rich assurances. In fact the entire psalter, all the gospels—yes, all Scripture is filled with them and they are by no means to be scorned but should be highly valued, such as Psalm 55 [:22], "Cast your burden on the Lord and He will sustain you; He will never permit the righteous to be moved." And Psalm 22 [27:14], "Wait for the Lord; be of good cheer; do not despair and wait for the Lord!" Furthermore Christ Himself says, John 16 [:33], "Be of good cheer; I have overcome the world."

This cannot be wrong—I'm sure of it—that Christ, the Son of God, has overcome the world. Why do we tremble before the world as before a triumphant conqueror? It is worth going to Rome or Jerusalem on one's knees to obtain those words of Christ. Just because we have so many such words we pay no attention to them. That is not good.

[163] The Reformation.

9

Though our faith is weak, let us pray earnestly along with the apostles, Luke 17 [:5], "Lord, increase our faith," and with the child's father in Mark 9 [:24], "Lord, I believe: help my unbelief!"

10

The cause of Christ was in greater peril in the times of the Roman emperors Diocletian, Maximinius, and others who persecuted the Christian Church in horrible ways and attempted to destroy it completely,[164] and likewise in the times of John Hus and others, than it is in our own times.

11

Though the cause be great, He who has brought it about, who directs and guides it, is great too, yes, the Almighty Creator of heaven and earth. This is by no means our cause, so why should we keep on tormenting ourselves over it or plaguing ourselves to death?

12

If this cause, this doctrine, be a mistaken one, why do we not recant? But if it be a righteous cause—and as true as God lives and will remain in eternity, it is such—why do we make lies out of God's many comforting, unchanging, and eternal promises? He bids us be of good cheer and joyful, Psalm 32 [:11], "Be glad in the Lord," and Psalm 145 [:18–19], "The Lord is near to all who call upon Him, to all who call upon Him in truth. He fulfills the desire of all who fear Him. He hears their cry, and saves them." And Psalm 91 [:14–16], "Because he cleaves to Me, I will deliver him; I

---

[164] Diocletian decreed the most severe of the Roman persecutions of the Christians in 303–5. This persecution was continued by Maximinius Daza, a short-lived Eastern Roman ruler, in 311, shortly before the legalization of Christianity under Constantine and Licinius.

will protect him, because he knows My name. I will be with him in trouble, I will rescue him and honor him. With long life will I satisfy him and show him My salvation."

13

Even though we worry and fret so much, such needless anxiety will avail us nothing. We only plague and trouble ourselves and make matters all the worse. God wants us to look to Him as our God and Father in Christ, to call upon Him in every time of need and to be confident that He will provide for us, as St. Peter says, quoting Psalm 55 [:22], "Cast all your anxieties on Him for He cares about you" [1 Pet. 5:7], and as Christ Himself says, Matt. 6 [:31], "You should not be anxious."

14

The devil and his cohorts can do no worse than slay us bodily. They cannot touch our souls at all, as Christ says when He comforted His own, Matt. 10 [:28], "Do not fear those who kill the body but cannot kill the soul."

15

Christ, our dear Lord and Savior, died once for our sin, as it is written in Rom. 4 [:25] and 6 [:10], Heb. 5 [:3] and 9 [:28]. Henceforth He will not die again for the sake of righteousness and truth, but rules as all-powerful Lord over every creature. If this be true, as scripture continually testifies, what are we afraid of?

16

Though, if God so ordains, we ourselves might be destroyed for the sake of His Word, the Almighty and Merciful God, who in Christ has become our Father, will then be a kind and gracious father and guardian, defender and protector for our wives and children, our widows and orphans, and He will manage matters a thousand times better than we could if we were living.

17

Our forefathers and ancestors did not have this glorious, noble, precious treasure, namely, the true and pure understanding of the Divine Word, which, God be praised, we now have in ample measure. Nor did they experience these days which have brought the Word to light again, just before Judgment Day. This indescribable blessing has been bestowed upon us as a gift of God's kindness and grace. This very same God will continue to be God and Creator after we are gone, as He has been before us, and to the end of the world He will always gather to Himself a little flock and uphold it. He will not die with us or cease to exist, as we of little faith imagine.

That is what Eli the priest thought when the Philistines had wrested the ark of the covenant away from the Jews. He thought that all of Judaism with its priesthood and monarchy would come to an end.

When Eli fell backward and broke his neck, 1 Sam. 4 [:18], things were better for the kingdom of the Jews by far than they had been during his lifetime.

Again, when King Saul tragically stabbed himself after his country was defeated and three of his sons had fallen in the same battle, 1 Sam. 31 [:4, 9], what else could one conclude than that this would be the end of the kingdom of the Jews? But afterward, in the time of David and Solomon, it came to its greatest power and glory. When the papists had burned John Hus in Constance during the council in 1416,[165] they were triumphant and took it for granted that they had really exalted the papacy. But the pope has never been more despised than from that time on.

18

Thus we are ever firmly assured by God's Word that after this wretched and fleeting existence, in which we are never safe for even one moment, there shall be an eternal and blessed life and kingdom. Otherwise we would have to blot out the First Commandment along with the entire gospel and Holy Scriptures. What

[165] Hus was executed in 1415.

PRAYERS, DEVOTIONS, AND HYMNS [347

would be the use of a God solely for this fleeting life in which they flourish best who have no God? But if there is a God, as all devout and pious souls firmly and steadfastly believe and in which faith they live and die, then we shall not only live here for a brief time but also eternally in the place where God is.

19

The First Commandment places our children and descendants under God's protection and providence, as God Himself says, "show mercy to thousands of those who love Me and keep My commandments" [Exod. 20:6]. We ought rightfully to believe these exalted and comforting words of the Divine Majesty.

Though our faith be weak, we nevertheless rely on God's honor that He can and will do what He says and promises.

20

If God were to announce all this through an angel we would not cast it lightly to the winds and ignore it, as unfortunately we do when it is brought to us by the spoken Word. But though we fail to believe it when it is preached, we dare not despise the prophets, Christ Himself, or the apostles, who preach to us in such rich measure and gently admonish us with words of consolation and encouragement and shower us with such words as, "Be glad in the Lord"; "Be strong and of good courage; do not fear"; "Put your hope in the Lord; pour out your heart before Him"; "Give thanks to the Lord"; "Be of good cheer, I have overcome the world"; "The Lord is at hand. Have no anxiety about anything," etc. [Ps 32:11; Deut. 31:6; Ps. 62:8; Ps. 107:1; John 16:33; Phil. 4:5–6.]

If we distrust such abundant and divine consolation, we would not believe it even if it were announced by not just one but many angels.

21

It is certainly true that even if our adversaries would kill all of us—if God so decreed—we should not remain unavenged. Before long, He who said to Cain, "Where is Abel, your brother?" [Gen.

4:9] would challenge them; He would pursue them and make the world too small for them.

22

Let us be calmly confident in this cause which has to do with God's Word. Christ, whose cause it is, will staunchly defend and uphold it against the cunning of the vile devil and the tyranny of the wicked and deceitful world. For those who confess Him before this evil and adulterous generation and must suffer much thereby, Christ in turn will confess them before His heavenly Father and requite them for their suffering with the delights of eternity [Matt. 10:32]. God Himself says, 1 Sam. 2 [:30], "He who honors Me, I will honor." Even if the waves of the sea are strong and huge billows rise up and roar furiously as though they would drown us, the Lord is still on high and has begun a kingdom as wide as the world, which He now rules and has decreed that it shall endure. He is greater, yes, almighty, and He will accomplish it. Amen.

There is no other way—if we desire to possess Christ, to live and to rule with Him in eternity, then suffering must first be endured.

Because this is so, why should we heed the rage and fury of such deadly powers, of whom Psalm 2 [:4] says God in heaven laughs at them and holds them in derision.

If the eternal and omnipotent emperor whose name is God and who lives to all eternity mocks and derides them, why should we fear them, or mourn and weep? Truly, God does not mock them in His own defense. He will always be the one dwelling in heaven no matter how they rage against Him. But He mocks them to encourage us, so that we may take heart and bravely laugh at their onslaughts.

Therefore the only thing necessary for us to do is to believe and to pray most confidently in Christ's name that God will give us strength, since He has erected His kingdom and this is His doing. It is He who without our help, counsel, thought, or effort has brought His kingdom forth and has advanced and preserved it to this day. I have no doubt that He will consummate it without our advice or assistance. Because "I know in whom I believe," as St. Paul says [2 Tim. 1:12], I am certain that He will grant me more, do far more abundantly, and help and counsel us beyond all that we ask or think [Eph. 3:20]. He is called the Lord who can and will help in a wonderful, glorious, and mighty way, particularly when the need is the greatest. We are meant to be human beings, not divine. So let us take comfort in His Word and, trusting His promise, call upon Him confidently for deliverance in time of distress and He will help.

That is all there is to it; we have no alternative; otherwise, eternal unrest would be our reward. May God save us from that for the sake of His dear Son, our Savior and eternal Priest, Jesus Christ. Amen.

TEN HYMNS

A New Song Here Shall Be Begun

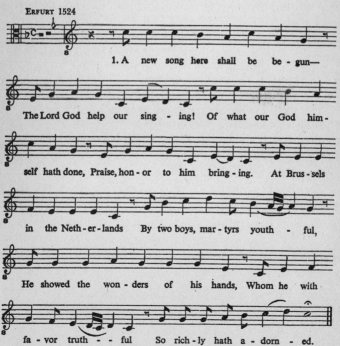

ERFURT 1524

1. A new song here shall be be-gun— The Lord God help our sing-ing! Of what our God him-self hath done, Praise, hon-or to him bring-ing. At Brus-sels in the Neth-er-lands By two boys, mar-tyrs youth-ful, He showed the won-ders of his hands, Whom he with fa-vor truth--ful So rich-ly hath a-dorn-ed.

2 The first right fitly John was named,
  So rich he in God's favor;
  His brother, Henry—one unblamed,
  Whose salt lost not its savor.
  From this world they are gone away,
  The diadem they've gained;
  Honest, like God's good children, they
  For His Word life disdained,
  And have become His martyrs.

3 The old archfiend did them immure
  With terrors did enwrap them.
  He bade them God's dear Word abjure,
  With cunning he would trap them:
  From Louvain many sophists came,
  In their curst nets to take them,
  By him are gathered to the game:
  The Spirit fools doth make them—
  They could get nothing by it.

4 Oh! they sang sweet, and they sang sour;
  Oh! they tried every double;
  The boys they stood firm as a tower,
  And mocked the sophists' trouble.
  The ancient foe it filled with hate
  That he was thus defeated
  By two such youngsters—he, so great!
  His wrath grew sevenfold heated,
  He laid his plans to burn them.

5 Their cloister garments off they tore,
  Took off their consecrations;
  All this the boys were ready for,
  They said Amen with patience.
  To God their Father they gave thanks
  That they would soon be rescued
  From Satan's scoffs and mumming pranks,
  With which, in falsehood masked,
  The world he so befooleth.

6 Then gracious God did grant to them
  To pass true priesthood's border,
  And offer up themselves to Him,

And enter Christ's own order,
Unto the world to die outright,
With falsehood made a schism,
And come to heaven all pure and white,
To monkery be the besom,
And leave men's toys behind them.

7 They wrote for them a paper small,
And made them read it over;
The parts they showed them therein all
Which their belief did cover.
Their greatest fault was saying this:
"In God we should trust solely;
For man is always full of lies,
We should distrust him wholly":
So they must burn to ashes.

8 Two huge great fires they kindled then,
The boys they carried to them;
Great wonder seized on every man,
For with contempt they view them.
To all with joy they yielded quite,
With singing and God-praising;
The sophs had little appetite
For these new things so dazing.
Which God was thus revealing.

9 They now repent the deed of blame,
Would gladly gloze it over;
They dare not glory in their shame,
The facts almost they cover.
In their hearts gnaweth infamy—
They to their friends deplore it;
The Spirit cannot silent be:
Good Abel's blood outpoured
Must still besmear Cain's forehead.

10 Leave off their ashes never will;
Into all lands they scatter;
Stream, hole, ditch, grave—nought keeps them still
With shame the foe they spatter.
Those whom in life with bloody hand
He drove to silence triple,

When dead, he them in every land,
In tongues of every people,
Must hear go gladly singing.

11 But yet their lies they will not leave,
To trim and dress the murther;
The fable false which out they gave,
Shows conscience grinds them further.
God's holy ones, e'en after death,
They still go on belying;
They say that with their latest breath,
The boys, in act of dying,
Repented and recanted.

12 Let them lie on for evermore—
No refuge so is reared;
For us, we thank our God therefore,
His Word has reappeared.
Even at the door is summer nigh,
The winter now is ended,
The tender flowers come out and spy;
His hand when once extended
Withdraws not till He's finished.

Dear Christians, Let Us Now Rejoice

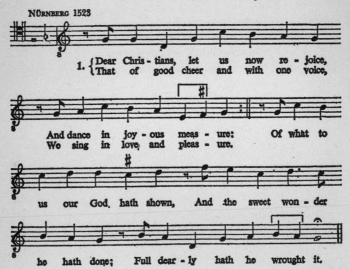

2 Forlorn and lost in death I lay,
   A captive to the devil,
   My sin lay heavy, night and day,
   For I was born in evil.
   I fell but deeper for my strife,
   There was no good in all my life,
   For sin had all possessed me.

3 My good works they were worthless quite,
   A mock was all my merit;
   My will hated God's judging light,
   To all good dead and buried.
   E'en to despair me anguish bore,
   That nought but death lay me before;
   To hell I fast was sinking.

4 Then God was sorry on His throne
   To see such torment rend me;
   His tender mercy He thought on,
   His good help He would send me.
   He turned to me His father heart;
   Ah! then was His no easy part,
   For of His best it cost Him.

5 To His dear Son He said: "Go down;
   'Tis time to take compassion.
   Go down, My heart's exalted crown,
   Be the poor man's salvation.
   Lift him from out sin's scorn and scath,
   Strangle for him that cruel Death,
   That he with Thee live ever."

6 The Son He heard obediently,
   And by a maiden mother,
   Pure, tender—down He came to me,
   For He would be my brother.
   Secret He bore His strength enorm,
   He went about in my poor form,
   For He would catch the devil.

7 He said to me: "Hold thou by Me,
   Thy matters I will settle;
   I give myself all up for thee,
   And I will fight thy battle.

For I am thine, and thou art Mine,
And My place also shall be thine;
The enemy shall not part us.

8 "He will as water shed My blood,
My life he from Me reave will;
All this I suffer for thy good—
To that with firm faith cleave well.
My life from death the day shall win,
My innocence shall bear thy sin,
So art thou blest forever.

9 "To heaven unto My Father high,
From this life I am going;
But there thy Master still am I,
My spirit on thee bestowing,
Whose comfort shall thy trouble quell,
Who thee shall teach to know Me well,
And in the truth shall guide thee.

10 "What I have done, and what I've said,
Shall be thy doing, teaching,
So that God's kingdom may be spread—
All to His glory reaching.
Beware what men would bid thee do,
For that corrupts the treasure true;
With this last word I leave thee."

From Trouble Deep I Cry to Thee

Phrygian Melody

1. From trou-ble deep I cry to thee,
   Thy gra-cious ear, oh, turn to me,
   Lord God, hear thou my cry - ing;
   O - pen it to my sigh - - - - ing. For if

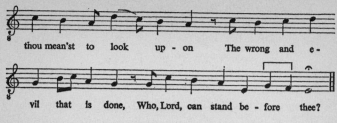

thou mean'st to look up - on The wrong and e -

vil that is done, Who, Lord, can stand be - fore thee?

F major Melody

STRASSBURG 1525

1. { From trou - ble deep I cry to thee,
     Thy gra - cious ear, oh, turn to me,

Lord God, hear thou my cry - ing;
O - pen it to my sigh - ing. For if thou

mean'st to look up - on The wrong and e - vil

that is done, Who, Lord, can stand be - fore thee?

2 With Thee counts nothing but Thy grace
   To cover all our failing.
   The best life cannot win the race,
   Good works are unavailing.
   Before Thee no one glory can,
   And so must tremble every man,
   And live by Thy grace only.

3 Hope therefore in my God will I,
   On my deserts not founding;
   Upon Him shall my heart rely,
   All on His goodness grounding.
   What His true Word doth promise me,
   My comfort shall and refuge be;
   That will I always wait for.

4 And though it last into the night,
   And up until the morrow,
   Yet shall my heart hope in God's might,
   Nor doubt or take to worry.
   Thus Israel must keep His post,
   For He was born of [the] Holy Ghost,
   And for His God must tarry.

5 Although our sin be great, God's grace
   Is greater to relieve us;
   His hand in helping nothing stays,
   The hurt however grievous.
   The Shepherd good alone is He,
   Who will at last set Israel free,
   From all and every trespass.

Were God Not with Us at This Time

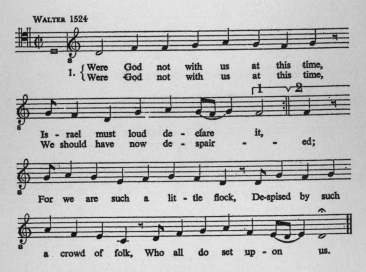

WALTER 1524

1. Were God not with us at this time,
    Were God not with us at this time,
   Is-rael must loud de-clare it,
   We should have now de-spair - - ed;
   For we are such a lit-tle flock, De-spised by such
   a crowd of folk, Who all do set up-on us.

2 'Gainst us so angry is their mood,
   If God had giv'n them tether,
   Us they had swallowed where we stood,
   Body and soul together.
   We were like drowning men, like those
   Above whose heads the waters close,
   And sweep them down with fury.

3 Thank God! their throat He did not yet
Let swallow though it gaped;
As from a snare the bird doth flit,
So is our soul escaped.
The snare's in two, and we are through;
The name of God it standeth true,
The God of earth and heaven.

Death Held Our Lord in Prison

ERFURT 1524

WALTER
1524

1. { Death held our Lord in pris - on,
    { But   he   hath up   a - ris - en,

For sin that did un - do us;
And brought our life back to us.   There - fore we must

glad - some be,   Ex - alt God, and thank - ful be,

And sing a - loud: Al - le - lu - ia!

Al - le - lu - ia! Al - le - lu - ia!

2 No man yet Death overcame—
   All sons of men were helpless;
   Sin for this was all to blame,
   For no one yet was guiltless.
   So Death came that early hour,
   O'er us He took up His power,
   And held us all in His kingdom. Alleluia!

3 Jesus Christ, God's only Son,
   Into our place descending,
   Away with [all] our sins hath done,
   And therewith from Death rending
   Right and might, made Him a jape,
   Left him nothing but Death's shape:
   His ancient sting—he has lost it. Alleluia!

4 That was a right wondrous strife
   When Death in Life's grip wallowed:
   Off victorious came Life,
   Death He has quite upswallowed.
   The scripture has published that—
   How one Death the other ate.
   Thus Death is become a laughter. Alleluia!

5 Here is the true Paschal Lamb
   Which God Himself attested.
   That was on the tree of shame
   In flaming passion roasted
   His blood on our doorpost lies;
   Faith holds that before Death's eyes;
   The smiting angel can do nought. Alleluia!

6 So we keep high feast of grace,
   Hearty the joy and glee is
   That shines on us from His face:
   The sun himself, ah! He is,
   Who, by His brightness divine,
   His light in our hearts makes shine:
   The night of our sins is over. Alleluia!

7 We eat—and so we well fare—
   Right Easter cakes sans leaven;
   The old leaven shall not share
   In the new Word from heaven.
   Christ Himself will be the food,

Alone fill the soul with good:
Faith will live on nothing other. Alleluia!

Come, God Creator Holy Ghost

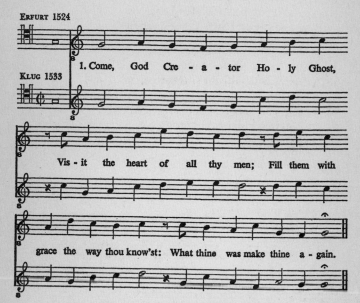

ERFURT 1524

KLUG 1533

1. Come, God Cre - a - tor Ho - ly Ghost,
Vis - it the heart of all thy men; Fill them with
grace the way thou know'st: What thine was make thine a - gain.

2 For Thou art called the Comforter,
   The blessed gift of God above,
   A ghostly balm our quickener,
   A living well, fire, and love.

3 O kindle in our minds a light;
   Give in our hearts love's glowing gift;
   Our weak flesh known to Thee aright
   With Thy strength and grace uplift.

4 In giving gifts Thou art sevenfold;
   The finger Thou on God's right hand;
   His Word by Thee right soon is told,
   With clov'n tongues in every land.

5 Drive far the cunning of the foe;
   Thy grace bring peace and make us whole,
   That we glad after Thee may go,
   And shun that which hurts the soul.

6 Teach us to know the Father right,
   And Jesus Christ, His Son, that so
   We may with faith be filled quite,
   Thee Spirit of both, to know.

7 Praise God the Father, and the Son,
   Who from the dead arose in power;
   Like praise to the Consoling One,
   Evermore and every hour.

In One True God We All Believe

KLUG 1533

1. In one true God we all be-lieve, Mak-er of the earth and heav-en; Who, us as chil-dren to re-ceive, Hath him-self as Fa-ther giv-en. Now and hence-forth he will feed us, Soul and bod-y will sur-round us, 'Gainst mis-chanc-es he will heed us, Nought shall meet us that shall wound us. He watch-es o'er us, cares, de-fends; And ev-'ry-thing is in His hands.

2 And we believe in Jesus Christ,
His own Son, our Lord and Master
Who beside the Father highest
Reigns in equal might and glory.
Born of Mary, virgin mother
By the Spirit's operation
He was made our elder brother
That the lost might find salvation;
Slain on the cross by wicked men
And raised by God to life again.

3 We all confess the Holy Ghost
With the Father and the Savior
Who the fearful comforts most
And the meek doth crown with favor.
All of Christendom He even
In one heart and spirit keepeth.
Here all sins shall be forgiven;
Wake too shall the flesh that sleepeth.
After these suff'rings there shall be
Life for us eternally.

In the Midst of Life We Are

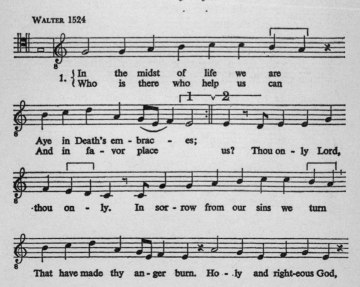

WALTER 1524

1. In the midst of life we are
Who is there who help us can

Aye in Death's em - brac - es;
And in fa - vor place us? Thou on - ly Lord,

·thou on - ly. In sor - row from our sins we turn

That have made thy an - ger burn. Ho - ·ly and right-eous God,

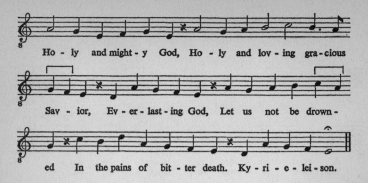

Ho - ly and might - y God, Ho - ly and lov - ing gra - cious
Sav - ior, Ev - er - last - ing God, Let us not be drown -
ed In the pains of bit - ter death. Ky - ri - e - lei - son.

2 In the midst of death behold
    Hell's jaws gaping at us!
    Who will from such dire distress
    Free and scathless set us?
    That dost Thou, Lord, Thou only.
    It fills Thy tender heart with woe
    We should sin and suffer so.
    Holy and righteous God,
    Holy and mighty God,
    Holy and loving gracious Savior,
    Everlasting God,
    Let us not be daunted
    By hell's hollows all aglow.
        Kyrieleison.

3 In the midst of pains of hell,
    Us our sins are baiting;
    Whither shall we flee away
    Where a rest is waiting?
    To Thee, Lord Christ, Thee only.
    Outpoured is Thy precious blood,
    For our sins sufficing good.
    Holy and righteous God
    Holy and mighty God,
    Holy and loving gracious Savior,
    Everlasting God,
    Let from Thee us fall not
    From the comfort of Thy faith.
        Kyrieleison.

Our God He Is a Castle Strong

KLUG 1533

1. {Our God he is a cas - tle strong,
{He sets us free from ev - 'ry wrong

A   good   mail - coat   and   weap - - - on;
That wick - ed - ness   would   heap   on.

The   old   knav - ish   foe   He means ear -

nest now;   Force   and   cun - ning   sly   His   hor - rid

pol - i - cy,   On earth there's noth - ing   like   him.

2 'Tis all in vain, do what we can,
   Our strength is soon dejected.
   But He fights for us, the right man,
   By God Himself elected.
   Ask'st thou who is this?
   Jesus Christ it is,
   Lord of Hosts alone,
   And God but Him is none,
   So He must win the battle.

3 And did the world with devils swarm,
   All gaping to devour us,
   We fear not the smallest harm,
   Success is yet before us.
   This world's prince accurst,
   Let him rage his worst,
   No hurt brings about;
   His doom it is gone out,
   One word can overturn him.

4 The Word they shall allow to stand,
   Nor any thanks have for it;
   He is with us, at our right hand,
   With the gifts of His Spirit.
   If they take our life,
   Wealth, name, child and wife—
   Let everything go:
   They have no profit so;
   The kingdom ours remaineth.

From Heaven on High I Come to You

SCHUMANN 1539

1. From heaven on high I come to you.
I bring a sto-ry good and new; Of good-ly
news so much I bring, Of it I must both speak and sing.

2 To you a child is come this morn,
   A child of holy maiden born,
   A little babe so sweet and mild—
   Your joy and bliss shall be that child.

3 It is the Lord Christ, our own God.
   He will ease you of all your load;
   He will Himself your Savior be,
   And from all sinning set you free.

4 He brings you all the news so glad
   Which God the Father ready had—
   That you shall in His heavenly house
   Live now and evermore with us.

5 Take heed then to the token sure,
   The crib, the swaddling clothes so poor;

The infant you shall find laid there,
Who all the world doth hold and bear.

6   Hence let us all be gladsome then,
And with the shepherd folk go in
To see what God to us hath given,
With His dear honored Son from heaven.

7   Take note, my heart; see there! look low:
What lies then in the manger so?
Whose is the lovely little child?
It is the darling Jesus child.

8   Welcome Thou art, Thou noble guest,
With sinners who dost lie and rest,
And com'st into my misery!
How thankful I must ever be!

9   Ah Lord! the maker of us all!
How hast Thou grown so poor and small,
That there Thou liest on withered grass,
The supper of the ox and ass?

10   Were the world wider many fold,
And decked with gems and cloth of gold,
'Twere far too mean and narrow all,
To make for Thee a cradle small.

11   The silk and velvet that are Thine,
Are rough hay, linen not too fine,
Yet, as they were Thy kingdom great,
Thou liest in them in royal state.

12   And this hath therefore pleased Thee
That Thou this truth mightst make me see—
How all earth's power, show, good, combined,
Helps none, nor comforts Thy meek mind.

13   Dear little Jesus! in my shed,
Make Thee a soft, white little bed,
And rest Thee in my heart's low shrine,
That so my heart be always Thine.

14 And so I ever gladsome be,
   Ready to dance and sing to Thee
   The lullaby Thou lovest best,
   With heart exulting in its guest.

15 Glory to God in highest heaven,
   Who His own Son to us hath given!
   For this the angel troop sings in
   Such a new year with gladsome din.

LUTHER'S EVENING PRAYER

My heavenly Father, I thank You through Jesus Christ, Your beloved Son, that You have protected me by Your grace. Forgive, I pray, all my sins and the evil I have done. Protect me by Your grace tonight. I put myself in Your care, body and soul and all that I have. Let Your holy angels be with me, so that the evil enemy will not gain power over me. Amen.

SUGGESTIONS FOR
FURTHER READING

ALAND, KURT, ed. *Martin Luther's 95 Theses: With the Pertinent Documents from the History of the Reformation.* St. Louis, Mo.: Concordia, 1967.

BAINTON, ROLAND H. *Here I Stand: A Life of Martin Luther.* Nashville: Abingdon-Cokesbury Press, 1950.

BOEHMER, HEINRICH. *Martin Luther: Road to Reformation.* New York: Anchor Books, 1961.

CHADWICK, OWEN. *The Reformation.* Vol. 3 of *The Penguin History of the Church.* New York: Penguin Books, 1990. (First published 1964.)

DILLENBERGER, JOHN, ed. *Martin Luther: Selections from His Writings.* New York: Doubleday Anchor Books, 1951.

EBELING, GERHARD. *Luther: An Introduction to His Thought.* Translated by R. A. Wilson. Philadelphia: Fortress, 1970.

EDWARDS, MARK U. *Luther and the False Brethren.* Stanford, Calif.: Stanford University Press, 1975.

ERIKSON, ERIK H. *Young Man Luther: A Study in Psychoanalysis and History.* New York: W. W. Norton & Co., 1958.

GRITSCH, ERIC W. *A Tragedy of Errors: Thomas Muntzer.* Minneapolis, Minn.: Fortress Press, 1989.

HILLERBRAND, HANS J., ed. *The Protestant Reformation.* New York: Torchbooks, 1968.

HOLBORN, HAJO. *A History of Modern Germany: The Reformation.* New York: Alfred A. Knopf, 1959.

JUNGHANS, HELMAR. *Martin Luther and Wittenberg.* Munich: Koehler and Amelang, 1996.

LORTZ, JOSEPH. *The Reformation in Germany.* 2 vols. New York: Herder, 1968.

LUTHER, MARTIN. *Luther's Works.* 55 vols. Edited by Jaroslav Pelikan (vols. 1–30) and Helmut T. Lehman (vols. 31–55). St. Louis, Mo., and Philadelphia: Concordia Publishing House and Muhlenberg Press, 1955–1986.

MCGRATH, ALISTER E. *The Intellectual Origins of the European Reformation.* Cambridge, Mass.: Blackwell, 1994.

———. *Justitia Dei: A History of the Christian Doctrine of Justification, the Beginnings to the Reformation.* Cambridge: Cambridge University Press, 1986.

MCSORLEY, HARRY J. *Luther: Right or Wrong? An Ecumenical-Theological Study of Luther's Major Work: "The Bondage of the Will."* New York: Newman Press, 1969.

MARIUS, RICHARD. *Martin Luther: The Christian Between God and Death.* Cambridge, Mass.: Belknap Press, 1999.

MULLETT, MICHAEL A. *The Catholic Reformation.* New York: Routledge, 1999.

OBERMAN, HEIKO A. *The Harvest of Medieval Theology.* Cambridge, Mass.: Harvard University Press, 1963.

————. *Luther: Man Between God and the Devil.* Translated by Eileen Walliser-Schwarzbart. New York: Doubleday Image Books, 1992.

OLIVIER, DANIEL. *Luther's Faith: The Cause of the Gospel in the Church.* Translated by John Tonkin. St. Louis, Mo.: Concordia, 1982.

————. *The Trial of Luther.* Translated by John Tonkin. London: Mowbrays, 1978.

OSBORNE, JOHN. *Luther: A Play.* London: Faber & Faber, 1964. (New York: Plume paperback, 1994)

OZMENT, STEVEN. *The Age of Reform, 1250–1550: An Intellectual and Religious History of Late Medieval and Reformation Europe.* New Haven, Conn.: Yale University Press, 1980.

————. *Protestants: The Birth of a Revolution.* New York: Doubleday, 1993.

————. *The Reformation in the Cities: The Appeal of Protestantism to Sixteenth-Century Germany and Switzerland.* New Haven, Conn.: Yale University Press, 1975.

PAUCK, WILHELM, ed. and trans. *Luther: Lectures on Romans.* Philadelphia: Westminster Press, 1961.

PELIKAN, JAROSLAV. *Luther the Expositor: Introduction to the Reformer's Exegetical Writings.* St. Louis, Mo.: Concordia, 1959.

————. *Reformation of the Church and Dogma (1300–1700).* Chicago: University of Chicago Press, 1984.

PLASS, EWALD M., compiler. *What Luther Says: A Practical In-Home Anthology for the Active Christian.* St. Louis, Mo.: Concordia, 1959.

RUPP, GORDON. *The Righteousness of God.* London: Hodder and Stoughton, 1963.

RUPP, GORDON, and PHILIP S. WATSON, eds. and trans. *Luther and Erasmus: Free Will and Salvation.* Philadelphia: Westminster Press, 1959.

SIGGINS, IAN. *Luther and His Mother.* Philadelphia: Fortress Press, 1981.

SPITZ, LEWIS W. *The Protestant Reformation, 1517–1559.* The Rise of Modern Europe series, edited by William L. Langer. New York: Harper & Row, 1985.

STEINMETZ, DAVID C. *Luther and Staupitz: An Essay in the Intellectual Origins of the Protestant Reformation.* Durham, N.C.: Duke University Press, 1980.

TAPPERT, THEODORE G., ed. and trans. *Letters of Spiritual Counsel.* Philadelphia: Westminster Press, 1955.

TODD, JOHN M. *Luther: A Biographical Study.* New York: Paulist Press, 1972.

————. *Reformation.* London: Barton, Longman and Todd, 1972.

Editors' note. A useful source of Luther texts and information is Project Wittenberg, whose Web site may be accessed at *www.iclnet.org/pub/resources/text/ wittenberg/wittenberg-home.html.*

RICHARD LISCHER has served as pastor of Lutheran congregations in Illinois and Virginia, and for the past twenty years has taught at the Duke University Divinity School. His most recent book is *Open Secrets: A Spiritual Journey Through a Country Church*. He is also the author of *The Preacher King: Martin Luther King, Jr., and the Word That Moved America*. He lives in Durham, North Carolina.

JOHN F. THORNTON is a literary agent, former book editor, and the coeditor of *Dumbing Down: The Strip-Mining of American Culture* and *Tongues of Angels, Tongues of Men: A Book of Sermons*. He lives in New York City.

SUSAN B. VARENNE is a New York City high school teacher with a strong avocational interest in and wide experience of spiritual literature. She holds an M.A. from the University of Chicago Divinity School and a Ph.D. from Columbia University.

138-43; "Third Sunday After Epiphany, 1533," pages 242-52; "Reminiscere Sunday—Second Sunday in Lent," pages 321-28.

Vol. 6, *Sermons on Gospel Texts for Easter, Ascension Day, Pentecost, Trinity, and the Fourteen Sundays After Trinity,* Second Sunday After Easter—Misericorias Domini," pages 73-78; "First Sunday After Trinity," pages 223-240; "Third Sunday After Trinity," pages 250-57; "Fourth Sunday After Trinity," pages 258-68; "Eleventh Sunday After Trinity," pages 387-94.

Vol. 7, *Sermons on Gospel Texts for the 15ᵗʰ-26ᵗʰ Sundays After Trinity, the Festival of Christ's Nativity, and Other Occasions,* "Twenty-Third Sunday After Trinity," pages 146-56; "Twenty-Fourth Sunday After Trinity," pages 176-83; "The Day of St. Mary Magdalene," pages 365-73.

3. "Psalm 23," pages 147-179, from *Luther's Works* Vol. 12 edited by Jaroslav Pelikan © 1955 Concordia Publishing House. Used with permission.

"The Sermon on the Mount (Sermons) and The Magnificat," pages 118-129, from *Luther's Works* Vol. 21 edited by Jaroslav Pelikan © 1956 Concordia Publishing House. Used with permission.

4. Letter "To John Hess, November, 1527." Reproduced from *Luther: Institutes of the Christian Religion* (Library of Christian Classics) by Theodore Tappert, pages 230-44. Used by permission of Wesminster John Knox Press.